The political psyche

In radical and original form, here is an engagement of depth psychology with politics that fully reflects the discoveries both participants make in analysis and therapy. Andrew Samuels shows that an inner journey and a desire to fashion something practical out of passionate political conviction are linked projects. He brings an acute psychological perspective to bear on public themes such as the distribution of wealth, the market economy, Third World development, environmentalism, nationalism, and anti-semitism. Our conception of 'the political' is expanded and enhanced.

But, true to his aim of setting in motion a two-way process between depth psychology and politics, Samuels also lays bare the hidden politics of the father, the male body, and of men's issues generally. Politics and depth psychology are not collapsed together. Nor is Samuels starry-eyed about the troubled relationship of depth psychology to the political events of the century. In the book he presents his acclaimed and cathartic work on Jung, anti-semitism and the Nazis to the wider public.

A special and fascinating feature of this extraordinary book is the light shed on clinical work by a *political* analysis. Samuels conducted a large-scale international survey of analysts and psychotherapists into what they do when their patients/clients bring overtly political material into the clinical setting. The respondents also revealed their own political attitudes and histories. The results of this survey totally destabilize any preconceived notions about the political sensitivity of analysis and psychotherapy.

Andrew Samuels is a Training Analyst of the Society of Analytical Psychology, London, and a Scientific Associate of the American Academy of Psychoanalysis. He is the author of *Jung and the Post-Jungians* (1985), *A Critical Dictionary of Jungian Analysis* (1986, with Bani Shorter and Fred Plaut) and *The Plural Psyche* (1989), as well as the editor of *The Father: Contemporary Jungian Perspectives* (1985) and *Psychopathology: Contemporary Jungian Perspectives* (1989).

'Andrew Samuels reconstitutes the relations between mind and power, in the wake of the splits in consciousness and society created by our Cartesian heritage. *The Political Psyche* brings together socially-concerned analytic writing (Fromm, Marcuse, Habermas), radical psychiatry (Lang) and the most recent criticism.

'As a therapist, Samuels restores to their political roots such clinical processes as countertransference, psychopathology, fantasy and sexuality; as a cultural critic, he speaks of the environment, nuclear war, capitalism, poverty and gender; as an intellectual, he reflects with philosophical precision upon these; and as a Jungian analyst, he introduces – respectfully – his metapsychological father's nationalism and penchant for National Socialism to "the political psyche".

'This is an ambitious, honest, radical and well-informed book written in a style free of jargon and warmly dialogical.'

Peter Homans, Professor of Religion and Psychological Studies (Divinity School) and Professor in the Committee on Human Development, The University of Chicago

'Few tasks are more necessary, and few more difficult, than finding adequate and useful ways of connecting an understanding of the psyche with political issues and analysis. Attempts to build bridges have always tended to collapse back into a social or, more often, a psychic reductionism. Today, many have abandoned the task altogether, leaving the study of psychic pain firmly within the clinic, and politics to the polemicists. In this book Andrew Samuels adopts a bold new approach to the task, ranging widely across depth psychologies and clinical experience to place them solidly within contemporary political debate. He seeks not just some type of interaction between clinicians and their political and cultural milieu, but real transformation on both sides. The originality of his ideas is most apparent as he keeps on moving in areas where others fear to tread. We find here a complex analysis of masculinity, fathering and paternal engagement, presented in rich detail in terms of their significance for pro- and anti-feminist goals and interests, and progressive and conservative movements generally. The book makes a passionate and compelling case for connecting inner and outer worlds, and for clinicians' greater political involvement – in their training, with their patients, and above all in the wider world.'

Lynne Segal, Principal Lecturer in Psychology, Middlesex University

'A splendid bringing together of Jungian, post-Jungian and Freudian thought in an effort to link psychology and politics. Samuels has not tried to reduce one field to the other, but instead has seen how they can benefit from each other. He is free of sectarianism, and absolutely up-to-date in the latest literature. It is a stimulating and thoroughly original book that is fully accessible to the general reader.'

Paul Roazen, Professor of Social and Political Science at York University, Toronto, Ontario

The political psyche

Andrew Samuels

London and New York

First published 1993
by Routledge
11 New Fetter Lane, London EC4P 4EE

Simultaneously published in the USA and Canada
by Routledge
29 West 35th Street, New York, NY 10001

Typeset in Times by LaserScript, Mitcham, Surrey
Printed and bound in Great Britain by
Biddles Ltd, Guildford and King's Lynn

British Library Cataloguing in Publication Data
A catalogue record for this book is available from the British Library.

Library of Congress Cataloging in Publication Data

Samuels, Andrew.
  The political psyche/Andrew Samuels.
  p.   cm.
  Includes bibliographical references and index.
  1. Psychoanalysis–Political aspects.   2. Political psychology.
  I. Title.
  BF175.4.S65S25   1993
  150.19′5–dc20   92-39941
                                                      CIP

ISBN 0–415–08101–7
      0–415–08102–5 (pbk)

For Joel and Lydia

The author is more modest and less obliging than the title of this piece might lead one to infer. Indeed, I am convinced not only that what I say is wrong, but that what will be said against it will be wrong as well. Nonetheless, a beginning must be made; for the truth is to be found not in the middle of such a subject but around the outside, like a sack which changes shape every time a new opinion is stuffed in, but grows firmer all the while.

(Robert Musil, 'Helpless Europe: A Digressive Journey')

Contents

Preface

As I understand it, the purposes of a Preface are to tell how the book came to be written, to position it in relation to the writer's previous work, and to convey the importance of the book to the writer on a personal level. Some explanation of terminology, especially in a discipline-crossing work like this, may also be helpful.

In *Jung and the Post-Jungians*, I used a politicized methodology to draw together an overview of the analytical psychology scene since Jung's death in 1961. Debate and dispute between the schools of post-Jungian analytical psychology delineated the field itself. In *The Plural Psyche*, I refined my approach and called it 'pluralism', extending my purview to straddle internal psychological life, theory-making in psychology, and the psychology of certain moral themes that I thought had social significance. This book takes up the wider issues touched on by *The Plural Psyche* and foregrounds them in an unambiguous attempt to create linkages between depth psychology and political theory and practice.

Why has my writing become 'political'? It can be seen that this has not been a sudden whim and that the roots of this book lie in the previous books (not forgetting anthologies on the father and on psychopathology, nor a dictionary of analytical psychology, which had as their 'political' project the communication of analytical psychology to non-Jungians). As far as I can tell, in answering the question 'why politics?', it has been a question of conscience. In simple terms, the worlds I live in, or have experienced on my travels, have disturbed me. Inequality, prejudice, violence and a lack of imaginative vitality have affected me and worried me. I felt I wanted to do something about it and could not contemplate going back to the left-wing splinter group politics of late adolescence. Then it gradually dawned on me that the profession I had 'chosen', for whatever reasons, offered a particular way of making the contribution that my conscience was demanding. Once embarked on the work, I found that the movements of mind and heart were in two directions: The planned one was from depth psychology to politics; the unplanned one, that grew and grew in power and significance, was from the political to the principles and practices of depth psychology.

The book does not follow some single-minded method, though there is method in it. Nor do I adhere to some absolute Truth, though there are truths herein that will survive if they survive healthy competition with other truths. Nor do I have a fixed version of human nature in mind, though I have passionately held ideas of what constitutes human beings.

That remark about the absence of a fixed version of human nature leads me to raise the question of the 'we' who are ubiquitous in this text. Sometimes, and uncontroversially, this 'we' refers to those reading my text in the here-and-now. But at other times, my use of 'we' may seem to reflect the usual tendency of a white, Western, Jewish, middle-class, heterosexual male to see himself as representative of everyone. However, I have tried not to fall into this inflation, making it clear when I do mean 'everyone', and when I mean 'people like me', 'analysts', 'political practitioners', 'men' and so on. This caveat is particularly important because, in these pages, I have tried to address some of the concerns of a wide spectrum of diverse groups of people: Psychologically aware politicos, mainstream politicians, some feminists, gay and lesbian activists, embattled members of ethnic minorities, environmentalists, certain artists, the poor in developing and industrially advanced countries, those living in presently unconventional styles of family organization. Since I do not have the fantasy of formalizing this spectrum into a federation, my text will not flourish (meaning *work*) unless the components of the spectrum are differentiated. 'We' will only be authentic to the extent that 'we' has been differentiated.

In the Preface to *The Plural Psyche* I made the point that what looks like new theory is often a description of cutting-edge practice. Based on the experience of writing this book, I can develop the point further. It is a question of raising something that is present in culture but unrecognized therein to the more conscious level of a text. If one does that, then the discourse of which that text is a part will be affected by the (new) text. So I do not now see it as primarily a question of describing untheorized practice, but rather I regard such practice as itself an expression of something worth 'texting'. My surmise is that the whole idea of factoring the psychological into the political is just such a bubbling-under phenomenon.

I will move on to provide the promised notes on terminology. There are three. First, I use the old-fashioned term 'depth psychology' because I do not want to use the more cumbersome phrase 'psychoanalysis and analytical psychology'. However, it is more than a question of saving space. As far as most of the themes touched on in this book are concerned, I think that the arguments and ideas arise from and are comprehensible to both psychoanalysis and analytical psychology. Moreover, this is certainly not a 'Jungian' text and the term 'depth psychology' is intended to offer me some protection from sequestration as a 'Jungian'. Depth psychology, as a tag, has its own imperfections and I discuss these in the book from time to time.

Second, I want to say something about my use of the words 'analyst', 'psychotherapist' and 'therapist'. Not all psychotherapists and therapists think and work analytically, so at times I have had to corral the analytical folk and refer to 'analysts'. But, given that clinical practice is mobilized in this book for political purposes, I must add that it is not only analysts who think and work analytically. Many psychotherapists and therapists do as well. That said, I do not have any intention of commenting directly on the vexed question of the similarities and differences between psycho-analysis 'proper' and psychoanalytic psychotherapy. In Chapter 2 and elsewhere I have used the term 'political analyst' because of the polysemous associations such a term inspires and not in spite of them.

Third, I have tried to be careful in my use of the words 'politics' or 'the political', 'culture', 'society' and the 'collective'. I attempt a definition of politics in the first chapter (pp. 3–4, below). By 'culture', I mean the assembly, limited in time and space, of the social, material, mental, spiritual, artistic, religious and ritual processes of a relatively stable and sizeable community. I use the words 'society' or 'societal' in the following senses: The means by which relations between individual and community are structured; the institutions that cause differences between individuals to acquire significances beyond those individual differences; whatever promotes learned forms of behavior and communication that excite support and approval or condemnation and punishment; relations between organizations and groups. The 'collective' implies what is held in common, ranging from a biological/phylogenetic use of collective to something like the collective atmosphere in a crowded theater or soccer stadium.

To conclude: I acknowledge that the book springs from depth psychology. But, as I confessed, there has been a two-way process. My passionate hope is that my work will also be read outside the depth psychological communities: In the universities, in departments of social science, sociology, politics, psychology, psychiatry, cultural and gender studies, law, and religion; in centers of artistic activity; by psycho-therapists and counsellors whose orientation is not depth psychological; by political activists in a wide range of fields of endeavor.

My overall perception is that depth psychology (broadly conceived) and politics (broadly conceived) are enriched by contact with each other. However, I trust that I have not totally confused the two disciplines by experimenting with a hybrid of them. For that would lead to the unforgivable delusion that simply publishing a text on depth psychology and politics is all that it is necessary to do.

London and Ashton, February 1993

Acknowledgments

Responsibility for the ideas expressed in this book is, of course, mine.

I would like to thank those patients who have given me permission to write about them.

The research project, carried out by means of an international questionnaire, would not have been possible without a generous grant, for which I am most grateful, from the Ann and Erlo van Waveren Foundation in New York. The project is described in Chapter 10.

The following professional societies of analysts and psychotherapists helped in a variety of ways with the sending out and return of the questionnaires. I have indicated the various 'contact persons'. I think I can say that, without exception, each organization helped me to the maximum extent possible for it and I am truly thankful: Society of Analytical Psychology (Jane Knight and Hugh Gee), British Psycho-Analytical Society (Anne-Marie Sandler), Institute of Psychotherapy and Counselling (WPF) (Lesley Murdin and Trevor Dawson), Association of Humanistic Psychology Practitioners (John Rowan), National Psychological Association for Psychoanalysis (Michael Vannoy Adams and Michael Eigen), San Francisco Psychoanalytic Institute (Robert Wallerstein), Chicago Society of Jungian Analysts (Peter Mudd), Society of Jungian Analysts of Northern California – San Francisco (Rick Steele), Society of Jungian Analysts of Southern California – Los Angeles (Allen Koehn), Centro Italiano di Psicologia Analitica (Luigi Zoja), Sociedade Brasileira de Psicologia Analitica (Helena Albuquerque), Russian Association of Practical Psychologists – Division of Psychoanalysis (Julia Aloyshina), Israel Association of Analytical Psychology (Eli Weisstub), Deutsche Gesellschaft für Analytische Psychologie (Gustav Bovensiepen and Arvid Erlenmeyer).

I am grateful to Luigi Zoja, Gustav Bovensiepen, Simona Panatta, Arvid Erlenmeyer, Helena Albuquerque, A. H. Brafman, Gottfried Heuer, and Julia Aloyshina for translating the questionnaires and/or replies. Most of all, I thank the respondents who took time from their busy lives and practices to work on a particularly demanding set of questions.

I do not think I could have written this book without the stimulus provided by invitations to lecture or conduct workshops and seminars from analytical, cultural, intellectual and academic institutions in Britain, the Republic of Ireland, the United States, Canada, Germany, Switzerland, France, Italy, Denmark, Holland, Israel, Brazil and Russia. I appreciate the invitations and continue to learn from such experiences.

Writing a book is both a lonely and profoundly social process. I have had support and feedback from so many people that it is almost impossible to list them all. I am thinking of: Henry Abramovitch, Mike Adams, John Allan, Karin Barnaby, Cathie Brettschneider, Sheila Butterworth, Carlos Byington, Andrea Ciecierski, Giles Clark, Coline Covington, Ian Craib, James Croghan, Kendra Crossen, Gustav Dreifuss, Musa Farhi, Nina Farhi, Ian Fenton, Karl Figlio, David Freeman, Paul Gordon, Rosemary Gordon, Jane Haynes, Birgit Heuer, Gottfried Heuer, Bob Hinshelwood, George Hogenson, Peter Homans, Judith Hubback, Raphael Kaplinsky, Jean Kirsch, Tom Kirsch, Jean Knox, Paul Kugler, Bruce Linton, Nancy McKenzie, David Mayers, Kitty Moore, Michael Munchow, Mary Nolan, Renos Papadopoulos, Roderick Peters, Ruthie Petrie, Fred Plaut, Michael Pokorny, Kevin Polley, Val Richards, Paul Roazen, Margaret Ryan, Cesare Sacerdoti, Janet Sayers, Ilene Serlin, Nathan Schwartz-Salant, Ann Scott, Sonu Shamdasani, Joe Smith, Martin Stanton, Averil Stedeford, Tom Steele, Murray Stein, David Stonestreet, Tessa Strickland, David Tacey, Matthias von der Tann, Peter Tatham, Richard Wainwright, Eli Weisstub, Edwina Welham, Richard Wilkinson, Don Williams, Elizabeth Wright, Wendy Wyman, Bob Young, Luigi Zoja, and the members of the Male Psychology Workshop that is under the aegis of the Society of Analytical Psychology. My thanks to all and I apologize if I have inadvertently left anyone off this list.

There are three individuals that deserve a special mention:

Jo Foster has word processed and re-processed what must seem like countless times. Yet her good humor, accuracy and incredibly speedy responsiveness have never deserted her. She has been a delight to work with and I thank her for it.

John Beebe brought his own particular brand of miracle-working editing to over half the book. He didn't just improve the text – by the depth of his understanding, he gave me confidence to push my ideas further on, and played a full part in the dialectic that developed between us.

Rosie Parker continues to be my most stringent critic at the same time as being my most important support. How she pulls this off, I shall never know. But I do know how much I owe to her and I am deeply grateful.

All of this book was written with the book in mind. However, some chapters or sections have been published in journals as 'work-in-progress', as follows: 'The mirror and the hammer: Depth psychology and political transformation', *Free Associations* 28 (1992); 'Parents as messengers', *British Journal of Psychotherapy* 7: 4 (1991); 'Counter-transference and politics', *British Journal of Psychotherapy* 9: 1 (1992); 'National psychology, National Socialism, and analytical psychology: Reflections on Jung and anti-semitism, Parts 1 and 2', *Journal of Analytical Psychology* 37: 1 and 2 (1992); 'Men under scrutiny', *Psychological Perspectives*, Spring 1992; and *Winnicott Studies* 7 (1993).

Permission to quote from the following works is acknowledged:

The Homeric Hymns (2nd edn, rev.), translated by Charles Boer. Dallas, Spring Publications (1979). Copyright Charles Boer (1970).

Surfacing by Margaret Atwood. London: Virago; New York: Ballantine; Toronto: General Publishing Company (1972).

'Gerontion' in *Collected Poems 1909-1962* by T. S. Eliot. London: Faber and Faber; Orlando, Florida: Harcourt, Brace, Jovanovich.

Against Nature by J.-K. Huysmans. Translated by Robert Baldick. Harmondsworth: Penguin Books (1959).

Part I

The political psyche

In Part I, I make some proposals about the relationship between depth psychology and politics. Far from abandoning what has been learned from clinical work, my ideas involve the discovery of new uses for clinical methodology in the making of political and cultural analyses. But, at the same time, the methods and theories of clinical depth psychology cannot remain unaffected by the new uses to which they are being put. I elaborate the idea of 'the political development of the person' and other related concepts as showing the viability of my attempt to politicize the clinical project.

I explore key contemporary political issues from a depth psychological outlook. These issues include the nature of politics itself, the psychological and political dynamics of the market economy, questions of economic inequality and the distribution of wealth, and an assessment of the cultural impact of environmentalism. To carry out the expansion of what is usually considered to be 'the political', I deploy collective, cultural figures such as the Trickster and Hermes.

Chapter 1

The mirror and the hammer
The politics of resacralization

DEPTH PSYCHOLOGY AND POLITICAL TRANSFORMATION

This book is about the depth psychology of political processes, focusing on processes of non-violent political change. It is a contribution to the longstanding ambition of depth psychology to develop a form of political and cultural analysis that would, in Freud's words, 'understand the riddles of the world'.[1] I will be trying to bring depth psychology as a whole, and the particular experience of clinical analysis, to bear on politics. An engagement of depth psychology with politics makes a contribution to social science, social theory and the other human sciences.[2] But the book is also oriented in the opposite direction. Bringing an understanding of the political world to bear on the theories of depth psychology and the practices of clinical analysis, leading to a concern for humankind as well as an absorption in one's personal problems.

By 'politics' I mean the concerted arrangements and struggles within an institution, or in a single society, or between the countries of the world for the organization and distribution of resources and power, especially economic power. Politics concerns the way in which power is held or deployed by the state, by institutions, and by sectional interests to maintain survival, determine behavior, gain control over others and, more positively perhaps, enhance the quality of human life. Politics implies efforts to change or transform these arrangements and efforts to maintain them. Economic and political power includes control of processes of information and representation to serve the interests of the powerful as well as the use of physical force and possession of vital resources such as land, food, water or oil.

On a more personal level, there is a second kind of politics. Here, political power reflects struggles over agency, meaning the ability to choose freely whether to act and what action to take in a given situation. This is a feeling-level politics. But politics also refers to a crucial interplay between these two dimensions, between the private and public dimensions of power. There are connections between economic power and power as expressed on an intimate, domestic, level. Power is a process or network as much as a stable factor. This version of political power is demonstrated experientially: In family organization, gender and race relations, and in religious and artistic assumptions as they affect the life of individuals.

Where the public and the private, the political and the personal, intersect or even meld there is a special role for depth psychology in relation to political change and transformation. The tragicomic crisis of our *fin de siècle* civilization incites us to challenge the boundaries that are conventionally accepted as existing between the external world and the internal world, between life and reflection, between extraversion and introversion, between doing and being, between politics and psychology, between the political development of the person and the psychological development of the person, between the fantasies of the political world and the politics of the fantasy world. Subjectivity and intersubjectivity have political roots; they are not as 'internal' as they seem.

The political tasks of modern democracy are similar to the psychological tasks of modern therapy and analysis. In both areas, there is a fight between consciousness, liberation and alterity on the one hand and suppression, repression and omnipotent beliefs in final truths on the other. Psychological and political processes share an uncertain outcome. Hence, the demarcation between the inner world of psychology and the outer world of politics has no permanent existence. The *Umwelt* is both inside and outside. This congruency of politics and depth psychology is demonstrated by the ubiquity of political metaphors that can depict personality: The 'government' signifies the ego, the 'citizens' signify constellations of object relations, social problems signify psychopathology. In this book, I do not in fact make use of notions such as 'the class system inside one's head', but I do draw conclusions from the existence of such notions about public referents of private matters.

From its beginnings, depth psychology has been interested in the world of politics. In his paper entitled 'The claims of psycho-analysis to the interest of the non-psychological sciences', written in 1913, Freud staked a claim for the proactive capacity of psychoanalysis

> to throw light on the origins of our great cultural institutions – on religion, morality, justice, and philosophy. . . . Our knowledge of the neurotic illnesses of individuals has been of much assistance to our understanding of the great social institutions.[3]

Jung made a similar point about the relationship of depth psychology and politics in a more reactive vein in 1946 in his preface to a collection of his essays on Nazi Germany:

> We are living in times of great disruption: political passions are aflame, internal upheavals have brought nations to the brink of chaos. . . . This critical state of things has such a tremendous influence on the psychic life of the individual that the analyst . . . feels the violence of its impact even in the quiet of his consulting room. . . . The psychologist cannot avoid coming to grips with contemporary history, even if his very soul shrinks from the political uproar, the lying propaganda, and the jarring speeches of the demagogues. We need not mention his duties as a citizen, which confront him with a similar task.[4]

At times, it seems that Freud and Jung were as interested in the broad sweep of cultural evolution and in an engagement with collective psychology as they were in their day-to-day work with patients. Certainly, there is a tension between their cultural and clinical projects and this is a tension that is still with their descendants today. In the last twenty-five years, we have witnessed the growth of psychoanalysis as an academic discipline, whether as a human, social or emancipatory science. The same is now beginning to happen in analytical psychology (inevitably, twenty-five years later). Of course, the origins of this intellectual movement go much further back to 'Freudian' writers like Harold Lasswell, Jürgen Habermas, Herbert Marcuse, Erich Fromm, and Norman O. Brown, or to 'Jungians' like Mircea Eliade and Herbert Read.

The gulf between depth psychology in the academy and depth psychology in the clinic is at its widest in Britain and in the United States, but even in Europe we can see signs of a similar rift. Academic depth psychology might involve a close textual study of Freud's writings or comparative work that sets Freud alongside Heidegger or other important thinkers. Literary and film criticism, cultural and gender studies, psycho-history and psychobiography, sectors within anthropology, sociology and political studies – all may quite fairly be reckoned as aligned with academic depth psychology. Research into the outcome of psycho-therapeutic treatment and diagnostic studies may also be understood as academic. Though academic depth psychology often seems more at home with an insertion into the political field than clinical depth psychology does, it lacks a vehicle for engaging with political issues in a pragmatic form while retaining a psychological orientation.

However, something new is rumbling within the clinical world. In 1991, just before the Gulf War, a protest meeting was called in London by the Medical Campaign Against Nuclear Weapons and the Study Group on

Psychosocial Issues in the Nuclear Age. It was held at the Institute of Psycho-Analysis, a highly significant fact in itself, and psychoanalysts were prominent on the platform. What is more, over a quarter of the members of the British Psycho-Analytical Society have joined a group called Psychoanalysts for the Prevention of Nuclear War.[5] In Britain, and all over the world, clinicians and some who have voluntarily given up clinical practice are arguing and writing about politics in a way that they did not just a few years ago.

It seems that the existence of a rupture between depth psychology in the consulting room and depth psychology in the political world is being challenged, if not exactly closed. One can tell that something significant *is* going on by the existence of fierce opposition to it from those who regard the clinical as an untouchable, privileged category, on the basis of its contribution to the alleviation of human suffering.[6]

Although I abhor that kind of clinical triumphalism, I do not suggest in this book that we should close all the consulting rooms. This is because I can see that clinical practice may be something other than a bastion of possessive individualism and narcissistic introspection. It is right to criticize myopic (and greedy) clinicians who cannot apperceive that their work has a political and cultural location and implication. But it is not right to indulge in simplistic thinking that would do away with the entire clinical project of depth psychology. *Without their connection to a clinical core, why should anyone listen to analysts at all?* The rejection of the clinical forecloses what is, for me, the central issue: The relations between the private and the public spheres of life. This foreclosure mimics the attitude of the most conservative, dyed-in-the-wool clinicians and mental health professionals. The high-profile apostates of therapy are as terrified of exploring the relations between the personal and the political as are the fanatical professional adherents of therapy.[7]

The patients who come to see analysts and therapists are playing a part in these debates. In Chapter 10, I give the results of a questionnaire that was sent to analysts and psychotherapists in several countries. The questionnaire concerned political material brought to the consulting room, its prevalence, and how it is handled by the practitioner. From the survey, it seems clear that such material is being brought more frequently than before to the clinical setting, that the range of themes and problems covered is immense, that these do not invariably reflect the social situation or obvious preoccupations of the particular patient, and that practitioners are a bit puzzled as to how to interpret such material. *Through this survey, I have found that practitioners are more reluctant than I thought they would be to interpret political material in terms of the internal world of the patient.* I can confirm this puzzlement from my own experience. During the Gulf crisis of 1990–1, I was struck, not only by how some patients employed war imagery to express their internal states (predicted by theory), but also by how some patients communicated what looked like inner world material when actually they had a deep desire to talk about the Gulf crisis (not predicted by theory).

Depth psychology's area of inquiry is moving on to make a new connection with the world of politics. However, I do not agree with the conceit that the unconscious itself has moved on and now resides outside the individual in the external world. The unconscious cannot be reified like that – and in any case who could doubt that the unconscious has always already been in the world as well as in the individual. The very idea of unconscious influence on action suggests that the unconscious itself influences the relations between the individual and the world. What has changed is our perception of what depth psychology can, and should do. (I return to the theme of the relations between the unconscious and the social world in Chapter 3.) Maybe it is now the turn of the external world to receive the ministrations of the depth psychologists. Maybe it is the external world that now clamors for our attention, for there is certainly much political pain and dis-ease 'out there' (as we say). But first we have to find out whether the political world *does* want something from depth psychology. (In the next chapter, I will unpack the word 'world'.)

In spite of these developments, it has to be admitted that there is an intense reluctance in the non-psychological community to accept the many and varied ideas and suggestions concerning political matters that have been or are being offered by analysts of every persuasion. I do not believe this reluctance can all be put down to resistance. There is something quite offensive about reductive interpretations of complex sociopolitical problems in exclusively psychological terms. The tendency to pan-psychism on the part of some depth psychologists has led me to wonder if any adequate methodology and ethos actually exist to make an engagement of depth psychology with the public sphere possible.[8]

Depth psychology concerns a person's subjective experience of social and cultural structures, and that is valuable in itself. But in this book I want to ask: Is there a special psychology of and for politics and culture? If so, what does the clinical practice of analysis and therapy with individuals or small groups contribute to the forming of such a psychology? And, conversely, I ask: What does a perspective taken from cultural or political analysis contribute to a clinical analysis of an individual or small therapy group? In what way is the personal political – and in what way is the political personal? Can these questions be answered without recourse to a totalizing politics, in a way that preserves and celebrates difference and diversity? A depth psychological approach to politics needs to be a humble one.

Depth psychology can help with these queries. In spite of claims that the age of psychology is over, we may be entering a period of cultural evolution in which it will become easier to work out the possible contribution of depth psychology to social science and politics. Modern social theory is concerned with identity, with difference, and with the relations between identity and difference. How am I wholly and unmistakably myself? How am I part of the mass, similar to or the same as others? These questions, which constitute the *cri de cœur* of what Anthony Giddens calls 'late modernity', shove us in the direction of psychology.[9] These are the pressing questions that the analytic patient brings to the consulting room – even in group therapy. And these are the crucial questions about that patient that the analyst has to contend with – to what extent can I encounter this person as a unique human being, to what extent must I react to him or her as a typical patient, to what extent as a combination of these? The political dimension of these psychological questions was summarized by Aristotle: 'Similars do not constitute a state.' Nor, we may add, do people with nothing at all in common.[10]

The characteristic of late modernity to try to make use of knowledge about itself can be recast as a struggle within our culture to become self-conscious; *our culture struggles to become psychological*. Moreover, the pervasive presence of *doubt*, even 'radical doubt', as a 'feature of modern critical reason' and as a 'general existential dimension of the contemporary social world', suggests that the psychology that is already being embraced by late modernity is depth psychology, the psychology of not knowing, of unknowing, of interpretation and reinterpretation.

The late modern (and, if you like, the post-modern) age has reorganized the categories of time, space and place, using technology to deliteralize and overcome them, permitting the exercise of power-at-a-distance. In its overturning of the laws of nature, the age itself more and more resembles the unconscious. The speedy and multilevelled tone of life at the close of the twentieth century means that we often do not know what it is that has hurt or disturbed us though we do know we have been hurt or disturbed. We may only know what it was after the event. Such 'deferred action', to use the standard mistranslation of Freud's *Nachträglichkeit*, means that we are condemned to afterwardness and retrospection, required to fashion our response to hurtful and disturbing social changes out of a backward-looking stance.[11] No wonder there has been an explosion of nostalgias.

PSYCHOLOGICAL REDUCTIONISM

Here is an example of the difficulty with psychological reductionism to which I referred earlier. At a conference, a distinguished psychoanalyst referred to the revolutionary students in Paris in 1968 as 'functioning as a regressive group'.[12] Now, for a large group of students to be said to regress, there must be, in the speaker's mind, some sort of normative developmental starting point for them to regress to. The social group is supposed to have a babyhood, as it were. Similarly, the speaker must have had in mind the possibility of a healthier, progressive group process – what a more mature group of revolutionary students would have looked like. This 'regressive group of students' stunned nearly every intellectual in France and also fatally wounded Marxism. The regressive group was so effective that it forced an intelligentsia already intimately concerned with political issues to throw up its hands and realize the urgent need to retheorize politics. Not bad for a psychologically immature group. (I return to the topic of group and institutional dynamics in Chapter 11.) Be this as it may, my main point here is to emphasize that complex social and political phenomena do not conform to the individualistic, chronological, moralistic, pathologising framework that is often applied in a mechanical way by depth psychological commentators.

The problem of reductionism does not stem from having a therapeutic *attitude* to the pathologies of culture as these are expressed in political issues. Rather, the problem stems from approaching an entire culture, or large chunks of it, *as if it were an individual or even as if it were a baby.* In this infantalization of culture, depth psychology deploys a version of personality development couched in judgmental terms to understand a collective cultural and political process. If we look in this manner for pathology in the culture, we will surely find it. If we are looking with a particular psychological theory in mind, then, lo and behold, the theory will explain the pathology. But this is a retrospective prophecy (to use a phrase of Freud's),[13] twenty–twenty hindsight. In this psychological tautologizing there is really nothing much to get excited about. Too much depth psychological writing on the culture, my own included, has suffered from this kind of smug correctness when the 'material' proves the theoretical point. Of course it does! If we are interested in envy or greed, then we will find envy or greed in capitalistic organization. If we set out to demonstrate the presence of archetypal patterns, such as projection of the shadow, in the geopolitical relations of the superpowers, then, without a doubt, they will seem to leap out at us. But so often this is just more of the maddening rectitude of the analyst who has forgotten that we influence what we analyze. Psychological reflection on culture and politics needs to be muted; there is not as much 'aha!' as pioneers, such as the Frankfurt School, hoped for.

I am sure that the book cannot solve all the problems or answer all the questions I have mentioned. In the 1920s the Russian Futurist poet Vladimir Mayakovsky wrote that 'Art is not a mirror to reflect the world, but a hammer with which to shape it.' I think depth psychology might try to reflect *and* shape the world, doing it as part of a multidisciplinary project, and in a mixture of styles ranging from exegetical sobriety to playfulness *to something quite frankly irrational*. In these diverse ways, we may find out more about the interplays between (a) personality development and social structure, (b) the private, intrapsychic world of an individual and the public, political system in which he or she is embedded, and (c) psychic reality and sociopolitical reality. The political world is today's uncanny (*Unheimlich*); something that was familiar (*heimisch*) has slipped out of the grasp of consciousness.

PSYCHE, CULTURE AND RESACRALIZATION

It has never been more difficult to make a psychological analysis of politics for, in our day, every institution and element in culture is undergoing fragmentation and Balkanization. It has become harder and harder to see what political arrangements can hold societies together. Moments at which one apprehends a social unity have become as precious and vulnerable as those revelatory and mystical moments when one experiences a personal unity.

Increasingly, the fragility and disunity of our culture provokes a reaction arising out of a sense of the underlying oneness of the world – a holistic response. But, for me, the problem with the re-emergence in our day of cosmic visions of a unified world is that a sense of oneness tends to generate only one particular kind of truth. Moreover, proclaiming the indissoluble unity of a world soul may be little more than a *defensive* reaction to atomization. Advancing holism as if it were *the* solution is not an adequate critical response to the drama of cultural diversity. Holism founders on the sea of the discontinuities of life, for holism is secretly highly rational and ordered and cannot abide irrationality or a messiness in which its Truth has to coexist with lots of truth*s*. A unified viewpoint has to find some kind of articulation with a diversity of viewpoints; this, holism finds difficult.

My approach here is not holistic. I want to take those anxiety-provoking ideas of cultural fragmentation, fracture and complexity, and re-imagine them as the very tools of the trade of psychological analysis of cultural political processes. Let us take our sense of fragmentation, fracture and complexity as *healing* as well as wounding to a sense of political and social empowerment. It follows that we have to try to engage with a diverse and fragmented culture by means of an analysis that sees through its own fantasy of homogeneity, is already itself diverse and fragmented, and seeks out complexity. Rousseau referred to 'the language of the heart' and I suppose that, in our day, we have to begin to speak the languages of the hearts.

Amidst the tragic anomie and baffling atomization, amidst the dreadful conformism of 'international' architecture, telecommunications and cuisine, amidst the sense of oppression and fear of a horrific future, amidst war itself, there is an equally fragmented, fractured and complex attempt at a *resacralization of the culture* going on. People have risen to the challenge and there are many diverse surface signs of resacralization: New Age or New Times thought, expressions of concern for the quality of life, green politics, feminism, demands for the rights of ethnic minorities, the human potential movement, liberation theology, gay activism, finding God in the new physics. I would even including trying to engage depth psychology with politics on this deliberately diverse list; I certainly do not want to leave myself out! It is suspicious that depth psychologists concerned with the public sphere have not paid much attention to *themselves* as a cultural phenomenon. I would go so far as to say that depth psychology itself may be regarded as one of the precursors of late twentieth-century resacralization. A depth psychologist has as a credo that he or she is 'in' whatever is being analyzed, whether patient, political problematic, or art work. I can readily understand objections to resacralization that find the linkage of depth psychology and fundamentalist religion difficult to stomach. It was hard for me, at first. But if one's goal is to track and speak up about such connections, then there is little alternative to leaving such shocking linkages out in the open. Perhaps the objections also have something to do with the differences between depth psychology and philosophy. While some philosophers might pay lip service to the impossibility of maintaining the observer/observed boundary, this often is not reflected in their experience-distant texts.

The groups and movements I have listed vary in the degree to which they seek fundamental changes in society as a whole; some of them have quite particular, sectional interests to pursue. Nevertheless, I see this heterogeneous phenomenon – resacralization – as held together by aspirational rather than by socioeconomic ties. In fairness, I do not assume that only left-leaning, so-called progressive political and religious movements partake in resacralization. Born-again Christians, Islamic fundamentalists and the Lubavitch Jews are part of the same trend. In different forms, of course, resacralization is also a way to describe what has been happening in Eastern Europe and the former Soviet Union. Across the world, people have risen to the challenge of resacralization. It is the spiritual longings of ordinary people that have fuelled these movements – and perhaps all the more progressive political and cultural projects of the twentieth century. The resacralizing perspective recovers a sense of the religious verities but these are played through a changing world view less dependent on religious organization. The resacralizing ethic may be plebeian in its roots, but it is sublime in its aspirations.

Clearly I think that all these developments are extremely important. They may contain elements of a successful resolution of some of our most vexing dilemmas. *But I also think that, in their present form, they are at risk of failing* and the consequences of failure will be serious even for those who feel out of sympathy with many or all of the facets of resacralization.

As I said, I think these spontaneous movements are surface signs that there is something politically transformative going on. I want to suggest that resacralization is our contemporary attempt to shift a sense of holiness into the secular and material world. Let us look at holiness. The roots of holiness do not only lie in God or in a transpersonal realm. They also lie in humanity's *making* of holiness. We make holiness by the designation and construction of sacred spaces (which we call temples). We make holiness by the performance of sacred acts (such as sacrifice and repentance). I doubt that contemporary resacralization will ultimately glorify God or lead to a new religion. But, along the way, most aspects of human culture will be touched by this attempt to connect to a feeling level that we sense once existed but we find has vanished from the modern world (hence *re*sacralization). I think that, at the very least, this involves a search for a new ethical basis for society. In its preoccupation with the discovery of meaning, depth psychology has vectored in on the same search.

The notion that holiness is located in the material, social world is not a new one. For many, religious and non-religious alike, the world has long held a Chassidic gleam. Since my childhood, I have been fascinated by God's detailed instructions to the Children of Israel about how to build the Ark of the Covenant (not to mention the Tabernacle, or, earlier, Noah's Ark). In the divine detail of the construction, we see how ineffable holiness depends on every single joint, bevel, dimension, and the material used:

And Bezaleel made the ark of shittim wood: two cubits and a half was the length of it, and a cubit and a half the breadth of it, and a cubit and a half the height of it. And he overlaid it with pure gold within and without, and made a crown of gold to it round about. And he cast for it four rings of gold, to be set by the four corners of it; even two rings upon the one side of it, and two rings upon the other side of it. And he made staves of shittim wood, and overlaid them with gold. And he put the staves into the rings by the side of the ark, to bear the ark.[14]

Bezaleel's name is hardly ever mentioned, not even in the film *Raiders of the Lost Ark*! Yet he is the collective image and cultural personification of resacralization, the contemporary drive to render the secular holy as a creative response to the fate of God.

This is why, for many, resacralization has indeed taken the form of a return to religion. Sometimes this is established religion, sometimes archaic (or apparently archaic) religion. However, as a depth psychologist, I have to engage with resacralization in a different way. To do so, it is not essential to support or to believe in resacralization, and many do not. What is essential is to try to pick up on the psychology of what is happening in this particular piece of cultural process. I want to make something psychological, but not exclusively or excessively psychological, out of a host of social and political impressions. The idea is to bring something up and out that is *already* there – so these words of mine about resacralization are intended to be description, chronicle and interpretation, not sermon or advocacy, nor anything beyond an indirect contribution to resacralization itself. The parallel is with clinical analysis, in which the analyst can do no more than foster a process in which potentials within the patient are brought into consciousness.

One specific impression is of a growing, collective sense of disgust, in both Western culture and the once-communist states, with the political world in whose making we have participated. Disgust is lurking alongside the shallowness and cruelty of much of modern life; our subjectivity is full of it. As Thomas Mann put it, 'Our capacity for disgust is in proportion to the intensity of our attachment to the things of this world.'[15] Disgust with our present politics leads us to aspire to a resacralized and reformed politics in which political openness and unpredictability lead to faith and hope rather than to fear and disgust. To achieve this, we need a new psychological valuing of the potential of political engagement itself. Involvement in the mess and confusion of the external world and passionate political commitment to that world are as psychologically valuable as an interior perspective or an intimate I–thou relationship.

Political involvement *can* certainly be a means of avoiding personal conflicts or acting out such conflicts, leaving others to do the changing. But political involvement can surely also be a means of expressing what is best in humans, acknowledging the fact of our social being, that we are not the isolated, solipsistic monads that some psychological theories might lead us to believe we are.

A more evolved and realistic attitude to politics is something to work on in the consulting room, just as we work on more evolved and realistic attitudes to sexuality, spirituality and aggression. In the course of this book, I will propose that analysts (and patients, too) begin to work out models that enable us to refer to a person's *innate political potential*, to his or her state of *political development*, and to a *political level of the psyche*. In clinical practice, such a model would enable us to generate new readings of personal and collective *political imagery*. We may even find that there is a *politics of imagery* and that *countertransference and politics* are linked. Political imagery will be as fluid and unpredictable in its display of what is (or claims to be) positive and what is (or seems to be) negative as any other kind of imagery. Not all political imagery presents the worst case for humanity. For example, in Chapter 4 I attempt a psychological analysis of the imagery in Machiavelli's political thought, to find out how an engagement with the political level of the psyche affects depth psychology and how depth psychology affects political theorizing. Here, I want once more to emphasize that *the core of my project is to move toward an end of the isolation of the consulting room, though not toward the end of clinical analysis itself*, and to work out the detail of a serious relationship between depth psychology and politics rather than huff and puff at the absence of such a relationship. (I will discuss the role of the clinical project throughout the book.)

Our culture (and not just our culture) is longing to atone for its social injustices and the sense of disgust it feels for them, longing to be able to think good thoughts about itself and rid itself of depressive preoccupation with its own destructiveness, longing for a resacralized politics. When depression infects a political system, the first victim is any capacity to find imaginative solutions to political problems. This is because depression leads to an awful literalism in which fantasy and actuality are hopelessly muddled. Collective fantasies of hate and aggression are taken literally, leading to depressive guilt (for example, over the possession of nuclear weapons) and mass delusional self-reproach. The problem is how to contain and integrate disgust on this scale without either repressing it or acting it out.[16]

On the political level, many are full of guilty contempt for capitalism (and for what passed for socialism in the East). But there is a lack of any cultural ritual by which reparation and repentance can be made. Lacking ritual and a symbolic language with which to express this unease and disgust, and the desire to atone, many resacralizers tend to make a split between the constructive and the cheating sides of capitalism and the market economy, preferring to see only the negative side. Perhaps in response, a group with a totally opposite ideology of support for capitalism and the market has emerged. If we do not do something about this split in our political culture, then, hard though it is to face, resacralization, so ardently sought by so many, will not take place; it will not work. To be specific: Resacralization seems to be characterized by an attempt to construct a shadow-free politics in which the dark side is located somewhere else – in men, in whites, in the market, and so forth. Even when resacralizers do get involved with politics, it is a half-hearted involvement, distinguished, psychologically speaking, by a fear of getting dirty hands. I want to explore the damaging contents of this split.

On the *negative* side, there are fantasies of an apocalyptic end, whether by nuclear conflagration, AIDS pandemic, or the greenhouse effect. All these are blamed on capitalism and the market economy. Certainly, these anxieties are rooted in reality and resacralizers are right to point this out. But taken as fantasies, they are the deepest signs of a self-punishing contempt for ourselves. Perhaps many people think we deserve to perish like this. On the *positive* side, there are other voices, not at all persuaded by the arguments of resacralizers, claiming to be 'realistic', extolling the virtues of capitalism and the workings of the market as the source of the material benefits that 'we' enjoy today and as the only economic system that seems to work.

Sometimes it seems that those involved in resacralization try to manage their disgust and guilt at the excesses of capitalism and the market economy by attempting to make reparation and repentance over-literally – by making it up to the entire planet. There will be many good things to come out of the environmental movement but a prudish and facile environmentalism may not have enough psychological depth, enough connection to the dirt it seeks to cleanse, to ease the unease and even the disease in the culture. In Chapter 5, I consider whether there is a way to transform the dreams of environmentalists into pragmatic politics and hence make social realities out of them.

THE MARKET

This form of negative/positive split can be very clearly seen in relation to the market economy. Is the market economy a socially divisive rich man's charter, as even erstwhile supporters of it are beginning to say in Britain or the United States? Or is the market economy the road to freedom and dignity as many now seem to think in Eastern Europe and the former Soviet Union? Or is it the best available synthesis, a good compromise? Or – and this is the line I intend to take – is it both a negative and a positive phenomenon *at the same time*, with the negative and positive verdicts each having a distinct psychology of its own that resists synthesis and compromise? In this way of looking at the market economy, our negative and positive images of it are not split off from each other; indeed, they each guarantee the existence of the other for there will be no chance of realizing the positive features of the market economy *without* accepting the *simultaneous* presence of the negative features of the market economy. It is relatively easy for a cultural critic to reject the Manichean, crude, psychologically primitive, split approach in which the market must be good or bad. But the approach that attempts a balanced view of the market is almost as problematic, psychologically speaking. In the so-called 'balanced' approach, which is supposed to 'heal' the split, there is a difficulty in integrating the undoubtedly unfair and ruthless features of free market economics, seeing how they *have to be* present for the benefits of the market to be available. Resacralizers need to come to terms with this. We are not talking of unfortunate byproducts of the market; according to this psychological analysis, they are its *sine qua non* and cannot be ameliorated. We need to know more about the psychology of the market as a negative phenomenon *and* about the psychology of the market as a positive phenomenon. Both psychologies are relevant for resacralization. Resacralizers cannot stay pure, above, or outside the economic world. Disgust cannot be transcended to order; *there is no shadow-free politics*. Resacralization will have defeated itself as much as having been defeated by patriarchal exploitation and other reactionary forces.

Many sensitive and intelligent commentators have pointed out that the apparent triumph of capitalism is a moment for self-reflection. This is because market forces have already invaded or colonized most aspects of life. There is a need now to work on the development of a sense of community: Caring, compassionate, reaching-out to the less well-off. But a sense of community that does not address the shadow of community – the totalitarian shadow of community – will be thin, dessicated, morally elevated classroom civics, and socially useless. We will not be able to limit or tame market forces unless we comprehend their psychological nature and the powerful imagery involved in such forces. To understand the market requires political imagination and imagination about politics. There is no either/or about politics; nor is there an average. Politics is certainly the art of speculating, calculating, secret agreements and pragmatic maneuvering. But politics is also the art of making the world and the people in it better. There are *some* connections between these two distinct and separate images of politics that we should not ignore.

Our inability to stay in emotional contact with the psychologically distinct and separate images of the market makes it difficult to concentrate on the psychological issues of resacralization that are central to notions of economic and political change. Here, I am sure that *economics* can be a *psychological* focus. Later, in Chapter 4, in order to concentrate on splits within the image of the market economy, I will enlist the aid of the myth of Hermes to help us to hold onto both sides, positive and negative, enthusiasm and disgust, of our evaluation of the market economy. A political reworking of the myth of Hermes can provide a base for an approach that avoids the dangers of splitting *and* of trying to reach a supposedly balanced view. To the extent that there are opposite feelings in the air about the market, it is very hard, emotionally, to hold on to these as necessarily existing opposites without having recourse to either a schizoid, judgmental retreat or to glib sloganizing about accepting the bad with the good. As I said, we do need to know more about the psychology of the market as a positive phenomenon *and* about the psychology of the market as a negative phenomenon. Then, perhaps, we could move on to try to work out the psychology of the market without the introduction of the categories 'positive' and 'negative'.

For the moment, we do have to let 'positive' and 'negative' structure our psychological response to market economics. But there is a hidden gain in this. For maintaining an attitude of evaluation and judgment enables us to see to what extent the preceding ideas about attitudes to and images of the market are relevant outside Western, capitalistic culture.

It sometimes seems that the *Zeitgeist* in what was the Soviet Union and in Eastern Europe is quite different from that of the West. In the West, criticisms of the excesses of free market economics are beginning to surface in circles that had, hitherto, been gung ho for the market. For example, it seems that the long sentence passed on Michael Milken, the 'junk bond king', was 'widely seen as public retribution for the excesses of the '80s', resulting from 'public anger over the ethics of the age'.[17] Kevin Phillips, a one-time senior aide of President Reagan, published a bestselling book in 1990 entitled *The Politics of Rich and Poor* in which he prophesied the end of an ethical and political climate that permitted 'the triumph of upper America – an ostentatious celebration of wealth, the political ascendancy of the richest third of the population and a glorification of capitalism, free markets and finance'.[18]

In the East (and in many parts of the Third World), things seem to be going the other way. In progressive circles, the free market is hailed, not only as the sole means to revive moribund economies, but also as a means to political and spiritual revival. However, I wonder if the two completely different political situations do not share some psychological features in common. Both kinds of society are fascinated, even obsessed by the market; the one eager now to condemn it, the other to praise and implement it. Both have the same difficulty in getting beyond a verdict that is either good or bad. Both seem to sense the limitations of the 'balanced' view. We see this in the former Soviet Union in the popular rejection of Gorbachev's idea of a 'third way' incorporating what was best in communism and capitalism. We see it in the United States in the almost total disagreement about what can be done to ease the plight of the so-called underclass (including intense argument over whether such a grouping actually exists).[19] Crucially, in both West and East, modes of economic and political organization are seen nowadays as inseparable from psychological, ethical and spiritual themes. One Russian commentator had this to say: 'The main thing is for people to learn to be human. If we have bread and still become beasts, there will be no reason for us to live.'[20] Surface differences between Western and Eastern attitudes to the market mask a deeper, psychological similarity.

Of course, we shall have to wait to see what, if anything, the psychosocial impact of a new Russian middle class will be.[21] But the psychological dimension is demonstrated in a comment made by a Russian political commentator in 1991: 'Our people are fed up with the free market without having lived in it for a single day.'[22]

I have not merely been proposing that our epoch *needs* resacralizing and encouraging people to do it. I am arguing that resacralization is already going on, and has a life of its own running underneath the development of technology and a hyper-rational way of life. As I said, I am trying to bring something to consciousness – to cultural consciousness – that is already there in culture. It is an analyst's way of making politics. And it is as an analyst that I have found myself thinking that, from a psychological point of view in which depth common denominators are given more weight than surface discrepancies, everything I have written about 'our' culture (meaning Western culture) is, paradoxically, *exemplified* by what has been happening in Eastern Europe since the late 1980s. The imagery from two differing contexts is not disconnected.

NUMINOUS EXPERIENCE AND SOCIOPOLITICAL CRITICISM

I feel that split-inducing collective disgust would be moderated by a sense that culture can be transformed through a resacralized politics. The psychic energy locked up in disgust and cultural depression would be employed in a less masochistic way – in a more practical way, like Bezaleel's, with his sacred box. When considering such a political commitment, it is unavoidable that religious language and imagery, if not religion itself, will have a part to play. Here, the role played by the churches in the political changes of Eastern Europe should be borne in mind. One cannot imagine an expression of the more caring and compassionate side of liberal democracy without religious terms. We need to look again, more psychologically and more generously, at what we regard as sacred. Beneath and within the fractured surface of contemporary Western culture lies a protoreligious culture (and this is also shown clearly by events in Eastern Europe and in the emergence of liberation theology in Latin America). We can see the culture's attempts to resacralize itself in its extreme openness to numinous experience – not always along decorous lines, and including the ritually pagan: Sexual experimentation, rock music, sports, food, fashion, money, collectible things. Maybe the best way to find the sacred today would be to submit and surrender to the apparently pagan.

However, political resacralization is not identical with religion or religious revival. In the latter case, there is usually or often a program to be followed, a prescription, a recipe. What I perceive in resacralization is the marking out and making of a place – a social temple – in which something politically transformative can be born. The resacralizing place is also designed for self-reflection and the recovery of personal dignity.

In religious, mystical or holistic experiences, the individual is seized and controlled by something outside himself or herself that is possessed of a fascinating and awe-inspiring power. Such a power, in Jung's words, makes one feel 'its victim rather than its creator'.[23] This kind of experience was described by Rudolf Otto in *The Idea of the Holy* in 1917 as numinous experience. Otto was at pains to stress the paradox that, though the numinous experience was irrational, it could be analyzed rationally; an important point to remember concerning depth psychological analysis of politics. We can be rational about the irrational and honor both dimensions while so doing; we can be secular and social about the holy and the sacred. Nevertheless, the irrational *is* irrational. Otto, in fine German academic style, lists his criteria for the irrational:

Pure fact in contrast to law, the empirical in contrast to reason, the contingent in contrast to the necessary, the psychological in contrast to transcendental fact, that which is known *a posteriori* in contrast to that which is determinable *a priori*; power, will, and arbitrary choice in contrast to reason, knowledge, and determination by value; impulse, instinct, and the obscure forces of the subconscious in contrast to insight, reflection, and intelligible plan; mystical depths and stirrings in the soul, surmise, presentiment, intuition, prophecy and finally the 'occult' powers also; or, in general, the uneasy stress and universal fermentation of the time, with its groping after the thing never yet heard or seen in poetry or the plastic arts – all these and many more may claim the names 'non-rational', 'irrational'.[24]

It is remarkable that Otto, the author of one of the most influential works on religious psychology and the psychology of religion, publishing in the revolutionary year of 1917, should perceive in the 'uneasy stress and universal fermentation of the time' a groping, not for a rational system as a form of panacea (such as Marxism) but for the nub of the irrational itself – the *numen*. I want to take this statement of Otto's as an account, not only of the raw material of a psychological analysis of political process, but also of the orientation of the political analyst. It is a kind of clarion call to pay attention to what seems absurd and trivial, as well as to what seems dignified and profound. What is 'deep' (as in 'depth' psychology) may be on the surface.

Reacting to Otto has led me to muse on the styles or, perhaps more accurately, the tropes of depth psychology in its attempt to do cultural and political analysis. We need to introduce the irrational into our discourse on politics: Measures of exaggeration, grotesquerie, vulgarity and broad comedy, making a social critique out of these just as the unconscious itself sometimes manages to. For example, the wild and compelling imagery of aggressive fantasy eventually promotes concern for other people. The hidden social *telos* of aggressive fantasy, the covert function it serves, the thing that it is secretly for, is the fostering of an emergence of concern. Without my base and sordid aggressive fantasies in the direction of another, there would be less need for concern about him or her on my part.

Similarly, the seductive and shifting fantasies of sexual selfhood that I call 'gender confusions' respond to a political and prospective reading, leading to a far more positive and welcoming evaluation than the one usually given by analysts. In the future, we will all become even more confused about gender. Provided we stay close to the confusion and the confused experience, and do not try for an instant escape by 'androgyny' or flee into 'gender certainty', and provided we keep our judgmental tendencies under control, then the earthy challenge to the established order represented by gender confusions may move onto an ever-more practical, collective, political level. (See Chapter 7 for a further discussion of gender confusion.[25])

As I see it, the tasks of depth psychologists who seek to engage with the political are to locate the enormous psychic energy that is presently locked up in collective and subjective self-disgust, and to try to release the energy so that it becomes available for political renewal. If depth psychology is to make a contribution on a political level to the processes of resacralization of which it is already an unconscious part, it must surely continue to engage with the irrational and numinous aspects of life. Depth psychology can attempt to work these into a social and political analysis of culture. But this fantastic and original project cannot always be carried on within a rational or moral framework. A politics of transformation can hardly be totally rational. However, working with the irrational and the amoral is the forte of depth psychology. In Donald Williams's words: 'The greatest possibilities for wisdom in the psyche come from its immediate aliveness to new, current and contemporary sources that take advantage of its innate adaptability and resourcefulness.'[26]

To be sure, as I mentioned, this brings up matters of style and, at the same time, something more than style is involved. For what looks like a matter of style is also relevant to the concrete contribution depth psychology can make to the social sciences, especially politics. It may be that it is the general areas of interest that depth psychology covers that earn it the right to be taken seriously by social scientists, as Ian Craib has suggested. He saw the central features of depth psychology as (a) its concern with the irrational, (b) its focus on emotions, (c) its apprehension of the complexity of personality, and (d) its concern for creativity (including, in Craib's listing, religion and artistic production) and for morality.[27] Depth psychology reaches the parts of human nature other disciplines, such as sociology, do not reach: 'The complexity and conflict of people's emotional lives, . . . the profound ambiguities of motivation and meaning, . . . the strange and often difficult relationships we have with our bodies.'[28]

I want to take this clarion call of Ian Craib's and rotate it through 180 degrees. The central features of depth psychology, meaning the areas it has staked a claim for in the knowledge-battle, may also be the ways and styles in which it should make its contribution to social science. Not only saying something *about* irrationality, emotion, personality, creativity, morality – but saying something *with and through* these thematics, and with and through dream, fantasy and passion. The style of a depth psychological contribution to an understanding of political process should be congruent with what depth psychology has habitually done, while not reducing one field to the other. We should focus on a particular political problem in terms of its irrational aspects, the emotions (and hence the images) it engenders in our subjective experience of the problem, the complexity of the issue as it impacts on people's evolving personal lives, and the ways in which what is going on speak of the fostering or negating of human creativity and moral sensibility.

This idea is strengthened by noting that many of the criticisms of attempts to link depth psychology to social and political issues have settled on the oversystematized, hyper-rational, mechanical nature of these 'applications'. In particular, the project of combining Freud and Marx to create a politics of the subject(ive) has degenerated into an obsession with Freud – the man and his texts – and a preoccupation with the work of Jacques Lacan that, for many, has cut psychoanalysis off from those very features of itself that could make a distinctive contribution to social science (as listed, for example, by Craib, above). While these failings are not going to be totally absent from my book, I have tried to be aware of them. Hopefully, this enables me to ask: Can social theory truly respond to the challenge of telling us who we are as subjects and what our place in cultural process might be *without* its taking account of a realm of interiority? This, in turn, leads to exploration of the various criticisms of depth psychological accounts of subjectivity that have been mounted.

Before concluding the chapter, I want briefly to make some distinctions about the ways I am using the overlapping terms 'subjectivity' and 'the personal' and how these relate to 'the irrational'. *Subjectivity* is a perspective on things that tends toward direct experience of them and an evaluative response fashioned out of direct experience, however illusory that might be from a philosophical standpoint. (I return to the philosophical problems with the idea of subjectivity in the next chapter.) The sensation of direct experience remains even when the intellect is aware that one experiences things through ideological filters and that subjective experience is itself culturally and politically constructed. In addition, I see the body as a prime source (and recipient) of subjective experience and of subjectivity.

I regard *the personal* as being implicated in the identity/difference theme that I referred to earlier in the chapter. This implies a sense of boundary, however permeable ('skin-ego'), and hence a potential for relationship. The narrative and mythology of people's lives contribute to their sense of what is personal of and for them.

The irrational can scarcely be comprehended without reference to its spouse: rationality. Moreover, what is and is not considered irrational is highly variable according to personal, historical and cultural features. However, when attempting to factor subjectivity and the personal into political discourse, there is little doubt that a sense of irrationality will (and ought to be) generated from time to time.

These distinctions are the background to the 180-degree turn I proposed earlier in which the central concerns of depth psychology are revisioned as the tools with which to make an analysis of a political problem: Irrationality, subjectivity, the personal dimension, and a focus on creativity and morality.

As I said, the way in which depth psychology engages with political themes is both a matter of style and, at the same time, something more. On the stylistic and on other levels, I will return to the topic at many moments throughout the book – a sign that I find myself unable to reach a conclusion about the balance between rational and irrational elements in my text. Perhaps what is needed at the present time is a more generous conception of what is 'serious' and 'scholarly' in writing. Maybe we are on the verge of a revolution in our understanding of what constitutes scholarly, academic and intellectual writing, based on the realization that many apparently discursive texts in the human sciences are full of rhetoric. An antithesis between scholarly and imaginative writing can itself be an obstacle to the success of a text in either mode. (The question of how literally I intend to be taken is addressed in Chapter 7.)

Sometimes depth psychologists will seek to accomplish their political tasks irrationally, making use of the least rational psychological function: intuition. Intuition provides a person with a subjective sense of where something is going, of what the possibilities are, without depending on conscious knowledge or empirical proof (though, hopefully, without downgrading these). Hence, intuition moderates the vicissitudes of *Nachträglichkeit*, the deferring of action that, in social terms, condemns us to study the impact of political change only retrospectively, only when it is too late. Though intuition may tend toward prophetic or oracular pronouncement, intuition also has the capacity to weave empathy, compassion and imagination into social theorizing. Crucially, intuition is required for the conversion of subjective response into sociopolitical criticism – and this is the topic of the next chapter.

Chapter 2

Subjectivity and political discourse
The contribution of the clinic

THE COUNTERTRANSFERENCE REVOLUTION

People who have never been analysts or therapists are often surprised to find that clinical practice is a red-hot emotional activity. It is not usually the case that a patient quietly reports a problem to an analyst who then explains its origins by reference to specialized knowledge about such matters as childhood or the significance of chains of association. In particular, the analyst's state of mind often shows signs of altered levels of consciousness and the presence of intense fantasy and aroused emotion. These may lead to disturbed bodily and behavioral functioning on the analyst's part. These central features of the analyst's experience, which are the regular currency of discussion among clinicians have, rightly or wrongly, been tagged as 'countertransference'.[1] *They are not usually referred to by those who seek to illumine political and social process by means of a depth psychological analysis.* I want to remedy this huge omission by supplying a political focus on countertransference. By so doing, I think I can give a novel and practical twist to the contribution depth psychology can make to an analysis of political and social processes.

Some years ago, I carried out a research project into counter-transference to see how analysts and therapists conceptualized the strange mental states into which they enter while doing their work. I garnered thirty-two respondents who told me of seventy-six examples of what they saw as countertransference. (I allowed them to define the term in their own way.) These practicing clinicians had had the most extraordinary range of experiences in their work and these could be divided into three groupings: Bodily and behavioral responses, feeling responses and fantasy responses.

Some bodily and behavioral responses were: Wearing the same clothes as the patient, walking into lamp-posts after sessions with a particular patient, forgetting to discuss something important, strange sensations in the solar plexus, pain, sexual arousal, sleep.

Some feeling responses were: Anger, impatience, powerfulness, powerlessness, envy, irritation, depression, manipulation, redundancy, being flooded, bored.

Some fantasy responses were: This is the wrong patient, there's something wrong with my feet, a large black pot, I killed her mother, I'm a prostitute, I feel reverence for her serious, private place, *he* has God on *his* side, all color has gone out of the room, I'm going to be involved in an automobile crash after the session, the patient will rummage through my books and papers if I leave the room, the patient is getting bigger and bigger and filling the room.[2]

Those of my readers who are in clinical practice will know something of the revolution in clinical theorizing that has taken place. This revolution has made it possible to review the analyst's subjective experience in a calm and considered way, underscoring its utility and resisting, but certainly not forgetting, the tendency to conclude that analysts are prone to mad responses to their patients. Because many readers will not be familiar with this revolution, I want to give a brief history of it. Although no hard-and-fast consensus exists about the *use* of the counter-transference, something which need not dismay us (as we will see), a definite historical trend in theorizing about it can be observed. In this trend, the countertransference experiences of the analyst are retheorized as communications from the patient and hence as being of clinical utility. Analysis and therapy *result from* an interplay of subjectivities – they are intersubjective phenomena; there is no subjectivity (no subject) without an Other.[3]

For Freud, it was apparently, but by no means exclusively, a problem that analysts reacted to their patients in ways that suggested neurosis or even psychosis on the analyst's part. Freud regarded these kinds of responses as undesirable and as something the analyst should overcome by more analysis or self-analysis. In the way Freud himself worked, it is clear that he did not function as a 'blank screen', as he seems to have had a strong personal presence in relation to his patients; this is apparent in his case histories. But it is also clear that, quite deliberately, from time to time he functioned *as if* he were a blank screen, a person without emotion or subjective life when seen from the patient's point of view. In this way, he argued, the patient's projections of problematic figures from the past could be more freely transferred onto the person of the analyst – hence, transference (which was also considered a phenomenon that interfered with treatment right at the very start of psychoanalytic endeavor).

By the 1950s, some analysts were, controversially, regarding countertransference as other than inevitably neurotic, seeing it as an informative phenomenon with distinct clinical value. Nowadays there are numerous analysts who see their subjectivity, carried by the counter-transference, as a central feature of the clinical encounter. Such analysts conceive of themselves as 'ready' for the experience of counter-transference.[4] There have been parallel debates in analytical psychology but there has been less of a sense of overturning the applecart because Jung constantly asserted that the analyst was 'in' the treatment just as much as the patient. Jung regarded countertransference as a 'highly important organ of information' about the patient and felt that analysts who could not let themselves be influenced by their patients' psychological emissions would be ineffective clinicians.[5]

There are many strands of post-Freudian theorizing about counter-transference. One strand lays emphasis on the analyst's emotions and emotionality, meaning his or her total involvement in the analytical process. The idea is that the analyst's unconscious somehow 'understands' that of the patient in an empathic, feeling manner.[6] This view is claimed, with justification, to stem from Freud who, in spite of warning against the possibility of neurosis in the analyst, also referred to the analyst's unconscious as a 'receptive organ' in relation to the 'transmitting unconscious of the patient'.[7] Psychoanalysts (and analytical psychologists) who have theorized treatment as an emotional encounter do not, on the whole, advocate simple disclosure of or sharing their emotional states with their patients.

Another strand of post-Freudian thinking about countertransference makes use of a form of communication theory. Everything that happens between the analyst and patient, whether originating in analyst or patient, may be regarded as a symbolic communication. This permits a further revision – in this instance, it is a revision of the role of the patient. The patient is regarded as a person who helps the analyst conduct the treatment, pointing out errors and misjudgments either directly or by communication with the analyst's unconscious. In the latter case, it is countertransference that provides the means by which the patient can communicate his or her corrections of the analyst's attempts.[8]

A third way in which contemporary psychoanalysis has modified Freud's views of countertransference also makes use of a notion of communication. But in this approach communication is understood as the interplay of projective and introjective processes, the movement of psychological material between people, out of one and into the other and, maybe, back again. These processes are understood as special variants of generally occurring psychosocial phenomena and so countertransference theorizing can be understood as part of a wider apprehension of how people communicate. The advantage of this theory is that it is possible to see how parts of the patient's psyche crop up in the analyst's subjectivity, and vice versa.[9] Post-Jungian theorizing about countertransference has made use of similar thinking about projection and introjection.

The concern and preoccupation with countertransference has reached a peak in Britain and Latin America, where it sometimes seems that analysis consists of nothing but an exploration of the countertransference. But the United States, Germany and Italy are rapidly catching up, as a review of the literature demonstrates.[10]

The situation in France is different. Jacques Lacan criticized (quite correctly, in my view) tendencies to fashion ego to ego communication out of the countertransference.[11] However, Lacan's view of what happens dramatically oversimplifies the experience and practices of those who pioneered a revision of Freud's methodological suggestions. Though the *question* of disclosure remains a pressing one, Lacan overlooks the issues of the level of the analyst's disclosure and the work he or she might do on what is to be disclosed prior to communicating it.

The purpose of this opening section has been to familiarize non-clinical readers with the background. I will indicate my own position later in the chapter.

COUNTERTRANSFERENCE AND POLITICS

The title of this section is a little enigmatic, so I will give my main argument in a nutshell. Psychotherapists and analysts have in their possession a precious attribute of which they are themselves unaware, something that would deepen and enhance our idea of the political. I am referring to the evolving body of clinical knowledge and practice that I described in the previous section concerning the countertransference. I mean especially the clinical valuing of a *practitioner*'s subjectivity as a royal road to *the patient's psychic reality*. I am going to detach the countertransference and theorizing about it from its clinical moorings and insert this professional jewel in a different setting: In the world of politics. I am going to politicize countertransference. *By so doing, I will reframe and revision clinical practice: As a potential link between depth psychology and society and not as the source of an isolation of depth psychology from society* (which is how critics of depth psychology usually depict its clinical project). The clinical can be a bridge to a new way to express and theorize political dissent. It will be a radical version of the clinical. Deconstruction of the opposition between the disciplines of depth psychology and politics leads to the advocacy of their occasional hybridization.

I hope to indicate a practical contribution that depth psychology can make to working through, in a positive but critical spirit, the insight of contemporary feminism that the personal is also political. That insight supports a political valuing of a *citizen*'s subjectivity as a royal road to *the culture's social reality*. I want to underscore the analogy I have made: In the world of the consulting room, the move is from the analyst's subjectivity to an understanding of the patient's psychic reality; in the world of politics, the move is from the citizen's subjectivity to an understanding of the culture's social reality. We can take a sentence from a clinical text like this one of Christopher Bollas's and rewrite it in more political terms: 'It is essential to find some way to put forward for analytic investigation that which is occurring in the analyst as a purely subjective and private experience.'[12] 'Analytic' becomes 'political', 'analyst' becomes 'citizen' and the analogy I want to draw is demonstrated.

Judith Hubback defined an analogy as 'a likeness in certain respects between things which are otherwise different'. As a 'device' or 'tool', an analogy can be used or abused and 'analogy is the basis or substructure from which image-making develops . . . a most powerful help in the constant effort to make sense of life'.[13] According to Martin Stanton, Sandor Ferenczi's idea about analogies was that they 'negotiate the inability of any philosophy to rid itself of the subjective and erect a purely objective view of the world'.[14]

An excursion into the complexities of countertransference means that we can find out more about, or 'negotiate', the linkage *between* psychic reality and social reality and even do this in a way that would satisfy Robert Musil's complaint that 'we do not have too much intellect and too little soul, but too little precision in matters of the soul'.[15] Precision and soul – two faces of psychotherapy and two faces of politics. Modern clinical practice in analytical psychotherapy can be dreamt onward as a template for a form of political analysis. And, as we will see, a political analysis illuminates the clinical encounter. I do not think that depth psychology can make a whole new politics. But, true to its functional role, depth psychology shows up problems in our habitual styles of making politics.

This is more than an attempt to demystify the practices of depth psychology and to show that the clinicalization of depth psychology is not 'natural' – in the sense that no other form of practice is possible. It is also an attempt to challenge wider power structures, showing that hyper-rational modes of making politics and policy are not 'natural' either – in the sense that no other ways of theorizing politics are possible. Perhaps this implies a fresh, depth psychological epistemology less wedded to Enlightenment values.

In the previous chapter, I argued that a new, politically sensitive spirit is abroad in depth psychology. This makes it easier to work out a political psychology and a psychology of politics. What therapists and analysts think about and do with countertransference gives us a fresh way of introducing the subjective factor into political discourse, of making the personal political.

THERAPY AND/FOR THE WORLD

I want to go on to explore a fantasy that I sense as moving depth psychology just now, to analyze the fantasy within which depth psychologists are functioning, to study what symbols and images inform their particular contribution to resacralization. When I speak of 'fantasy' I do not mean to bring in a pathological construct. Rather, I intend to refer to something that evokes the flavor, shape, direction, purpose – and shadow – of an enterprise.

The fantasy is of providing therapy for the world. I mean providing therapy for what is sensed as the external world, conceived of very broadly. Helping that world to resolve its conflicts, understand itself better, enjoy a healthier psychological trajectory. *The fantasy is of giving therapy to the world.* Yes, this is inflated, even oracular stuff. But it is also imaginative, creative and, most important, right now the fantasy of treating the world is empathic with, in tune with the world's desire to be treated, the clamor of the world for therapeutic attention that I referred to earlier. *What distinguishes a depth psychological analysis of the political world from any other kind of analysis is this fantasy of providing therapy.* In the clinical context, though we know that 'analysis' and 'therapy' are not synonymous, we tend not to regard them as totally separate activities.

Providing therapy for the world does not mean converting the world into a patient in the sense of a reduction of the world or an aggrandizement of the therapist. Anyway, that would not be true therapy. As we saw, it is still less helpful to treat the world as if the world were a baby requiring only good-enough mothering to flourish. But providing therapy for the world, which I am seeing as the fantasy that drives depth psychology today, does involve our taking up a certain attitude – a therapeutic attitude – toward the world. Therapists of the world might bring therapy into the world. A therapeutic attitude toward the world is most appropriate when we come to politics because politics is the dimension of social reality that contains the social world's pathology: Palpable injustices, such as an unfair distribution of wealth, skewed gender relations, racism, poverty, disease and a wrecked ecology. What connects depth psychology and politics is a preoccupation with therapy. The analyst of complexes is preoccupied with the therapy of the individual; the analyst of politics is preoccupied with the therapy of the nation or society or the world – hence the imagistic links that can often be observed between 'personal growth' and environmental concerns. Neither side of the private/public divide can flourish without affection for the other side. Marxism failed to take account of this.

Several art and literary critics refer explicitly to providing therapy for an art work or text.[16] Some historians also seem to regard themselves as offering therapy to their topics of interest.[17] As I noted, the imagery of psychotherapy permeates the entire environmental movement. *So it is not absolutely necessary to have a patient in human form in order to do psychotherapy and analysis.* It seems clear that one cannot simply evacuate the clinical element from so-called academic depth psychology. The clinical is *the* distinguishing feature of depth psychology. As John Forrester puts it, 'the conceptual system of transference–counter-transference is built around the questions: What is an analyst? What is his or her desire?'[18]

So – here are the depth psychologists: Ready, willing and able to treat the world. Ready to be therapists of politics, political therapists, even political analysts (with all the ambiguity of the term 'political analyst'). They are pretty sure that the world has asked for therapy or analysis. But, having issued them with a request for therapy, the world has not shown up for its first session. The world is ambivalent about its therapy, suspicious of its political therapists, reluctant to be a patient (or a baby). We can see just how suspicious the world is when we reflect on the limited role depth psychologists have played, or have been allowed to play, in the political happenings of our century. As I suggested in the previous chapter, it is quite reasonable that exclusively psychological understandings of the external world will be found unacceptable. If depth psychology wants to treat the world, then it had better do so as part of a multidisciplinary project.

Where is this leading? Should we give up on the idea, the fantasy, that depth psychologists might be of use to the world in a therapeutic way? Is their utility to be restricted to the positive impact made on the lives of their individual patients? Is there anything in that psychological medicine chest that has not been tried so far?

I think that the answer to this last question – Is there anything depth psychologists have not tried so far? – is 'yes'. There is something that has not been tried so far in an attempt to treat the world. I want to suggest that it is not in metapsychology, nor in models of the psyche or the unconscious, nor in schemas of personality development, and not even in the analytic attitude itself, that our usefulness to the political world might be found. Rather, it may be analytical and psychotherapeutic *methods* – modes and techniques of therapy – that we should be exploring as the means to move the fantasy of treating the world onto the level of a concrete and practical political engagement. In particular, those aspects of clinical practice clustering around the concept of countertransference may be the most liminal with politics – that is, lie on the threshold between depth psychology and politics. As Nietzsche put it, 'the most valuable insights are methods'.[19]

Let us consider the parallels between the typical clinical set-up and a depth psychological engagement with a political problem; what I have been calling 'political analysis'. As in clinical analysis and psycho-therapy, the political analyst gets into a transference–countertransference relationship with the problem she or he is trying to treat. As in clinical analysis, fostering this relationship means allowing himself or herself to be influenced by that which it is hoped to treat – accepting both transference and the experience of countertransference. Acknowledging the value of countertransference does not mean denying that it is in countertransference that we find the political analyst's own unresolved cultural and political problems and prejudices, evidence of unfinished political development on her or his part (the analyst's 'political neurosis').

Continuing the parallel, the political analyst can try to understand the behavior of a political problem in terms of its antecedents. Such an understanding means trying to find out the history of whatever problem is being treated, including the collective fantasies or myths that have become attached to the problem. The political analyst would then try to raise the level of the problem's consciousness so as to allow the problem to gain a degree of knowledge and control regarding itself. This task is accomplished to some extent, and as is usual in clinical analysis, by interpretation. Political and social problems, like human patients, will respond to therapy in differing ways. But accepting that the political analyst has a countertransference to the problem she or he seeks to treat avoids the well-known self-deception that a so-called 'objective' analysis of politics is possible. An objective analysis of a political problem would, following the analogy I am working out, be equivalent to the worst kind of high-tech or high-minded psychiatric approach. A similar failure to grasp the unconscious dimension of the treatment relationship between political analyst and political process marred much Marxist analysis of politics.

Employing the techniques and methods of clinical analysis, especially techniques and methods that foreground the experience and use of countertransference, provides a model for a political analysis that *makes use* of the political analyst's affective, subjective involvement rather than merely pointing it out. In such a way, the personal and the political are brought closer together. Looked at like this, maybe all social and political inquiry could be therapy.

When I write of the *use* of a countertransference by the political analyst or therapist, I do not mean to advocate reliance on an instant response – any more than I would advocate such a thing in clinical analysis. I am not in favor of 'that makes me feel' statements on the part of clinicians. I do mean that, as I will detail later, someone attempting to bring depth psychology to bear on political problems accepts that her or his experiences embody, or reflect, or are relevant to aspects of the 'patient's' experience. The relevance is based on the joint immersion of the political analyst and the political problem in a shared world that transcends the boundaries of private and public, subjective and objective. There is no clinical imperialism in this. I am not trying to tell politicians what to do. The point is that depth psychologists have acquired power and legitimation to operate out of a feeling state, to 'use' feelings. Groups that are relatively powerless could also be granted access to this kind of power and legitimation. My conception of depth psychological political analysis is that its clinical element is not something to be restricted to the 'official' clinicians. Clinically inspired political analysis is, potentially, open to all to practice. It could provide an access route to political process for those who, currently, are effectively disenfranchised: Blacks, women, the poor, homosexuals, the disabled.

It may seem curious that I use the term countertransference to indicate this particular take on politics and I would like to explain why I do so. There is certainly more to therapeutic interaction than countertransference or transference–countertransference. And, to be sure, we should not merely equate countertransference and subjectivity. But the notion of countertransference focuses on what is happening in the analyst's subjectivity – the part of that subjectivity that is somehow connected or relevant to the patient. If clinical method is to provide the inspiration for a novel form of politics outside of the clinical setting, then it is experience and theorizing of countertransference that is the area of clinical method on which we must concentrate.

The idea of countertransference brings with it a penumbra or residue of neuroticism in the analyst – his or her unresolved neurotic conflicts and so forth. This, too, is important for my theme. Whenever there is an experience of countertransference, there is uncertainty about whose 'stuff' it is – the analyst's (the citizen's), the patient's (the political problem's), or a mixture of the two. This uncertainty is not in itself a handicap. Quite the opposite is the case. The uncertainty is an inevitable outcrop of the impossibility of uttering a statement in terms of 'this is subjective' or 'this is objective' whether the field is psychology or politics.

By using the term 'countertransference' in relation to what a citizen might do with his or her subjective response to a political problem, I am quite deliberately putting that citizen in the analyst's seat, in full consciousness of the authority and power that often attaches to the role of analyst. While the patient certainly does have power over the analyst to some extent, and patients undoubtedly influence the growth of their analysts, there is an unavoidable asymmetry in analysis. *I want to place the experiencing citizen in the analyst's place and not in the patient's place*, where the citizen would have to be regarded as having a *transference* to society. If the citizen is to participate in social transformation, then this is to be on the basis of being analyst not patient. Most psychoanalytic approaches to politics cast the citizen solely in the role of patient (or baby) with a transference to society.

By locating the political referents of the clinical process within the analyst and not within the patient, I have problematized the analyst. Hopefully, this will help to reduce the possibility of an arrogant, from-on-high, experience-distant psychologizing of politics – which has tended to mar some previous attempts to link depth psychology and politics.

I want to relocate the very idea of countertransference so that it lies *between* clinical analysis and political analysis. For instance, I would say that, just as in clinical analysis, in political analysis the analyst's bodily reactions are an important part of the picture: The body is an organ of information. Bodily reactions to the surface of modern life, its sounds, smells, textures and shapes; bodily reactions to the demands of modern life, its crush, bustle, hassle and artery-blocking stresses. Bodily reactions, worked on and distilled in ways familiar to the clinical analyst, lead the political analyst to the heart of the culture and its political problems. The body of the political analyst leads in a spontaneous political analysis.

Bodily reactions and an understanding of them are starting to figure in the clinical literature on countertransference. Can the body be an instrument of *political* analysis? If so, then it is to the wisdom of the body that we must turn as one way of politicizing what we know about

countertransference. In existing political discourse, there is no psychologically valid account of how we can take fear, disgust, a sense of
contamination, anger and all the rest of the somatic lexicon as indicators
of our political judgments. It is up to depth psychologists to provide such
an account, an account of the body as a discourse of power, even a record
of power (especially in the case of the female body).

Though a body-based analysis of political themes and problems will
take place spontaneously, it is nevertheless possible to sketch out three
stages or rather levels of a somatic analysis of the political. First, a
thorough exploration of the bodily state, both the body as a whole and its
constituent parts. I think this requires practice and training, and an
atmosphere and setting that is friendly to the enterprise. Second, we have
to learn the particular language of the body when it engages in political
discourse. We need to focus, clarify, differentiate and describe the somatic
vocabulary and the bodily imagery. Third, we would make explicit the
implicit meanings of such imagery in an act of interpretation. (I believe a
start has been made on each of these three stages or levels within the
relatively new discipline of dance movement therapy, in which I have
recently become interested.)[20]

I am arguing that analytic and psychotherapeutic methods serve as a
base for a form of political analysis, or approach to political problems, that
goes far beyond the rationalistic limitations of much political theory.
Political analysis that is infused with depth psychology is a way to make
the personal political, highlighting the relationship between individual and
society. *Affect, bodily sensations, wild fantasy, are all reframed and
re-evaluated as the tools of political analysis* – just as, via our theorizing
about countertransference, they have been reframed and re-evaluated as
the tools of clinical analysis.

Up to now, having empathy with a political problem has been seen from
the standpoint of conventional politics as having an 'emotional' reaction
to the problem (and nothing kind is meant by the word emotional in this
context). Being emotional about politics is too often seen as being biased,
unreliable, 'unsound', and sometimes even as having a 'feminine' attitude
to politics (again, nothing kind meant by feminine here). My position is
that, by accepting the parallels with countertransference in clinical
analysis, the realism and utility of a politics that incorporates a subjective
(and maybe an irrational) inquiry is established.

There are many implications in the advocacy of a subjective politics, a
politics over which hovers that charged word 'feminine'. A subjective
politics is available to both sexes – as is an 'objective' politics – but this
recognition needs to be coupled with a sense that one of the features of a

subjective politics is to back up the necessity for women to find a collective voice in relation to a male-dominated social reality. A subjective politics, in which women may have a significant role, must surely mount its challenge to injustice and oppression in diverse ways according to personal, socioeconomic and other circumstances. This diversity lessens the chances of replacing one hegemony by another. Making a subjective politics enables us to look at how women are denied access to political power as well as working out how to marry subjectivity to political discourse. To paraphrase Juliet Mitchell, if femininity in politics is by definition subjective, feminism is the demand *for* the right to be subjective in politics.[21]

The 'masculine' cast of so-called objective political analysis may have its roots in the psychological need of children to move away from a dependent relationship with either mother or father or both. To help themselves achieve personal boundaries, some individuals tip over into a rather rigid attitude to the world with an accent on distance and precision. This comes through as political 'objectivity' and is experienced as incontrovertibly objective even when its objectivity is exposed by others as being a disguised subjectivity. There are many in politics with such an outlook which I see as having been adopted for identity-saving reasons and not as a rejection of the mother or of femininity (though it can look and has been theorized like that). The feeling of being politically objective imparts a bleak political strength. But those who continue to maintain their political objectivity are uncomfortable with feeling deeply *involved* in social and political problematics. They fear that muddled feelings will inevitably lead to a return to the parental corral. So politics can only be approached from outside, as it were, because staying outside avoids a merger with the parent/political problematic – a merger that is experienced as identity-threatening. Subjective politics will or will not come into practical being depending on whether the psychological seductions of political objectivity can be overcome.

A question is bound to be raised concerning the untrammelled use of subjectivity in political discourse. Does this not lead to undesirable mass hysterias, such as Nazism or racism, or to markedly populist leaders such as Mrs Thatcher? And you want *more* of this? As far as mass movements go, I think the exact opposite argument can be made: That they destroy rather than foster the space for subjectivity in politics, in that mass movements are hostile to whatever is peculiar to an individual subject and his or her psychological functioning.

Thinking of populist leaders, if one sees them as therapists of the world, then they resemble those guru-like therapists who approach their patients with assumptions as to what constitutes wellbeing and how to achieve it. We know that those kinds of therapists are not working out of alterity and empathy at all, nor are populist leaders like Mrs Thatcher. They are not *responding* to the patient; they're *imposing* something upon the patient out of their own systems of belief. Just as guru-therapists often get good results in the very short term, so, too, populist leaders seem to offer quick solutions to political problems. But, in both instances, before very long the complexity and incorrigibility of psychological or political problems defeats these magical cures. You could say that the problem starts to resist a solution that does not arise from itself – its history, its distinguishing features, its needs, its goals and so forth.

A NOTE ON SUBJECTIVITY

I am aware that there are problems with my (or anyone's) use of the term 'subjectivity'. However, I argue that the need to retain the idea of subjectivity is pressing when we consider the political dimensions of life. To continue to refer to subjectivity is not as naive as it seems. It does not bring with it a belief in an innate, autonomous, single viewpoint arising from the heart of a person, independent of social institutions and relations. However, it must be admitted that some psychoanalytic usages of the notion of subjectivity do seem to imply just that. In contrast, my usage of the idea of subjectivity involves the recognition that subjectivity is indeed constructed, polyvalent and heterogeneous. Else why bring the idea into politics at all? Nevertheless, we can do much more with the idea of subjectivity in politics than remain on this rather dull definitional level.

We certainly have to take on board the notion of the decentered subject and the ideological coloring of subjectivity. We can do this but, at the same time, could we not explore what other versions of the subject and of subjectivity might be possible? I cannot accept that it is somehow unprofessional to refer to 'the subject' or to 'subjectivity' – as if it were some kind of intellectual sin.[22]

We should not forget that *all* discourses are fictional (i.e. imaginative) discourses. I concede that it can be difficult to write about subjectivity without a collapse into liberal humanism taking place. Nevertheless, the subjectivity of the countertransference is not an autonomous, 'authentic' subjectivity – quite the opposite when we recognize that the source of such a subjectivity (politics) lies outside the subject (the analyst). The subjectivity of the countertransference is part of an interrogation of subjectivity, part, in a sense, of a performance, of an act. The links between imaginative acting and political action are strong.

I feel that there are two aspects of subjectivity that have been relatively neglected. First, subjectivity has a monitoring function, scanning social and political reality, as well as having been fashioned by such realities. Of course, subjective monitoring of politics is influenced by the politics being monitored but this does not mean that the function of monitoring is not taking place. The deconstruction of the subject is not the same as a deconstruction of the political – and the political subsumes the subject who monitors it.

The second neglected aspect of subjectivity concerns its wounded and grieving nature. In late modernity there is scarcely the possibility of subjectivity divorced from a sense of marginality, woundedness and an accompanying grief – that is, subjection. Hence, the ubiquity of depth psychology, characterized by its fantasies of healing. The wounded and grieving subject behaves affectively, emoting from below, calling out from the psychological and also from the social depths. Such a subject is bound to be critical of its leaders.

In sum, subjectivity in the political area does not mean more of what we already have and don't want; it may mean less. It cannot be denied that subjective political analysis involves risk, nor that it is often essential to make rational political choices. However, I feel that there is always a creative element of danger or risk in the making of choices, especially moral choices. Every encounter with politics is a moral encounter, underscoring the central experience of choice. Before long, given that politics is a collective activity, any one person's subjective politics will have to rub up against the subjective politics of others. And what starts off as a subjective politics, a personal confession, will soon acquire an extraverted life of its own – just as psychological theories, rooted in the personal circumstances of their authors, move beyond what we regard as the usual limits of subjectivity (hopefully without sundering themselves from their subjective origins).[23] Then the subject may become an agent, capable of acting in the world just as the analyst 'acts' in the countertransference script provided by the patient.

I am suggesting that there is a powerful fantasy abroad of providing therapy for the world, and that this is a response to the ills of late modernity that I discussed earlier. The notion of therapy and the clinical dimension distinguish depth psychological analyses of cultural process from all other kinds. The fantasy of providing therapy highlights the role of countertransference. Building on the clinical experience of counter-transference, we are able to address the question of subjectivity in politics and political discourse. Then we might be more able to translate the Utopian politics of passion, dream and desire into the pragmatic politics that gets things done. Here it is a question of 'translate' rather than 'transform' because it gradually dawns that Utopian politics and pragmatic politics resemble each other.

SUBJECTIVITY AND POLITICS

I will be returning to the idea of countertransference as a tool of subjective political analysis. But now I want to give some examples of what I am getting at and discuss them.

I was on the subway. It was crowded and hot. I had a sudden fantasy of staying all day with the people who were in the carriage. We would go to lunch as a group and become friends. I wanted to call out and suggest this plan. I really felt in love! I wanted to embrace everyone. I had an erection. I don't think this was just polymorphous sexuality or a manic response to underground miseries. For, if we take my bodily reactions and my fantasies as a kind of countertransference to the social issue of transport, then perhaps this was one way of embodying my need and desire for movement with my need and desire for stasis and continuity.

During the Gulf War, there were images on TV of military aircraft, filmed through a heat haze. In spite of her conscious anti-war attitudes, a patient found that there was a kind of beauty locked up in these martial images. I suspected that this was her personal reflection of the prevalent collective war fever, an inner world fascination with our own capacity to be deadly and destructive, a syntonic excitement spawned by the facile victories of the bully. This would be rather a different understanding from one that relied on an interpretation of the patient's projection of her own aggression.

Watching the regular TV report of parliament one evening, I screamed at the parliamentarians 'Shut up!'. This total response was concordant with what I now see as *their* desire that we, who are outside the charmed circles of power, should stay shut up. Certainly, this could be taken as an example of my own authoritarian tendencies. Or I could have been merely expressing a general unease with the nightly spectacle. But my reaction gave some unthought but known specificity to the unease: Parliament as tending to silence and marginalize other fora for debate – for instance, at the workplace or within groups defined by common interests – not to mention other styles of debate, more modular and conversational and less adversarial.

The fourth example is interactive and I will give it in some detail. During the writing of this chapter, I discussed its contents with a friend and colleague.[24] What follows is taken from a recording of our conversation and discussions that she and I have had since.

My colleague talked about a group of young, single mothers on the dole in the northeast of England in the 1980s, described by Beatrix Campbell in her book *Wigan Pier Revisited*.[25] Beatrix Campbell represented the tendency for young unemployed women to have babies without a permanent relationship with a man as providing a partial and admittedly ambiguous source of strength for the women. My colleague had had a set of equally ambiguous reactions to this idea. Somewhat to her surprise, and mixed in with a sympathetic appreciation of the women's situation, she found herself having an anxious and super-egoic reaction toward what came across to her as their psychic *defiance*.

I suggested to her that, as well as super-ego, she might use one of the many modern theories of countertransference. What would these theories say about her response, in the most general terms? Maybe that her apparently super-egoic reaction arose in her via communication from the social problem of which she was an unwitting therapist. Moreover, as is usually the case in such situations in clinical analysis, never mind political analysis, there was probably a hook on which the communication could hang itself.

If my colleague can be regarded imaginatively as a therapist of the cultural and social phenomenon known as young, unemployed motherhood, then her reaction could be seen as a countertransference. This would not be a countertransference of the neurotic or self-defensive kind, but a politically useful countertransference, a communication from the so-called patient – in this instance, young, unemployed mothers. (It is not really important for my purposes here which theory of counter-transference a reader finds most useful – as long as it is acknowledged that the countertransference is a much theorized phenomenon.)

Would a therapist of politics/political analyst engaged with the problematic of young unemployed mothers (or with transport, or war, or parliament) say to the patient 'You worry me' (or 'let's stay together in this carriage', 'war is beautiful', 'shut up')? No, of course she or he would not because, by analogy with clinical practice, those responses, apparently the therapist's, have, to some extent, been placed in the therapist by the various 'patients'.

Young, unemployed mothers who have their child in the absence of a man give off a sense of defiance. My colleague developed a comple-mentary countertransference to young, unemployed mothers – one that embodied the culture's attitude to them that young, unemployed mothers will certainly have internalized. The parallel is with the way a clinician understands her or his reactions to an individual patient as in tune with, fitting in with the patient's inner world. In my colleague's 'case', an intersubjective interaction arose between the inner world defiance of the social problematic known as young, unemployed motherhood and her apparently private response. She had to decode the response in herself in terms of the defiance to which it was complementary. (And, incidentally, she may have strengthened Beatrix Campbell's thesis by this total response of hers.) *Her subjectivity – maybe like all subjectivity – was constructed as countertransference within her in part by what lay outside her.*

In the four examples, I managed to work in references to six distinct theories of the analyst's use of her or his countertransference: complementary and concordant countertransference (Racker), syntonic countertransference (Fordham), fitting in with the patient's inner world (Winnicott), intersubjective interaction (Atwood and Stolorow), total response (Little) and embodied and reflective countertransference (which are my own ideas).[26] The fact that political and social problems do not have an unconscious in the same way that humans do does not stop them communicating with our unconscious and being illumined and hence analyzed by what we make of our unconscious reaction. Moreover, who is to say that political and social problems do not have an unconscious?

On the tape of our conversation my colleague went on to make two remarks that I want to take as further highly usable and relevant diagnostic countertransferences to my whole thesis. ('Diagnostic counter-transference' is Casement's term,[27] so I have actually incorporated seven different theories here.) First, she commented on the absence of a historical or class perspective in depth psychological writing about mothering, leading to a somewhat normative and, hence, potentially moralistic attitude to social practices. This would be neurotic counter-transference on the part of depth psychology to subversive ideas about family organization in general and tendencies like young, unemployed motherhood in particular.

The second remark linked my project with that of feminism because one of the aims of feminism is to create a vocabulary for phenomena that had not previously been named. I am sure that my particular goal of deploying countertransference theorizing as the means of inserting subjectivity into political discourse also suffers – and enjoys – the consequences of there not seeming to be a ready-made language in which to do it.

I could have given numerous other examples of the use of the political analyst's subjectivity in political discourse. I want to explain why I have chosen to give this particular example of interaction between two people who know each other quite well. Is this not unnecessarily messy and confusing and foreign to social science? I would reply to this by saying that the messiness and many-layered nature of this intersubjective example is its whole strength. It is an advantage and not a disadvantage that the example is clouded in so many ways. Isn't this what the worlds of both clinical and political analysis are like? Isn't contamination the norm? Why invoke neutrality at all, in clinical analysis or even in social science, if there isn't constant pressure toward partisanship? Both clinical and political analysis are messy, confused, partisan, struggling to keep the boundaries, suffused and yet somehow also terrified by the strength and energy of the imagination. We cannot be ideologically pure. The society that we criticize is the source of the material out of which we seek to fashion that critique.

There are bound to be some who will react to what I have been saying with a 'so what?' or a 'big deal' or with a 'what's new?' or with 'don't we know that already?'. Precisely! What I have been doing in this chapter *can* eventually be related to concepts and language that are familiar to us all. What I have been doing is bringing up and out – we say bringing to consciousness – something that is already present in the professional unconscious of depth psychology as a potential contribution to political and social analysis; something clinicians have been doing without knowing that they have been doing it; something hidden in the open. I am referring to the as-yet-unrealized potential of clinical experience and theories of countertransference to validate and legitimatize a style of political engagement that lacks validation and legitimation in our political system. I mean much more than the recognition that objectivity in politics is impossible. I mean the affirmation of a personal, subjective, emotional, irrational, bodily, fantastic style of making politics. I am not saying that there have never been politics of this kind, for there have been: May '68, happenings, the Yippies, Situationists, Rock Against Racism, the Greenham women's protest against the stationing of US cruise missiles in Britain, just to give a few scattered and unrelated examples from the past twenty-five years. As with resacralization, it is hard for depth psychology to distinguish itself from those movements without, at the same time, recalling that, at times in its past, depth psychology has also tried to make a politics of the non-rational kind. There is a line stretching from Otto Gross to Wilhelm Reich to Herbert Marcuse that has not considered itself bound by the tenets of rational discourse. Otto Fenichel was dismayed at the possibility that psychoanalysis would ignore social reality and define itself as exclusively a science of infantile fantasies.[28] This line – broken as it is, and repressed by the psychoanalytic establishment – demonstrates that the support of depth psychology for non-rational political discourse would also be a support for its own project.

But what has the greater part of depth psychology done, what has psychoanalysis done, what has psychotherapy done, in relation to these non-rational political manifestations? Depth psychology has colluded with the dominant political culture when we condemn such politics as primitive or regressive, as not being in accord with the reality principle, as not having achieved genitality or the depressive position, as foreign to the spirit of individuation, as the politics of the negative Trickster. *Our collusion may have contributed to the failure of these movements*. Maybe we indulged in this collusion because of our own conservatism, or to protect our own avenues of access to power and resources, or in a kind of cowardice. But, in their ordinary clinical method, depth psychologists have their own ecstatic equivalent of this devalued politics of subjectivity, their own claim for the humaneness and generosity of subjectivity and a personal response to someone or something *other*.

Recently, I have had the opportunity to lecture in St Petersburg and Moscow. I tried to communicate some up-to-date clinical thinking to Russian psychologists and therapists. Let me say immediately that, for Russian therapists, depth psychology, in the absence of anything else to trust or believe in, is a tool of political analysis and social criticism *at the same time* as inspiring methods of treatment. These Russian professionals just did not feel the academic–clinical divide in the way that Westerners do, nor, of course, the divide between the personal and the political. Moreover, I found that the more irrational the kind of psychological thinking I introduced, the more seriously they tended to take it. They seemed to know that depth psychology is a discipline of excess and transgression and hence they responded to a tricksterish blend of the vulgar and the numinous, the grotesque and the divine, the sexual and the spiritual, the tragic and the comic, the rational and the irrational. In Russia in the long term, in contrast to Britain and the United States, affect and emotion have been seen as the prime sources of progress whereas reason was seen more as a source of destruction. Russian writers had, for two hundred years prior to the Revolution, inveighed against Western rationalism, whether in the form of British industrialism, German orderliness, French logic, or American money. Maybe the Russian nineteenth-century rejection of reason went too far, creating a space for the disastrous reversal (or *enantiodromia*) into the crazy rationality of twentieth-century communism.

The point I want to make is that, by supporting our own system's official espousal of rationality in politics, depth psychological clinicians may have sold their souls. After all, rationality is only a special case of fantasy! As I suggested in the previous chapter, our discourse on politics may, with advantage, reek of hyperbole, blemish, crudity and farce, making a social critique out of their very irrationality.

We need a more plural approach to rationality and we need to rethink our epistemic values when it comes to the political, social and even the academic fields, as shown in this comment by the historian Ludmilla Jordanova: 'Historians have little occasion to allow their subjective selves to take part in their work, yet to do so would open up vast new territories.'[29] Vast new territories! Opened up by subjectivity! How exciting it is to hear from someone in the world of the liberal humanities about such a prospect. But depth psychologists *already* 'allow their subjective selves to take part in their work'. Moreover, depth psychologists already have an ethos, ideology and method which specifically allow their subjective selves to take part in our work. It is the ethos, ideology and method of the countertransference that should be shared with colleagues in other disciplines, rather than models of the psyche, lists of defense mechanisms or schemas of personality development. Then we can engage with modernity's totalization of reason, the oppressive, transcendental privileging of the rational. Factoring subjectivity (back) into discourse transforms depth psychology's habitual concentration on the roots and even the causes of subjectivity into a deliberate project of setting subjectivity free in the political world – subjectivity terminable *and* interminable.

To do this we have first to work out texts that can serve as the deepening vehicle for such a sharing with colleagues in other disciplines. Without texts and their liberating and legitimizing influence, the countertransference treasure will remain very private property. Moreover, depth psychologists of all persuasions will remain in a complicit relation with oppressive, hegemonistic and marginalizing political tendencies. I suggest that these ideas about forming a political text out of countertransference practices are likely to benefit those marginalized and dispossessed groups whose most urgent need is to translate their subjective misery into pragmatic and effective political terms. In addition, if these ideas influence social theory and the processes of policy formation, there would be a 'trickle-up' effect.

We certainly need countertransference theory as well. The Greek word *theoria* means 'looking about the world', 'contemplation', 'speculation'. But we might also gain something by considering the meaning of an adjacent word in Greek: *theoros. Theoroi* (in the plural) were emissaries sent by the Greek city-states to consult distant oracles or participate, on behalf of their own city, in important far-off religious rituals. That is, *theoroi* travel, and, on their travels, they relate to and work with people from outside their own community; it's their job. If depth psychology is going to engage with politics, it needs the kind of *theoria*, the kind of texts, that *theoroi* can take with them. The culture of the Enlightenment bequeathed to us deterministic, rational, objective theoretical systems. We have to try to create psychologically grounded political theories that are not only functional but also satisfying to us on the subjective level.

In this chapter, I have been continuing to look at what depth psychology can contribute to an understanding of politics, working the field between the personal and the political. I hope I have shown that depth psychology has always been interested in the world of politics and that the interest has burst into bloom in recent years as part of a more general attempt to resacralize culture. The underlying fantasy is of providing a therapy for the world, and, if this is not taken too ponderously or concretely, the apparently inflated fantasy has considerable social utility. However, it is not in models of the psyche nor theories of development that the utility is found. Rather, it is clinical method in general, and the use of counter-transference in particular, that depth psychology has to contribute to political discourse and to share with other disciplines. Countertrans-ference theory is a validation of the subjective element when engaging with a particular political problem or theme. We need to pay attention to the countertransference communications given off by any particular political problem or theme for, as with individual patients, the communications given off will vary. Depth psychology can contribute toward a politics that has made a new place for the irrational and, in so doing, depth psychology is true to its own roots and its knowledge that there are differing modes of consciousness. Russell Jacoby points out that the potential of depth psychology to frighten the institutions of an oppressive society has leeched away: 'Over the years the ghost has become a ghost of itself.'[30]

CULTURAL, CLINICAL AND POLITICAL DEBATES

I want now to take this whole argument a step further. I have been suggesting that experience and theorizing of countertransference, derived from the clinical set-up, can be a template for a rather unusual kind of politics and also contribute to the techniques of other disciplines such as history. I have been proposing that we take something from one area (the clinical) and make use of it in another area that is apparently different (the political). But an awkward question arises. Are these two areas as different as they seem? And, if they are not as different as they seem, what are the connections that already exist between them? By exploring some connections between the clinic and the political world, I want to return at a more profound level of political theory to the problematic of the countertransference. This return to the topic of countertransference is going to be more demanding of the concept. Up to now, I have been celebrating countertransference as if it were a gift from 'us' in the clinical world to 'them' in the political world. The new demand I will make of the idea of countertransference is that it start to function more and more as a link or bridge between 'us' and 'them', between clinical analysis and political analysis.[31]

Scanning the literature and talking to people in the field, I sense five main areas of anxiety about countertransference, and debates about the clinical utility of countertransference have tended to be located within these areas of anxiety.

1 *Anxiety about the analyst's or therapist's neurosis.* How do you tell that the countertransference is a communication from the patient and not part of an unresolved issue for yourself? Indeed, and this may be the most anxiety-producing point of all, can the two ever be separated? Can the practitioner ever see the patient save through her or his own needs, wounds, desires and gratifications?

2 *Anxiety about the legitimacy of understanding countertransference as communication.* I think this is truly a political anxiety because the analyst's actual power is highlighted. Is there not a risk – runs this anxiety – of shoving everything back into the patient, of making the patient responsible for everything, even for the analyst's subjective life?

3 *Anxiety about the accuracy of depending solely on the counter-transference without historical collateral.* Isn't working out of the countertransference alone merely indulging the patient's fantasy of the analyst's magical omniscience, or, conversely, persecuting the patient with his or her penetrative mind?

4 *Anxiety about breaking the frame of analysis and psychotherapy.* This is an ethical anxiety. No matter how disciplined the practitioner intends to be, employing countertransference in the ways that modern clinical theory suggests are possible raises the specter of disclosure of the countertransference state to the patient. It is felt by many that this is unethical in that the clinical frame will be broken. Yet the idea of disclosure of the countertransference has had a long and respectable history within depth psychology.

5 *There is anxiety about getting confused.* This anxiety can be expressed in a logical format: If you value countertransference as communication,

and if the experience of countertransference means getting confused about yourself or accepting confusion between you and your patient, then are you not valuing confusion? And, if you value confusion so much, is it not the case that, in advocating the use of counter-transference, you are advocating confusion? And is not this completely contrary to the overall accepted aims of psychotherapy and analysis to make things clearer? I have myself recently been a victim of this particular anxiety on the part of others. I had written in an earlier book of the ways in which the countertransference experience resembles mystical experience, drawing the parallels between the analyst's working things out and the mystic's working things out. In a review of the book, it was stated that I was *advocating* analysts entering into mystical states during the session.[32]

So there are these five anxieties about countertransference: Anxiety about the analyst's neurosis, anxiety about the political legitimacy of using countertransference, anxiety about the ethical consequences of breaking the frame, anxiety about the accuracy of depending solely on counter-transference which could also feed patients' fantasies about the analyst's magical powers, or persecute the patient, anxiety about getting confused. Yet, in spite of the existence of these anxieties, many if not all of the clinicians that I know continue to understand their subjective reactions to the patient as if they were, in the broadest possible metaphorical terms, communications from the patient's unconscious. In other words, *in spite of the anxiety and the shadow issues, we go on working with counter-transference*, no matter what terms we use to define this process or what caveats we enter about it.

What I would like to do now is to see what happens if we recast all these professional worries that clinical analysts and therapists have about the countertransference into political terms. This will show up the objections to a subjective, personal kind of politics. Please remember that the overall idea is that struggles with issues in the world of the consulting room speak to, are relevant to, and link up with issues out there, in the political world.

An imaginative recasting of the five clinical worries in political terms goes something like this:

1 *The worry about neurosis becomes*: Look, your viewpoint about equal opportunities and reverse discrimination simply reflects your own experiences and problems in this area – you're just not being *objective*.
2 *The worry about legitimacy becomes*: Look, you're putting too much onto the existence of capital markets and other financial institutions in our system. These are not inherently repressive or evil – there's no plot.

You're simply *shoving the blame* for a complex socioeconomic problem like unemployment onto one thing.

3 *The worry about accuracy and magic becomes*: You can't make a policy for the environment on the basis of feelings – it is all too emotional, anecdotal, esthetic. That would be fine for poetry but not for practical politics. What we need are *facts* and detailed proposals.

4 *The worry about ethics becomes*: Look, it isn't sound to make policy about resource allocation in the National Health Service without due process. There have to be rules and conventions about how we do it or there will be a bear garden in which some groups will lose out. We have to do things *properly*.

5 *The worry about confusion becomes*: Look, what you're saying about the Gulf War is too subjective, too shapeless and too formless – it will only lead to confusion when what we want is clarity and a clear head. These are the only possible bases for action. *Getting emotional won't help*; it isn't even political at all.

When I re-read this attempt to shift the worries about the use of subjectivity in analysis over into a political context I was a bit shocked at how well the parallel worked. I was alarmed at how powerful and confident the objections to the political analyst's use of counter-transference sounded. Do the political worries, which I derived from clinical worries and debates, mean that the personal can never be political, that the nature of the political necessarily excludes subjectivity? Or, just as clinical analysts manage to work through their worries about countertransference and make use of it for the furtherance of the analysis or therapy, is there a way to make space for, acknowledge and even integrate these worried concerns about the subjective factor in political discourse?

We may begin to answer these questions by exploring what factors make countertransference communication possible at all. The way I look at countertransference phenomena is to see that there is a shared imaginal world constellated in psychotherapy and analysis. The imaginal world is a world of images with human and social properties. The imaginal world both creates and is created by relationship; therapeutic and, indeed, all social relationships have a potential to bring an imaginal world to life. The therapeutic relationship between political analyst and world is no exception. Though the idea of the imaginal world originates in religion and mysticism, it is not hard to see the parallel with the social and political world in which people share, being both creators and creatures of it. Image is primal; feeding into, and back from, clinical and political practices.

I am arguing that clinicians can suggest how to accommodate political worries over subjectivity by stating what it is that they actually do with their subjective countertransference reactions. This means that everyone in clinical practice is bound to have a different point of view, deriving from their own way of working! My own idea is that there is a need to make a general distinction between two kinds of countertransference communication. One of these I call *reflective countertransference*. The analyst's countertransference reaction reflects the patient's here-and-now psychological state of which the patient is currently unaware. This might also include aspects of the patient's transference to the analyst. Reflective countertransference suggests that I may be feeling depressed in my work with this particular patient because this particular patient is currently depressed. The second kind of countertransference communication I call *embodied countertransference*. The analyst embodies someone or something in the patient's internal world that has been active therein over time. I feel depressed, in this second kind of countertransference understanding, as an embodiment of the patient's mother's depression, or as a hint that the patient has a longstanding fear that being depressed is unacceptable. Sometimes, embodied countertransferences do not conform to the patient's history and have a mythopoetic cast. My depression leads to thinking about the archetypal constituents of depression and how these might be relevant to my patient: Delusional guilt, unmanageable destructive aggression, and interference with thought and action.

I try not to be too rigid about this distinction between reflective and embodied countertransference because many countertransference reactions respond to both kinds of understanding. When I have identified the kind of countertransference that might be going on, and always allowing for my own neurotic wounds, I begin a process of association to the reactions I am aware of in my thoughts, fantasies and bodily sensations. This process, which can often be playful as well as totally irrational, I have come to call the process of *distillation*. Associations to refining, purifying, something valuable dribbling down drop by drop are intended. So, too, are associations to the typical moves in distillation from liquid to vapor to liquid. The base liquid is my countertransference reaction, the vapor is what I do with that reaction in a disciplined and professional way, the new liquid is the use to which I may put the outcome of my work on my subjectivity, whether silently and in a contained way, or actively, as an ingredient in interpretation.

As I said, this is a (brief) description of my own ideas and practices and every clinician will have her or his own equivalents to offer to political analysts who hope to make use of their own subjectivity in political discourse. Such an ambition may have got discouraged by the strength of the objections to this thrown up by the existing political order, such as those that I sketched out above.[33]

The countertransference experience of depth psychologists should be deployed to state that people are not as cut off from each other as they seem to be. (I return to this point in detail in Chapter 11.) The profound, pre-existing link between people in a social context, to which depth psychologists can attest, sheds a completely new light on those five anxieties or worries that I listed earlier. If there is a primary mutuality between people, on the political level as well as on the personal level, then one person's neurotic preoccupations are no less (or more) reliable than another person's apparently objective study of a problem. Similarly, the objective test of whether or not political subjectivity is dangerous (for example, racism) will be in people's reactions to it, especially their negative reactions and refutations; subjectivity assesses subjectivity. The legitimacy of a subjective politics is not affected by tendencies to shove blame onto institutions, for each person is implicated in those institutions, no matter how powerless they are in relation to them. This means they have a *right* to shove blame onto institutions and whatever is blamed has the right to defend itself. Nor is it unethical to try to subvert the system, to try to out-smart or out-negotiate other people or other groups. Negotiation and bargaining are profound and passionate forms of relating. Finally, the worry about confusion can be utterly reframed. No clarity exists save in relation to confusion; confusion is the bedrock of clarity, instability leading to temporary stability (as chaos theory suggests). What belongs to whom is gradually being established. Our daily experience shows us that making use of subjectivity is neither mad nor impossible – though it is very hard to do in a disciplined way, very hard to integrate precision and soul. Even Karl Popper argued in favor of retaining some undefined and hence confusing terms!

Just as worries about countertransference can be read politically, so, too, we can *make a political theory and practice out of what clinical analysts have done with those worries.* Worried objections to the role of subjectivity in political discourse can be integrated into political discourse. I have tried to do this in a way that resembles the manner in which clinicians try to integrate worried objections to the use of countertransference into their practice with individual patients.

Depth psychology and the wider culture are linked in a two-way process, and this is exemplified by the unresolved and unresolvable debates within depth psychology and within cultural process generally. If what depth psychologists think is relevant in a wider setting, then it is worth noting what worries depth psychologists have had to overcome while continuing to make use of their own subjectivity in the counter-transference. The anxieties about countertransference in the clinical context and the anxieties about countertransference in the political context are very similar anxieties. And there really are some serious objections to be heard to making the personal political. These are analogous to the worries among clinicians over countertransference. But these objections to the role of subjectivity in political analysis can be integrated in the same way that clinical analysts have integrated their worries about the role of subjectivity in political discourse.

CONCLUDING REFLECTIONS

I will end the chapter by completely reversing its poles. Instead of merely suggesting that depth psychology offer its work on countertransference to the political world, let us also explicitly entertain the possibility that it is joint membership of and participation in a political order that makes the psychological experience of a countertransference reaction to the patient possible in the first place. This is a political analysis that is intended to illumine the clinical process. Analyst and patient are subject to the same repressive forces. There is no personal outside of the political; the political is itself a precondition for subjectivity. That is perhaps why there is so much politics in depth psychology, the profession of the subjective.

The work I have done on a pluralistic approach to depth psychology has convinced me that there is a benign form of the politics and practices of the profession. So often, the opponent contains or represents the missing bit of oneself or what is needed to round out one's own idea. But what of possibly malign aspects of the politics and practices of depth psychology? If it is felt that the institutions and practices of depth psychology are technocratic and apolitical, how can they promote and contribute to a libertarian and progressive politics? I am not sure and so I intend to explore the matter in the following chapter.[34]

Chapter 3

Depth psychology and politics

INTRODUCTION

There would be little point in our having worked on the orientation of depth psychology to the world if its own basic theories and practices remained completely unaltered. I support the continuing practice of analysis with individuals and small groups. This is because I do not agree that therapy inevitably syphons off rage that might more constructively be deployed in relation to social injustices. In fact, I think that it is the reverse that often happens: Experiences in therapy act to fine down generalized rage into a more specific format, hence rendering emotion more accessible for social action. Even when this is not what happens, the potential remains for a move from private therapy to public action within the institution of therapy – and I propose to discuss that potential in this chapter.

The key question concerns whether analysts and therapists are going to change their theory and practice, or not. Have the many analysts who have written on politics and culture been able to change what they think and do as clinical analysts? Does a politically aware analyst work differently from one whose perspective is confined to the inner world? In what ways, if any, is my work affected by my ideas about depth psychology and politics? Have the one-quarter of the members of the British Psycho-Analytical Society who have joined Psychoanalysts for the Prevention of Nuclear War changed the way they think about and practice with their patients? Or is it possible to divorce a political interest from analytical theory and clinical practice? Maybe some would argue that such a divorce is desirable.

In this chapter I focus on *the political development of the person* and on public implications of private imagery. Elsewhere I have written about the politics of the analytical encounter and the politics of the discipline of depth psychology itself.[1] These are still concerns of mine but they are not the focus of this particular chapter.

The idea is to continue my portrayal of the clinical setting as a bridge between depth psychology and politics rather than as the source of an isolation of depth psychology from politics. As I said, critics of the clinical project of depth psychology have noted the isolation – and this is not a totally wrong observation. But I want us also to see the potential links and to take further the radical revisioning of clinical work begun in the previous chapter.

For me, there certainly is a pressing need to reflect on what I do clinically and to consider what changes, if any, I might make. It seems that I am not alone in reaching this position. The editors of a remarkable book entitled *Psychoanalysis and the Nuclear Threat: Clinical and Theoretical Studies*, all of them members of the American Psychoanalytic Association, write:

> In the best of circumstances, analysts may assume that considerations of politics are irrelevant to the analytic space. We raise the possibility here that the potential of nuclear weapons for destroying the world intrudes into the safety of that space. We no longer live in the best of circumstances. Thus, the construct of a socially, culturally, and politically neutral analytic setting may be a fantasy, one that embodies the wish that the outside can be ignored, denied, or wished away.[2]

In a major review of the book, Alexander Gralnick noted that

> Unfortunately, few of the contributors to the theoretical part of the book deal with the many important assumptions and unsettled issues in psychoanalytic thought and clinical practice that the editors hoped consideration of the nuclear threat would prompt them to discuss. A bit of a challenge is raised, however, in that two of the authors advocate encouraging patients to think about the nuclear threat and to relate it to their own problems. They also favor an 'active' political role for themselves in the analytic process – which is, of course, contrary to traditional practice. . . . Some authors . . . call for new techniques to deal with the subject under discussion, but would favor maintaining their 'neutrality'. Thus, though bound by traditional concepts, they seem to recognize that psychoanalysts may not be as neutral as they believe themselves to be. . . . These psychoanalysts are plagued by their own resistances and anxieties about the further changes they face and how creative they dare be; they are naturally limited by being at *the earliest stages* of changes that we all face and, like the rest of us, are *handicapped by lack of a needed new language.*
>
> (My emphases.)[3]

This chapter represents a start on the creation of that needed new language and this will – hopefully – lead to the evolution of research techniques, literature, training and monitoring that are informed by the new language.

THE POLITICAL DEVELOPMENT OF THE PERSON

I am not so omnipotent nor so optimistic as to expect major breakthroughs or new paradigm shifts within the field of depth psychology. The golden age of theorizing is surely past. But every now and then one perceives gaps in the theory, lacunae in the practice of depth psychology, and then one is obliged to plunge into the void to see what lies therein.

One such gap, lacuna, void concerns what I have come to call the political development of the person. Although I have been working on this idea since the beginning of the 1980s, I have not felt confident enough to publish before now. I am sure that this is going to turn into a vast area of research and theorizing and I am very much aware that what I am sharing here is only a small start.

I expect many would agree that the analytic patient's material cannot remain linked only to his or her personal situation, or to the working through of innate, instinctually based fantasies. Links have to be made with the patient's culture, *its* traditions and history, and to the patient's social, racial, ethnic, religious and national origins. But how might this be done, and what changes in theory and practice will be necessary? What happens if we factor the political into our narratives of the psychological development of the person?

An individual person leads not only his or her own life but also the life of the times. Jung was supposed to have said that 'when you treat the individual, you treat the culture', meaning that persons cannot be seen in isolation from the cultural matrices that played a part in forming them.[4] Acknowledging that there is such a thing as political development makes us build into our apperception of the person the impact of the political events of his or her life – *the political history of the person*. These will have contributed, over time, to the state of political development that has been arrived at. Taking a historical, hermeneutical, or even an old-fashioned etiological approach helps to give the analyst confidence in moving into an area fraught with worries about bias, suggestion and disagreement. Although I shall argue that such worries are, to a great extent, delusive, the need for the relative safety of historical, hermeneutic and etiological approaches to political development is something to acknowledge. For example, when confronted with a patient whose views are repulsive, an analyst's best bet might be to focus on the emergence, effects and origins of such views. Of course, such explorations will take a variety of different forms. We have to consider the politics an individual has 'inherited' by reason of family, class, ethnic, religious and national background, not forgetting accidental, constitutional, typological, fateful and inexplicable influences; the non-rational element.

As we will see in Chapter 13, where I discuss the psychology of cultural difference in greater detail, caution is needed when assessing the part played by the cultural background in the political development of the person. Analysts need to be careful not to rely on pre-existing generalized conclusions. These are usually based on what is supposed to be empirical evidence about the 'typical' psychology of this or that grouping. But an analyst's concern should be with the experience of difference, not with the defining of difference; each patient has his or her own difference. I think that I am after a kind of Foucauldian archeology of politics, but on a personal level.[5] Certainly, I recognize that there is unlikely to be one single, total explanation for a person's politics.

Each patient may be seen as struggling toward a recognition, expression and celebration of his or her own difference. If we do not bear this caveat about predefinitions in mind, then sets of delusive complementarities may come into play. For example, Jewish psychology will be contrasted with German psychology, black psychology with white psychology, Catholic psychology with Calvinist psychology, homosexual psychology with heterosexual psychology, female psychology with male psychology. This will be done without paying sufficient critical attention to the processes by which terms such as 'Jewish psychology' and the others arise.

The important point is that groupings like these are not homogeneous. Though members of the group will have some political experiences in common, the exact nature of the impact of such experiences on political development cannot be predicted. Moreover, there are going to be some ways in which everyone is like everyone else and some ways in which everyone is different – again, it is impossible to say in advance which set or combination of conditions will hold.

There is a second implication of that gnomic utterance of Jung's 'when you treat the individual, you treat the culture'. He is saying that treating an individual indirectly, and maybe inadvertently, provides some therapy for the culture of which that individual is a part. Perhaps this is because of the impact the analyzed individual will have on his or her culture, as a sort of 'change agent'. Now I do believe it is possible, in partnership with others, especially social scientists, to treat the culture, to offer therapy to the political and social systems. But I do not believe that clinical analysis produces 'special' individuals who will then go out into the world and heal it. What analysis can do is to assist a person to achieve a degree of agency on the private and personal level, and, as I suggested in the previous chapter, this cannot be cut off from emancipation on the public and political level. But I find it hard to accept that every analysand acquires special political powers or prowess or that, as a group, people who have been in analysis constitute the vanguard of a politically transformative movement. The idea that those who have become individuated will have a decisive effect on the world scene does seem to have been in Jung's mind, and one can also detect the same kind of notion cropping up throughout the evolution of psychoanalysis.[6] The person who, via analysis, conforms to the reality principle, has achieved ego mastery, become genital, or reached the depressive position, is often represented as belonging to an élite that is not susceptible, or is less susceptible to the group psychological pressures of the social and political world that they inhabit.

If there is élitism in my way of thinking, then it is not an élitism based on the special properties of clinical analysis to produce more politically developed individuals. My élitism involves a belief that depth psychology (that is, my own discipline) itself has something unusual to offer a multidisciplinary attempt to make an analysis of culture. For example, one interesting implication of these thoughts is that political organizations should pay more attention to the psychological development of their members, for reasons of effectiveness as much as for humanitarian reasons.

To refer to the political development of the person is to challenge the boundary that is conventionally accepted to exist between public and private. If we follow the challenge through, then we will have to consider how psychopathology, usually a discipline confined to the private and interior realms (though often measured by visible behavior) also refers to the public and political realms. If there is a psychopathology of politics, then, as I suggested, it is valid to think in terms of providing a therapy for politics – but without getting too excited at the mere discovery that there *is* psychopathology in politics.

In many respects, the ground has been prepared for the challenge to the boundary between public and private by what has happened in depth psychology as well as in sociopolitical movements such as feminism. As far as depth psychology is concerned, our notion of the intrapsychic, internal world includes the part played by relations with other people. At the same time, relations with other people are enriched and expanded by internal processes and images. Internal imagery links people and fosters their relationships. It follows that to divorce work on the apparently internal and work on the apparently interpersonal is false and limiting. Offering this formulation in terms of there being *a political level of the psyche*, we reframe political processes in terms of psyche speaking, and internal processes in terms of politics. The field of reference is seamless and continuous. Of course, the field is also partial and divided in that differences between these realms will always exist and require acknowledgment rather than being permanently submerged in a cosmic holism.

Even the unconscious itself may be understood as having some origins outside the individual person, not only of an archaic, phylogenetic kind, but also resulting from the internalization of social institutions and political processes. Language plays a special role in the making of the unconscious; at once, direct and indirect. Unconscious perceptions of the world will not find consciousness without language and language will influence what is perceived and how it is perceived. But even language cannot claim permanent primacy, for language is itself affected by social and political institutions and relations. There is an interplay between language, social and political institutions, and phylogeny. But all lie outside the individual human person and all constitute a kind of contingency for the unconscious of an individual.

It follows that any conception of the unconscious or the psyche that omits to refer to social institutions and political processes will be inadequate. The individual develops on the terrain of social and political relations and hence there is a political level of the unconscious. One consequence of the internalization of political and social factors from the environment is that the full flowering of an individual's political potential may be repressed so that his or her contribution to political process is stunted and distorted. Here, there is a similarity to what internalization of moral prohibitions stemming from parents and society does to the innate drives such as sexuality or aggression. In addition to a similar stunting and distorting of political potential, internalization of political and social factors influences parent–child interaction and, hence, the development of object relations. For example, the political climate concerning the balance between self-reliance and state provision may influence the duration and quality of the period of dependence enjoyed by a child. The parallel is with the way in which, on the family level, parental psychology and values form a moral climate in which intense relationships acquire a particular moral tone.

The ideas of political development and a political level of the psyche have implications for other areas of psychological theorizing. We may come to see aggression as a politically reparative drive, understanding that aggression often incorporates not only intense wishes for relatedness, but equally intense wishes for participation, in a more cooperative or communal mode, in political or social activity. To be authentically aggressive, angry in the belly, and still be able to be part of social and political processes, is a psychological and ethical goal of the highest order. Moreover, the idea of the political development of the individual will influence our ideas about sexuality. I am thinking of the politically destabilizing functions of the polymorphous Trickster, and the politically creative functions of the pluralistic father's erotic playback (discussed in Chapters 4 and 9 respectively).

I have to admit that it has been very tempting to refer to a 'political drive', meaning that there is something innately political in human beings and that the political is not a derivative of something else – and hence not inevitably some kind of sublimation. Should we talk of a 'political drive'? I am not sure. On the one hand, the last statement of Freud's about the life and death instincts need not be regarded as written in stone. Moreover, object relations theorists do not refer much to drives anyway. Hence, there is no hard and fast intellectual reason to desist from calling the innately political 'something' a drive. On the other hand, a theoretical innovation of that magnitude might distract attention from the overall implications of my theorizing on the role of the political. Perhaps what is necessary is to protest any premature attempt to displace the political as a category in depth psychology by translating it into other 'languages'. It may be useful here to recall that social psychologists have asserted that there are up to twelve basic instincts and that some of these are social in nature.[7] A regularly occurring criticism of depth psychology is that it makes little place for the social dimension as a primary factor. This is certainly true of analytical psychology and maybe Jungian theory could be expanded so that a political channel could be postulated for the flow of libido, alongside biological, moral and spiritual channels.[8] Anyway, for the moment I should like to refer to an individual's innate political potential.

If political potential is innate, then it may be expressed as a quantum, regarded as having been inborn in the person. (This is one way of expressing the constitutional, accidental, fateful factor in the patient's political history that I mentioned earlier.) If we take as a starting point the idea of an inborn quantum of political potential – meaning, in simple terms, an amount of energy of a political kind – then there are fascinating byproducts of the idea. To begin with, not all individuals would have the same quantum of political potential or political energy. Then one could ask: What happens if a person of innately high political potential/energy has parents with a low level of it? Or vice versa? What is the fate of the political potential born into an age that does not value a high level of that kind of energy? What will be the consequences if an individual's innate level of politicalness is not in tune with that of the society into which he or she is born? I think that situations of this kind are as likely to produce problems in political development as are specifics such as infantile traumas, maternal and paternal insufficiency, and so forth.

There are numerous other questions which now become askable: Did your parents foster or hinder the flowering of your political potential? If they hindered it, what was the destiny of that repressed political energy? Could we say that some people sublimate their political energy in ways that invest the sexual or aggressive areas of their psychology (turning the usual formulation on its head)? The important result of this kind of inquiry is that it becomes ever more difficult to render the political into other terms such as those of conventional drive theory or object relations – which does not deny the many articulations between political development and sexuality, aggression or object relations. But a partial, limited, focused approach has its advantages. Moreover, working on the political history and the political development of a person might open out into a wider discovery of unconscious material and processes.

If a culture does not allow a flowering of political potential to occur and express itself and the political self to flourish, then that culture loses one of the most productive avenues for personal growth and individuation. The individual loses out as well as the prospects for transformation and healing of psychopathology within the political system. We may find our private selves in the public sphere, just as we find psychopathology, hitherto thought the province of the individual, on the collective scene. If making politics is innate in humans, then we cannot speak in terms of deciding whether or not to join in; we are ethically involved as part of the human condition.

I would go further to say that there is an innate desire in humans to change social and political reality. The argument builds up like this: Social and political institutions constitute a form of reality. We know that desires can never be fully realized in reality. Therefore, social and political institutions are *not* exclusively constituted by desire. Hence, the relation between desire and existing social and political institutions is most likely to be an inimical one. This dissonance is expressed in humanity's recurrent attempts to change its social and political institutions. There is a sting in the tail here for political activists: At times of rapid social and political transformation, the desire for change can take the form of opposing and obstructing whatever political activity is going on. Taking 'desire' very loosely, perhaps that is why, during periods of political and social upheaval, sexual relationships become more urgent than ever, and are often experienced as a contradiction of the call to political action. This is shown quite beautifully in Alexandra Kollontai's novel *Love of Worker Bees* set just after the Russian Revolution. The heroines are torn between their sexual and emotional needs on the one hand and, on the other, their political commitment. Kollontai, writing in the period 1917–21, concluded that this problem can never be resolved unless and until there is a transformation of the family and the sexual and emotional relations between women and men.[9]

An individual can be said to suffer from repression of political potential if he or she cannot engage with a political theme that, consciously or unconsciously, is exercising that individual. *My clinical experience is that people are already much more engaged politically than they think they are.* Does such engagement have to be active, or would excitement and sympathy be enough? Or, paradoxically, might not good-enough political development mean withdrawal from political engagement for a period of time?

Why do I refer to political development? Might this not be rather conservative, from an intellectual standpoint? There are now numerous books on 'moral development', 'spiritual development', 'religious development', and 'the development of personality' is a well-researched and much argued-over field. So the general idea of development seems to be in the *Zeitgeist*.[10] The idea of development is obviously intended to be applied as non-normatively and non-judgmentally as possible, though it will be as well for me to admit immediately that my own personal political beliefs and values will enter the picture and help to bring a kind of hierarchy into play. This is absolutely unavoidable but I do not believe that my having beliefs and values of my own makes me any less neutral than or different from theorists in the fields of moral, spiritual, religious and personality development who undoubtedly have moral, spiritual, religious and psychological positions of their own to defend and privilege. Nevertheless, my interest is *not* in what might be called 'political maturity'. No such universal exists. My interest is in how people got to where they are politically and, above all, in how *they themselves think, feel, explain and communicate about how they got to where they are politically*; a subjective narrative of political development. Moreover, they may turn out not to be where they thought they were politically, or to have got to where they are by a route that they did not know about. We ask how, in the British political scene, a person *became* a Hampstead liberal not whether being a Hampstead liberal is a good thing in itself – but not denying that we have a viewpoint about Hampstead liberals. Moreover, not all Hampstead liberals became Hampstead liberals in the same way. We want to know how Hampstead liberals have experienced their becoming Hampstead liberals.

When a patient describes his or her political experiences, in the sense of formative or crucial political experiences, an analyst would listen with the same mix of literal and metaphorical understanding with which he or she would listen to any kind of clinical material – but with the idea of political development in mind as a permanent heuristic presence. Sometimes, the most productive path to follow would be to accept the patient's account of his or her political history; at other times, what the patient has to say may be understood as image, symbol and metaphor; at other times, as defensive and/or distorted; sometimes, it will be a mélange of these ways of understanding; sometimes, a competition between them.

The idea of development does not have to be used as if it were an exclusively linear, personalistic, causal-deterministic idea, characterized by regularity or predictability. (I wrote at length about this elsewhere.[11]) Development is a creative fantasy with extraordinary utility – and, by fantasy, I (once again) do not mean anything pathological or lacking connection to reality. Rather the reverse. Political development is a fantasy that enables us to look at an area of the psyche and at an aspect of the person that have been relatively neglected. The fantasy of political development helps us to access the politics of the person in the here-and-now, as the warring elements in personality clash and conciliate. For phases of development do not just fade away. Each phase remains active in the psyche in competitive relation to phases which only seem to us to be successive. Therefore, to the concepts of the political history of the person and the political development of the person we should add the concept of *the political here-and-now of the person*.

The implications for depth psychology of taking in these ideas about political development could be profound. In 1984 I suggested to my fellow members of the training committee of a psychotherapy organization that we should start to explore with candidates something about their political development – its history, roots, antecedents, patterns, vicissitudes and current situation. Just as we looked into sexuality, aggression and spiritual or moral development. At that time, the idea was regarded as slightly way out but more recently it has evoked a favorable response. Similarly, if political and social factors are part of personality and psychological development, should analysts and therapists not explore those areas in initial interviews with prospective patients? In throwing out these ideas on the political development of the person, I am aware that I have done no more than sketch out ways of engaging with what promises to be a fruitful – and vast – area of research.

As with 'subjectivity' I am aware that there are problems with my (or anyone's) use of the term 'person'. I think that the need to retain some idea of the person is necessary when we consider the political dimensions of life. Paradoxically, this speculation about the political development of the person is part of, not in opposition to, attempts to 'decenter' the 'habitual focus of psychoanalysis on an individual' by 'evoking the place of the between, thus dissolving the logic of inner and outer'.[12] Nor am I forgetting the wounded and grieving nature of the late modern or post-modern person that I mentioned in the previous chapter.

I conclude this section on the political development of the person by saying that we need to envision a new relationship in clinical practice as well as in theory between the private and the public, the intimate and the crowded, the secret and the open, the vulgar and the numinous – analysis as a kind of theater. In the theater of analysis, we need a crowd on the stage and a crowd in the audience. On that crowded stage are individuals who offer their most secret truths to individuals within that crowded audience, sharing a collective experience with them. Workshops on 'the political development of the person' facilitate such sharing and, with the help of workshop participants, I have developed a set of experiential exercises that illuminate political development.

THE POLITICS OF IMAGERY

It has often been suggested that our political culture has reached the point where the politics of imagery is the only politics there is. This is an important psychological point about politics. My sense is that a constructive response to the debasement of politics should take the form of making a political point about psychology in general and about imagery in particular. Concerning a political analysis of imagery, I have a suggestion to make: That we try to revise notions of imagery so that imagery is given a primary and not a secondary status. All too often, we tend to regard images as *products* – whether of relationship, or of instinct, or of conflict, or of emotions or of institutions. This view accords with common sense. Harder to see is that imagery *runs* relationships, *evokes* the goal of the instinct, *promotes* conflict, *engenders* emotion and *infects* institutions. I think the difficulty with keeping imagery as a first-order concept reflects a stultifying preoccupation with a substructure/ superstructure dichotomy in thinking, that insists on the very notion of underlying structure. From an experiential point of view, images are the things we experience most directly; this given-ness of experience in terms of images is as true of our bodily sensations, as pain studies show, as it is of our political experiences. If there *are* structures, scaffolds on which images hang, then it may be that images, the contents of those structures, have created them in the first place. Certainly, without the image, we would not be able to hypothesize the existence of the scaffold in the first place.

There are implications of this crash course in phenomenological psychology for cultural and political analysis. Let me give an example. An Italian patient dreamt of a beautiful lake with clear deep water. He said this represented his soul and then immediately associated to the pollution on the Italian Adriatic coast. The image of the lake, and the association to coastal pollution, suggested, in the form of one symbol, the patient's unconscious capacity for depth and his present state of which he was all too conscious – a state of being clogged up by 'algae', like the coastal waters of the Adriatic. When disparate psychological themes are thrown together like this, the symbolic image makes a powerful impact on the individual, who cannot ignore it. If he or she can hold on to the symbol that has emerged from the unconscious, keeping it available to consciousness and without idealizing the image, then the ego is itself strengthened or enhanced. But the capacity to retain a hold on symbolic images depends on ego strength and, if the ego is weak, the symbol remains unavailable to consciousness. Then the newly emerging interpretive synthesis, and the patient's new self experience, quickly fades from the picture. In this particular instance, the notion that there was possibly a 'solution' for the clogging up of his lake-soul potential, and the idea that being clogged was a state he had gradually got into over time and was not a witch's curse, together with the vision that depth and clarity and beauty were options open to him, were powerful and liberating thoughts for the patient to entertain. He made a choice to return to Italy, to tell his father that he was homosexual, and, in his words, to 'get more involved' – perhaps in environmental politics, it was not absolutely clear.

It was Jung who discovered the crucial property of imagery to face in two or more directions at the same time. In 1916, he termed this property 'the transcendent function', meaning that apparent opposites could be linked by images, provided these transcending images were understood symbolically: 'Opposites' such as the real and the imaginary, rationality and irrationality, consciousness and the unconscious, spirituality and sensuality, could be linked in this manner. According to Jung, the one-sidedness of many conscious attitudes could be transcended by new psychic products generated from the unconscious. This idea, termed 'compensation', meant that opposites could dialogue and engage in mutual influence. For instance, someone may have a preoccupation with sensual and material things. But the absolute opposite of this attitude – that is, spirituality – will probably be present as a potential in the unconscious and, given a facilitating environment, may become available to consciousness. What is involved is more than reaction formation or a crude combining of two possible attitudes. In individual analysis, the transcendent function mediates between a person as he or she is formed and the possibility of change. We see, not so much an answer, but the presentation of a choice or series of choices with all the attendant risks. The 'opposites' (sensuality and spirituality) were never as 'opposite' as they seemed.[13]

Returning to the dream of the lake, I would like to suggest an alternative reading, couched in more political terms. *I think that this re-reading constitutes a further transcendent function, a further statement about another crucial property of imagery.* The images of the dream can be approached via their individual presence, or via their political presence, or via the movement and tension between the two. In the dream of the lake, the tension between the individual and the political presences of the image was prominent and insistent; after all, the patient was Italian. What, the patient and I asked together, is the role of pollution in the soul, or even in the world? What is the role of pollution in the achievement of psychological depth? Can the soul remain deep and clear while there is pollution in the world, in one's home waters? Did the lake, with intimations of mystery and isolation, clash with the popular, extraverted tourism of the Adriatic? Eventually, the patient's concern moved onto the social level: Who owned the lake? Who should have access to such a scarce resource? Who would protect the lake from pollution? These were his associations. From wholly personal issues, such as the way his problems interfered with the flowering of his potential, we moved to political issues, such as the pollution of natural beauty, not only by industry but also by the mass extraversion of tourism. And we also moved back again from the political level to the personal level, including transference analysis. I do not mean to foreclose on other interpretations, but to add in a more 'political' one so that the patient's unconsciously taken up political commitments can become clearer.

I think imagery can be understood as performing this further transcendent function: Bridging the gap between the apparently individual, private, subjective and the apparently collective, social, political. Much of this book argues for the general thesis that there is a constant relationship and articulation between the personal/subjective and the public/political dimensions of life. Can we discriminate these separate dimensions in such a way that this newly transcendent function can, on a more conscious level, better bring them together? I think that we are finding that private, interior imagery carries a political charge. Moreover, we need to be better placed to make practical, clinical use of the by-now conventional observation that the external world, particularly its social and power relations, has an effect on our subjective experience.

Applying this approach to imagery to a psychological analysis of politics, we would try to discriminate the individual and the cultural aspects of an image and see whether, by means of a kind of transcendent function, they can be brought to an equal level of consciousness. This process would increase the range of choices available, rather than collapsing them into a solution. In the example, the question of ownership of the lake at first seemed a distant 'political' concern. But gradually the patient's social sensitivity came to the fore: He asserted that the lake, like his soul, was not a commodity to be owned by anyone. Then a celebration of his social conscience came to the fore. He addressed the fate of his 'Italian-ness' on a personal, individual level. Finally, as the transcendent function in his imagery continued to pulse, he discovered more collective, cultural and political associations to pollution on the Adriatic. I hope it is clear that the public/political and private/subjective dimensions were both thoroughly alive.

I have noticed that the choice of imagery in the language of political theory sometimes shows the operation of a transcendent function of this kind, as it moves between the individual and the collective dimensions, trying to connect them. The language of politics, like the language of depth psychology, is often treated with extreme suspicion as if it were somehow fundamentally negative. I feel this depreciation besmirches and represses political process. When we think about themes such as political obligation, negotiation and bargaining, we see that an additional positive connotation of the imagery in political language cannot be avoided, just as it is not possible to deny the positive side of the unconscious and its creative productivity.

This reworking of the transcendent function onto a sociopolitical level provides the beginnings of a model for tracking moves between individual and collective realms and a means of studying conflicts and harmonies between culture and individual. For individual and culture are not the crude opposites that many, including Freud, have taken them to be. Both terms enjoy the complex interaction produced by their dynamic relationship; the relationship changes the nature of the original 'opposites'. The more deep and personal the experience, the more political and public it may turn out to be.

The politics of imagery now operates, in the external world, at a pace that often precludes rational debate. If we are to avoid being permanently after-the-event – the unending social *Nachträglichkeit* – then we have to try to engage, not only with the politics of psychological imagery but also with the politics of depth psychology itself.

ON CHANGING PRACTICE

As I said at the start of the chapter, changes in the orientation of depth psychology to the world lead to a consideration of changes in the basic practices of clinical analysis. One extreme position would be to drop the practice of analysis altogether in favor of large-scale group psychological teaching.[14] I feel, in contrast, that, if we accept the human subject as located between so-called inner and so-called outer worlds, then the political necessity of continuing to meet him or her in the consulting room remains. It is true that the individual human subject is not the alpha and omega of political action. Nevertheless, giving up analysis on the (incorrect) grounds that it operates only in a solipsistic frame is, as I suggested in the previous chapters, just a different inflation from the one that forces psychotherapy in a hyperprofessional direction, following slavishly an absolutist clinical path. Where depth psychology is deployed in non-clinical analysis, as in film, art or literary criticism, there is simply no problem. Such critics are lucky, perhaps. But how are ordinary clinical analysts to change their practice?

It may be useful here to offer an amplification from another field of intense praxis, in which political consciousness deeply affected a worker.

I think we can learn a great deal from Bertolt Brecht's struggle to evolve the kind of theatrical practice that would really embody his politics. Brecht's ideology is most acutely expressed, not in his extra-theatrical activities or in his 'message' – but in his *practice itself*. Of course, Brecht did not invent the idea of drama with a social conscience, but it is mainly to him that we owe the notion of theater as an arena for social and political debate. Above all, Brecht's goal was to change the status and role of the audience. The paradox is the creation of the active spectator, participating in an argument rather than identifying with a heroic character. In the old theater, the heroic, individual human being was taken for granted, but in Brecht's epic theater that notion is under the microscope. As Galileo says, 'unhappy is the country that needs a hero'.

For Brecht, the characters in a play are not heroic individuals, frozen in time, but ordinary persons in a social context, engaged in an episodic narrative. They are part, as we would say nowadays, of a larger text. In analysis, as in the theater that Brecht encountered, we are much caught up with heroisms. We see this in Jung's heroic version of mother–infant separation or in Freud's heroic version of father–son rivalry. But heroism is also present in analysis itself, as when the patient is required to 'overcome' something, 'achieve' something, 'sacrifice' something, 'integrate' (that is, take possession of) something, even 'work' through something. The imagery of analysis is all about struggle *within* the patient and I would not say, from my experience, that this is always a wrong conclusion to draw. But the idea of struggle has resonances and relevances that are political, reflecting the collective's accurate fantasies about the nature of politics. Can they be amplified and picked up? Can, for instance, the changing nature of the patient's parental imagery be interpreted on an appropriate political level? (I attempt this in Chapters 6 and 7.) Such shifts might involve questions of concern for the environment or other political topics. Similarly, can analysts alter their own interpretive thrust, their own heroism, away from 'you, the patient', away from 'we the analyzing couple', so that the patient's conflicts are more rigorously connected to the political world? This would be a modulation of feelings outward as well as inward toward ego absorption. 'Ex-volvement' as well as involvement? To answer such questions, it helps to be able to envision the patient as undergoing political development alongside his or her sexual or aggressive development, as I discussed earlier.

This makes practical clinical use of the idea that any image brought to analysis can be approached via its cultural and public presence as well as via its individual and private presence. Sometimes, it is the movement and tension – the articulation – between the individual and the cultural perspectives that is important. Let us recall the patient who dreamt of that beautiful lake with clear, deep water and interpreted it as referring to his soul, further associations being to coastal pollution in his home country. The articulation between the individual and the cultural associations was marked. The key question concerned the role of pollution in his soul. We asked how *his soul* could remain clear while there is *pollution on the Adriatic coast.*

With thoughts of this further transcendent function in mind, Brecht's 'alienation effect' and his idea of 'distanciation' can help us here. The analyst might, in some circumstances, completely reverse the poles of what he or she ordinarily does and work also to *distance* the patient from the emotions engendered by the patient's personal situation. In a sense, the patient is not to identify with himself or herself as hero, not to be self-empathic, not even to aim for insight or self-understanding. The patient tries to locate what is public about his or her private conflicts, anxieties, relationship problems. This would be a radical course to take and implies the *deprivileging and reframing of the personal dimension* in analytical ideology. Feelings would not only be important on the personal level. Just as the Brechtian actor is both Hamlet and Hamlet's critic, so a Brechtian mode of analyzing would disassemble the falsely unitary nature of the analytical project, moving away from catharsis and self-knowledge as the highest goals.

I cited the patient's dream of the lake as illustrative of the *problem*, showing why this work has to be done rather than as a model solution. When discussing these ideas with colleagues, a worry has often been expressed that one might be influencing the patient or, dreaded word, using 'suggestion'. Sometimes I have been accused of wanting to foist my own political prejudices onto the patient. These arguments are advanced as if suggestion was completely out of the question, and hence absent from an average, normal, good-enough analysis and as if topics like sex and aggression never excited an analyst's prejudiced responses – whereas politics does.

Of course, there is always a risk of discipleship in the analytical situation as those who have had training analyses know. But I feel confident in saying that there is a huge amount of uncritically accepted suggestion in analytical practice already and that, from a certain point of view, the more 'professional', 'bounded', 'contained' and 'disciplined' the behavior of the practitioner, the more suggestion is taking place in his or her practice. I think this is inevitable. The technical rules of analysis are not politically or culturally neutral; they do more than facilitate the unfolding of the self. They have themselves cultured (or facilitated) depth psychology in a permanent way, and they have themselves done it to a certain extent by suggestion. On the basis of the replies received to my questionnaire on political material that is brought to the consulting room, it is clear that a good deal of discussion goes on in ordinary analysis – probably more than is revealed in supervision, wherein 'discussion' can be a dirty word. (The survey itself is reported in Chapter 10.) If analysts are already discussing politics with the patient, this would be to bring 'the political' into the consulting room as well as to stimulate an interchange on one particular political topic. It is clear that, in the words of a colleague of mine, 'the hygienic sealing of the consulting room from politics is a virginal fantasy' on the part of analysts and therapists.[15]

Following Brecht's project, perhaps we need to think about how to engage some of our patients in political, social and cultural discussion and argument. Sometimes, we have to take a frankly educative model for our work (often, assuredly, the patient is educating the analyst). Sometimes, we may even argue with the patient (usually regarded as a *grave* technical error). We should not go on as if all our ideas about the internalization of the culture, the disunity of the human subject, the meaningfulness of symptoms, were all a new kind of metaphysics and hence not of immediate practical relevance. Like Brecht, we have to interrupt a smoothly running narrative – in our case, by disputing the claim of the inner world for a disproportionate level of analytical attentiveness. Like Brecht, we have to discourage identification with the hero – in our case, to discourage identification with ego, self, depressive position, the symbolic order, individuation.

The worries about excessive suggestion expressed by those who have argued with these ideas of mine are actually very important and I do not seek to minimize them – for instance, by pointing out that Freud could cope with the idea that suggestion played a part in the talking cure, provided the patient was, in fact, disposed to be suggestible.[16] Above all, these worries do highlight our lack of a map or model by which to approach whatever individuals sense their *political* development to have been, or whatever their present political state might be. We have such maps and models to guide us in the fields of sexuality, aggression and object relations. But are we not by nature political animals, as Aristotle thought – and, hence, as I have been hinting, is not politics a drive, just as sex or aggression are? By maps or models of political development, I do not mean something expressed in the language of the issues of the day, though that might form the raw material for political development.

One particular question that I would like to discuss concerns the impact of these ideas upon what clinical analysts actually say to patients, on interpretation. I like to work in terms of plural interpretation, of saying to the patient: 'I think this material refers to such and such *and also* to such and such, but I am not sure which path we should explore.'

The giving and receiving of plural interpretations is a highly problematic technical issue. But there are critical political issues as well. As far as technique is concerned, it may be that the differing interpretive views would have to be spaced out over time so as to make their assimilation easier. On the other hand, the impact of interpretation is on an inner world level and not through intellectual understanding and it is difficult to see how such impact would be interfered with if an interpretation were plural in nature – unless we are going to say that the unconscious can only deal with clear-cut messages. The difficulty that may exist with plural interpretation could be more to do with adherence to what are felt to be the technical rules of analysis. Here, we might recall E. H. Carr's comment that, even for a historian, whatever he offers as an interpretation of events is always the outcome of the establishment of a hierarchy of interpretations. Note that Carr did not go on to say that all interpretations save the main one are discarded.[17] So, to an extent, all interpretation is plural interpretation.

The political issues are highlighted when the analyst makes *his or her uncertainty* concerning a multiplicity of viewpoints the central plank of an interpretation. Politically speaking, this is far more democratic and likely to lead to dialogue and negotiation than crudely offering the patient several options and letting him or her tick the preferred one. Many single-strand interpretations of psychological material are themselves concerned with conflict and dissent; in such cases, plural interpretation may be stylistically closer to many-layered political reality. The risk of intellectualizing need be no greater than with single-strand interpretation, and could even be less.

The weakness of plural interpretation is undoubtedly that it could degenerate into infinite and unreal tolerance and acceptance of any viewpoint whatsoever. But it is as possible to experience a change from the plural (tolerant) as it is from the singular (incisive). In any case, we would hardly want *all* interpretation to be plural. (See Chapter 9 for a fuller discussion of pluralism.)

We can speculate as to the effect on the transference of making plural interpretations. Negatively, the analyst may be seen as woolly, hedging his or her bets, not providing value for money and so forth. More positively, the idea of analysis as a partnership or corporate activity would be promoted, without its acquiring a radiance of spurious equality or becoming a two-person discussion group.

It may well not be necessary for the analyst to do very much (or anything) more than provide a safe place for the political aspects of the patient's psychological potentialities to unfold. This would be a con- firmation of what we already know about holding, containment and the *temenos*.

I would like to bring in a final cautionary note about changing practice, gleaned from another cultural area – this time, feminist art practice. Women artists quickly found that it was not possible to make art out of women's experience and challenge the patriarchal ways in which the idea of 'art' has been constructed *without* considering changes in art practice as well. However, tracking the debates within feminism over the past twenty years underscores the near impossibility of producing a definitive statement of feminist art practice.[18] The same will undoubtedly be true for depth psychological analysis of politics. *And this ambiguity should be the case.* It would be tragic if 'political' depth psychologists deluded themselves that there's only one way to go, for this would simply give ammunition to those who want depth psychology to stay politically 'neutral' and 'objective'.

POLITICS AND THE CASE HISTORY

I am trying to make a psychology which operates on a political level so that something extrapolated from the individual situation would refer to the more collective aspects of a patient's material. I am thinking of the presence of cultural influences on the unconscious (or the corollary: The driving power of mythopoetic imagery in relation to cultural performance). However, the typical feature of depth psychology is its case-by-case approach, exemplified by the case history, nowadays referred to by many writers as the case 'illustration'. We need to discuss whether the case history genre is relevant to cultural and social analysis or not. At the outset, I must say that, for me, the issue is not at all connected with the truth or objectivity of the case history. *For I never doubted that they were fictions, and that apparently radical notion was widely accepted even in my rather conservative training as an analyst.* To critique clinical narratives as if, these days, 'scientific' claims were being made of their incontrovertibility is to tilt at windmills.

Feminism has engaged in a similar debate. That the personal is political is a central tenet of radical feminism. Such feminist theory may be said to have come to terms with the case history approach, for all the inadequacies of that. Theorists such as Martha Rosler have addressed the question 'Is the personal political?' in terms which scarcely require any translation into the language of depth psychology and analysis.[19]

There is another sense in which the retention of some kind of case history approach is valid and this concerns the use of psychopathology. When discussing psychopathology, there is a spectrum that stretches from what might be called a professional approach to a poetic approach. Making diagnoses such as 'narcissistic personality disorder' or 'anal character', or discussing normality and abnormality, represents the well-known, professional pole. However, there is also a poetic style of pathologizing to consider. Before doing that, I would like to make a few comments about this spectrum, which is itself a creative falsehood, offered by me for its heuristic value. There is no reason for the poles of the spectrum to be in opposition. No one analyst will occupy one pole exclusively; indeed, many will claim that they make explicit use of the whole spectrum in their work. There may even be a level on which the two poles turn out to be identical: The poesy of consummate professionalism, and the professional cutting edge of an acute poetic imagination.

What represents the poetic end of the spectrum? Provided we do not get seduced by cheap professionalism, and provided we do not attempt an artificial division between normal and abnormal, then the study of psychopathology acquires a poetic cast: The individual case, or even symptom, contains a microscopic version of the culture, including its power relations. The smallest part (symptom) contains the greatest whole (politics). The clinical situation is not to be regarded as finite and the political milieu as infinite, for the opposite is also the case.

Therefore we need not abandon the familiar jargon of case-by-case psychopathology. But we have to try to use it imaginatively so that it starts to function once again as psyche's language, psyche's words, psyche-ology. I suggest that there is a sense in which this kind of psycho-pathologizing may have an effect on social and political analysis. Judicious argument on the basis of what is found with the individual patient may lead to something that is generally true for society.[20]

Yet, in spite of the potential helpfulness of the case history approach, there are also major problems with it. I have already mentioned one of the more obvious: That case history is a form of creative writing. What is more, much case history is propaganda for one theoretical view or another and the presence of that kind of reductionism has proved a serious obstacle for psychobiography and psychohistory to overcome.

From a more philosophical angle, there are certain objections to the case history approach which, parodying Wittgenstein, I would call the 'second-person illusion'. Wittgenstein's 'first-person illusion' is the claim that one knows one's own mental states better than one knows other people's mental states because one observes one's own directly. The second-person illusion would be that one (an analyst) can be more certain about another's (patient's) mental states than that second person can be because one does not suffer from that second person's repression, denial, or lack of training. But neither the first-person *nor* the second-person case gives us certainty. According to Wittgenstein, they have no meaning at all without reference to the fact that 'there are people in the world besides oneself and [that] one has a nature and form of life in common with them'.[21] Wittgenstein stands, then, as an unlikely starting point for moves into political psychology which do not retain features of the case history approach.

PSYCHOID ASPECTS OF POLITICAL PROCESS

Most Jungian essays in collective psychology, while acknowledging cultural diversity on the surface, end by stressing the universal impact of 'archetypal' patterns on group processes.[22] Certain themes figure promi-nently in such psycho-anthropological analyses: The role of religion, the ritual significance of politics, the mythical functions of the offices and officers of state, the presence or absence of fulfilling initiatory experiences, and where these are absent, perverse searches for such experiences, such as drug addiction. In this kind of archetypal analysis, the gods and goddesses often emerge as providing a fundamental hermeneutic framework. For example: 'The massive technologizing of contemporary culture, far from moving without purpose or form, is playing itself out according to the stories of Prometheus, Hephaestus, and Asclepius', 'the military-industrial complex is Hera–Heracles–Hephaestus'.[23] Such an approach works best when accompanied by as scrupulous as possible a recovery of the particularity of the god or goddess (something I will myself attempt in Chapter 4 with regard to Hermes).

Sometimes the employment of collective psychology follows a different path. In this alternative appreciation of what 'collective' means, psychology is seen as an analog of the instincts, as something akin to biology.[24] The focus is not only on what is universal but on those psychological events and processes deemed to lie closest to the biological realm of the instincts. So the ground covered is that of early infancy – though the mother is often the Great Mother and the child the Divine Child. The idea is that psychology at the start of life is somehow more instinctually determined, hence more collective, than at any other time. (I'll dispute this viewpoint in Chapter 11.)

There is a possible third way in which the notion of the collective unconscious could be deployed in political and cultural debate. I would like to explore this new idea in detail here. I start from Jung's concept of the psychoid level of the unconscious. This concerns a level of the psyche that is so submerged and yet so fundamental that it would be an error to regard it as deriving solely from a biological base. Jung's psychoid category represents a complete interpenetration of matter and psyche to the point where they may be regarded as two sides of a coin: Psyche-in-matter, matter-in-psyche. Jung cautions, no doubt correctly, that at this level, the psychoid level, things are 'unfathomable'.[25] However, the search in modern physics for a force that would unite the four forces known to operate in the physical universe may also be seen as a search for a kind of 'psychology' in matter (as in action-at-a-distance). The existence of the scientific parallel suggests that Jung's concept of the psychoid has possibilities beyond those he himself saw in it, leading to approaches to political and social theory that are more pragmatic than those that a mere revival of the medieval doctrine of the *unus mundus* would offer.

The more I have reflected on the idea of the psychoid, the more I have become aware that the concept can be extended to invoke a set of profound political, social and cultural issues. *The psychoid is also political, social and cultural in nature.* We are not only talking of the psyche's influence on the political, social and cultural worlds, but also of the political, social and cultural worlds' influence on the psyche. All these worlds show a degree of identity as well as difference. The psychoid level, by definition collective, but, equally by definition, neither exclusively psychological nor exclusively social, can be seen as a (or the) vehicle for the transmission of cultural and social practices. We flesh out the adage that 'when you treat the patient, you treat the culture'. If this idea holds water, it could be of use in depth psychology's project of providing therapy for the political culture. For, up to now, we have only the concept of internalization to account for such transmissions; this operates exclusively on the individual level: A person takes in the received social and relational order and it becomes part of that person's mental set.

Positing a psychoid level, and doing this in a social language, could obviate the difficulties of an individualistic approach to cultural transmission. The problem remains: How to develop a social or political language that reflects the psychoid factor – that is, accepting the unity of the psychic and political realms while at the same time maintaining their separateness and diversity. For I would be unconvinced if my introduction of the psychoid factor led to an untrammelled holism, a claim that there are no differences between the three differing realms of human, cultural and material existence. The paradox of holism is that, if the realms *are* identical, then it becomes ever more necessary to disentangle them in order to permit any kind of discourse at all. Holism is a provocation to analytical thinking! The psychoid interpenetration of society and psychology is a perspective that helps us to see personal pain as a statement about social conditions – pain as a spur to analyze those conditions, and pain as the motive force in changing those conditions.

TELEOLOGY AND POLITICAL ANALYSIS

The teleological viewpoint (from *telos*, meaning goal) is based on Aristotle's idea of *causae finales* (final causes). Sometimes it is referred to as the prospective approach. In psychology, this approach means considering a phenomenon from the standpoint of what it is for, where it is leading, for the 'sake' of what it is happening. All these dimensions were more interesting to Jung than the effects of the situation of causes located in the chronological past (Aristotle's *causae efficientes*). Jung's emphasis on teleology led him to propose that symptoms, and indeed mental illness itself, may often signify something of great potential value for the individual. For example, Jung saw depression as a damming up of energy, which, when released, may take on a more positive direction. Energy is trapped because of a neurotic or psychotic problem but, if freed, actually helps in the overcoming of the problem. A state of depression is, according to this view, one which should be entered into as fully as possible, so that the feelings involved may be clarified. Seen teleologically, depression may have a regenerative and enriching aspect. It may take the form of 'the empty stillness which precedes creative work'.[26]

Jung pointed out that in everyday life the teleological viewpoint is taken for granted alongside the strictly causal factor. For example, if a person has an opinion and expresses it, we usually want to know what he or she means, what is being got at, rather than the historical origins of the remark alone. According to Jung, psychological phenomena ought to be approached as if they had intention and purpose – i.e. considered in terms of goal-orientedness or teleology. Jung grants the unconscious a kind of knowledge or even foreknowledge. If we are not to descend into fortune- telling, we must be careful how we adapt the idea of teleology to cultural and political processes. We must try not to make teleology an instrument of closure, denying the modern predicament in which there seems to be no *telos*.

The idea that there is a 'knowledge of the unconscious' makes it possible to think that there may be a 'knowledge of the political and social collective'. Obviously, mass consciousness is not remarkable for its good taste and political sophistication. But it is possible to determine occasions in mass movements and movements of the mass when a goal seems to be functioning as a cause, dragging or leading the situation in a certain direction. I have in mind the events in the former Soviet Union and Eastern Europe that took place in the 1980s and early 1990s.

Teleology cultivates a certain kind of question: What's this for? Where's it going? What does it mean? Not, What are its roots? What made it happen? *The question 'who benefits?' is a teleological question that is absolutely crucial for political analysis.*

The adoption of a teleological attitude is particularly useful in the kind of political and cultural analysis I am describing. Ever more teleological questions will be asked of disciplines already directly engaged with problems in the human sciences. For example: What is moral philosophy for, socially speaking? Where is literary criticism going, from a cultural perspective? What is the economic significance of modern theology?

PSYCHOPATHOLOGY AND POLITICS

Clinical and political analysts are equally the victims of their own hypotheses. It is very hard to get it completely wrong in depth psychology and the risk is of ending up with a tautological display of correctness. I want to suggest that, rather than looking for psychopathology in culture, which is so easy to find, we try to look *with* psychopathology, with a psychopathological eye. We should not only search for hidden depression in the culture, or for paranoid projections between nation states, or for the sado-masochistic patterns in pornography. Rather, let us see how our own depression makes us regard things in a certain way, through a lens preoccupied with our own destructiveness. Let us see how an envious eye makes us see envy everywhere, making us accept that what is good in modern culture can be rubbished by a weary intelligentsia. Let us see how our own paraphilias make us, as analysts, probe and pry into areas of life that used to be sacred, profoundly fetishizing their contents. This is more than self-reflection or self-analysis; it is using the psychopathological part of our selfhood as a way of seeing, and then as a way of analyzing. It is a new use of the project of depth psychology – to move outward armed with the tools of the trade, which are not methods, theories and interpretations alone, but also the very symptoms, syndromes, illnesses and problems without which depth psychology would have no social function.

Can we develop the kind of eye for psychopathology that would enable us to enter more deeply into political and social illnesses? An 'eye of understanding'? This would be imaginative understanding and making use of imagination in psychological analysis of culture demands an *esthetic approach* to political and social illnesses. New terms such as 'social esthetics' or 'political esthetics' would approximate to what I have in mind. Political esthetics would not be an esthetics of connoisseurship, though an apprehension of beauty would still reside at its core.

In the orthodox Jewish and other religious traditions, repentance of sin is often expressed as an esthetic reaction to the revulsion caused by one's own corrupt behavior. Sin is not only wrong, but also disgustingly ugly. If sin looks beautiful to you, you will be a sinner. If you cannot discover the often-hidden beauty of virtue, you will never be virtuous.

There is a marvellous cartoon in Gary Larson's 'Far Side' series which is apt here. There are two pictures. In the top picture, a man arrives in heaven to meet St Peter. In the bottom picture, a man arrives in hell to meet the Devil. St Peter says 'Welcome to heaven – here's your harp'. The Devil says 'Welcome to hell – here's your accordion'. I say that we should play the harp when we can but we should not be afraid to play the accordion when we must. A political esthetics is going to be more convoluted than an esthetics of art.

THE LIMITS OF PSYCHOLOGY

Should we be attempting a psychological analysis of politics? My answer is: Not directly. Direct application of depth psychology to cultural themes is clearly not the best way of going about things. I am sure that depth psychologists should not try to be historians, anthropologists, philosophers, political theorists, biographers or scientists. What a depth psychologist *can* do is offer a psychological partnership to all these disciplines, respecting the ways of working already developed therein. Such an indirect role means a fresh engagement with a corpus of knowledge and practice that *already* has made a direct engagement with culture with its own specific tools.

When I first thought about this particular idea, it depressed me. I think I was fond of the notion of an activist analyst, prominent on barricade and in newspaper column. Then I perceived that to be *indirect* is a particular contribution of depth psychology – a grasp on reflection and the ability to deepen any issue that it touches. To insert depth psychology sensitively into a discourse where it has not been present is by no means the same as to try to operate within that discourse or to take over that discourse. Surely it is desirable for depth psychologists to stick to what they do well, but do it in a different manner and in different settings? This seems more realistic than depth psychologists becoming amateur members of other disciplines.

Of course, this would not stop those who are already competent in other disciplines from making use of depth psychology. But I think it would be a more effective realization of the subversive potential of depth psychology to suggest that, in distinction to direct action in the political and cultural spheres, there might be this more reflective modality. In any event, a depth psychologist is as free to be as politically active as he or she likes, or as is possible given the constraints of belonging to a somewhat conservative profession.

As I suggested in Chapter 1, it is crucial to avoid a reductionism which perceives everything as psychological. I will give two brief examples of this danger becoming manifest. First, Jung's insistence on 'the nation' as an exclusively *psychological* fact trapped him in an uncritical acceptance that there were really such things as 'German psychology' and 'Jewish psychology'. These he presented as mutually antipathetic and this led him to make statements, beyond his conscious intention, of a fundamentally anti-semitic kind. In his references to *the* German or *the* Jewish psyche, rather than to the psychological experience of being a German or a Jew, Jung sought too much living-space for depth psychology. (Questions of Jung's anti-semitism are discussed in detail in Chapters 12 and 13.)

Similarly, some of Freud's remarks in *The Future of an Illusion* concerning the 'suppressed' members of a culture demonstrate the same tendency to misjudgment of cultural and religious phenomena based on a hypertrophy of psychology. Freud argues that politically and economically suppressed people do not, and cannot, internalize 'cultural prohibitions' (i.e. the cultural super-ego) because they are so irrevocably hostile to the culture as a whole.[27] The illogicality of this position seems obvious to us now; it is the suppressed people who have internalized the largest dose of cultural prohibition. Above all, suppressed people accept (internalize) the idea that there have to be suppressed people.

I want to end this section on the limits of psychology with a comment on *doing and saying nothing as a means of cultural and political analysis.* Generally speaking, such political analysis would avoid a quiet acceptance of things as they are, or meditative emptiness, or 'Eastern' ways to cure the madness of 'Western' society. But even these tropes should not be ruled out. 'Sometimes I sits and thinks and sometimes I just sits', was the rural sage's solution. Drawing on clinical experience, an analyst can offer the men and women of action – though the most brilliant of them know it already – a trained sense of timing: When to speak and act and when to keep silent and do nothing.

Chapter 4

The lion and the fox
Morality, Trickster and political transformation

MORALITY AND MACHIAVELLI

In Chapter 1 I mentioned the importance of paying attention to political imagery. After the opening chapters about resacralization, politics and the market economy, I now want to move on to a psychological analysis of the imagery in the political thought of Niccolò Machiavelli. The idea is to explore what an engagement with politics does to psychology and at what psychology can bring to political theorizing. Machiavelli is important for us precisely because he does not look like a modern resacralizer. There is no deep ecology in Machiavelli's Prince, no upbeat spiritual optimism, not a lot of femininity or feminine consciousness. He's a meat-eater, isn't he? He can be dishonest, unreliable, impure, worldly – and, perhaps because of these things, he is very effective in the worlds of psychology and politics alike. What we find in Machiavelli is the kind of bleak realism and sense of civic duty that sees things through. If only resacralization could tap into Machiavellian energies. . . .

In Machiavelli's short book *The Prince*, written in 1513–14, we find a psychological analysis of the political process. Machiavelli blends wanton subversiveness, subtly buried morality, and relentless imagination. It is possible for us to encounter his encounter with the political culture of his time, seeing 'the Prince' as a metaphor for a certain kind of political psychology, or psychological approach to politics.

We can make psychology in a Machiavellian way, think Machiavellian thoughts, see with a Machiavellian eye. The opprobrium heaped on Machiavelli's head for nearly five hundred years is also something to muse about. Depth psychologists, such as Freud or Jung, also stir up similar reactions when they bring their psychological theories to bear on the political and social scene. As with Machiavelli's writings, what depth psychologists have to say often appears to subvert every generally held decency. But it is the peculiar quality of the subversiveness found in an apparently reactionary thinker that is the compelling quality in Machiavelli's writings. The subversiveness is not contrived or adolescent but argued out rather logically.

The prince is a person who is subject to history and, above all, to Fortune. His job is to make sure that Fortune does not mar his attempts to write his own script, be a successful ruler, and achieve glory. So, at the same time as noting that the prince is a contingent and constrained person, Machiavelli emphasizes that the prince also has creative autonomy. His future, and that of his people, is bound up with how comprehensively he can create his own Fortune.

In classical political theory and also in the new Renaissance humanism, the prince's task was to develop in himself the four cardinal virtues: Wisdom, justice, courage and moderation. In addition, there were many other virtues which the prince was also supposed to possess. The phrase 'honesty is the best policy' summarizes the tenor of this way of thinking about politics. In *The Prince*, Machiavelli completely rejects these virtues. His *virtù* is that the prince should follow the dictates of necessity. The rejection of humanistic political morality is given dramatic and precise imagistic form: The prince should follow the fox and the lion. Not God, not the inner voice; the prince should learn from animals:

> A prince is forced to know how to act like a beast. He should learn from the fox and the lion; because the lion is defenseless against traps and a fox is defenseless against wolves. Therefore one must be a fox in order to recognize traps, and a lion to frighten off wolves. Those who simply act like lions are stupid. . . . Those who have known best how to imitate the fox have come off best. But one must know how to color one's actions and to be a great liar and deceiver.[1]

Machiavelli is not content simply to ignore humanism; he does not seem much troubled by Christian morality either. The prince is never admonished to take care lest he be judged in the afterlife and the usual Christian virtues of forgiveness and gentleness are explicitly ruled out: The prince should punish his enemies instantly and with public ruthlessness. The ideology to be found here is the deliberate rejection of ideology. I mean that there is a rejection of ideology as a rational system, a reliable and predictable way of getting through the chanciness of the world. However, Machiavelli is not advocating a patternless mode of behavior for the prince. Nor is a conception and recognition of human moral capacity missing from Machiavelli's outlook: The prince's morality should, above all, be of a flexible nature; he is required to *choose* to be evil, to be evil in spite of himself:

> And so he should have a flexible disposition, varying as fortune and circumstance dictate. . . . He should not deviate from what is good, if that is possible, but he should know how to do evil, if that is necessary.

The act of choice, of temporarily suppressing the dove in favor of the hawk, takes us onto a subtle moral plane. Problems of choice lie at the heart of political and moral philosophies. Being 'Machiavellian' means more than being ruthless or always allowing ends to justify means.

In modern psychological language, what Machiavelli is doing is to make an ideology and a morality out of the shadow, out of those aspects of human psychology that we would rather disown. Most political theory seeks to combat and deal with the shadow.[2] Machiavelli's approach is to embrace the shadow and go *with* its energies rather than against them. This is what we today find so difficult – to accept that even resacralizers have motives such as greed and the desire for power:

> One can make this generalization about men: they are ungrateful, fickle, liars, and deceivers, they shun danger and are greedy for profit; while you treat them well, they are yours . . . when you are in danger they turn against you. A prince who has come to depend entirely on promises and has taken no other precautions ensures his own ruin. . . . The bond of love is one which men, wretched creatures that they are, break when it is to their advantage to do so; but fear is strengthened by a dread of punishment which is always effective.

To adopt this as a *conscious* base for government was truly revolutionary, at least in the West. For Machiavelli, political actions are enclosed in a conception of human psychology. The message for cultural and political analysis is clear: A perception of what people are like precedes a conception of political change. Perhaps we cannot follow Machiavelli in his bleak generalization as to what human nature is. Maybe he is wrong, or his view is one-sided and incomplete in leaving out the positive side of human potential. But Machiavelli is right to place psychology at the heart of the political process. One reason why I have been drawn to Machiavelli is his eschewal of easy answers. Nowhere in his work is there anything that resembles a modern psychodynamic medicine, such as genitality or individuation or the depressive position, which is claimed to 'cure' the political system of its psychopathology. Machiavelli's stand here is to take no stand, to go with the flow of what we usually reject or cannot face, to stay with the dirt rather than try to make gold out of it. Remaining disillusioned about the possibility of political and cultural transformation is a hard path to take. But the point for political and cultural analysis is that

Machiavelli is dealing with what is possible and also with what is the case
– that is, politics – and doing this from a psychologically realistic point of
view. Hence, he has a realistic chance of changing things.

Paradoxically, Machiavelli's realistic angle on political morality leads
us to the legendary figure of the Trickster. When we explored
Machiavelli's morality, we noted that 'if a prince wants to maintain his
role he must learn how not to be virtuous, and to make use of this or not
according to need'. The prince, it seems, must overcome his innate virtue.
However, at the same time as being bad, he must not *appear* to be bad:

> A prince should be so prudent that he knows how to escape the evil
> reputation attached to those vices which could lose him his state . . . To
> those seeing and hearing him, he should appear a man of compassion,
> a man of good faith, a man of integrity, a kind and religious man. . . .
> Everyone sees what you appear to be, few experience what you really
> are.

It's a trick, you see. Perhaps it needs to be made clear that this is not
Satanic, nor perverse, not Machiavelli taking evil as his good, nor foul as
fair. For this unavoidable tricksterism lies at the heart of the *political*. By
exploring the psychology of Trickster, I intend to test the insight about
links between the Trickster and political processes. The aim is to gain a
deeper understanding of the depth psychology of political process in
general and the depth psychology of political change in particular. What
have we done to ourselves by evacuating the shadow from accounts of
political motivation and by shunning the Trickster in politics?

POLITICS AND THE TRICKSTER

Trickster figures and stories appear in many cultures, as has only quite
recently become accepted. For the Greeks, the arch-Trickster was
Hermes, with his tendency to play jokes, to lie, to cheat, to steal, to deny
reality, and to engage in grandiose fantasy. (We will be turning to Hermes
in the next section of the chapter.) Genuine Tricksters, from Coyote in
North America to Ananse or Eshu in West Africa, follow that pattern,
undermining the prevailing organization of power and even the perceived
structure of reality itself. Tricksters can certainly be seen as personifications of primary process activity, challenging and disregarding the
laws of time, space and place. Rather, let us speculate about why Trickster
mounts this challenge. He does it *precisely to test the limits of those laws*,
the bounds of their applicability, and, hence, the possibility of altering
them. At the moment we say this, the political referents of the Trickster

are revealed. Challenging the limits of laws, their applicability and the possibility of altering them – and doing this in an ideological climate that is hostile to such a challenge – is *the* classic progressive political project. Claiming the Trickster for politics might seem like the most crass over-interpretation. But if Trickster's political theorizing can retain his own capacity for shock and irony then no more than a little damage will have been done to him. Later in the chapter, when I try to imagine what the female Trickster looks like, I think I play a trick on Trickster, which should make him happier (see pp. 95–6, below).[3]

In the Middle Ages, carnivals began to take their present form and there would usually be a portrayal of some disturbance in the hierarchy. For example, an unsuitable person, such as a child or the village idiot, would be dressed up as the bishop. In fairy tales, we find figures like Tom Thumb parodying our usual conception of the hero. Tyl Eulenspiegel and Pulcinella have similar attributes. Parapsychology is full of tricky poltergeists who strain the boundaries of what we take for reality by living out the dramas of the unconscious itself. Sometimes, animals represent the Trickster (Machiavelli's fox is a good example). According to Jung, many aspects of God's behavior in the Old Testament show Tricksterish features, as does Zeus's behavior in Greek mythology.[4] When the world doesn't conform to expectations, when Sod's or Murphy's law prevails, when things get jinxed, when the Emperor, though not the small boy, is deceived by his own vanity, when tummy rumbles uncomfortably punctuate a silence, when we laugh at the clown – Trickster is present.

The question of Trickster's sex radiates undecidability. His representations are not conventionally male in either an anatomical or a behavioral sense. But he is not a straightforward hermaphrodite either. Moreover, to refer to Trickster as bisexual is already to make far too definite a statement, while the term 'polymorphous perversion' leads us to regard Trickster either as a baby or a damaged grown-up. The one thing that *can* be said about most, if not all, traditional images of Trickster is that they are not usually presented as female and that there is an emphasis on phallic prowess in Trickster stories. One common theme involves Trickster cuckolding an earnest, respectable husband. For example, the West African Trickster Ananse manages to trick Akwasi so that Akwasi ends up actually ordering Ananse to make love to his wife Aso.

I find myself wondering where the images of the female or proto-female Trickster are to be found. I do not think that Trickster as a 'he' is irrelevant to women's issues (in fact, I think the opposite), and feminist scholarship has demonstrated that the absence of things female from a discourse is rarely of no significance. So, throughout this chapter and the next, I weave into my text a search for the figure that I will continue to refer to as the 'female Trickster' even though I am aware that she will be no more an ordinary woman than the male (or proto-male) Trickster is an ordinary man.

One of the most studied Trickster stories is the Trickster Cycle of the North American Winnebago Native Americans, brought together by Paul Radin in 1956 at a time when the ubiquity of the Trickster figure was first being recognized.[5] The Winnebago Trickster lacks even rudimentary body unity: His intestines are outside his body, his penis is autonomous, enormously long, sometimes kept in a box, sometimes wrapped round his abdomen, each hand regards the other as a mortal enemy (like Dr Strangelove in Kubrick's film). Trickster's odyssey is a picaresque one – organized episodically, full of fortunes, misfortunes, violent attempts at punishment and surprisingly resilient opportunism on the part of the protagonist who survives his mishaps. In picaresque fiction, all the characters suffer greatly as they play out the tensions between unaccommodated man and a hostile society and the fact that the picaroon is usually a scoundrel of low birth adds to that tension. Trickster's suffering is itself an occasion for new Tricksterism, and further resourcefulness.

One episode of the Winnebago Trickster Cycle will illustrate the kind of thing that happens. Trickster has sent his penis into a tree to punish a chipmunk who has been teasing him. When he withdraws, he finds that only a small piece of the penis is left. He gets hold of the chipmunk and tears him open . . .

> There, to his horror, he discovered his penis all gnawed up. 'Oh, my, of what a wonderful organ he has deprived me! But why do I speak thus? I will make objects out of the pieces for human beings to use.' Then he took the end of his penis, the part that has no foreskin, and declared, 'This is what human beings will call the lily-of-the-lake.' This he threw into a lake near by. Then he took the other pieces declaring in turn: 'This the people will call potatoes; this the people will call turnips; this the people will call artichokes; this the people will call ground-beans; . . . this the people will call rice.' All these pieces he threw into the water. Finally he took the end of his penis and declared, 'This the people will call the pond-lily.' He was referring to the square part of the end of his penis.
>
> What was left of his penis was not very long. When, at last, he started off again, he left behind the box in which he had until then kept his penis coiled up.
>
> And this is the reason our penis has its present shape. It is because of

these happenings that the penis is short. Had the chipmunk not gnawed off Trickster's penis our penis would have the appearance that Trickster's first had. It was so large that he had to carry it on his back. Now it would not have been good had our penis remained like that and the chipmunk was created for the precise purposes of performing this particular act. Thus it is said.

Well – is Trickster really the creator of lilies, potatoes and so on? Or is he the creator only of an illusion that he is? Is he a kind of Adam, an original man, whose morphology determined ours? Or is he the prototype of the infant, who has to work out a fantastic explanation of the origins and limitations of the body which he or she inhabits? The passage certainly supports Jung's view that during a cycle of such stories 'the marks of deepest unconsciousness fall away from [Trickster]; instead of acting in a brutal, savage, stupid and senseless fashion the Trickster's behavior . . . becomes quite useful and sensible. The devaluation of his earlier unconsciousness is apparent even in the myth.'[6] It would seem that involving the Trickster in political discourse does not injure the Trickster. What does it do to our conception of politics?

Given the conventionally moralistic nature of most depth psychological analysis of politics, the Trickster, like Machiavelli, often gets a bad press as symbolizing the antisocial personality. Trickster's mendaciousness and self-deception are placed in the foreground, obscuring his transformative and generative aspects and, in particular, masking the way in which Trickster acts as a sort of yardstick and spur to consciousness. Sometimes people take a rather patronizing attitude, one that is full of knowing laughter at Trickster's antics, evacuating their political pointedness. Of course, a sense of humor is necessary when relating to Trickster but not for the purpose of depotentiating him.

If we try to interpret the Winnebago Trickster Cycle from a conventional psychodynamic angle, the main themes are the absence of a coherent body schema (the mobile penis), projection and splitting (for example, of aggression into the chipmunk), and pathological grandiosity (Trickster as Creator). However, if we recover our sense of irony and suspend judgment for the moment, then these themes lead to certain psychological questions which can be seen to have a political flavor – such as the following:

Do the erotogenic zones ever constitute a fixed body schema? Human sexual attraction seems to rest on the interdependence and even interchangeability of the zones: A kiss on the mouth, a cute bottom of either sex, big breasts, a well-stuffed wallet. Similarly, is a split object always so pathological? I wonder whether it is always as necessary or desirable for splits to be healed, for loving and aggressive impulses to be brought together, as psychodynamic theory usually suggests? Or is Trickster's so-called primitive fantasy of a split-off object worthy of positive consideration? Finally, what about Trickster's grandiosity? After Kohut's revaluing of grandiosity, how can grandiosity be omitted from any account of human creativity?[7]

These questions are of interest to analysts and therapists for they contribute to a revision of what constitutes developmental maturity. But, as I suggested earlier, there is a *political* reading to be made of these psychological questions. For, in revaluing the psychology of Trickster, we revalue the politics of Trickster, maybe even revalue politics itself. Those boring psychodynamic questions about body schema, projection and splitting, and grandiosity have themselves had fascinating *political* consequences in our own time.

If the bodily zones can be quite healthily muddled, then no established order is safe, anything can be muddled: The personal can be political, the fixity of gender roles probed, tyranny challenged (if not always overthrown). If love and hate do not always have to be linked in so-called normal ambivalence, then there is a place for both community spirit and ruthless selfishness. They do not have to be seen as cancelling each other out. If grandiosity is respected and taken seriously, then what is condemned by the wise old man (*senex*) as immature (*puer*-like) fantasies of global solutions to the world's problems can be reframed as an excursion into practical politics.[8] We can see that it is not really the grandiosity of such solutions that is the problem, as is so often thought; it is *lack* of grandiosity that makes for political compliance. Watching the Rumanian revolution on TV in December 1989 (which is when I wrote the first draft of this chapter), watching unarmed workers and students refuse to leave the streets, getting shot while the army fought the *Securitate* (security police), drove the point home: That grandiosity of aim can be the healthy ground of realizable ambition. Unhappily, the Rumanian people will have further need of their grandiose courage. Trickster's denial of mortality is a political statement, for the fear of death plays a part in maintaining the political *status quo*; it is feared that any change will lead to the elimination of life itself. The need to accept the inevitability of death makes one think of the corollary need to celebrate life when one has it. This means a passionate yet socially responsible engagement with the erotic and sensual dimensions of life, art, religion, tradition, the life of the intellect, and play. Gray is not the only color.

I am arguing that the genuine Trickster should not be omitted from a psychology of the political. I want us to stop accusing others of being Tricksters, using the term only in a derogatory sense when applied to politics. The Trickster is compatible with order and organization on the one hand, and with chaos and fluidity on the other. Trickster's order is created *through* chaos; his stabilizing influence on human culture (lilies, potatoes) is an outcrop of his destabilizing influence. Is Trickster the first chaos theorist? Recently, the Trickster has even been given a role in management – the need for ambiguity and paradox, for dissonance in place of coherence, decentralization in place of coordination, have all been recognized. What is more, as John Beebe has pointed out, we should be very careful about *not* trusting Trickster. If, as usual, we don't trust him, then he will trick and betray us in an unexpected way and turn out to be absolutely worthy of confidence and trust.[9] This facet of Trickster maybe explains why so many fathers, in myth and family, are trustworthy/untrustworthy Tricksters. (We will encounter the politics of the Trickster father in Chapters 6 and 7.)

We should not look to the Trickster for signs of individuation, achievement of the depressive position, maintenance of firm boundaries, or consistency. I am all too well aware of what he cannot do. But I am trying to develop a depth psychology of politics in which we are not hamstrung by rigid orthodoxies. We tend to accept without question that what seems the most psychologically mature will turn out to be the most socially useful and true, and to assume that this kind of balanced insight is what constitutes a psychological contribution to politics. Trickster challenges this assumption. Nevertheless, many may want to know whether a political apprehension of Trickster means that anything goes in politics, that every view, no matter how irrational, should be given equal weight, that political tolerance of subjective responses should be infinite, that there is no political morality.

I think that political morality incorporates a ceaseless dynamic between a passionately expressed, codified, legally sanctioned set of principles and certitudes (original morality) – and a more open, flexible, improvised, tolerant kind of morality that is basically code-free (moral imagination). These two aspects of political morality are both present in varying degrees in any political system and it is important to resist the temptation to see one of them as somehow more advanced, rising from the ashes of the other. Certitude and improvisation are *equally* valuable and, even assessed from a conventional psychodynamic perspective, they are equally mature. It is easy to see that a political morality based exclusively on improvisation would be too slippery by far and would contribute to a climate in which anything goes. But a political morality based exclusively on principle, law and certitude would be equally problematic (in psychological language, equally 'primitive'). To begin with, laws are not politically effective on their own; legal codes reflect and depend on the distribution of wealth and power. Moreover, political principle easily becomes ossified and used to gain control over others. Finally, codified political and moral prohibitions do not always work, as the prevalence of theft or adultery demonstrates.

Trickster *is* aware of the existence of moral and political certitudes but they do not constitute his particular trajectory. If you think about it, in moral process exceptions are the rule. There is a Taoist saying: 'The reason why one does not wear a leather coat in summer is not to spare the coat but because it is too warm. The reason one does not use a fan in winter is not disdain for fans but because it is too cool.'[10] Yes, there are fundamental truths (even Truths with a capital letter T), but for each diverse context there is a separate and diverse fundamental truth. Trickster's political morality is anything but phallogocentric.

Even if orthodox political and moral principles are the windmills against which Trickster tilts, he does not deny them their existence as he tries to undermine them. Can the serious, respectable world of economic, political, and psychological theory and organization extend the same emotionally-complex generosity toward the Trickster?

I accept that Trickster's discourse may seem like garbage to some readers. Yet his refusal to say definitively that *this* is the only reality (for example, an unjust social and economic system) and *this* is Utopian fantasy (for example, reform or revolution) is in itself a profound, political statement.

During the Gulf War in 1991, the image of Trickster kept cropping up, usually in relation to Saddam Hussein.[11] While I think it is significant that people are sensitive to the Trickster's presence when things are changing or transforming, I want to say that Saddam Hussein was *not* a Trickster. And, in keeping with my overall thesis, I would add that the leaders of the coalition were not Tricksters. For tricksters do not cheat and lie as part of a program; they are not tricky to advance policies; they do not have goals as such. They just lie and cheat because that is how they are and who they are.

Citizens in most countries are faced with leaders who lie and cheat as part of a program and to advance policy. Here in the West, we have to learn from the experiences of the dissidents of Eastern Europe and the former Soviet Union who developed a profound cynicism that enabled them to read between the lines. We need to acquire this skill urgently.

The Trickster exists in political culture but he or she is not acknowledged therein and hence is not theorized about. Hence, instead of

Trickster's admixture of fantasy, practical ingenuity and transformation, we get a kind of repressed and distorted trickster (that's Saddam Hussein as Trickster, bribery and corruption, dirty tricks).

It certainly is not a question of needing more Trickster if more Trickster means more violence, more bribery and corruption, more dirty tricks. It is a question of an integration of a more complete – less repressed and distorted – version of Trickster, and at a deeper level. This would be an integration of the irregular psychology of Trickster into the regular psychology of political theorizing. Just as I have tried to revalue subjectivity in political discourse, I do not want to leave the Trickster on the level of unlicensed stalls selling rural produce by the side of the road in city centers, to use an image familiar in countries as disparate as Russia and Brazil. I do not want to sideline the Trickster like that. After all, the 'black economy' or 'parallel economy' plays a huge part in the socioeconomic life of developing countries. On the basis of official figures, everyone in a country like Somalia should have starved to death during the 1980s, so low was the official per capita income. Yet at the same time, new taxis regularly appeared on the streets of Mogadishu, and sales of petrol increased every year. Somalia's measured and stagnating official economy could be seen as an appendage of an unmeasured and dynamic informal economy. The success of informal economies all over the world requires a new kind of psychological explanation or interpretation of economic behavior, one that is informed by the experience of functioning in a black or parallel economy. This is where Trickster comes in, so different from conventional, psychodynamic explanations or interpretations of economic behavior. Psychodynamic understandings are, perhaps, the equivalent of the economic literature on the Third World written 'from above' by the World Bank and similar institutions.

If we are to integrate the Trickster into political discourse, then we have to explore why he is on the scene in the first place – what is Trickster's *telos*, Trickster's goal? Surely this is more than the promotion of devious and corrupt political practices? Anyway, I am going to try to show that it is.

HERMES AND THE MARKET ECONOMY

Hermes is a Trickster of a different order than the Winnebago Trickster and we grasp something more specific about power politics from his myth. We grasp something about capitalism, the market economy and relations between capitalism and the market because, in a sense, Hermes helps us to rescue the idea of the market from capitalism. Hermes is certainly deceitful and criminal, but, as we will see in the myth, the accent is equally on his constructive and transformative nature. After all, Hermes is a god: Guide of souls to the underworld, the divinity of olive cultivation, athletics, boundaries, commerce, and messenger of the gods. Hermes stands as a liminal presence, on the threshold or boundary of depth psychology and politics, of psychic reality and social reality, of the personal and the political. Hermes also articulates a relationship between the Trickster and the market economy – that particular political phenomenon causing confusion, idealization and splitting across the late twentieth-century world. In Chapter 1, struggling to get a depth psychological angle on resacralization, we saw that a split in the image of the market economy lessened the chances of converting dream into pragmatic politics. Most resacralizing movements are too one-sided in their evaluation of the market economy and this one-sidedness is also to be found in the enthusiasms of the gung-ho free marketeers. In short, there is a psychological problem with our politics and it is a problem to do with opposites – opposite evaluations of the market. Nobody actually *advocates* a one-sided view but, as we saw, taking an average does not help us because we miss out on the quite specific and suggestive psychologies of the market as negative and the market as positive. Merely holding those opposites in mind strikes me as far too passive, which is why I want to work out a means of developing each side separately, thus permitting ongoing interplay between them.

The tale of Hermes is, in many ways, the pattern of our particular socioeconomic epoch which, like him, is a shape-shifter with numerous names to match its myriad presentations: Late capitalism, late-late capitalism, post-capitalism, post-Fordism, the information culture (Hermes as messenger), post-industrialism, post-modernism, late modernity and so forth.

In the myth, we hear of the deceit and lying of Hermes. This inspires associations to the ruthlessness of economic inequality, stock market fraud and insider trading. We also hear of the capacity of Hermes to bargain and negotiate in a compassionate and related style. That inspires associations to the need of any political culture to avoid oligarchic hegemony and gross injustice. Let's consider each of these in turn, trying to hold on to them in imagination. Then we can let the two sides of Hermes come together. This is the first step in an approach to those crude splits in our image of the market economy that could ruin the prospects for resacralization. As I suggested earlier, there is a necessity to overcome *both* schizoid tendencies to make an either/or split between positive and negative assessments *and* the temptation to reach an uncritical synthesis. If we can manage that, then we can establish a credible psychological analysis of economic themes that are not usually approached by depth psychologists. This is a tragic lack when one considers the colonial and neocolonial connections between economics, economic inequality and war. We have to try to address the underlying psychology, the depth psychology, of our political compulsions. Can we introduce a depth psychological dimension into a questioning of our dependence on existing levels of consumption, personal mobility and comfort?

Difficulties with images of the market economy are of central concern in both West and East as both struggle with their confused reactions to the market economy. In the rich countries of the West, we have to face that, in spite of growing disgust, we are still caught in a collective love affair with a rotten social order and an unfeeling culture. We made our commitment to this order of things a long time ago, and however much we may know intellectually that it does not work for us on the ethical level, however much we may know about the psychodynamics of greed and envy, we cannot seem to break our tie to our lover: economic inequality.[12] It is a deep guilt over the undeniable fact of our love of economic inequality that takes us to the cheating heart of global capitalism, the partner we refuse to leave, having never really chosen, remaining locked in an enigmatic relationship whose tensions drive us crazy.

Perhaps we should now take a closer look at the mythic patterns of this dilemma. Myths open issues up when they are understood as expressive of mutable external and social forces rather than of immutable internal patterns. Joseph Campbell regarded this aspect of myths as 'social dreams'[13] and I would add that myths may also be cultivated as political fantasies that have, over time, shown themselves capable of surviving the inevitable violence done to them by appropriating them for all kinds of purposes. Their ambiguity is their strength. Nevertheless, those who adopt a hyper-kosher academic approach to myth – for example, one that insisted on knowing the precise social origin of a myth on grounds of cultural relativity, or constituting a refusal to listen to a source fatally flawed by its patriarchal roots – are not going to be well pleased with what follows. But, even if myths depend on ideology they are not the same as ideology. Myths alter and new ones come into being; as the historian Ludmilla Jordanova puts it, 'as stories about human doings they are overtly powerful and emotionally dense. In this respect they differ from ideologies. . . . Hence, to speak in terms of myth need not imply an ahistoricity of any kind, because myths are perpetually put to work in different, historically shifting ways.' Jordanova argues against the suspicion that exists in academic circles of 'anything not rooted in particular circumstances [and] historical specificity'.[14]

As far as interpretation is concerned, myths do not normally admit of an unchallenged reading. They are characterized by 'density and complexity, imaginative depth and universal appeal. . . . Myths are on the one hand good stories, on the other hand bearers of important messages about life in general and life-within-society in particular.'[15]

In *The Homeric Hymn to Hermes*, on the first day of his life, Hermes leaps up to look for meat. Pausing only to kill a turtle and fashion a lyre from its shell, he steals fifty head of cattle from the herd of Apollo, his half-brother. Hermes drives the cattle backward so that their tracks seem to point away from his stables. According to the *Homeric Hymn*, Hermes was the inventor of fire and he roasts two of the animals he has stolen and makes a sacrifice of this meat to the other gods.

Understandably, Apollo is very upset that his cattle have been taken and quickly works out what must have happened. Charles Boer's brilliant, modern translation[16] conveys his agitation: 'Listen kid, / lying in your cradle, / tell me where my cows are, / and quick! / We're going to fight this out / and it won't be very pretty!' Hermes is innocence itself – how could a milk-sucking baby do such a thing and, as he says, after all, 'I was just born yesterday.' Doesn't fool Apollo, though: 'You trickster, / you sharpie, / the way you talk / I bet you have broken into a lot of expensive homes / in nights past.' In humorous vein still, Apollo prophesies that Hermes will come to a bad end. Hermes sticks to his guns and goes on denying the theft. The two Gods present themselves before Zeus. Apollo accuses, Hermes declares himself not guilty. But, to Zeus, all is clear and, with a laugh, he orders the two Gods to try to sort out their differences.

We shall be returning to the narrative of the *Homeric Hymn*. Let us now react psychologically to the story so far and reflect on its political implications.

The myth amplifies my earlier remarks about our devotion to the economic realities of capitalism, how we seem to want – really want – inequality, cheating, and injustice between individuals, groups, nations and regions. The fact that there is no reference in the *Homeric Hymn* to Hermes actually eating the meat makes me think of the non-productive nature of the capital markets. They feed no one directly and yet accumulate wealth invisibly and inequitably.

What is the depth psychology of economic inequality? I mean something more than its psychodynamics. If we free ourselves from interpretations that depend on the psychology of the individual, then we can say that economic inequality maintains the social structures of desire. The baby Hermes covets Apollo's cattle even when he can only suck at the breast – he has no truck with psychodynamic narratives of infancy. That he does not eat the meat tells us that the cathexis, the emotional investment, is on the wanting and on the sense of incompleteness. Such a sense of incompleteness is by no means a wholly negative phenomenon for it acts as a spur to constructive activity. However, the nagging and gnawing in Hermes's spiritual stomach, which our epoch surely can recognize, are settled only when, by acquisition, by takeover, by theft, he gets into a relation with another.

Some might argue that tricksterism cannot constitute a type of relating. But it is clear that Hermes's magical introjection of food is more than just a phase or passage on the road to 'true' internalization. Economic inequality itself is tied up with a devotion to primitive magic, amorality and even criminality, all of which belong to the introjective attitude: It's there, I want it, I don't want to ask for it, I'll take it.

Apollo really responds to Hermes and, as we will see, things deepen between the two brothers. Hermes gets Apollo's attention and this, too, is part of the psychology of economic inequality. Not only stirring up envy, but really being seen, and even mirrored.

Our devotion to the differences displayed by means of economic inequality has something to do with space for symbolization. What I mean is that the wealthier the individual, family, clan, class, nation, region, the greater the space for symbolization seems to be. One can afford movies, the theater, opera, eating in restaurants, driving in automobiles, and even personal analysis. These are activities which secure and provide the space for symbolization. Of course, this display of differentiation is illusory. I am not saying that the space is really taken advantage of. I am certainly not saying that the well-off are enjoying richer inner lives or that the richer countries are spiritually richer. But the illusion that they are is hypnotic. In economic inequality, there are located personal and national hopes for the richness of the symbolic life. We believe this emotionally even though we know intellectually that such richness cannot be bought by women, men, corporations or governments.

Another factor in economic inequality that makes this condition psychologically attractive to us is the fantasy that the other does not amount to much, particularly if he or she has less money. The poor other does not count. Hermes does not worry about Apollo's reaction or even think about Apollo at all when he steals the cattle. If one's space for symbolization expands, it can eliminate the other's space for symbolization, and hence can eliminate the other, or seem to. Economic inequality does away with the anxieties of alterity, of having to relate to people who are psychologically other; it encourages fantasies of insulation and isolation. Rich people do not necessarily have rich consciences. Another

Taoist saying is apt here: 'If you are not satisfied with yourself, even if you have a whole continent for your house with all its people for your servants, this will not be enough to support you.'[17]

We see the link between economic inequality and emotional isolation in the modern legends of Howard Hughes and Paul Getty – and also in the *Homeric Hymn* when, after the theft, Hermes elects to spend the night alone, kicking dust over his fire and generally covering up. The fantasy plan is of concealing the crime altogether so that its perpetrator can walk away. In Hermes's case, and here he truly does represent the unconscious motivation of the modern business tycoon, he walks home to his mother. He tells her of his plans to be the most successful capitalist ever: 'I'm capable certainly / to be thief number one.'

So far, we have been looking at one part of the Hermes story. We saw the myth as a psychological patterning of the unjust and inequitable aspects of market economy capitalism. The myth illumined our investment in such corruption. Yet the rest of the myth brings out that there is another side. For there is more in humanity that a collective love of a rotten world order and an unfeeling culture. There is also in humanity a collective love of a healthy world order and a commitment to a just culture concerned with alterity and the wellbeing of all its members. *There is absolutely no contradiction.* Both exist side-by-side at the same time, and in permanent competition with each other. Both sets of human traits are patterned in the Hermes story. I want to state my argument once more: In our age, in both the capitalist West and the once communist East, it is very hard to go beyond our split emotional attitude to the market economy.

What follows next in the Hermes story may be taken as a metaphor for the kind of constructive and creative relationship the market supports rather well. The I–Thou aspects of market relations between people or peoples are revealed alongside the ruthless aspects, compassion functioning alongside competition.

We return to the narrative of *The Homeric Hymn to Hermes* at the point where Zeus tells Apollo and Hermes to come to terms. Zeus has made it impossible for Hermes to conceal the theft any longer. Apollo, reunited with forty-eight head, decides to tie Hermes up, perhaps as a prelude to further punishment. To the Sun God's amazement, the thongs he has placed round Hermes's ankles suddenly extend to tie up all the cattle! (This trick of Hermes's can be compared with Trickster's use of his penis in the Winnebago Cycle of stories.) To placate his older brother, Hermes then plays a tune on his lyre. Apollo is quite transfixed by its beauty, which is unlike any music known before. At this point, Apollo relents. He states his intention to make Hermes his protégé. Apollo will be a kind of theatrical agent for Hermes. He will be an impresario for his musical gifts. Apollo promises Hermes the roles of soul-guide and messenger of the gods. But, in the pecking order, Hermes will most certainly be *under* Apollo. Apollo wants the kind of deal Colonel Parker struck with Elvis Presley. The god of capitalism is to be a wage-slave.

Hermes's response to this offer is to come up with a revolutionary counter-suggestion: He will give the lyre to Apollo, if Apollo will give him the cattle. Hermes also takes Apollo up on the job of soul-guide and messenger. *They make a bargain* – the first bargain – and the imaginative implications for the market economy, for liberal democracy and for global politics are immense. Exchange and mutuality are now highlighted by the myth; Hermes the Trickster makes a constructive contribution to political thought. It may be objected that there is plenty of deal-making around, perhaps too much. Yes, there is too much deal-making outside of alterity, outside of relationship. Admitting Hermes to cultural consciousness at least gives the potential for related deals.

Apollo installs Hermes as 'being in charge of / exchanges among men / on the nourishing earth'. Being no fool, Apollo also makes Hermes swear an oath not to steal anything from him again. Hermes does so and Apollo gives him the caduceus, the famous staff of the messenger. In this transaction, neither god is altered; gods do not change. It was a bargain not a transformation but the point is that it would not have occurred without the earlier cheating, stealing and lying. Apollo remains the oracular god. Hermes remains the liminal god, the Trickster god, moving freely between Olympus and the earth, helping the gods (saving Zeus's life once in a battle with the giants), lubricating the orgy of trade he has set in motion. But, as the *Homeric Hymn* soberly reminds us, 'even though he helps a few people, / he cheats an endless number'.

HERMES AND SOCIAL THEORY

Both sides of our image and evaluation of the market economy have equal existence and equally significant psychologies. As we have seen, to be able to develop two distinct though limited psychologies of the market economy means something different from striving for a conjunction, synthesis, or balance of them. What is required is a profound emotional recognition of the ineluctably negative aspects of the market that cannot be done away with or averaged out. They will always exist and flourish alongside and in competition with more positive aspects and we need to know more about them – especially if we seek to combat them. We cannot even begin to identify the positives of the market without identifying, working through and coming to terms with the negatives of it. A synthesis is by no means the only psychological or political option available to us. For, in a synthesis of our split image of the market economy, the psychological specificity of *either* its cheating *or* its constructive aspects is lost. *We cannot just dispense with the problems of the psychology of theft because we want to enjoy the fruits of the psychology of bargaining.* There is a psychological co-existence, acceptance of which opens up the possibility of exploring the social and political realities of these sibling economic modes and of transforming their relationship. That is why, earlier, I stressed the need to integrate the Trickster into our conception of the political. He steals for sure – but he also transforms the political scene by his souk-like skills.

THE POLITICAL SIGNIFICANCE OF THE FEMALE TRICKSTER

It is important not to idealize the bargaining process. To begin with, Apollo and Hermes do not cease to eye each other cautiously. Moreover, there are many different styles of bargaining. Bargaining should not be seen as something pertinent only to men and money. One can conceive of a negotiatory approach to knowledge and, maybe, this is something that, for reasons of acculturation and socialization, women in Western countries do anyway. Certainly, even if the evidence exists only on an anecdotal level, the capacity of women to bargain and derive pleasure from it in a commercial setting seems to have been established. It is possible to take the idea of bargaining to the point where bargains are struck with reality itself – and this would include social reality. It may be that it is in this kind of bargaining that we will find the missing female Trickster. Or is it that life for women is always already constituted within Trickster's discourse as the only way to flourish within a male-dominated socioeconomic system?

   This point is strengthened by an understanding of Trickster stories as depictions of what social life ('real' life) is like for the people who enjoy the story. Trickster's capacity to make us laugh is a depiction of the tragicomic cast of life itself, his or her undermining of pomposity and received wisdom a depiction of what we would all like to do to parental figures, his or her sexual and gustatory excess a depiction of how to follow a certain kind of bliss, his or her economic and mercantile ingenuity a depiction of what is required to keep one's head above water. Put like this, the Trickster can be seen as exemplifying what Eliade called 'the mythology of the human condition'.[18] Now, to the extent that women's condition has not been written into accounts of the human condition, the female Trickster remains *terra incognita* (though she is beginning to appear in movies). My hunch is that her emergence will be in the economic sphere and her methods will be those of the politics I have been sketching out: Subjectivity and refusal to accept social reality as the only reality there is.

I can think of one political enterprise, undertaken exclusively by women, which demonstrates the female Trickster in political action. The Mothers of the Plaza de Mayo in Buenos Aires assembled in the plaza each day during the period of 1976–82 to protest at the 'disappearance' of their children at the hands of unofficial elements directly connected with the military dictatorship in Argentina. It has been estimated that at least 6,000 and maybe as many as 20,000 persons, mostly under the age of 40, 'disappeared' during this time. As Jean Bethke Elshtain has shown, the Mothers politicized the collective, cultural images of motherhood that were central to Argentinian family and public life. The Mothers were extraordinarily effective – in my view – because they tapped into a Tricksterish format for their political intervention.[19]

The Mothers did not reject the dignified, stately, caring, elemental role assigned to maternal women in Argentinian culture. But they expanded upon, parodied and utterly transformed that role in a Tricksterish way. The trick was to ensure that their mobilization of a mass positive, maternal transference to themselves, in Argentina and abroad, was never interfered with by the premature or careless revelation of the degree of radicalization and politicization that had taken place among them. The trick, the masquerade, was to use the Holy Mother to destabilize the junta.

The Mothers wore traditional scarves on which the names of their children and the dates of the 'disappearance' were embroidered – a striking example of what Rozsika Parker has called 'the subversive stitch'.[20] The Mothers presented themselves as sacrificial victims and as the victims of sacrifice, deploying traditional maternalism for decidedly non-traditional ends. And, crucially, they did all this in a public place. The gender solidarity of the Mothers constituted a Tricksterish kind of organizational sophistication. The Mothers were not overtly involved in politics at all but, as Elshtain points out, 'staying "above" politics may well be a way of *doing* politics that is far more effective than entering the arena on established terms'.[21] The Mothers were both faithful and unfaithful to the traditional image of the mother in their country. Yet their Tricksterish achievement was to politicize that tradition and, ultimately, the image of Woman in Argentinian society was affected and – who knows? – may have been transformed.

It is important not to approach the bargaining process with a jaundiced eye, with the prejudices of old-style socialism or new-style eco-politics. The purpose of these psychological reflections on the market is to do something to tame and temper the power of the market *by facing up to its negative features and seeing what we can do with them*, rather than fulminating against them. Whether this leads to the 'social market' concept of European social democrats, or to a 'socialized market' as proposed by some socialists,[22] or to a concept of the market with a more psychological tone, remains to be seen. Facing the negative features of the market enables us to celebrate its positive features and its variegated potentials. I am not saying that what is unmarketable does not exist or has no value and I am aware of the possibility that a market tyranny may have developed in Western and other cultures. But it is the very possibility of a tyrannical global market that, from a psychological angle, should make us hesitate before indulging in knee-jerk protest about the market *per se*. Something potentially (or actually) so powerful as to become a global ideology with practical implications for everyone on the planet must also be regarded as the most concentrated and dynamic source of creative energy that we possess on the social level.

I am not one of those who think that socialism is dead but, in company with many others, I recognize that we have to try to think in terms of there being a plurality of socialisms, each resisting the hegemonistic impulses of the other brands, but all somehow linked. As Karl Kautsky put it in 1918, 'Socialism as such is not our goal, which is rather the abolition of every kind of exploitation or oppression, be it directed against a class, a party, a sex, or a race.'[23] To achieve these ends, I agree with those who argue that socialist thought has to engage with what is implied by the market. It seems to me that socialism is already moving on to do just that. Hence, what is needed (if anything at all is needed) from depth psychologists is a contribution concerning the depth psychology of the market. Depth psychological critiques of the market should expose what R. W. Johnson called the 'warmed-over wishfulness of so many on the left'.[24]

I have not suggested that we 'chose' capitalism but rather that people are invested in certain ways in maintaining economic inequality. Nor have I assumed that, in a bargaining or negotiating situation, everyone starts from the same place. The psychosocial consequences of the destruction of free collective bargaining in the United States, Britain and elsewhere have been immense. But it is amazing how often current left-wing texts, for instance in the British journal *New Left Review*, return to the question of the 'socialized market', meaning some way of factoring compassion, social justice and alterity into market economics.

Unfortunately, no body of knowledge exists that gives a satisfactory and satisfying account of the relations between, for instance, a class-based analysis of social and economic conditions and an unconscious phantasy-based analysis of the internal world. My text displays what will be, for some readers, an almost relentless concentration on economics, if not in the language that some old-fashioned socialists would have preferred me to use. As I said earlier, this has been a Hermetic attempt to recover the idea of the market from capitalism and make a contribution to notions of a socialized market. My Tricksterish expansion of what we take as 'the political' was informed by the realisation that there is a fundamental interdependence of the market (or the markets) and politics (or the political).

Perhaps the left will have to be content with a more modest role in relation to this interdependence of the markets and the political. As Jürgen Habermas put it, socialism will become 'the radically reformist self-criticism of a capitalist society which, in the form of constitutional democracy with universal suffrage and a welfare state, has developed not only weaknesses but also strengths'.[25]

Depth psychology offers a new gloss on the protests about the triumph of the market that are beginning to emerge. Some of these protests emanate from Eastern Europe, supposedly the seat of the market's triumph. One Rumanian commentator claimed that the market economy was a 'big hoax'.[26] Growing foreign debt arising from the marketization of the economy and from the built-in inequities of the East–West trade structures slewed the whole system in the West's favor. These developments caused great instability and unhappiness in the society concerned – 'the initiation of the technological revolution actually goes against the interests of the working class . . . the market generates a large middle class that gets all the goodies'.[27] Here we are most certainly confronted with the economic and psychological products of the negative side of the market. However, the psychology of the negative side of the market is not a stagnant psychology – it is too orthodox to restrict the expectation of psychological movement to positive psychologies. We can work out some rather pragmatic political ideas on the basis of the negative depth psychology of the market. The global market has created a global community composed of all those communities that are suffering because of the negative aspects of the market – its social injustices, wastage of talent, privileging of the already wealthy and its general political pathology. The global poor are linked by a common set of experiences whether these are in debt-laden Latin America with its vast fetid cities, declining rust-belt communities in Europe and the United States, or the starving in the Horn of Africa. I wonder if it is possible that a political consciousness born out of global poverty, out of the negative psychology of the market, will emerge in the next quarter-century. This would be a 'poor' politics, characterized by a psychological orientation, for the psyche itself can only be commodified with the greatest difficulty. If, as I will argue in Chapter 9, the psyche can be construed as an autonomous source of social change and movement, then *its active presence in poor politics, blended into subjective political discourse, may spawn modes of organization and production that we are not at present familiar with.*

There is a human level to be considered here. For, alongside the desire to make a good deal, the bargaining process supports and fosters compassion for the other, without whom there would be no bargaining possible. As Montesquieu put it, 'Wherever the ways of men are gentle, there is commerce, and wherever there is commerce, the ways of men are gentle.'[28] The bargaining process can be exhilarating and fun, even sexy – and the eroticism of the negotiatory process is an important part of its psychological viability and peace-making potential.

The relevance of these ideas about negotiation and bargaining for the resolution of warlike conflict was ably summarized during the Gulf War of 1991 by my then four-year-old son. I do not recall him hearing me speak about it but one day he said: 'Daddy, I want to tell you something. A bargain. A bargain is all standing round in a circle and asking if we can stop fighting.' I am not sure I can fully explain why bargaining, too, cannot be split off from stealing, cheating and lying. But that seems to be the way it is in the collective psyche.

A collective psychology that is infused with a tricky but related mercantile spirit may help a society to avoid tyranny and enjoy an active and diverse political and social life. Competition and bargaining are ways of resolving conflict as well as generating it. But they do not close down options; that is why I stress the emancipatory potential of doing deals. Bargaining is an alternative to potlatch – the explosive evacuation of personal wealth undertaken by the Northwestern Native Americans. The world does not have easy access to such surpluses. Bargaining is different from the distribution of gifts.

These comments on the process of bargaining and its political psychology should not obscure the fact that the two bargainers in the myth have very different standpoints and political philosophies. Apollo stands for order, harmony, hierarchy and the unavoidable knowledge of the oracle. Hermes stands for Tricksterism, revolution, panic and intuitive knowledge. Apollo stands for the deep *status quo*. Hermes stands for its subversion. The political tension between Apollo and Hermes will always be culturally significant.

The image of the two brother-gods bargaining makes me wonder how a society should seek to achieve a greater degree of economic equality. To what extent should a society demand of its members that they accept responsibility for the economic wellbeing of others? Depth psychologists rarely address the questions that arise from an inequitable distribution of wealth. Therefore we do not know very much about the depth psychological implications of seeking a more equitable distribution. Bargaining between 'haves' and 'have-nots' might seem to have only one outcome were it not for the possibility of the apparently weaker uniting together, and maybe even taking extra-constitutional action, a form of poor politics. The image of bargaining is, therefore, not an unrealistic basis for a rectification of economic injustice.

That there is injustice is not in doubt. In countries like Brazil, less than 20 per cent of the population are covered by minimum wage legislation and general conditions, along with the real disposable income of 70 per cent of the population, are worsening year-by-year. In 1961, it was estimated that 38 per cent were malnourished and the estimate for 1991 from the same source is almost 70 per cent. There are 14.5 million handicapped people in Brazil (almost 10 per cent of the population) and somewhere in the region of 10 million abandoned children. (It is these abandoned children who are being exterminated by vigilante hit squads formed by disaffected police officers as a horrendous response to the soaring crime rate.)

In Britain, the poorest million of the population have suffered a decline in real living standards of at least 10 per cent and, in some cases, as much as 15 per cent since 1980. (The lowest paid tenth of British families saw their real income decline by 7 per cent in the same period. In the United States, the average after-tax income of the poorest 10 per cent of the population declined by 10.5 per cent in the period 1977–87.)[29] I do not want to claim an equivalence for conditions in Britain and America and conditions in Brazil – after all, in Britain infant mortality rates continue to decline while in Brazil the opposite is true. But there is one particular socioeconomic pattern that does seem common to Britain, the United States and Brazil (and can also be observed in the evolving once-communist countries such as the former Soviet Union).

This pattern in which the gap between rich and poor gets larger leading to an ever-increasing concentration of wealth was exemplified in the United States in the 1980s. It is this polarization that should be highlighted when we talk of economic inequality – not just the material gap between rich and poor but their *relative* wealth, meaning the scale of income differences within a society. The point is that, in recent years in many countries, after a certain level of economic development is reached, and this does not seem to be a particularly advanced level, all subsequent reward goes to the section of the population that already possesses a disproportionate share of resources, thereby increasing their political power. It follows that increasing productivity beyond a certain point benefits fewer people than would be expected. Worldwide, it is this particular economic configuration that has been reached and many countries are at a point where trickle-down prosperity ceases to occur to any great extent.

Some recent research shows that income distribution, the gap between haves and have-nots, is the most important determinant of health standards in the developed world (and I can see little reason why the same arguments should not be valid for a country like Brazil).[30] The research highlights the psychological aspects of economic inequality which will be deleterious in terms of self-esteem.[31] That, in turn, means that the poor will be less able to develop a sense of agency and hence be less effective on a political level. Not forgetting the simple point that living in poverty is incredibly stressful.

In the *Wealth of Nations*, Adam Smith explored how competition can work in favor of the less powerful, provided that competition is permitted to exist. For example, if manufacturers raise their prices too high, a chance is created for one of them to make an increased profit by selling at a lower price. In this way, competition acts as a kind of regulator upon selfishness. Adam Smith's attitude to self-interest was very even-handed. He observed that self-interest was *the* primary economic motivation but, Machiavelli-like, he never said that self-interest was a virtue. He saw competition as a means of transforming a socially destructive aspect of human behavior into something more benevolent and useful. In the Parable of the Talents, the good servant *trades* with the money – he does not merely save it. This suggests, not only the well-known linkage of religion and capitalism, but also an emphasis upon outcome and utility.

RECAPITULATION

As I have been saying, questions of economics are at the heart of psychological engagement with processes of political change, especially non-violent political change. The problematic of a more equal distribution of wealth has everything to do with the power relations within a single society, or in the world as a whole, and hence with its political organization. But political reorganization, in its turn, cannot be cut off from whatever psychological processes of resacralization might be taking place. Therefore, at this point, it makes sense to try to relate the content of this chapter to the themes that have already been generated in Part I.

There is a process of resacralization going on in Western culture, and the same is true of Eastern Europe and the Soviet Union as well as of the Third World, though the surface signs may be different in different societies. Those who seek to link depth psychology with politics should admit that they too are caught up in a resacralizing process. Resacralization is essentially a secularization of the holy, following the pattern of Bezaleel, master craftsman of the Ark of the Covenant. But resacralization is threatened by a massive split in our image of and attitude toward the market economy. Disgust with ourselves, and confusion about the inequalities of world capitalism and the market economy fuel the urgency of addressing the split if resacralization is going to occur. Machiavelli addresses many of these issues in *The Prince*. Here we find that the essence of politics is to know how to be evil when necessary, without anyone thinking you are evil: a trick. Machiavelli's politicization of the shadow led us to the Trickster and his role in processes of political change. Hermes is a special kind of Trickster and exploring the Hermes myth helps us with our splits and confusions about capitalism and the market economy. Hermes speaks for both the inequitable, unjust, cheating side – and the creative, transformative, compassionate side of the market. Hermes is a passageway to a depth psychological engagement with the political dynamics of the economic system.

Returning to the connecting tissue between depth psychology and politics, I want to add that it would be a pity and a mistake to restrict the political significance of Hermes to the impersonal, collective, global levels of political and economic theory and organization. There is also a pressing, personal and individual level. By engaging with Hermes, we also have to engage with the warring sides of our Hermes-selves: On the one hand, our fraud, our criminality, our belief in magic, our love of economic inequality, our own depression-inducing violence. On the other hand, our capacity for exchange, integrity, relatedness, flexibility, our own love of dignity and freedom, our desire to reject coercion and bullying, our skill at making peace.[32]

Chapter 5

Against nature

In this chapter, I discuss environmentalism and ask: Must the environmental movement fail? I suggest it will fail unless it becomes more conscious of the authoritarianism and depression within it, and the idealization of nature is somehow moderated.

Criticisms of the authoritarianism of the environmental movement, referring to its 'eco-terrorism', could wreck it by playing into the hands of entrenched industrial and financial institutions.[1] I think we should begin by admitting that there is a degree of accuracy in such criticisms. For there is a hidden authoritarianism in much of the new environmental politics which are the latest manifestation of the Enlightenment belief in perfectibility. Whether this takes the form of a downgrading of humanity to the level of fauna (or flora) or the issuing of a whole set of edicts about what is 'good', the tendency is clear to see. And already a backlash is going on. I think that environmentalist authoritarianism stems from a deeply buried misanthropy and, unless challenged, will itself turn out to be secretly and horrendously destructive. In Jungian terms, this is the shadow of the environmental movement and it would be helpful to become more conscious of it. Then the advantages of the unquenchable human thirst for a better world can be enjoyed – for only things of substance cast a shadow.

Casting an analyst's eye over the information and education material put out by organizations like Greenpeace and Friends of the Earth, I am struck by the one-sided portrait of humanity that is presented. Certainly, there is much to feel guilty about, much thoughtlessness and destructive behavior to be owned, much acquiescence in horrid developments to be confessed. But the unremitting litany of humanity's destructiveness may not be the way to spur movement in a more creative direction. The result of too much self-disgust may be the cultivation of a deadening cultural depression that would interfere with environmental action. This is because fantasies of being all-bad and all-destructive usually lie at the heart of depressive illness. Therefore environmentalists should try to avoid any presentation of ideas about the environment that reflects humanity in an exclusively harsh light.

Instead, they might also celebrate what careful tending of the earth there has been over millennia. They might reaffirm the goodness, gentleness and esthetic sensibility of humanity's artificial, cultural productions – our buildings, cities, art works and so forth. As an instance of what I am talking about, I think of the continuity to be found in the relations between humans and the environment in England. There is a sense in which the landscape itself has been made and remade over time as each succeeding generation leaves its mark. Emphasizing this cultural layering means that a more positive estimation of our environmental potential is brought into being.

It is vital not to represent environmentalism as a concern of the privileged classes, cut off from wider issues of social justice. To begin with, we have already seen that the greening of politics is going to be painful, both within Western societies and in terms of the relations between the developed and the undeveloped worlds. A whole host of moral decisions arises when we in the industrially advanced countries call for limits on deforestation in poor countries or advocate their controlling of their birthrates. We need an educational program that faces people with these decisions and choices rather than letting them to be made for them by experts who will offer protection from the moral implications of what is being done. Otherwise we will end up with a new Western hegemony: We will be OK but the poor of the earth will be even worse off.

What is more, we must not look to things like changes in consumer spending patterns to bring about improvement. Are we to say that when the going gets tough the greens go shopping? If substantive issues of social justice are not addressed then we *will* just be doing a landscaping job.

The question of economic redistribution within advanced societies is going to have to be addressed. If the polluters are to pay, then prices will rise enormously. The knock-on effects will be dramatic and many goods that we take for granted will be priced out of reach. *I want to suggest that this is a marvellous opportunity!* We are going to have to think about how we live and about how resources are distributed within our more advanced societies – and this will mean challenging the awesome power structures that exist. The problems confronting the world force a critical engagement with the banks, the multinational corporations, the IMF and with governments.

Calls for a return to traditional forms of homeworking or the setting up of *ersatz* agrarian-style communities should be treated with caution. For, in such situations, the lot of women has been and would continue to be an unhappy one. Instead, we should think of greening the cities we already have, making them safer and more pleasant for the groups they oppress – women, children, the elderly. For it has never been demonstrated that agrarian, parochial life is inherently superior to urban, cosmopolitan life. Advocating the tearing down of cities so as to foster the triumph of nature would be the way of a Khmer Vert.

Our young people will see through any educational campaign that idealizes nature, leaving out its frightening, harsh and bloody aspects and our ambivalence toward it. Such a campaign would resemble those commissioned portraits of the eighteenth century in which the lady of the manor is pictured dressed up as a milkmaid. The effect was to make nature an acceptable decorative element in the salons of the rich. Nature is itself not 'natural' but a culturally constructed idea. Moreover, the environmental movement still has to work on a balance between its 'anthropocentric' middle-of-the-roaders and its extreme wing – sometimes called 'ecologism'. Are we doing this for ourselves, for our own benefit and that of our children and other humans? Or is that simply a new gloss on the old exploitative attitude to nature? Should we not be acting for the benefit of an entire planetary organism? Battle lines are even now being drawn up between green extremists and the rest of the community, including 'ordinary' environmentalists. The argument that trees and rivers have rights needs to be assessed so that we can distinguish between its potential to inspire action and its gross oversimplifications. Does the HIV virus have 'rights'? Is it ethical to destroy dams or insert into trees spikes that injure loggers?

In the chapter, I will question some of the underlying assumptions and practices of the modern environmental movement by exploring the tensions between nature and artifice revealed by a critical comparison of two very different yet somehow complementary novels that seem to mark out this particular patch of psychological, cultural, and socioeconomic territory. The novels are Margaret Atwood's *Surfacing* (1972)[2] and J.-K. Huysmans's *Against Nature* (*A Rebours*, 1884).[3] The interplay between Huysmans's hymn to artifice and Atwood's celebration of a woman's journey to a profound encounter with nature turns out to have political and social resonances. In addition, I suggest that in *Surfacing* we have a beautiful account of the progress of a female Trickster. I hope that the results of making this juxtaposition of two unrelated novels will justify the transgression of ordinary academic norms. Certainly, these are very different books. But they both engage with the idea of nature, they both present definite though complicated visions of sexuality, and they were both written at times when the relations between humanity and industrial-ism, and between women and men, were displaying rapid changes. Atwood was writing at the beginning of contemporary feminism, during the Nixon era with the Vietnam War in progress. Huysmans was working in the ferment of Paris in the 1880s, a time when the functions and forms of art were undergoing the most radical revision. Yet Huysmans, whom one would have thought of as the quintessential Artist (with a capital A), spent his entire working life in a government office and, in retirement, attempted to join a Trappist monastery. I hope the books can indeed bear the burden I am placing upon them. However, the chapter is more than a literary critique of two novels.

I assume that readers are broadly familiar with the current debate associated with environmentalism: The possibility of global warming, deforestation and species depletion, damaging of the ozone layer, acid rain and other pollutions, the limits to growth, the need for sustainable growth, the debate about population limitation, the general decay of urban civilization. I assume, too, an awareness of the gap in wealth between the industrially advanced countries and the developing countries, with the latter group heavily in debt to the former and often economically dominated by global corporations based in the industrially advanced countries. The tensions between the two kinds of country have also been written about so often that, allowing for differences of opinion, most readers will be aware that many developing countries assert their own right to the technological and industrial features that provide the consumers of the developed world with all their goodies. It is all very well for the industrially advanced countries to worry about pollution or deforestation in the developing countries but there is a certain irony in the fact that those who protest about what is happening to the rain forests of Amazonia themselves live in countries that consume a disproportionate amount of the earth's resources. In 1986 the United States was the only country to vote against the Declaration on the Right to Development passed in the General Assembly of the United Nations, and at the Earth Summit of 1992 the United States was also out of step with the rest of the world.

I am sure I am not the only one to be bewildered by the competing claims of groups of scientists that the situation is very grave indeed, or that it is grave but not disastrous, or that the warnings of planetary collapse are greatly exaggerated. It was partly to think my way through a thicket of information that I began the work that now forms the chapter.[4,5]

SURFACING

Surfacing is presented in the first person. The anonymous narrator is returning to the northern bushlands of Canada because she has been informed of the mysterious disappearance of her father. She is a city-based commercial artist who has lost touch with her family and has not been 'home' for many years. Some time previously, she has left her marriage and child, and is travelling with three companions: A couple, Dave and Anna, and her lover, Joe. Dave and Joe are supposedly making a film in a *cinema verité* style. The four are depicted, not uncritically but also with humor, as creatures of the late 1960s or early 1970s, with the typical linguistic affectations and cobbled-together values of the middle-class rebels of that era. However, the novel's repeated mention of 'Americans' is not simply to be taken literally. 'Americans' are signifiers of all that is crass, destructive of natural beauty, and threatening. This is a particularly Canadian referent, connected to Atwood's concern over the fate of Canadian culture and letters shown in another book of hers also published in 1972 – a book of literary criticism entitled *Survival*.[6] Moreover, as we saw, today's environmentalism has to deal with its own literal and metaphorical 'Americans'.

Drawing a blank at the homestead of an old farmer who was the narrator's father's best friend, the group of companions take a boat to the isolated cabin on an island in the lake in which the narrator had lived with her mother and father (her mother is dead). At the cabin, there is still no clue about what has happened to her father but, instead of returning to the city, the group decides to stay on for a further week, a decision which the narrator at first does not like. She organizes the others so that they can live relatively comfortably in the deliberately simple domestic arrangements her father has chosen. She takes them on blueberry-picking and fishing trips and, in general, acts as a kind of wilderness guide for the other three.

All the while, she is studying her mother's photograph albums and the scrapbooks she and her brother had assembled. She is swamped by memories. Then she finds some drawings that her father has made. These are crude representations of human-like, exotic creatures. She concludes from the drawings, and his comments on them, that her father had gone mad. She is forced to change this view when she finds a letter from an anthropologist regarding material her father had collected and sent to him on ancient Indian rock paintings in the locality. The drawings must be of these paintings. She realizes by now that her father is probably dead but is impelled to make use of a map she has found that seems to indicate the whereabouts of the rock paintings.

She goes out onto the lake and dives beneath the surface, for the map shows that some of the paintings are under water due to a rise in the surface level of the lake. There she finds, not a rock drawing, but her father's body, weighed down by his heavy camera. However, in the shock of that moment, she confuses his swollen and waterlogged body with the fetus she had aborted many years before when her then lover, her teacher and about the same age as her father, convinced her to get rid of the baby:

> It was there but it wasn't a painting, it wasn't on the rock. It was below me, drifting toward me from the furthest level where there was no life, a dark oval trailing limbs. It was blurred but it had eyes, they were open, it was something I knew about, a dead thing, it was dead.
>
> . . . it was in a bottle curled up, staring out at me like a cat pickled; it had huge jelly eyes and fins instead of hands, fish gills. I couldn't let it out, it was dead already, it had drowned in air.

Following this catalytic experience, the narrator begins a *nekyia*, a kind of descent,[7] in which she seeks to reverse her acculturation and attain a state of merger with nature. She persuades Joe to impregnate her, but does it in a way marked out as a meaningful ritual, an initiation rite.

> We go over the ground, feet and skin bare; the moon is rising, in the greygreen light his body gleams and the trunks of trees, the white ovals of his eyes. He walks as though blind, blundering into the shadow clumps, toes stubbing, he has not yet learned to see in the dark. My tentacled feet and free hand scent out the way . . .
>
> I lie down, keeping the moon on my left hand and the absent sun on my right. He kneels, he is shivering, the leaves under and around us are damp from the dew, or is it the lake, soaking up through the rock and sand, we are near the shore, the small waves riffle. He needs to grow more fur.

By now the narrator has disappeared from the sight of her companions who return to the city in frustration. Acting on implicit knowledge that she is on some kind of significant journey, the narrator sinks into, embraces, and identifies with the earth and its animals, with *nature*.

> Something has happened to my eyes, my feet are released, they alternate, several inches from the ground. I'm ice-clear, transparent, my bones and the child inside me showing through the green webs of my flesh, the ribs are shadows, the muscles jelly, the trees are like this too, they shimmer, their cores glow through the wood and bark.
>
> The forest leaps upward, enormous, the way it was before they cut it,

columns of sunlight frozen; the boulders float, melt, everything is made of water, even the rocks. In one of the languages there are no nouns, only verbs held for a longer moment.

The animals have no need for speech, why talk when you are a word
I lean against a tree, I am a tree leaning

I break out again into the bright sun and crumple, head against the ground
I am not an animal or a tree, I am the thing in which the trees and animals move and grow, I am a place

Right at the end of *Surfacing*, Joe returns on his own to look for her and, like an inquisitive but cautious beast, she watches him from the trees. The frame freezes.

Perhaps more than any other single artistic production of the past twenty-five years, *Surfacing* deepened and highlighted questions about the cultural and psychological linkages of women and nature.[8] These questions have mainly been taken up in two contradictory ways. First, as referring us to a power and knowledge of nature held exclusively by women, based on their reproductive and nurturing capacities. Thus, women are the true guardians of nature, creatures of the earth goddesses, emblems and purveyors of all that is fecund.[9] The second view is that the equation of women and nature is one of the main processes that bind women into their oppressed place in patriarchal culture. For, as the subjugation of nature by (male) science proceeds, the subjugation of women, equated with nature, will proceed in parallel. *Surfacing* appears, superficially, to come down on the side of the first viewpoint, supporting and celebrating a twinning of woman and nature. But, as we will see, it is not as straightforward as that and *Surfacing* is not at all an essentialist tract.

It is interesting that, in the intense debate between feminist circles over these issues that were and are highlighted by *Surfacing*, there has been (quite rightly, in my view) very little space for the facile line beloved of the rote Jungians that at-oneness with nature is a 'feminine' capacity or quality, meaning a femininity capable of being developed internally by any woman or man. This metaphorical femininity is not the theme of *Surfacing*, nor the basis of what has been termed 'eco-feminism' – the perspective that sees correspondences between a despoiled planet and the exploited and ravished female body.[10] The equation of women and nature, whether taken as an indication of female potential and female gifts, or as an indicator of culturally driven female inferiority, cannot be split off from flesh-and-blood women.

Of course, there are many layers in a polysemous novel like *Surfacing* and, as Francine du Plessix Gray says, 'Atwood's genius rises above these debates'.[11] However, I do not agree with du Plessix Gray that the novel has to be taken as a religious quest or as the working out of a female religious vision or, as other critics have claimed, as part of a typical, 'Jungian', 'individuation' process, following the 'archetypal' stages of a (or the) shamanic journey.[12] Undoubtedly, the narrator does go through a trans-formative process in which psychologically heightened exposure to the material world of her childhood functions so as to transcend the materiality of that childhood and, indeed, the materiality of the physical world itself. But this is quite specifically a transformation downward: Down into the lake, down into the animal world, down (if you will) into the unconscious. This journey downward involves the narrator in nothing less than a transcendence of her human body:

> the footprints are there, side by side in the mud. My breath quickens, it was true, I saw it. But the prints are too small, they have toes; I place my feet in them and find they are my own.
>
> I am part of the landscape, I could be anything, a tree, a deer skeleton, a rock.

Transcending the body, and doing it downward not upward toward spiritual planes, implies a transcendence of ego-consciousness itself, or rather an assumption of a kind of 'natural' consciousness, a fathomless Nature consciousness – so that there is a paradox of total unconsciousness acting as a phantasmagoric *consciousness*. It is a paradox we have met before, when we met the Trickster who challenges the habitual division: Below, matter; above, spirit.

Let us review the particular features of the narrator's transformations: The downward moves to an embrace with inferiority, the absolute bodily fluidity, the naive but magical omnipotence, the unconsciousness that is revealed as a treasure-chest of natural consciousness, even the ambiguous ending of the book (will she, can she go to Joe or not?). Taking all of these features into account, I suggest that we are indeed in the realm of the female Trickster. As I noted in the previous chapter, in our culture the female Trickster lacks texts, lacks recognition, and yet one senses her readiness to be texted, to be recognized, if only for a millisecond.

The oft-discussed equation of women and nature now takes on yet another set of implications. It ceases to be a question posed in terms either of the celebration of women or of the subjugation of women. The equation of women and nature, taken on the level of the female Trickster, viewed as a trick, is revealed as having as its goal or *telos* nothing less than the social transformation of women. In Atwood's words:

> [The Americans] can't be trusted. They'll mistake me for a human being, a naked woman wrapped in a blanket: possibly that's what they've come here for, if it's running around loose, ownerless, why not take it. They won't be able to tell what I really am. But if they guess my true form, identity, they will shoot me or bludgeon in my skull and hang me up by the feet from a tree.

This is a trick because a woman who is by now not a woman but really an animal is pretending to be a woman lest in her true form she be treated as an animal by American men who have come to hunt in the Canadian wilderness. The female narrator of *Surfacing* quite literally 'drops out'. Ceasing to be a woman, she cannot be subjugated *like* nature because she *is* nature. But, to the extent that nature threatens people, especially men like Joe, or Americans, as a woman still she acquires nature's deathly powers – woman as 'Ice Woman', to use a phrase from Atwood's other book *Survival*. But we know it is still an illusion, because men still have the 'real' power, the socioeconomic power, the political power. It is no accident that, in the carefully crafted ghost story that is *Surfacing*, Atwood assigns all the pioneering skills – fishing, fire-making, tracking – to a female.

Reflecting upon the image of the female Trickster as agent of political change, especially of change in our attitudes to and dealings with the environment, offers an opportunity to break away from those three problems I mentioned at the beginning of the chapter: Authoritarianism, depression, and an idealization of nature. Environmentalism is itself subjected to a critique modelled on the upside-downness of the Trickster.

The trick is to use the most eternal, the most 'natural' formulation but to orientate that usage in the direction of social change. The eternal points up the mutable. Atwood is neither extolling woman as nature nor critiquing the notion: She is using it to reinforce a political project. The power of nature is, as we say, harnessed – but under a different egis than that of phallogocentric industrialism controlled by 'Americans'. Tricksters push the logic of a particular piece of cultural oppression to the point where it implodes. We saw the same thing in the emancipatory effectiveness of the Mothers of the Plaza de Mayo (in the previous chapter), and we will witness the same capacity in des Esseintes, hero of Huysmans's novel *Against Nature*.

I must emphasize that my claim that *Surfacing* refers to a female Trickster and her socially transformative potential is not intended to depreciate its version of female potency. Quite the reverse. For, as we saw in the previous chapter, there is a neglected political capacity in Tricksters of whatever sex to transform passion and dream into the germ of a pragmatic political program. The female Trickster's impressionistic manifesto deploys what seems to be an intrapsychic identification with nature as a template for changes in a different but related area of reality, namely the sociopolitical realm. Here, Atwood's concern with the survival of Canadian letters in the face of American cultural imperialism needs to be brought back into the picture. The relationship between the novel *Surfacing* and the critical work *Survival* is an extraordinarily complex one, not least in Atwood's own mind. But I think it is justifiable, at least in imagination, to propose that the female Trickster narrator of *Surfacing* is part of a response to the political problem of cultural and environmental survival depicted in *Survival*. In her critical book, Atwood points up the difference between 'nature as woman' and 'woman as nature'. As one who is both poet and novelist, she tells us that prose writers incline toward 'woman as nature', thereby confirming, if in code, that it is *women* on whom she wishes to focus in the prose work *Surfacing*.[13] Hence, perhaps, these lines:

> This above all, to refuse to be a victim. Unless I can do that I can do nothing, I have to recant, give up the old belief that I am powerless and because of it nothing I can do will ever hurt anyone. A lie which was always more disastrous than the truth would have been.

NATURE AND ANXIETY

Woman as nature makes many of us anxious. Yet, on the cultural level, the equation of woman and nature may itself be seen as a *response* to anxiety. In his seminal book, *Man and the Natural World*, Keith Thomas argued that the snowball of industrialism, Enlightenment and modernity created a profound anxiety in European cultural consciousness, to the point of neurosis, over what was being done by civilized humans to the natural world.[14] Between 1500 and 1800, massive doubts emerged over the changes brought about by science and technology in the ways the natural world was perceived. There were many expressions of this counter-cultural sentiment. Theologians altered their notions about the relations between humanity and the rest of creation so as to gentle those relations and accommodate a certain decentering of humanity. Naturalists tried to understand and classify other species in non-anthropomorphic terms, thereby respecting their separate existence. Scientists explored links between humans and animals. Moral philosophers urged kindness to animals. In the city, the land came to be regarded as a thing of beauty, fit for contemplation, not as a useful resource. In sum, by 1800, people had responded to the anxiety engendered by the brutalizing path on which the world seemed embarked. The list of cultural and intellectual developments I have cited is evidence of the anxiety-driven shift in consciousness.

Today's concerns over the limits to growth, animal welfare and the fate of the environment may be regarded as descended from these earlier expressions of cultural anxiety. Yet we should temper our admiration for those who could not stomach 'progress'. They did not actually stop its march. Today, animal experimentation and factory-farming have to coexist with the supreme idealization of the animal: The child's toy furry animal. As Thomas says, these cuddly creatures 'enshrine the values by which society as a whole cannot afford to live' – an observation he extends to include nature parks and conservation areas.[15]

The revolution in consciousness that Thomas writes about constituted a kind of underground resistance to what was being done to the natural world. This resistance went beyond a reaction to the ruination of nature. The perception of slaves, non-Europeans, children and women also underwent profound changes. As far as women were concerned, the form that liberal anxiety about modernity's denigration of women took was of an oppressive (and convenient) idealization that restricted women to private and domestic roles. The idealization of women and the idealization of nature share similar roots in cultural history in the West: They are both reaction formations. But women and nature remain deeply threatening because the idealizations of them are based on such flimsy and anxiety-ridden foundations. Hence the swiftness with which the image of the 'natural' woman moves from one who soothes a crying child or makes beds neatly into one who, transparent and web-footed, gazes at the man she commanded to fertilize her from behind a screen of trees.

So the cult of the countryside has this she-demon at its heart. Gaia[16] tips over into the Terrible Mother and the proud, human illusion of serving as Gaia's physicians is replaced by the starker reality of our being her slavish attendants, her Cabiri.[17]

AGAINST NATURE

Any difficulty with summarizing the plot of *Surfacing* fades into insignificance compared with having to summarize the plot of *Against Nature*.

Duc Jean Floressas des Esseintes admits that he suffers from 'une névrose', a neurosis. At the age of thirty – Atwood was thirty-three when she wrote *Surfacing* – des Esseintes, the scion of a degenerate aristocratic family, decides to leave the debauched, big-city life of Paris and retreat to a 'desert equipped with all modern conveniences, a snugly heated ark on dry land in which he might take refuge from the incessant deluge of human stupidity'. We are told that

> try what he might, he could not shake off the overpowering tedium which weighed upon him. In desperation he had recourse to the perilous caresses of the professional virtuosos, but the only effect was to impair his health and exacerbate his nerves.

Even prior to his move, des Esseintes has a reputation as an eccentric. For example, he gave the by-now notorious 'black banquet', a dinner modelled on a funeral feast:

> The dining room, draped in black, opened out into a garden metamorphosed for the occasion, the paths being strewn with charcoal, the ornamental pond edged with black basalt and filled with ink, the shrubberies replanted with cypresses and pines. The dinner itself was served on a black cloth adorned with baskets of violets and scabious; candelabra shed an eerie green light over the table and tapers flickered in the chandeliers.
>
> While a hidden orchestra played funeral marches, the guests were waited on by naked negresses wearing only slippers and stockings in cloth of silver embroidered with tears.
>
> Dining off black-bordered plates, the company had enjoyed turtle soup, Russian rye bread, ripe olives from Turkey, caviare, mullet botargo, black puddings from Frankfurt . . . .
>
> On the invitations, which were similar to those sent out before more solemn obsequies, this dinner was described as a funeral banquet in memory of the host's virility, lately but only temporarily deceased.

By the way, thinking of those invitations, Huysmans made up des Esseintes's name from railway timetables to avoid the possibility of being sued for libel.

Having constructed his retreat, des Esseintes sets out to lead a life devoted to the experience of the highest forms of artifice and artificiality. Using the finest and most expensive materials, he builds for himself a replica of a monk's cell in which he will sleep. The point is that great expense is employed to create the *appearance* of humble poverty. Des Esseintes also constructs what he calls his 'mouth organ', a machine that dispenses liqueurs in tiny quantities, thus permitting a kind of blending to go on within the blender's own mouth:

> The organ was then open. The stops labelled 'flute', 'horn', and 'vox angelica' were pulled out, ready for use. Des Esseintes would drink a drop here, another there, playing internal symphonies to himself, and providing his palate with sensations analogous to those which music dispenses to the ear.
>
> Indeed, each and every liqueur, in his opinion, corresponded in taste with the sound of a particular instrument. . . .
>
> Once these principles had been established . . . he even succeeded in transferring specific pieces of music to his palate . . . .

Surrounding himself with exotic hot-house flowers, specially chosen for giving the appearance of being artificial flowers, des Esseintes spends many hours blending perfumes, seeking to reproduce, by artificial means, exact replicas of natural odors: 'One aspect of the art of perfumery fascinated him more than any other, and that was the degree of accuracy it was possible to reach in imitating the real thing.'

If des Esseintes wants to travel to London, he does not actually go there. He constructs a room on gimbals that reproduces artificially the rolling motions of the cross-Channel ferry and he has his servants make splashing sounds with barrels of salt water outside the window, using fans to waft in the salty smell. He travels to Paris so as to eat English food in an English restaurant, claiming that this is as 'real' as doing it in London. He wears a fur coat in hot weather, forcing himself to shiver, admires the convolutions of Decadent Latin poetry, adores the play of gorgeous colors on his walls, and praises the marvels of modern manufacture above all the works of nature in a passage which is surely the ideological heart of the book:

> Nature, he used to say, has had her day; she has finally and utterly exhausted the patience of sensitive observers by the revolting uniformity of her landscapes and skyscapes. . . . In fact, there is not a single one of her inventions, deemed so subtle and sublime, that human ingenuity cannot manufacture . . . .
>
> There can be no shadow of doubt that with her never-ending platitudes the old crone has by now exhausted the good-humoured admiration of all true artists, and the time has surely come for artifice to take her place whenever possible.
>
> After all, to take what among all her works is considered to be the most exquisite, what among all her creations is deemed to possess the

most perfect and original beauty – to wit, woman – has not man, for his part, by his own efforts, produced an animate yet artificial creature that is every bit as good from the point of view of plastic beauty? Does there exist, anywhere on this earth, a being conceived in the throes of motherhood who is more dazzlingly, more outstandingly beautiful than the two locomotives recently put into service on the Northern Railway?

I have given what must necessarily be a partial list of the things des Esseintes gets up to in the privacy of his own home. Perhaps the *pièce de resistance* is des Esseintes's adoption of a system of rectal feeding by means of peptone enemas. He fantasizes about all manner of delicious meals that might be consumed in this way. Thus, by artifice, basic biology is transcended.

How are we to understand des Esseintes's story, one hundred years later? We have our own *mal de siècle* with which to contend. Certainly, he acts with a directed energy quite foreign to his enervated and dilapidated physical state. He acts strongly so that his weaknesses may be pursued – the enemas were actually recommended by his doctor as a last resort for his drastically failing health. Des Esseintes, as I understand him, is merely doing something *natural* by creating an *artificial culture* for himself; for making culture is 'natural' for humans. Huysmans's genius is to hold a mirror up to ourselves, to disabuse us of the notion that we can separate nature from culture – and, thinking thoughts that hark back to *Surfacing*, to disabuse us of the notion that we can clearly separate so-called feminine (i.e. natural) and so-called masculine (i.e. cultural) capacities.

For sure, des Esseintes is not made happy by his experiment. Torn by vicious nightmares, he contemplates a return to the Catholic church. In the ecclesiastic yearnings of des Esseintes, the Trickster artificer expresses his religious instinct – just as 'I', the narrator in *Surfacing*, apparently on a religious quest, expressed her Trickster self.

Des Esseintes bears a message for our epoch about the ambivalence toward, and fear of nature that no environmentalism can disguise. His neurosis is not merely a personal condition but a symbol of a collective malaise. Des Esseintes is both terrified of the body and seemingly quite at home with its febrile gestures. His mouth organ and his perfumery show that, within his own self-designated limits, he remains a perfectly sensual man. Moreover, throughout *Against Nature*, in his diatribes against nature, do we not hear des Esseintes calling out for some kind of connection to her? In his manipulated, artificial delights do we not perceive a recognition that no direct experience of nature is possible? (Nor direct experience of anything else, for that matter.) Nature is an artificial entity, a constructed phenomenon, existing in the hearts and brains of human beings. And here, does not des Esseintes anticipate Jung's idea that everything that exists exists first in psychic reality? Or, in more modern vein, is not *Against Nature* an anticipation of the virtual reality of the computer game and a screen-bound, theme park culture? *Nature can be improved on by means of culture.*

Like Margaret Atwood, Huysmans cannot resist the move (almost a 'natural' move, it seems) from an engagement with nature to an engagement with the social – though, for Huysmans, artifice serves as the essential mediator. What could be more *engagé*, not to say *enragé*, than these lines from *Against Nature*?

> Under the pretext of encouraging liberty and progress, society has discovered yet another means of aggravating man's wretched lot, by dragging him from his home, rigging him out in a ridiculous costume, putting specially designed weapons into his hands, and reducing him to the same degrading slavery from which the negroes were released out of pity – and all this to put him in a position to kill his neighbour without risking the scaffold, as ordinary murderers do who operate single-handed, without uniforms, and with quieter, poorer weapons.

But Huysmans wouldn't be Huysmans and des Esseintes wouldn't be des Esseintes if these anti-war sentiments were not immediately followed by this remarkable *non sequitur*:

> Ah! If in the name of pity the futile business of procreation was ever to be abolished, the time had surely come to do it.

FLEXIBLE SPECIALIZATION

Viewed imaginatively, des Esseintes stands as a kind of economic and technological pioneer rather than an omnipotent narcissistic type seeking to control nature. His 'work' is carried out at home, not in office, factory or field. He makes constant use of technology – the mouth organ, the perfume-making apparatus, the room on gimbals, the syringe for rectal feeding. Following trends in development economics, des Esseintes uses technology that can be characterized as 'appropriate technology', operating on a small scale and with regard to environmental and social costs.[18] From the standpoint of the 1990s, it is hard at first to share des Esseintes's enthusiasm for technology, yet, in spite of ecologistic alterations in cultural consciousness, we in the West remain committed to and dependent on technology. Technology is, for us, a part of nature. Des

Esseintes seems to know just which technology or, more accurately, which level of technology to apply to his consciously chosen tasks. In this sense, he can act as an imaginal bridge between a perspective that would restrict appropriate (or intermediate) technology to developing countries and one that could sense that the same pragmatic, modest approach might have applicability in the industrially advanced countries.

Another concept, also taken from development economics, which finds symbolization in des Esseintes's activities, and even in his personality, is that of 'flexible specialization'.[19] When I first heard this term, I thought immediately of human psychology because the capacity to perform many separate tasks according to the quite specific dictates of consciousness is characteristic of our species. In fact, the theories of flexible specialization are a response to the limitations of models of industrialism founded on mass production. In mass production, purpose-built machines are used by semi-skilled workers to produce standardized products. Standardization of the product permits economies of scale and helps to maximize profits. Flexible specialization, on the other hand, requires a combination of craft skill and flexible equipment – maybe electronics-based machinery that can be reprogrammed. As Kurt Hoffman and Raphael Kaplinsky put it, we are at a transitional point between the eras of 'machinofacture' and 'systemofacture'.[20] It may be that we are entering an era of technological Darwinism. It is important, for the developing countries *and* the industrially advanced countries, that flexible specialization kill off mass production because flexible specialization could then come into its own as the globally appropriate approach to technology for the last decade of the century.

That this should happen is important when we consider the possibility that environmentally linked conflicts may well erupt in the developing world in the near future – for example, conflicts over scarce supplies of water or large-scale migrations caused by desertification. The Gulf War of 1991 may also have been a precursor of other resource wars.

However, none of this will mean anything, and we run the risk of staying on a des Esseintes level of practicality, if we do not address the contemporary form of slavery represented by international debt. Developing economies need emancipating from the burden of debt and this will be facilitated by changes in mindset in the industrially advanced countries. The debts of the Third World were not incurred – are not being incurred – under a system of rules of fair play. Flexible specialization and appropriate technology may produce export-led growth, but the foreign currency never reaches the producers. If we consider a development problem such as the feminization of poverty, the trend in which women's economic lot often worsens as the wealth of their community increases, then the disaster that is going on right now is a deathly disaster for women and children.[21] The human rights of women and children are integral to effective and sustainable development. People have some 'right to development', no matter how artificial or against nature that turns out to be. Even the arch-dandy, esthete of esthetes, hyper-misogynist Duc Jean Floressas des Esseintes would agree (at least I think he would).

SPECTRUM

Let me review some of the links between *Surfacing* and *Against Nature* that I have been conjuring into existence. First, there is the interplay in both novels between Trickster and the person on a religious quest. Second, there is a searching examination in both novels of the relations between culture and nature, leading to all manner of destabilizations of our habitual diagrams of these relations. Third, in both novels the protagonists explore the possibility of a transcendence of the body. Fourth, there is in both novels an explicit search, by means of excess, whether natural excess or artificial excess, for a more fruitful relation to nature. As far as I can tell from empathic identification with both writers, the result should not interfere with the fullest possible living out of an unbalanced, supposedly one-sided position: 'I am a place' says Atwood's narrator; 'But I just don't enjoy the pleasures other people enjoy' says des Esseintes. Fifth and last, both writers are concerned with the relation between depth and the surface, the particular depth to be found on the surface, when surfacing; the unnatural depth of the environment.

What I have been trying to do is to construct a spectrum of responses to environmentalism out of the narratives, imageries, and underlying ethoses of the two novels *Surfacing* and *Against Nature*. What happens if we allow Atwood's narrator and des Esseintes to have a baby? What if des Esseintes were the father instead of Joe? What would *that* baby be like?

ENVIRONMENTALISM AND EDUCATION

Unlike Margaret Atwood, I have had to combine in one piece imaginative, fantasy thinking and pragmatic, directed thinking. What follows is both a depth psychological contribution to the many debates about environmentalism and an attempt to answer the question with which I ended the previous section: What *would* the baby look like?

The ideogram that is born out of this joint presentation of fantasy thinking and pragmatic thinking is that of *change*. Maybe the image of change always underpinned my argument already. One message of the environmental movement has been that we must change the way that we live and this will have to be done on the basis of changes in the ways we apprehend our relation to nature. It is hard to say succinctly whether the environmental movement is truly 'for' or secretly 'against' change. In the sense that environmentalism represents an opposition to the forms of social organization established in the industrially advanced countries in the past two centuries, the environmental movement supports a change. But in the sense that environmentalists, along with everyone else, have not caught up in consciousness with the techno-industrial revolutions of the past two hundred years, and are rooted in a pre-industrial cultural matrix, environmentalism may be seen as being against the very changes that have already happened. Hence, environmentalism may be regarded as deeply conservative. (It is a good example of the operation of *Nachträglichkeit* on the cultural level.)

But the key question, in all its school debating society naivety, remains: Does, or can, human nature change? We saw how Atwood developed the eternal to point up the mutable. Des Esseintes does artificially what comes to us naturally by creating a new micro-culture. Oscar Wilde, profoundly influenced by Huysmans, wrote in his tract 'The soul of man under socialism' that 'The only thing we know about human nature is that it changes. Change is the one quality we can predict of it. . . . The systems that fail are those that rely on the permanency of human nature, and not on its growth and development.'[22]

I think that what our thinking and feeling lacks most is a unit – I mean a unit of size and space – which is a comfortable one to have in mind when discussing environmental concerns. The temptation is to propose the world itself (as in the Gaia theory) or, at the other extreme, to focus on the bottle bank in one's own neighborhood. We are, after all, embarking on nothing less than an exploration of the psychology of the earth, of what in Britain is called soil and Americans call dirt. How does the very ground on which you stand, on which you grew up, contribute to who you are?[23]

NOT A CONCLUSION

There can be no conclusion to a chapter such as this one. I am aware of its dissonances and jerkiness. The making of pragmatic suggestions when confronted with insoluble problems is itself an act of faith; there is an undecidability that cannot be denied. So the move on which I want to end is to salute the conception, or rather the construction, of a new kind of actor, an environmental actor with an environmentally attuned political consciousness.[24] Atwood's words from the closing passage of *Surfacing* chime with this:

> I bring with me from the distant past five nights ago the time-traveller, the primaeval one who will have to learn, shape of a goldfish now in my belly, undergoing its watery changes. Word furrows potential in its proto-brain, untravelled paths. No god and perhaps not real, even that is uncertain; I can't know yet, it's too early.

Or, in des Esseintes's words, at the end of a meditation on the evil triviality of the power held by the bourgeoisie whose only interest is the accumulation of wealth:

> Well, crumble then, society! Perish, old world!

Part II

The political person

In Part II, I move the argument of the book onto a more personal plane. I begin with two chapters that present a view of fathers that highlights their positive psychological, political and cultural roles. In these chapters, I critique depth psychology's narratives and theories of the father and widen my study to challenge the heterosexist assumptions and prejudices of developmental psychology. The interplay between psychic reality and sociopolitical reality is a *leitmotif* that is also present in the following chapter on men. Here, I try to work out a strategy for recognizing and protecting the diversity of men's life and experience. I am suspicious of recent attempts to hegemonize male psychology. The last chapter in Part II is a theoretical essay that explores the conceptual background to this section of the book and links Parts I and II.

Chapter 6

Fathers

FOCUSING ON FATHERS

This chapter and the next one concern the claiming or reclamation of ordinary, personal experience and imagery of the father for a psychological analysis of politics. This is achieved by means of a political reading of such personal imagery. *The goal is to provide a political recuperation of the father–child relationship rather than the more usual psychological aim of understanding politics in terms of father–child relating.* Hopefully, this opening of another way of thinking about the political permits something fresh to be said about the relationship between political and social reality on the one hand and psychic reality on the other.

We have drawn out the political and economic implications of the mythic imagery of the Hermes story and the psychological implications of Machiavelli's political philosophy. A similar kind of job can be done in relation to the more ordinary images of fathers that are present in most people's experience of him, whether in terms of his presence, his absence – or the presence of his absence. The plural 'fathers' is deliberate here, as it is in the chapter's title. This is because a preliminary historical and sociological reading suggests that there was not and is not a monolith 'father' of the kind to which we have grown accustomed to refer. Hence, I will not be discussing the decline or advocating the restoration of the father's authority, or weighing the pros and cons of a return to the father as the king of the family. In a way, I see *these* traditional facets of the father as contributing to his wounds and, hence, as something to be healed. Not a lot has been written about the father's desire to be loved.

Nevertheless, it is very hard to avoid the tunnel-vision, stereotypical version of the psychology of the father when political matters are being addressed, particularly when issues of conflict and power are prominent. This conventional symbolization of the father is one that I and others have continued to observe clinically during the Thatcher period in which Britain had a female Prime Minister. Cultural images of fatherly power meld with intrapsychic images of the father. It is an interplay of socio-political reality and psychic reality that is worth tracking. But I have also noticed that there is a side to the father, when his image is explored with the political dimension in mind, which does *not* radiate an aura of social control, castrating tyranny and unreachable authority. *We need to bring into the open the father's hidden political sanctioning of the cultural diversity of others, particularly his children.* Though it has become common to note the mobility, enfranchisement and emancipation of men in contrast with the oppression and subordination of women, very little has been said about the father's positive attitude to mobility, enfranchisement and emancipation for others. I want to suggest that father imagery carries a secret symbolism *for* social and political movement and change, alongside the far better known symbolism of an oppressive and repressive political order. But we cannot make any use of a text that tells of the father's reinforcement of political and social change until we first acknowledge the existence of such a theme and raise it to a level of consciousness that allows for entry into cultural discourse. To do this, we have to allow ourselves to be preoccupied, hopefully for a limited period, with the father, and to focus our psychological and political attention on him, rather than on the mother.

In spite of careful delineations like these, depth psychologists who write about the father are often accused of ignoring the mother, or of attacking women. (I write from personal experience here.) Of course, none of these critics would even go so far as to deny that there is a need for depth psychologists to focus on new or different areas of interest. But it sometimes seems as if analysts, including myself, have become caught up in a struggle between two gigantic, competing parents. The political logic of this is that it has become very hard to write about the positive, loving, flexible father and *his* political impact as well as about the sexually abusing, violent, abandoning or absent, authoritarian father and *his* political impact. We are cut off from the veiled symbolization of political regeneration that the father also carries. Perhaps this loss would be made up if those who write about the politically progressive father protested more vehemently when they themselves are put in the role of the bad and repressive father, pilloried as attacking the good mother and her innocent children, or as trying to take over the role of mother.

It is necessary to do more than *protest* at the accusation of neglecting the mother. Why *do* I focus on the father and father imagery in a chapter on political readings of imagery? Are there perhaps special features of fathers and father imagery that should be mentioned as grounds for this focus on fathers?

Some justification for focus on the father as a political image has already been explained in the preceding chapters. One image which attaches itself to fathers is that of the Trickster. John Beebe has demonstrated the existence of Tricksterism in the father; an example of his, taken from the Bible, is the Tricksterish way Jacob deals with the intra-familial problems caused by Joseph's special talents, including those of dreaming and dream interpretation. Superficially, Jacob acknowledges Joseph as special and valued by the gift of the coat of many colors, but also stirs up the brothers' envy by asking Joseph if his dream about the sun, moon and stars making obeisance to him is to be taken as an allegory for the family situation.[1] We can see examples of the Trickster father beyond the Bible: Zeus, King Lear, Jung and Freud – all of these operated as fathers in their relations with others and moved in the kind of Trickster territory mapped out in the previous chapter. The peculiar Trickster blend of unconsciousness, grandiosity and a kind of wild, politically transformative capacity are, to some degree, locked up in father imagery on the ordinary, human level.

Fathers may be Tricksters in order to sublimate their infanticidal impulses toward their children, especially their sons. In myth, Kronos ate his sons, forgetting how Gaia, his mother, saved him from being buried alive by his own father Uranus; Laius cast Oedipus onto the mountain slope to die. The energy required for child murder has to be dealt with somehow. I can recall raising my arm with fist clenched above my small son's head when his back was turned after some row or other. I was certainly furiously angry but sure I would not bring my fist hammering down. I was alone with him at the time and, turning to leave the room (itself an aggressive act), I noticed I had a broad grin on my face. This was a rather schizoid moment because I was still feeling murderous; the grin was a kind of counterpoint to the hate I was experiencing. However, I was getting pleasure and satisfaction, leading to gleeful amusement, out of the fact that my action was a secret and my son had not seen the infanticidal gesture. I had played a trick on him. Another fatherly trick copied from a friend that comes to mind was showing both my son and daughter how to program the burglar alarm but omitting to tell them of the final procedure necessary actually to arm it. The uncomfortable thing is that the more involved with his children the father becomes, the greater his hate for them will grow. After all, Winnicott drew up a list of seventeen reasons why *mothers* might hate their babies![2]

There is another way that fathers deal with their murderous impulses toward their children: By projecting the impulses outward. I can think of three typical instances of this: Projection of the murderous feelings onto women in general, and the female partner or wife in particular; projection onto colleagues in the rat race; and projection onto the physical environment resulting, on a global level, in its despoliation (as we saw in Chapter 5).

Of course, the father's infanticidal impulse is complemented by the son's equally aggressive posture: Kronos, in his role as son, with the father-castrating sickle provided by Gaia, and Oedipus's slaying of the unknown father Laius on the road are examples of murderous sons. The results of these confrontations are impressive – the birth of beauty, as Aphrodite rises foamily from Uranus's dismemberment; and the mythic origin of guilt when Oedipus cannot bear to look at what he and Jocasta have done, and so blinds himself.

The linkage of the father, the Trickster and political change can be sharpened. If, as I will argue, there is a sense in which the father is the pluralistic parent then, when we read his as yet uncharted political imagery, we will find that his functions and behaviors tend toward pluralistic outcomes. This idea will be developed in the course of this chapter and the next one, but at this point my intention is to say why I focus on the father and to explain why I do not see the pluralistic charge as being carried by the image of the mother in quite the same way. Political readings of maternal imagery lead to radically different under-standings of the interplay of psychology and politics.

I am not suggesting that the mother is reactionary while the father is revolutionary, nor that the mother is only a comfortable, stable, even static figure while the father is daring, fluid and transmutative. But images of the mother refer to her capacity to contain *alternation between psychological fluidity and stability*. This alternation is one reason why the Kleinian psychological positions, paranoid–schizoid and depressive, are often notated ps ⟵——⟶ d, to indicate alternations between them as they share the role of the dominant descriptive metaphor for mental functioning. The image of the father is, perhaps, a less containing one and hence represents the *warring simultaneity of stability and fluidity*, which is why I argue for the father as carrying a pluralistic charge. We will see repeatedly that father imagery and personal experience of the father reflect this tension-rich simultaneity: A constant sense of identity, coherence and contained stability – *and*, at the same moment, a tolerant fostering of a community of selves, constructive abandonment of the reality principle, ambiguity and fluidity. Politically, the father stands for reaction *and* revolution at the same time; the mother's symbolic capacities cover the same range of possibilities but they are organized more around an alternation of the various political positions. Mother psychology expects schizoid splits to be overcome by bringing them together. Father psychology does not share that expectation.

LITERAL AND METAPHORICAL FATHERS

I expect that, by now, the reader will be wondering how literally I intend to be taken in these remarks about father and mother and the different political readings I am giving to their texts and their imagery. I know that there is a confusion in what I write and I want to explain why I leave the confusion in and why I think that the confusion is valuable and even politically significant in its own way. At one point in the evolution of my ideas, I used to be very careful to clarify at each and every moment whether I meant my statements to be taken literally *or* metaphorically. I would indicate either that I was referring to a flesh-and-blood man doing something that only a person with such an anatomy could do – or, conversely, that I was referring to some great psychic theme within a person or culture for which the father is a metaphor. Unfortunately, things were very rarely so clear-cut.

Then (and this was the next step) I thought I had resolved the problem of an over-rigid division between literalism and metaphor, or at least made a move toward resolving it, by taking the view that everything one said about the father (or the mother) could, in sequence, be understood literally and then, subsequently, be understood metaphorically.

Gradually, I have realized that even such a broad statement (literal and metaphorical understandings in sequence) cannot remain as the last word on the subject. To begin with, the literal and metaphorical realms do not like each other very much, though they cannot shrug each other off. The two perspectives have to bargain and negotiate. Metaphor asserts that there is no original literalism at all, that the notion of a flesh-and-blood parent, and even the idea that there are direct personal experiences, are themselves metaphors. Literalism seeks to say that the original raw material for the metaphor remains imprisoned within the metaphor, and will continue to shine through the layers of metaphorical elaboration, thoroughly infecting the metaphor. If the original raw material does have such a power, then, asserts literalism, citing the father as a metaphor for some great psychopolitical theme cannot be done without something of the characteristics of the flesh-and-blood personal father being actively at work. Picasso once wrote that the 'reality' that started an abstract artist off would always remain as a 'prisoner in the work . . . integral even when its presence is no longer discernible. . . . There is no abstract art.'[3]

I am not suggesting that metaphor (or psychic reality) is more important than literalism (or social reality) or vice versa. I am trying to demonstrate how it is that two modes of understanding can function *at the same time*. Then we have a base from which to show how it is that (a) the unconscious contains internalizations of social reality *and* (b) that psychic reality has always already played a part in creating social reality.

IN PRAISE OF GENDER CONFUSION

Though the simultaneity of metaphor and literalism can be confusing, this is a valuable confusion. It is important to theorize in supple vein about gender, for gender is itself pliable and fluid. There is a great danger that, given our current preoccupation with gender, we might become too clear and too organized (for example, assigning phenomena to 'orders': This is 'Symbolic', this 'Imaginary', as some rote Lacanians do). It is a reaction formation to the anxiety and pain we experience at finding what we thought was solid and fixed is perforated and shifting; a counterphobic response to the fear of psychosis. I sometimes think that humanity is not just divided into women and men, but also into those who are certain about gender and those who are confused about it.

Yet we live in a culture that, in its language and political organization, proclaims that it is quite certain about gender, at least in public. The links between gender certainty and gender confusion at the private level are much more complicated. The problem of gender certainty is more than its sometimes being a surface manifestation or compensation for deeper gender confusion – for example, in the way a gender-confused person sometimes assumes a gender-certain persona. When we try to get behind surface symptoms of apparent gender confusion, we often find an *unconscious* form of gender certainty exerting an influence. Behind many sexual and relationship problems that *seem* to stem from confusion about gender, there is often a pernicious, unconscious gender certainty at work. Unconscious gender certainty is rigid, conventional, and persecuting.

A person who is in the grip of unconscious gender certainty is going to appear – and consciously to feel – confused. Who wouldn't, faced from within with such a massive amount of certainty? The confusion may be measured *in comparison* to the certainty; one's intense unconscious certainty complements one's equally intense conscious confusion.

I no longer think, as I once did, that it is possible to harmonize gender confusion and gender certainty in a spirit of animated moderation: Not too certain, not too confused, somewhere in the middle, just a little mixed up. I now see gender confusion and gender certainty as warring elements in the formation of gender identity. In this pluralistic formulation, gender confusion and gender certainty have their own psychologies, separate from each other. They also compete for sovereignty. But they are also both part of that one state we call gender identity. They are competitively diverse and parts of one and the same thing.

We are confused about the degree of confusion over gender; we are certain only of a lack of certainty. Our anxiety about gender puts us under great strain, but there is also a certain usable pleasure in not knowing. The recognition of unconscious gender certainty lying behind apparent gender confusion is a radical revising of conventional kinds of psychodynamic formulations. These are usually content to reach the unconscious gender confusion that lies behind apparent gender certainty. Moreover, just as there needs to be movement between consciousness and the unconscious, or between the neurotic and psychotic parts of the personality, so, too, there needs to be movement and competition between gender certainty and gender confusion. What Lacan called the Symbolic order cannot resist being affected by this process which also takes place in the realm of social behavior. The existence of gender confusion in itself suggests that neither the Symbolic nor social behavior are givens, and hence can be challenged. (I return to this topic in the section on 'Fathers in depth psychology'.)

LANGUAGE AND THE FILTER

These speculations of mine about the father, part of present-day pre-occupation with gender, are sometimes literal in nature, sometimes metaphorical, sometimes an alloy of these, sometimes – pluralistically – both. But sometimes the question I posed earlier, 'Is this to be understood literally or metaphorically?', seems to be more of a riddle, or just too limiting, and we have to consider questions of language in greater depth. The absence of a consensual language with which to discuss late modern parenting is not something to despair over. It is a marvellous moment to be alive and thinking. The absence of good language suggests in and of itself that these themes are of the greatest importance in cultural evolution. There is a gap waiting to be filled but the gap is also an abyss into which one might tumble.

What terms do we use to suggest that an understanding is *neither* literal nor metaphoric? I do not think a term for this category exists and I am reluctant to try to provide one. What happens is that one particular social or psychological theme becomes culturally and psychologically attached to 'father' or to 'mother'. The theme itself may often be relevant when discussing the other parent, but such discussion does not seem to happen save through the agency of the parent with whom the theme has *already* been more strongly connected on the cultural level (and on the level of social reality, of statistics). So if one is trying to discuss incest, it is more or less inevitable that the dynamics of the father–daughter relationship will intrude into the discussion *even if* the incestuous relationship being discussed is that of mother and son. This is not to say that mother and son are ruled out as participants in incestuous relating – how could they be? – but that the history of our culture, and hence of depth psychology, has highlighted or been fascinated by or has been 'led' by the father–daughter relationship when it comes to incest. It is as if the father–daughter relationship forms a *filter* through which one cannot help but look when trying to say something about incest, even when it is the incestuous dynamics of a completely different relationship that are being investigated. Cultural expression and psychological theorizing about the father–daughter relationship are the filters for cultural expression of and psychological theorizing about the incestuous properties of the mother–son relationship. Similar examples can be found of the expressive and theoretical dominance of one particular familial relationship. For instance, expression of, and theorizing about, trust between father and child is perceived through the filter of the more culturally sensitized expression of, and theorizing about, trust within the mother-child relationship.

One form of words which fits in with this way of thinking is to speak and write of 'the father of whatever sex', 'the mother of whatever sex', 'the son of whatever sex' and 'the daughter of whatever sex'. To avoid this cumbersome post-modern formulation, I often continue to use the terms 'father' and 'mother' and, if the confusion generated leads to questions about the limits of anatomy and biology when it comes to parenting, so much the better. What is more, such confusion challenges the primacy of heterosexuality as the overall frame in which these kinds of subjects are discussed. *Paradoxically, by working it through in a form of words that reflects the influence of biology and heterosexuality, one is forced to consider the limits of biology and heterosexuality.*

For these reasons, my own preference is to keep close to the old terms, rather than go for New Age tags such as 'Sky Parent' and 'Earth Parent', though noting what ideas and ideals are being aimed at by using such terms. I stay confused because there is something of value in the confusion, in having to work through the mixture of tradition, cultural overlay, modern aspiration and psychological theory that is the current gender and parent-role state of affairs. I do not want to settle important problems on a facile, terminological level only, eliminating confusion but running the risk of losing the cultural psychology locked up in the confusion altogether.

THE FATHER OF WHATEVER SEX

A question that undoubtedly arises is: How does a woman perform the father's functions – in particular, the function I have picked out, that of fostering psychological pluralism by twinning stability and fluidity? When a woman performs functions traditionally ascribed to fathers, is that woman functioning as a father or as a mother or as neither? This inter-weave of sex and function is also highlighted by the similar but perhaps better known, worried question: Is a man who nurtures a very small baby doing some mothering? In engaging with questions like these, one sees the consequences of the impossibility of finding a language that fits with our contemporary situation, itself underpinned by language. My view is indeed that a woman bringing up children on her own, or a woman bringing up children in a homosexual relationship, or a woman in a conventional marriage can perform what are usually regarded as paternal functions. But to state that this is *simply mothering*, part of an expanded female psychology, leaves no space for crucial cultural and political associations to the term 'father', nor for the possibility of any differ-entiation in parental role; our cultural reality is denied. To state that this is *simply fathering* that just happens to be carried out by a woman leaves no space for any importance to be given either to the biological sex of the woman or to female psychological experience; cultural reality is denied in another way. 'The father of whatever sex' is supposed to be a way of starting to discuss questions like these.

Of course, if one's view is that the absence of a male called father in and of itself exercises a decisively negative effect on the psychology of the situation, then there is much less of a conceptual problem. However, my action/research work with single parents suggests that there are no *inevitable* psychological outcomes of the single-parent state.[4] We have also to distinguish between different kinds of single parenthood and, what is more, bear single fathers in mind. Nevertheless, if single parenthood were to be taken on an absolutely literal level, and there is no father or male figure present, then, *reductio ad absurdum*, it would follow that nothing at all pertaining to the psychology of the father–child relationship will be going on in such a family.

I find this position totally unsatisfactory. I would not deny that single parents and their children experience particular problems but these are not 'purely' psychological; there are political, economic and cultural constraints on successful single parenting.[5] When a man fathers, or a woman mothers, there may be less strain but even two-parent families do not find these matters plain sailing. 'Father' and 'mother', those most fleshy of creatures, are also, and at the same moment, metaphors for different and overlapping aspects of parenting. We need to go on trying to retain a hold on the non-literal dimension so as not to be blinded by what seems like common sense, or deceived into accepting that what currently goes on is 'natural'. Here, we need to exercise extreme restraint about appealing to tradition. For tradition is easily employed to promote a notion of order – which usually means that women's activities, in particular, are decisively limited.

For instance, there is cultural furore and moral panic at the idea that two women living together in a homosexual relationship should feel themselves entitled to try to adopt or foster a child. Indeed, two women in such a situation are often regarded as bound to fail to provide 'adequate parenting'. I reject this view utterly on the basis of my clinical experience and my observation of all-female parents/couples in action. This is also an example of the kind of social development to which depth psychologists have failed to adjust. Yet we are going to see an increasing number of all-female parental couples in future as women who have had children in heterosexual relationships feel more free to translate into action their desire not to live with a man again. Of course, not all pairs of women bringing up children together are homosexual, but the moral panic I referred to does not spare these same-sex friendships between hetero-sexuals. Here, as in so many other instances, I am dismayed by the tendency of analysts and therapists to convert prejudices that they share with the non-psychological world into authoritative theory. (Everything I have written above applies to male homosexual couples as well with the additional feature that social disapproval takes the form of a fantasy about child sexual abuse, as if all homosexuals were abusers and heterosexual men were free of this taint.)

Clearly, if there is a marital or relationship breakdown, it is necessary for the adults in the picture to behave with psychological sensitivity. Children need age-appropriate information about what is happening, to remain in contact in most instances with the parent who is no longer there and to be allowed to continue as children and not become inappropriate partners to the parent who remains. An awareness of the problems attendant on remarriage or a new relationship is also important. But there are psychosocial dimensions beyond these precautionary measures that need to be addressed. What happens to children's levels of self-esteem and to their attitude to themselves if they lose a parent in a society that stigmatizes single parents and their families? Does the theory of a single-parent dominated underclass have no social effect on the lives of those about whom it theorizes? Does the low social status of a single parent have no impact at all on the way he or she relates to the children? The way in which single parenthood cultures family dynamics has to do with social as well as psychological factors. For example, the view that members of the underclass have been conditioned by generations of welfare receipts to be feckless and workshy has been contradicted by recent research.[6] It has been found that persons who are unemployed and living in single-parent households are more likely to want a job than unemployed persons in households containing two adults of working age plus children.

Hopefully, we need not remain in confusion for ever, only for as long as is necessary. Out of our confusion on the linguistic, emotional and cultural levels, all manner of discriminations and differentiations can take place. Consider the incestuous relationship between the father of whatever sex and the daughter of whatever sex. How is this different when the person designated the father is a man and that father person is a woman? If there are significant emotional differences, then these should be acknowledged in our theorizing. And if there are aspects of incestuous dynamics that are similar, whatever the sexes involved, then we need to know of them as well. What is more, given the ineradicable argumentativeness of depth psychology, which picks up on that identical tendency in the human psyche itself, a battle of perspectives will ensue. In one perspective, differences of tone in line with the actual sexes will be stressed. In the other perspective, common themes will be highlighted irrespective of the anatomies of the people involved. At the present time, we simply do not know the exact balance between differences introduced by the sex of the parent and those aspects of parenting that are the same for both sexes. Nor do we know much about differences introduced by the differing sexes of observers and theorists. I say this because, however these arguments work out, we should not overlook the ways in which psychological theorizing about parenting both mirrors and plays a part in hammering out cultural processes that lead to possible redistributions of political power.

FATHERS IN DEPTH PSYCHOLOGY

It is difficult to stay close to positive images of the father without tipping over into denial and idealization. There is very little description of ordinary, devoted, good-enough fathering; our preoccupation is with the sexually abusing or violent father. I can instance this problem by recounting something that happened to me. I published an article in a serious London newspaper in 1990 on positive aspects of the physical relationship between father and daughter. The editor asked their in-house illustrator to provide an illustration for the piece. This man was described as sophisticated and intelligent and he worked regularly on psychological and health features. He produced a picture of a grotesque, slavering head, part-dog, part-boar, part-man, despite the fact that it was the 'good father' he was supposed to be depicting. He had heard 'father and daughter' and reacted accordingly. The editor was mortified and I felt badly undermined. At first, in a spirit of complaint, I claimed this as an instance of the difficulty in getting heard when one wants to talk about anything other than the scandalous, scabrous father. Then, when I had got my sense of irony back, I could see that, between us, quite unwittingly, and in the spirit of Trickster, the illustrator and I had unearthed a more profound truth: That the pool of images out of which we construct our experiences of good and bad fathers is the same pool no matter whether the judgment is positive or negative. It follows that, in order to stay with positive images of the father, one has to stay with the negative images as well. This is somewhat different from having both extremes in one's mind at the same time, working across a positive–negative range of options. There is a seductive illusion that there is a spectrum of imagery divided by the midpoint of the range. Rather, I now understand the mix-up at the newspaper as showing that any description of the positive father that does not employ the very language and imagery of the negative father is going to be unrealistic and stunted. *Sex and aggression constitute the good father as well as the bad father.* The central implication of this is that we are required to pay maximum attention to *the father's body.* When the media concentrate on incest, they are expressing a fascination with the father's body. In its positive form, frolicking in the swimming pool; in its negative form, touching the child in an abusive way in the pool.

Cultural analysis of fathers needs to strike a balance between the psychological and the social methods of exploration. Often, it is not easy to strike this balance. For instance, it seems clear that, in spite of rhetoric to the contrary, the behavior of males in the home has not changed very much in recent years. Yet something clearly has changed in the aspirational atmosphere. So there is a contradiction between something internal and private, such as the ideal of sharing the tasks within a marriage, and what can be observed and tabulated by social scientists as the actual behaviors of men and women. From a psychological angle, the image of the father as an active player in the domestic drama is important. From a social science angle, the domestic oppression of women is something that still waits to be overcome. As a depth psychologist, I believe that the aspirational level is as interesting as the level of social reality, which is not at all to say that it is more important. For I also think that sociological observation of what is going on is required in an age of politically charged generalizing about the function and destiny of the family. (I return to this theme in Chapter 8, which is about 'men'.)

Having delineated the psychological and non-psychological methods of exploring what is happening to fathers, I want to say something specifically about the state of depth psychology today in relation to the father. There seems to be general agreement that Freud's version of the father – prohibiting and castrating – is altogether too negative.

With the rise of object relations and self-psychology theory in psychoanalysis since the 1940s, and the consequent emphasis on the mother–infant relationship, male analysts have had to accept that, within the clinical relationship, via the transference, they are experienced as female. Female analysts, to the contrary, do not report with anything like the same frequency that they are fantasized by their patients as having penises and beards. There may be other reasons for this than theoretical biases. One reason could be typical male arrogance: A man in our society can do anything he wishes to turn himself to – and being a mother in the transference is no exception! However, I think the predominance of theories which place mother–infant interaction at their core is the main factor with which to concern ourselves.

We should admit that, in spite of some efforts to rectify the situation, we lack an adequate account of the early, direct, 'pre-Oedipal' relationship of father and infant. In particular, there is a huge gap or silence over the part played by the father's body in an early, direct relationship with a baby. I would like to criticize what I see as the main strands in depth psychology's theorizing about the father's role in infancy. I think there are four main approaches. I will not say much about the first two because I go further into them in Chapter 11, which addresses the implications of depth psychology's current fascination with the mother–infant relationship.

First, there is what I call the 'insertion metaphor'. This can be most clearly discerned in Margaret Mahler's work. Like a huge penis, the father inserts himself between baby and mother so as to break up the symbiosis or fusion of which they are supposed to be unconscious. (The existence of such a fusionary state is itself disputed by many who have carried out observational studies of mother–infant interaction.) The idea seems to be that father, sternly but gently, turns the baby toward the world, toward 'his' world.[7] *It is claimed that his first contact of a significantly emotional kind with his child is to deprive the child.* In the insertion metaphor, the father is depicted as a somewhat isolated figure. I place this idea of Mahler's first because, to a considerable extent, it (or a version of it) represents a present-day consensus of opinion concerning father–child relating.

Second, there is a conception of paternal holding, derived from D. W. Winnicott's ideas about the mother's holding function in relation to a very small baby. Briefly stated, in this theory the father holds the mother who holds the baby. His access to the baby is via the mother and his main role is that of support. This idea of Winnicott's is contradicted by the findings of researchers into infant attachment patterns: 'Contrary to psychoanalytic expectation, the infant's relationship to his father cannot be predicted from the nature of his relationship to his mother. It is independent of it and reflects the qualities which the father himself had brought to the relationship.'[8] It is therefore vital not to see the father through Winnicottian eyes, through the eyes of a mother-centered psychology.

At times, Winnicott's ideas about the father seem rather strange. At one point, in a paper of 1959 entitled 'The effect of psychotic parents on the emotional development of the child', he seems to discount the effect of having had a psychotic father:

> Fathers have their own illnesses, and the effect of these on the children can be studied, but naturally, such illnesses do not impinge on the child's life in earliest infancy, and first the infant must be old enough to recognise the father as a man.[9]

On another, earlier occasion in 1944 the father is depicted as a totally remote figure whose function, even in connection with older children, is to disclose life outside the home:

> [The children] get a new world opened up to them when father gradually discloses the nature of the work to which he goes in the morning and from which he returns at night, or when he shows the gun that he takes with him into battle.[10]

To those who protest in Winnicott's defense that these statements reflect the mores and conditions of the times in which they were written, I can only reply: 'Precisely!'

Third, we can identify a dematerialization of the father so that he crops up in accounts of development solely as a metaphor, just a name or Name in a complicated psychosocial theorem, a third term. This approach, particularly in Lacan's writings, lacks a sustained recognition of the interplay between father's concrete, literal presence and his metaphorical function.

For Lacan, as John Forrester says,

the father's function is *strictly metaphorical* – he functions neither as real father (flesh and blood) nor as imaginary father (though he later figures in fantasy as an ideal or punitive agency) but as the Name of the Father, with his name assigning the child a place in the social world and allowing the child to become a sexed being through the phallic function (i.e. sign of sexual difference) to which the Name of the Father refers.[11]

As we saw earlier in this chapter, it is not really possible to divorce the literal and the metaphorical as Lacan does, neither for purposes of description nor as a mode of understanding. Hence, references by Lacan to the phallus cannot dismiss the fleshy actuality of the father's penis as the raw material from which the metaphor has fashioned itself.

According to Forrester's authoritative account, Lacan 'affirms the centrality for the subject's history of the triadic Oedipus complex' and gives us a 'revised version of Freud's Oedipus complex'.[12] While this is certainly so, we should not overlook the way in which the Lacanian Oedipus complex and Lacan's account of the father's role rests utterly on a simplistic and highly arguable narrative of mother–infant relations. Lacan is a prisoner of psychic determinism; if the Oedipus complex follows earlier stages of development, then it cannot avoid having been conditioned by them. Lacan is not totally in thrall to chronology, for the unconscious is not structured like a clock. But the Lacanian Oedipus complex requires the pre-existence of a state of symbiosis or fusion between mother and infant. That symbiosis would not, or could not, dissolve or rupture without the father's insertion of himself between mother and infant. Lacan is no more than a crude Mahlerian here: The mother–infant relation is assumed not to contain any capacity *within itself* for the separating out and subsequent psychological development of the infant. The father–infant relation is assumed not to exist, or is not mentioned, until the mother–infant relationship, taking place within a fantasy of non-differentiation, is firmly established. Paradoxically, the centrally important father–child relationship is only constellated and brought into being by its target: The fused, 'dual unity' of mother and infant.

Do these various ideas and assumptions stand up?

There is a suspiciously neat symmetry in Lacan's theory, and he falls victim to the seduction of morphological analogy. Mother and infant enjoy an imaginary fusion. This fusion is broken up by (a) the father as the third term on an inexorable road to the Oedipus complex, and (b) language, bringing with it a plethora of social and cultural imperatives. Therefore, because (a) and (b) seem to fulfill the same function, language and the father are claimed to be more-or-less the same. Language certainly operates in the closest possible concert with the social and political status quo. This means that language is both creator *and* creature of the social system. It follows that the father, too, is both representative and builder of a repressive and static social reality, and constrained and limited by social reality, which has power over him. But Lacan fails to notice the lack of power of the individual father in the face of social reality, and so Lacan consequently fails to notice that society's repressive 'father' is not the only father there is. That is why, for Lacan, *le nom du père* is generally *le non du père*. Hence, there is no possible place for a subversive and radical account of the father. This is but one problem with Lacan's theory of the father.

The claim that infants fuse with their mothers in early development does not stand up as an objective account of what goes on at that time. The point is that, if fusionary states do *not* exist in the way Lacan presupposes them to exist, then the father *cannot* have the functions that Lacan ascribes to him, portrayed in a contradistinctive and even complementary manner to the functions of the mother. And they do not. Observational work on mother–infant interaction has seriously undermined theories that postulate some kind of 'normal autism' or 'primary narcissism' as the earliest mental state of the infant.[13] Instead, what is nowadays being noted is the existence of an intense conversation or proto-conversation between mother and infant, and, where this can be observed, between father and infant as well. The extent of mutual communication is massive. *Even the small baby is not necessarily operating in a world of fantasy.* In my view, babies may well fantasize that they are 'at one' with their mothers and fathers but these fusionary fantasies exist in an interplay with more communicative and interactive styles of functioning. That is, the presence and healing function of at-oneness is guaranteed by the implicit knowledge of mother and baby that this is phase-appropriate fantasy. In short, there is nothing that needs breaking up by the father. Separation from mother need not be a bloody business.

The last point requires underlining. The claim by Lacan (not to mention Mahler and Winnicott) that there is a mother–infant fusionary relationship that the father must rupture for mental health to result simply does not recognize that babies *themselves* desire to grow and separate from the mother as well as to rest in permanent oceanic bliss. Mothers, too, may sense that they have other things to do with their time than remain immersed in primary maternal preoccupation, characterized by devotion to their baby, and with the goal of achieving a good-enough fit between environment and inner world. Where would Lacan's theory be if the capacity of the early fusionary fantasy state to overcome itself were acknowledged? There is an inbuilt capacity of symbiosis to self-destruct. *Babies and mothers have an investment in separation* and to overlook this is to insult babies and mothers.

Crucially, where is there in Lacan an account of the pre-Oedipal father–infant relationship? I suggest that Lacan was as culture-bound as anyone else. Could a conscious recognition of the positive, direct, physical, affirming father–infant relationship, dating from the earliest moment, have been possible in the France either of Lacan's childhood (born in 1901) or during his adult life of psychoanalytic theory-making?

Although Lacan's position seems anti-essentialist, and this is one reason why there has been enthusiasm for his ideas in feminist and other political circles, there is also an element of eternalism in the theory. Lacan confuses what is the case now with what has always been the case, and with what will always be the case. If this were not so, then Lacan would have no difficulty with the idea of a more positive image of and role for the father in the psychological development of the individual. There is a lack of reference to social and political factors as these impact on psychic reality, and a lack of reference to historical mutability. For Lacan, power often seems to be a purely symbolic factor and this omission undermines the contribution he can make to debates about gender relations. Moreover, the ways in which fathering is affected by class or ethnic factors are not entered into. I agree with Page du Bois's criticism of Lacan (and of those feminist thinkers who have been influenced by him):

> To continue to consider the phallus as the transcendental signifier, to accept the inevitability of the 'idea' of transcendence, . . . to believe that the phallus and language control us . . . all this seems to me only to perpetuate a metaphysics of wholeness, presence, deism, and worship of the symbolic father. On the other hand, to see how such an ideology supports relations of male dominance, class and racial hierarchy, and the humility of the universally castrated might perhaps allow us to imagine democracy.[14]

Reading Lacan on the father, I have been struck by a resemblance to the ways in which Jung writes about the psychologies of men and women. (This is the *fourth* strand of depth psychological theorizing about the father.) There is the same conflation of the specific or cultural moment and what is claimed to be eternal or universal. There is the same attempt to move the debate in a metaphorical direction – Jung writes of 'the masculine' and 'the feminine', both of which are, in principle, available to people of either sex. There is the same misunderstanding of the role of anatomy in the emergence of symbols. Lacan's perception of his particular social situation, in which fathers do not have an early nurturing role, may have led him to depict the phallus, undeniably the symbol of the father, solely as signifying a penetrative penis. Similarly, Jung's perception of dream and fantasy images of the other sex, which he called animus and anima, overlooked the culturally contingent nature of the symbolic communication in the dream or fantasy. Images of men in a woman's inner world and images of women in a man's inner world refer to unconscious potentials as yet unrealized and not to specific characteristics of literal men and women.[15]

At times, the psyche employs images of the present-day social reality of men and women to express psychic reality. If, in our culture, there are more and easier ways for a man to express aggression than there are for a woman, then a woman's unconscious might represent her aggressive potentials by means of a male personification. But it would not be 'male' aggression that has engaged her; nor would it be 'female' aggression, even though she is a woman. It would merely be aggression. However, the fact that images of her aggression are encased in a man's body is far from unimportant for a political analysis. Indeed, this highlights the need to get to grips with the interplay between metaphor and literalism and, hence, between psychic reality and social reality as these are experienced by males and females, fathers and mothers, sons and daughters. We do not know enough about the articulations between social and psychic realities. As Teresa Brennan says:

> How changing the sex of either the intervening third party or the primary care-giver, or the actual father's social position, would affect the process of differentiation is another matter; but real changes in either parenting patterns or the social position of women and men must have consequences for the symbolic.[16]

While I would not think of these matters mainly in terms of the 'consequences for the symbolic', her Lacanian terminology should not obscure the fact that the explicit and implicit questions in Brennan's statement constitute my project in this chapter and the next one. I *am* concerned with 'the intervening third party', 'the primary care-giver', 'the actual father's social position', 'the process of differentiation' (particularly mother–daughter differentiation and the father's role therein), 'real changes in parenting patterns' and 'the social position of women and men'.

Continuing this survey of post-Freudian depth psychological

approaches to the father, we come to Jung's theory of the father archetype. Concisely, Jung ignores the *cultural* construction of the father–child relationship as he seeks to identify its essential and universal features.

If we explore the father–infant relationship, we see that it is a culturally constructed relationship. The father–infant relation is constructed out of the interaction of two other relationships: The primary bond between mother and infant, and the pair bond between man and woman. A male person does not become a father in any full sense unless there is interplay between these two other relationships. For the man's role could easily cease at conception. Realizing that the father is culturally constructed leads to all kinds of rather exciting possibilities. If the father relation is a product of two other relationships, and hence of culture, then it cannot be approached via absolute definition; it is a completely relative and situational matter. Once this is accepted, then a new judgment is required concerning what sometimes seems like hopelessly idealistic attempts to change the norms about the father's role. The father's role can change because, written into the definition of the father's role is the power to refuse absolute definition. This refusal is possible because of male power and because of the cultural construction of the father relation and, hence, its historical mutability. *The archetypal element is that there is no father archetype*; the father relation features a lack of innate features.

There are implications of this discussion of the father archetype for the ideas of animus and anima and for the possibility of change in what constitutes 'the father', 'the mother', 'the son' and 'the daughter'. As I stated earlier, animus and anima images are not of men and women because animus and anima are 'masculine' and 'feminine'. For an individual woman or man, the anatomy of the other sex is a metaphor for the richness, potential and mystery of the other. A man will imagine what is 'other' to him in the symbolic form of a woman – a being with another anatomy. A woman will symbolize what is foreign to her in terms of the kind of body she does not herself have. Animus and anima signify unconscious potentials within a person – the kind of *psychological* characteristics they do not themselves (yet) have. They do this as part of a *physiological* metaphor.

Socialization means that there will be certain behaviors that are, typically, unavailable (or said to be unavailable) to women. Inasmuch as these behaviors do become available to a person, they become the behaviors of that person and not the behaviors of the animus or anima that symbolizes them. If and when a father extends his range of behaviors within the family in relation to his children, we should remember that it is his achievement and responsibility, not that of his anima.

UNCOMPLEMENTARITY

At the base of each of the four approaches I have outlined is an attitude to the father based on *the complementary role* he plays to that of the mother. The complementarity of mother and father is taken for granted – and I want to dispute the assumption of complementarity. Any expression of complementarity usually requires two lists, and this instance is no exception.

The following lists were drawn up by a female colleague for a symposium in which we both participated on 'The Father's Role in Institutions':

Mothering	Fathering
care (and its envy)	power (and its envy)
nurturance	affirmation
sameness	difference
togetherness	aloneness
subjectivity	objectivity
emotion	knowledge
acting out	interpretation
equality	inequality, rivalry and competition
informality	formality, law and order
fear of intrusion (depletion)	fear of punishment (castration)
introjection and projection	repression and resistance
fantasy	language

I propose to spend some time discussing these lists and the complementary approach. The lists are particularly interesting for a number of reasons. To begin with, the symposium was not confined to the arena of the family; the social dimension was built into its title. Therefore the categories listed had outer world as well as inner world relevance. The list-making method rests on our seemingly ineradicable tendency to think in terms of binary pairs. In this instance, the fact that the mother was given the left-hand column is important for, given that we read from left to right, this makes her the parent on whom the complementary comparison is based. When it comes to a depth psychological account of parenting the tables are turned and the usual gender hierarchy is reversed: It is *the father* who is now the permanent Other, the other parent. I recall an impassioned discussion in my own family about whether it was appropriate or humiliating to refer to me, the father, as doing some babysitting! Does a father babysit his own children? The father is usually portrayed as the other parent, and this has disastrously handicapped other possible excavations of his role.

When my colleague presented her lists, I was cautious and critical for the reasons I have just outlined. But if the lists are *themselves* taken as indicative of a divide or tension within any human being engaged in parenting, irrespective of the sex of the person, then a different utility for them appears. The tension between the two columns is a tremendous tension within a parent, not a tension between two parents. What is more, within each separate pair of terms, it is possible to remove the 'mother' and 'father' tags altogether. So the tension between emotion and knowledge, say, irradiates anybody's parental experience and may play a distinctively enriching part in that experience. Initially, mother and father lists do need to be made, and then rejected as definitory statements. After that, the residue of complementarity can be used creatively to illuminate the original problem. I am certainly not suggesting that all these opposite qualities can simply flourish in any parent; rather what any parent experiences and exemplifies are *the contradictions themselves*.

Another way of addressing the issue is to ask from where in human ideation such lists come. If one single person encompasses such formidable tensions, then a high level of anxiety is likely to follow. Humans deal with anxiety in a number of ways; two of these are splitting and projection. What happens is that the anxiety spawned by these contradictions is handled by projecting the split within each of us onto the most convenient receptors for the projection: women and men. At the same time, historical economic and social forces constitute the material base for some kind of division. Putting the intrapsychic and the socio-economic factors together, an irresistible pressure for a clear, indeed overclear, line of demarcation based on complementarity builds up.

Although I have indicated that we can use the list-making tendency, it has to be employed with care and discrimination. Otherwise we end up with statements by psychoanalysts like this one of Meltzer's:

> The concept of husband, as provident manager of the overall space of the community, would seem to be in keeping with psychic reality. As provider and guardian of the space where the mother rears the children, a differential of spheres of influence and responsibility is clear-cut. One might say that it is his estate and her children, in the sense of responsibility rather than possession, as he faces outwards towards the community and she faces inwards towards the children.[17]

Now, it is not enough merely to want to overturn such a statement, either as theory or as description of (psychic or social) reality. I would not argue that, at the present time, such a description is factually wrong, or dispute that it fits many if not most families. But I do want to reveal that such statements have a persuasive intention and to dispute that the statement describes something 'natural' or offers a full, or even full-enough account of the father's role in infancy and childhood.

For depth psychologists, the problem is not primarily one of changing the social facts but of changing our psychological interpretation of them so that the full range of the father's role is revealed, including his so-far repressed political capacity to free-up the inner and outer processes of other people.

Nor is it enough to advocate a state of androgyny as a cure for problems caused by rigid gender divisions, for there will always be two sexes and, hence, the social and psychological conditions for cultural bifurcation will always be present. The human need for differentiation will play its part as each sex fantasizes about what distinguishes it from the other sex.

Though appeals to androgyny do represent wishful thinking, it is certainly important to challenge the heterosexist frame within which most discussions about fathering and mothering are conducted. Throughout the chapter, I have tried to maintain such a challenge. This is not a challenge to the existence of heterosexuality (or homosexuality) but a fierce resistance to the prepackaging of depth psychological interpretations of human sexuality. Frankly, at the moment depth psychology lacks a theoretical approach to homosexual development that takes account of its specifics and recognizes that 'homosexuality' is not a unitary state and that there are numerous differing kinds of homosexual relationship, many of which cannot be understood simply by tracing off maps of heterosexual development (themselves equally suspect).

It is certainly not enough to move the whole matter onto an exclusively interior level, so that each father is said to have an inner mother inside him and each mother to have an inner father inside her. I used to think well of such an interior perspective but I have grown deeply suspicious of its facile nature. What is most problematic in such approaches is that they are bound to deploy a kind of universal heterosexuality to explain how it is that fathers can mother and vice versa. So a father's nurturing capacity is said to be available to him via his 'feminine' element, the anima. But nurturance is a male capacity – just as aggression is available to women – and does not require anything 'feminine' for its coming into being.

FATHER PSYCHOLOGY AND MOTHER PSYCHOLOGY

It is tempting to try to construct a presentation of the mother relation in terms that are complementary to the way I have presented the father relation. The mother relation would then seem redolent of biology, archetypal foundations and innate features rather than of cultural mutability. But the more one works on the father relation as a cultural construction, the clearer it becomes that the mother relation *also* resists being defined in biological or sociobiological terms. Once we acquire a culturally sensitive eye with regard to parenting, then the whole edifice of motherhood as a natural phenomenon can be freshly investigated. And then Luce Irigaray's question becomes pressing: 'Without the exploitation of the body-matter of women, what would become of the symbolic process that governs society?'[18]

Acknowledging the cultural construction of the father relation, as Winnicott, Lacan and Jung, among others, fail to do, does not mean that the father's connection to his children must lack the emotional intensity of the mother's relation to her children. And this brings us to a political point. If the lack of nature, but not of intensity, in the father relation hints at a lack of nature in the mother relation, then everything we think about families, and the kind of family psychology we make, becomes an open rather than a closed field. This means that families with marginal, deviant styles of organization take on yet another burden: That of pathfinders, explorers of differing ways of running families and of thinking about them, a form of laboratory for the majority.

Undermining the edifice of maternal psychology is more than the work of a dissident child. It is a political move, for the most devastating argument against any change is that change is, *a priori*, out of the question. When we look at single-parent families, we can see how these various political points can be welded together. That is, single parents help us to reveal the lack of nature in the mother relation. Once the mother is released from her 'natural' prison, then questions about the organization of families and societies can be asked – the kinds of questions usually deflected by reference to tradition, biology, unconscious phantasy, orders, archetypes and common sense. To turn to Irigaray once again: 'Woman [is] reproducer of the social order, acting as the infrastructure of that order; all of western culture rests upon the murder of the mother . . . . And if we make the foundation of the social order shift, then anything shifts.'[19]

For the moment, we are still working the father's field, the field of the murder of the father. We require an approach to the father that is simultaneously literal and metaphoric if we are to shift *his* particular reproduction of the social order. As I admitted earlier, this will indeed have to be a confused approach. In order to communicate despite the confusion and to pay heed to the 'filters' on our theorizing, I have decided to retain a culturally conventional framework in which to present the next chapter. First, father/daughter/sex, and then father/son/aggression.

Hopefully, the fluidity embedded in these terms, at least as I use them, means that the limitations of this approach are not too oppressive. The structure may even constitute a special kind of subversion. Maybe the medium is the message here, and frustration at the heterosexist way I have organized the following chapter can be seen as reflecting ineluctable frustrations dwelling in the issues themselves; I return to this point in due course.

Chapter 7

Political readings of paternal imagery

ON FATHERING DAUGHTERS

At the height of the Cleveland affair (a child sex abuse scandal in Britain), my next-door neighbor confessed to me that he was frightened to cuddle his two-year-old daughter in public. The moral panic over child sexual abuse was reinforcing difficulties which many fathers have over physical aspects of their relationships with their daughters. Years later, when some daughters enter analysis, past inhibitions about bodily contact and the apparent failure to establish a warm, shared physical contact with the father turn out to have been very wounding. In a sense, these wounds are at the opposite extreme from the wounds caused by actual incest, but they generate their own brand of profound psychic pain. The understandable stress on the avoidance and detection of incest masks this other, more subtle problem.

In a determinedly heterosexual world, boys have an easier time of it than girls. This is because, for cultural reasons, their mothers are more used to being physical in relation to children of either sex. They are not as alarmed by the bodily dimension and by their feelings about their sons as fathers generally are by their feelings about their daughters. I am thinking of the physical experiences of pregnancy, childbirth and feeding and the ways in which women have to process such experiences.

What kind of damage results from the exclusion of physicality from the father–daughter relationship? There are three developmental issues to consider here. First, when the girl is a baby or small child, her father's inhibition, expressed in his handling of her, cannot help in the formation of a positive attitude toward her own body, a sense of its 'rightness', beauty, power and integrity. The image many women have of themselves as weaker than they are may stem in part from this particular lack.

Second, when the girl reaches adolescence, the physically inhibited father can have a destructive impact on her emerging sexuality. This can be seen happening in many ways: Excessive prohibitions about her activities with boys, mocking her sexuality, and general up-tightness. Of course, a degree of jealousy may be no bad thing, in that it confirms to the daughter that her father does have a positive regard for her. For there is no doubt that one sort of attack that a father can make on his daughter's emerging sexuality is to ignore it altogether, leaving 'that sort of thing' to the mother.

The third kind of damage that results from physical inhibition between father and daughter is more difficult to portray. It has to do with the positive side of romantic, even sexual fantasy, such as is typically found in most families – wishing to marry the parent of the opposite sex, or to have babies with them. This normal fantasizing is not to be confused with actual incest, although – and this is a problem with writing about these matters – actual incest may result from incest fantasies that have got out of control.

Such fantasies cannot be adequately understood as the child wanting intercourse with the parent and a response to them on that level is totally inappropriate. Adults who take them as such are mistaken and destructive. We need to understand these fantasies on the part of the child symbolically and metaphorically. Many years ago, Jung developed the idea that the child's fantasies and wishes concerning the parents express a longing to grow by means of being regenerated, or even reborn.[1] The purpose of such fantasy is to make contact with the grounds of one's being, a kind of refuelling that makes subsequent maturation easier. The parents represent the refuelling station.

Getting really close to someone who is psychologically more developed than you are leads to enrichment of the personality. We grow inside to a very large extent by relating to someone outside. In childhood, that 'someone' is usually the mother or father, though in single-parent families the child may be more likely to involve other adults to aid the growth processes. But what is it that enables us to get that close in the first place? *It is the physical, bodily, erotic element in family relationships that helps psychological growth to occur.*

I use the word 'erotic' deliberately because the range of associations is in itself important. References to the erotic *do or do not* conjure up images of genital sexuality depending on one's outlook, the particular context and ideology. It is significant that Freud chose a term with sexual connotations (Eros) to encapsulate the life instincts.[2] Jung, too, covers surprisingly similar ground. For Jung, Eros is sometimes equated with sexuality.[3] But, at other times, Eros is an archetypal principle of connectedness, relatedness and harmony.[4] It seems that the physical dimension and the psychological and spiritual dimensions cannot be divorced. Therefore we should be careful of accounts of 'the erotic' that are over-precise, seeking to make a sharp differentiation from sexuality and referring to 'love' or 'intimacy'. Such accounts can be a form of resistance to accepting that incestuous sexual fantasies are mixed in with the human impulse toward psychological growth via the agency of interpersonal relating. The genitals are implicated in every level of psychological growth.

As I said in the previous chapter, I am not trying to deny the mother's role in the complex pattern of processes that enter into psychological development. But if our focus is quite deliberately on the father, then we must say that the erotically inhibited father is going to be useless as an assistant in his daughter's inner growth. He cannot actually stop her from fantasizing about him, but he can send a message, on the bodily level, that such fantasies are not welcome.

PSYCHOLOGICAL PLURALISM AND THE DAUGHTER

A social and political problem faced by many women (and, increasingly, men are sensing that the same is true for them as well) is how to enjoy and suffer the many and varied facets of life while, at the same time, retaining a coherent and integrated sense of being a woman (or a man). How to be a mother, wife, lover, career woman and how to individuate – develop psychologically – via (or in spite of) all these roles.[5] *As far as this particular political problem is concerned, I think that the part played by the father is crucial.* The outcome of a woman's struggle to feel psychologically and socially whole and integrated at the same time as being psychologically and socially diversified is, to a great extent, fashioned within the father–daughter relationship.

In my practice I have seen several women who seem to occupy a cultural and psychological position somewhere between the traditional and the contemporary. There is often a pervasive sense of failure. Let me recount the story of a woman patient from whom I learned a great deal about the father–daughter relationship. When Beatrice came to see me for analysis, she told me she was having trouble 'holding it all together'. At home, she was finding it increasingly difficult to cope with her seven-year-old son whose emotional demands often seemed like a form of cannibalism. Her relationship with her husband (a struggling sculptor) was torn by power struggles and colored by Beatrice's growing fear that she was losing her sexual allure and that, at any moment, he would leave her. At work, she suffered from a crippling lack of self-confidence in dealing with colleagues (mainly male) of far less ability. She would become tongue-tied and blush. But on her own, in her office, she had no such problems and her scientific papers and books were beginning to win her an international reputation. One consequence of her growing fame was the opportunity for foreign travel to conferences or to give lectures – which made the domestic frictions even worse. Sometimes Beatrice fantasized giving up work altogether and settling down to be a *hausfrau*; at other times, she would imagine leaving home and family to dedicate herself to work.

Beatrice's father had been a prisoner of war. She did not have a regular relationship with him until she was six. When the family started to live together, he seems to have assumed a paternal authority which, as Beatrice saw it, he had not earned. One of her early memories was lying in the bath when her father returned from the war and, meeting him as if for the first time, saying that she would call him 'uncle' if he was not nice to her. As Beatrice could not or would not acknowledge her father's dominant position within the family, his attitude to her remained distant, disapproving and prohibitive. For example, he found her interest in science inexplicable and was hostile to it. Beatrice's mother was a successful businesswoman who constantly complained to Beatrice about how awful her married life was. Eventually, when Beatrice was in her teens, her parents separated. Her mother died when Beatrice was twenty-five and she found herself having to steer her father through the stresses and strains of old age. She hated having to visit him and I think it would be fair to say that the role of 'daughter' was yet another diversification – and one that was much resented.

My view is that the father's affirming physical response to his daughter at all stages of her life helps her to achieve a kind of psychological pluralism (to be one person and many persons). It is the father who communicates to his daughter that 'You can be this . . . and this . . . and this . . . and still be your (female) self.' I am not suggesting that the father gives *permission* for his daughter to flourish in a career, or that the daughter's perception of her mother's behavior is irrelevant. But when it comes to a matter of *combining different behaviors into a satisfying whole without losing the special satisfactions attached to each*, then the father's role is important, as we see in Beatrice's case.[6]

When these various processes are going well enough, the daughter is receiving confirmation from the father that, in his mind, she is not restricted to the role of mother. This is a political message. One hopes it is not accompanied by downplaying the value of motherhood. But the crucial thing is that a physical, even erotic connection between father and daughter is what signifies that she is *not* only a maternal creature. The erotic requires a political re-reading: The erotic factor as a kind of gateway to the various paths that are, or might be, available to a woman, even in our culture. The daughter is not *liberated* by the father in the sense of being led into pastures new. Rather, his positive physical and erotic communication fosters and brings out potentials in her which are already there. 'You are this . . . and this . . . and this . . . and you're still you.'

There is a social, cultural and political importance to be brought out of this description. Acknowledgment and acceptance of the daughter's bodily integrity and sexuality helps her to differentiate herself from the role of mother. In other words, the father acts as an influence on the daughter so that she can begin to explore her full potential, not restricted to the role of mother. To explore the spiritual path, the vocational path, the path of solidarity with the travails of other women, the path of an integration and acceptance of her assertive and aggressive side, the path of sexual expression, and to retain a sense of personal identity.

A good-enough father–daughter relationship supports the overthrow of restrictions placed on women. Once a girl, or woman, learns in the relationship with her father that she is something other than a mother, she can begin to explore just who it is that she might be, without losing sight of the fact that, if she desires it, she *can* be a mother. This would be a realistic extension of the slogan 'a woman's right to choose'.

Women have suffered enormously from narrow definitions of what it means to be female, from the requirement that they be unaggressive and selfless creatures who relate, who are responsive to the needs of others, who *react* but do not *act*. True, as *mothers* of small children, maybe something like this has to be done at times. But as *persons* women can sniff out other vistas and ways of being. It is the young woman's apperception of herself as an erotic creature, facilitated by her bodily connection to her father, that enables her to spin through a variety of psychological pathways, enjoying the widest spectrum of meanings inherent in the ideogram 'woman'. The father's first, literal, fertilization with his female partner helped to make the female baby. His second metaphorical fertilization with his daughter helps to conceive the female adult, *who is then free to drop her father when and if she needs to.*

There would be little point in replacing a femininity which pleases Mummy with a femininity which pleases Daddy. Moving beyond mother and father, though obviously in relation to them, today's female adult can, more than before perhaps, be considered as a multifaceted, plural woman-person, able to grow in all manner of unpredictable ways.

This is a vulnerable business, and not just because of an unsympathetic milieu. A mother who cannot understand what is happening can destroy it by jealousy, whereas a mother who has herself had this kind of experience will support erotic playback. A father whose own sexual development has been damaged may not be able to keep the physical element within bounds. But there's a paradox here: The father–daughter relationship has to be *physical* enough to allow for the experiential – and political – outcome I have been depicting. I call the mixture of physical, physiological and political communication 'erotic playback' and the good-enough father plays a full part in providing it.

This means that, alongside our interest in the father who delivers an excess of erotic communication and attention, we should also try to focus on a less apparent form of paternal deprivation. Quite understandable concentration on erotic excess, for example child sexual abuse, has made it very hard to stay with erotic deficit. Moreover, as I mentioned, there is a risk of being misunderstood as advocating incest. Therefore I suggest that we begin to think of *an optimal erotic relation between father and daughter and, hence, of the pathology of a failure to achieve that.* Eventually, the daughter and her father have to renounce their admitted longings for each other, and such mutual renunciation is itself an affirmation of the daughter's erotic viability.

These ideas about the physical father–daughter relationship are intended to sustain a less literal reading and to point up the existence of the psychological and cultural filters through which we see similar processes in other relationships. Erotic playback is something provided by the father of whatever sex for the daughter of whatever sex. Daughters need erotic playback from their mothers, and sons need it from their fathers. But whichever dyadic relationship we are discussing will be inflected by the erotic dynamics of the father–daughter relationship functioning as a filter. Later, we shall see how concentration on aggression within the father–son relationship acts as a template and a filter for ideas about aggression in the mother–daughter, mother–son, father–daughter and sibling relationships. We can only reach the psychological specificity of each relationship if we become aware of the presence of the template and filter of another more culturally recognized relationship.

The emotive importance of the question of women's ability to combine different behaviors into a psychological coherence is illustrated by the preoccupation of women's magazines with it: The famous subject of a lifestyle profile talks of the 'balancing act' she has to perform in order to meet her needs, her children's needs and her husband's needs. The grotesque yet fascinating oversimplification of 'superwoman' or 'supermom' underlines how much guilty energy is being consumed.

Beatrice's lifelong fight with her father was the sole source of erotic playback, and it was not enough. She tried hard to keep her aggression out of her marriage and under control at work but was consumed by a terror that there would be a catastrophic explosion. What she found difficult to face was the sense of satisfaction she attained via her aggressive impulses and fantasies. In the analysis at least, she did not discover ways of achieving intimacy other than aggression. For, when negative feelings toward the analysis and toward me began to surface, she withdrew.

I must stress that erotic playback is not dependent on whether the father is recalled as having been nice and understanding toward his daughter, though a loving father is more likely to be an optimally erotic father than, say, a physically violent one. But I have encountered numerous women who have had the erotic playback from fathers who do not fit a liberal, bourgeois description of a 'good' father.

Taking these ideas on board suggests a new and more political reading of clinical material concerning incestuous fantasy and, above all, the erotic transference. Despite Freud's original understanding of an Oedipal developmental phase, the erotic transference is often regarded nowadays as a secondary eroticization of something to do with feeding, or with the mother–infant relationship in general.

FATHER AND SON: THE PLURALITY OF AGGRESSION

'Aggressive playback' exists alongside erotic playback and aggression is the main focus of this section on the father–son relationship. The aggressive father plays back to the aggressive son that there is a plurality of aggressive styles and that movement between the styles of aggression is possible. I see the main problem with aggression on both the personal and the political levels as that of being trapped in one particular style of aggression. Much fear of the consequences of aggressive fantasy can be understood as a fear of playing permanently on one aggressive note.

Neither depth psychologists nor social scientists have done enough work on the phenomenology, imagery and details of aggression. A great deal has been written about *defensive* processes that handle the anxiety caused by unmanageable aggressive impulses and fantasies, but depth psychologists have not explored aggression in itself as fully as they have explored sexuality.

Whether we like it or not, aggression and the father are linked in our minds. For example, many writers have concluded that men are innately more aggressive than women for genetic and neurophysiological reasons. Our culture takes this for granted. However, more recently, numerous researchers, with whom I am in agreement, have disputed this consensus.

For example, Gerda Siann found that the evidence does not show any clear and unambiguous relationship between male hormones and the propensity to display violent behavior or feel aggressive emotion. Siann points out that environmental and social variables have a good deal to do with the secretion of male hormones and also emphasizes evidence that discovered a role for female hormones in violent behavior and aggressive emotion.[7]

A depth psychological approach to social phenomena means that one has to take cultural generalization and consensus into account at the same time as offering a critique of these. The risk in the present instance is that discussing the father–son relationship in terms of aggression will itself be taken as reinforcing the cultural prejudice concerning male aggression. This is not my intention, as I hope my comments above made clear.

Many divisions of the term aggression can be made. There is creative, self-assertive aggression, and then there is destructive or sadistic aggression. The difficulty with this division concerns who is to say which it is! Or one can regard aggression in terms of erotogenic zones and identify aggressions developmentally, noting, for instance, the biting aggression of early oral fantasy. Other aggressions pertain to other developmental phases of life such as the aggression that promotes the infant's separation from extreme physical dependency on the parents.

A somewhat different and more imaginative way to particularize aggression is to employ the human body as an index for aggression. Then we can observe and experience head aggression, a verbal onslaught, for example. Or chest aggression, exemplified by the ambivalence of the bear hug. Or genital aggression – pornography, Don Juanism or the materialistic sexual thrills of the acquisitive tycoon. Arm aggression suggests a whole range of images and acts: From striking a blow with a weapon to strangulation with bare hands. Leg aggression is often practiced by fathers against their sons; leg aggression means running or walking away. Anal aggression smears another's achievements, perhaps by snide comments – what the early encounter group jargon called 'coming out sideways'.

When father and son confront each other aggressively, the potential range of aggressions will be immense. But this does not always operate in a neat symmetry: The son's anal aggression might be met by his father's head aggression. The son makes a mess and the father calls him messy. The father's leg aggression is often countered by the son's chest aggression, and the child's hold on the father's lower limbs as the latter leaves the room should not be taken as implying only true love.

In the relationship between fathers and sons of whatever sex, a whole range of aggressive experience is being mapped out – without losing sight of the fact that it is all still 'aggression'. This is why I speak of a plurality of aggression, or of aggressive pluralism: Many different styles of aggression, with many different features, and yet having *something* in common by being part of the larger, more unified idea of aggression. Pluralistically, the different styles of aggression are themselves in a competitive, aggressive relationship with each other. So, for example, head aggression and leg aggression struggle with each other to be the primary or even sole mode of aggressive performance. In the example I gave at the start of the previous chapter, playing a trick on my son out-competed the alternatives of shouting, smacking or lecturing him – and out-competed all the non-aggressive options as well.

Aggression, and competition *between* the aggressions, are important in themselves, and also as the means of guaranteeing that there can be movement between the various styles. As far as the father–son relationship is concerned, movement between the styles of aggression is crucial. However, the father–son relationship is not only the beneficiary of such movement between the styles of aggression, so that father and son do not get hooked up on experiencing one style of aggression to the exclusion of all the other styles. *The father–son relationship is also the place in which movement between the styles is worked upon and developed.* Hence, the father–son aggressive relation provides the possibility of there being transformations *within* aggression. This means that antisocial, sado-masochistic, unrelated aggression can be transformed, by the physical and non-physical agency of the father–son relationship, into socially committed, self-assertive, related aggression.

Many male patients, and not a few female patients, report experiences of a 'dry' father. This father concentrates on getting the son of whatever sex to conform to ideals and values held by the collective. Thus even a dry father himself conforms to what a father is supposed to do – to deal with matters of conscience and morality within the family. But the dry way of going about this lacks a passionately spiritual element, lacks a certain kind of aggressive spirituality. There is no aggression in the dry father's playing of the father's role and this raises massive problems for the son concerning the fate of his aggressive impulses and fantasies, particularly those directed against the father. Dry fathers seem to select one way of communicating aggressively and stick to their guns; they miss out on the mercurial aspects of aggression and hence whatever creative potential might ultimately emerge. One patient whose experience of his father fitted this description was troubled by recurrent fantasies of dismembering women and stuffing their amputated limbs into the vagina. This particular fantasy differs only in its extreme viciousness from the aggressive fantasies directed against women that have emerged in my clinical work with numerous male patients. The patient who fantasized dismemberment of women entered a collusive relationship with his father in which their joint and unexpressed aggressions against an apparently dominant wife and mother served as a shield behind which their mutual aggression remained hidden. The father was not absent, not violent, not unreasonable. In fact, he was loyal, decent, progressive – but lacking in a particular kind of energy and commitment toward his son's evolving patterns of aggression.[8] The point is that, often, there *are* no evolving patterns of aggression. There is aggressive fantasy and even aggressive discharge but it does not go anywhere; it is a stuck, untransformed aggression.

I want to go in more detail into the question of transformations within aggression. How does the father transform the son's aggression in such a way that it remains aggression but is no longer confined to one particular style of aggression? Here we have to borrow and adapt some concepts from psychoanalytic thinking about the psychological role of the mother in early development. To begin with, we do not yet have a worked-out sense of what *paternal* reverie is like. By this I mean the manner in which a father uses his mind to make sense for the son of the son's aggressive fantasy. The father, on the level of unconscious-to-unconscious communication, transmitted through the body perhaps, cultivates a sense of there being a point (a *telos*) to aggression, bringing about a state in which it is possible to experience aggressive fantasy as being *for* something. This includes, but is something more than, 'valuing' the son's aggression.

Similarly, we need to start to theorize about *paternal* holding. This may be different from maternal holding as Winnicott described it. The aim of maternal holding is to establish securely within the baby an age-appropriate sense of his or her own omnipotence, making it possible for the baby to take good and bad events into his or her own potency, thereby converting mere events into personality-enhancing experiences. Perhaps paternal holding supports the efforts of the son of whatever sex to develop confidence (even faith) in the possibility of there being transformations within aggression, as opposed to the transformation of aggression into something else that would win an easier social acceptance. This could be understood as a special kind of play: The father–son dyad play experimentally across the entire aggressive spectrum, including playing with the fire of absolutely awful, destructive, unrelated, untransformable aggression. Aggression, reviewed in the context of father–son holding, remains aggression but a more plural conception of aggression and a more evolved capacity to experience aggression emerges between them. I think the idea that aggression cannot be transformed into something other than another kind of aggression shows that I am not romanticizing the phenomenon.

In my vision of aggressive playback, father and son take it in turns to be victim and aggressor and this, too, contributes to a fluidity in aggression. Aggression becomes something more liveable-in. It is not the same as managing aggression by containing it or a parent proving to a child that aggression is not always toxic by surviving the child's onslaught.

At this juncture, I want to suggest to the reader that, if he or she is interested in exploring the ideas of transformation within aggression and the plurality of aggression, it might be worthwhile to attempt an experiential exercise. The purpose of this exercise, which I have suggested to participants in several workshops on 'Fathers', is to strengthen the conviction that aggression can be moved out of one style and into another style. The exercise is therefore one of faith, to use the word I introduced earlier, faith in the capacity of aggression to respond to transformative endeavors. We are going to practice, to play at moving aggression round the body. You are asked to imagine and visualize the different aggressions that can be associated with the different parts of the body.

Let us begin at the top of the body. I would like you to recall a time when you yourself employed 'eye aggression', seeing the worst in somebody or something. Now, quite consciously and deliberately, move the physical locus of aggression over into your ears: Think of a time when you expressed aggression by not listening to someone. Now move the aggression into your arm or hand, transforming it into any one of the enormous range of possibilities that suggest themselves. Perhaps at some point you have used an instrument to carry out arm aggression. Focus on that. Now, let's try to transform arm/hand aggression into belly aggression, the deep, visceral, totally justified roar of rage. Consider a time when that happened in your experience (or the times when you wished you had let rip in the way I am describing and did not). The aggression of the genitals comes next and I would like you to muse on your experiences of sex without love. Also, have you ever been unfaithful – was this in the context of aggressive feelings?

These possibilities are not intended to be exhaustive and everyone will find their own material. Hopefully, the exercise strengthens the conviction that there is a plurality of aggression and that one aggression can be transformed into another. A final step in the exercise would be for the reader to review the relationship he or she has or had with their father and, thinking of themselves as the father of whatever sex, the relationships they may have had or may be having with their sons of whatever sex. Of course, what I mean here is to encourage the reader to look at the whole range of familial relationships *through the eyes of aggressive playback*, remembering my suggestion that it is necessary to filter our theorizing about aggression (and sex) through the relationships that are in each case the most culturally sensitized – here, with regard to aggression, this is obviously the father–son relationship.

A focus on aggression confirms the validity of two differing but compatible ways to theorize the father–son relationship: In terms of their intergenerational conflicts *and* in terms of their intergenerational alliance. Freud's Oedipal theory contains such a dual viewpoint. Psychoanalytic theory has had less to say about the alliance of the father with his son, as I noted earlier. Yet the interplay of alliance and conflict is crucial to any kind of organic cultural development and to politics itself. Aggressive conflict and competition between father and son are themselves not always politically negative for such aggressive interaction promotes the possibilities of social change, cultural vitality and a healthy check on excesses of both a reactionary and revolutionary nature. The good-enough relation of father and son provides a framework for aggression within which all this can happen. To use the mercantile imagery developed in Chapter 4, it is as if father and son have to try to strike a bargain, using aggression and trickery to do it. If the son renounces his claim on the mother, the father will help him in life.

The negative father should not be undervalued. If the incest taboo, carried by the negative father, is not effective, then cultural process will be impaired, drowning in a sea of what Jung called 'kinship libido'. Castration anxiety has a cultural function. Maybe we should take castration anxiety less literally, as Ernest Jones tried to do with his idea of *aphanisis*.[9] This term was intended to refer to the father's capacity to strip the son, not only of the means to express sexual desire, but also of the capacity to feel desire itself. We can adapt *aphanisis* for political discourse: The (reactionary) father threatens the (revolutionary) son with the removal of the capacity to feel a sense of political agency. This stimulates the politically constructive energies of the son. Both father and son suffer the aphanisic consequences of a failure to achieve workable levels of aggressive communication and aggressive playback or enjoy the consequences of a satisfying level of aggressive communication and aggressive playback.

At this point, I want to return to the idea that certain themes can only be approached through a filter which arises from cultural preoccupation and psychological theorizing. If we take the father–son relationship non-literally, then the father–son relationship stands as the filter through which all other dyadic aggressions have to be viewed. For instance, mother–daughter aggression may have differing features (in fact, I am sure it does) but we approach mother–daughter aggression through our collective, cultural experience of father–son aggression, carried out by the father of whatever sex with the son of whatever sex.

Moving the father–son connection onto a metaphorical plane means that applications of these ideas outside the family are possible. Consider soccer hooliganism. This constitutes one particular aggressive style. Many of the young British men who carry out violent acts at soccer games come from areas of the country and social classes that have not enjoyed much economic prosperity in recent years. Generally speaking, previously they would have expected to find employment in old-style rust-belt, manufacturing industries. But the silicon chip and the industrialization of Third World countries has meant that these industries have collapsed. What is more, the bourgeoisification of British cultural life has damaged the sense of cultural continuity that these young men might have expected to experience. It is inevitable that they will be angry. Yet the anger, which could be understood socioeconomically, as I have just explained, is not expressed through any kind of political channel whatsoever, but through hooliganism at sporting events. It follows that, psychologically, this is a completely untransformed kind of aggression.

Politicians and the media foster this miring in one style of aggression by responding solely in the language of moral condemnation, social control and policing. Moreover, explanations which try to communicate the subjective experience of the soccer hooligan are dismissed as the work of do-gooders and naive idealists. Recently, there has been a significant shift in opinion following an official report on a disaster at a soccer match when many supporters died in a horrendous crush. The report was written by a senior judge who pointed out that soccer supporters are not treated well within the stadia. Conditions are appalling with virtually no sanitary or refreshment facilities. The supporters who died in the disaster were, as usual, penned in large cages like animals. It is no doubt important that the judge concluded that it was the police and not the supporters who were responsible for the disaster. For the first time, the 'hooligans' had some sympathy from the wider community. The judge could also see why the police had developed expectations about the violent behavior of the supporters. The headline of a newspaper article on this subject shows the shift in public attitudes: 'Fans Welcomed Back To The Human Race'.[10] In that piece, the judge got the credit.

Of course, the judge was not only operating on the level of a cultural father providing aggressive playback. Nevertheless, his paternal reverie played a significant part in changing opinion about the etiology of soccer hooliganism by reframing the context for the aggression and so helping the rest of the community to see it differently, possibly as a form of sociopolitical dissent or protest. That in turn may have led to a trans-formation within aggression as apperceived by the cultural collective. Aggressive playback can, therefore, be important on the political as well as the personal level. Sometimes aggressive playback can have socially useful results, as the example of the judge's report shows. Erotic playback, translated into the cultural realm, may turn out to be a crucial element in the factoring of alterity into deal-making (referred to in Chapter 4). The father who communicates erotic playback helps to render the market economy more compassionate and sensitive to the plurality of needs assembled therein. The father who communicates aggressive playback sanctions dissent and protest at the injustices perpetrated by the negative side of the market. *This* father, Dionysian as much as Hermetic, could inspire a vision of a socialized market, the elusive, ubiquitous present-day grail of social and political theory and practice.

WHAT FATHERS DO

It is important to use aggressive playback or erotic playback in a depth psychological analysis of political process in a way that ensures that these ideas do not become *ideals* or goals rather than descriptions and tools. Everything I have written about erotic and aggressive playback is not intended as prescription or proscription. I am writing about ordinary paternal reverie and holding: What the personal father does, with mind and body, to allow the hidden political potentials of incestuous sexual fantasy and aggression to emerge and be available for the use of his children of whatever sex. In principle, none of this is difficult for a father to do; fathers already do it without being in the slightest trendy or striving to be good fathers. Even the judge did it. *But until a description of erotic and aggressive playback is formed into a text, and until we become conscious of these processes, we cannot enjoy their benefits to the full whether in the familial or the political spheres.*

In the previous chapter, I confessed the inadequacy of the heterosexist approach I would be taking in my account of the father-child relationship: Father/daughter/sex; father/son/aggression. But I also was careful to prepare the ground for a reversal of the main poles of this overstructured account. Mothers communicate erotic playback and aggressive playback and they do it to their children of either sex. Fathers certainly provide erotic playback for their sons and aggressive playback for their daughters.

Children supply erotic and aggressive playback for their parents. But, as I have argued, these subtleties will stay on the level of slogans unless we accept and respect cultural traditions that make it absolutely necessary to approach any of these themes through the most travelled and hence most sensitized routes.

Then we can return to those fascinating contemporary questions: How is parenting different when the sex of the parent and the sex of the child varies from the more theorized combination? How does a father's very early nurturing differ, psychologically and socially, from a mother's very early nurturing? And how does it differ when the baby is a boy or a girl? I wish I could give hard and fast answers but, in all honesty, I must fall back on the theme of identity/difference, mentioned in my opening chapter. In some ways, nothing changes when the combination of parent–child changes; in some ways, some things do change when the combination of parent–child changes; in some ways, everything changes. It is not an answer that will win an easy following but it is the best I can give. 'Some' – the keyword in Jamesian pluralism – is a difficult intellectual and emotional goal at which to aim. Family psychology seems to prefer absolutes: *Everything* changes when the combination changes; *nothing* changes when the combination changes.

If we do focus on this problem, then we have to examine the possibility that mother psychologies express the dynamics of containment and therefore provide a clarity, cohesion and relative lack of contradiction that father psychologies cannot. For incest fantasy (part of the father filter) breaks moral taboos and hence, by analogy, leads to a challenging of the social taboos that defend the political status quo. Incest fantasy and the political imagination are linked. Similarly, as Tom Steele puts it, 'aggression wants to bite, tear, smash, explode, find alternatives and push on to new territory'.[11] I have used terms like 'paternal reverie' that are based on terms like 'maternal reverie'. It may well be that pursuing the parallels between fathering and mothering (while noting possible differences) is *not* the only way to proceed. However, given that the father is the Cinderella-child of developmental psychology, this could well be all that is possible in present circumstances. I think there is still much to be got from redeploying the concepts of mother-dominated developmental psychology into a patrix. For instance, Steele has begun to examine the possibility of a paternal mirror stage of development, paralleling Lacan's notion of the maternal mirror stage of development.[12]

When lecturing on these themes in Latin countries such as Italy and Brazil, men in the audience have often claimed that worries about insufficient erotic playback are rooted in the physical inhibition of Anglo-Saxon males. My reply has been that it is not a question of how many times a day a father touches his daughter but of what the message contained in the touching might be. It has often turned out that I need not have replied at all because women in the audience have stated emphatically that (a) being touched frequently by a 'Latin' father is a sign of *ownership* not emancipation, (b) such touching does not make them feel erotically or socially viable but rather dependent, and (c) that the contradiction with their sexual oppression is what we should be focusing on.

SOME CLINICAL IMPLICATIONS

The implications for female therapists and analysts of all these ideas and speculations about the father are immense. For female therapists and analysts, particularly at the start of their practice, it is often difficult to accept that the patient's image of them in the transference is as 'father', with father's body, penis, and stubble. When that is the image the patient has of the therapist, then the father's role in terms of erotic (and aggressive) playback will also be highly relevant. As I suggested in the previous chapter, perhaps male therapists have less of a problem here since, after forty years of object relations and the focus on mother–infant interaction, male therapists 'know' for sure that, in the transference, they also have female bodies, breasts and womb. Optimal erotic playback from the father is a crucial factor in a female's envisioning of herself. This can be in a sufficiently broad and non-literal way so as to move beyond a self-conception limited to 'mother'. It follows that the female therapist's capacity to envision herself as other than mother in the transference, and even other than woman, connects with her own personal experience of erotic playback. How her own relationship with her father has been explored in her personal analysis, especially if this has been with another woman, becomes a critical concern. If her father failed to contribute erotic playback and if her analysis fails to get to grips with the meaning of that, she will remain mired in the equation therapist equals mother.

FATHERS AS MESSENGERS

I do not think we have begun to tap the political potential of metaphorical understandings of parental imagery. To interpret parental images as a result of memories of reality, unconscious phantasy or archetypal activity is still to confine understandings to the literal and personal realm. If we interpret parental imagery as representing *parts* of the self, then the full social *autonomy* of these figures, and the collective *functions* they perform, will be overlooked. But what if we rotate the interpretive lens so that the focus is on *social function* and *political action* – and even on *goal* and *aim* – on *telos*, in other words?

What is the social function and political aim of father imagery? There are pressing reasons to go deeply into the nature of paternal images that appear in analytical material, going beyond the obvious answers to that question, valuable though they may be. What is paternal imagery *for*? What is the father *doing*? Just to ask these questions is to disagree with those who see experience in personified form of the multiplicity and plenitude of the psyche only as a kind of madness.[13] What is more, we begin a profoundly self-critical and self-reflexive process by questioning, not the personal origin, but the public outcome of the kind of analytical material we take most for granted.

My one-line answer to the question 'What is the father doing?' is that *he is performing the function of a messenger*. Hermes-like, he carries messages which contain the wisdom of the psyche (and, occasionally, in good Tricksterish fashion, its fatuousness or indifference). Images of the father may be understood as a form of political self-monitoring, generated out of the psyche itself. The father is a messenger, and sometimes, again like Hermes, he is a guide. The father does not simply *bear* a message, like a document; it is often the father as he presents himself just as he is in narrative, memory, fantasy and dream that constitutes the message in personified form.

PATERNAL IMAGERY AND POLITICAL CONFLICT

I would like to make two proposals about political readings of imagery of the father as they crop up and are reported in analysis. The *first proposal* is that paternal imagery tells the analyst something about the individual's political capacity, broadly conceived. By political capacity, I do not simply mean the patient's capacity to win elections. Rather, I see the quality and tone of the father image that emerges as an indicator of the state of the patient's political development and therefore as an image of his or her attitude toward the world. As I suggested in Chapter 3, people are far more 'political' than they realize and it is possible to refer to the level of political development at which they are operating. Just as their sexual energy is something from which they may have got cut off, so, too, they can be unconscious of political standpoints and commitments which they have taken on. Once again, by 'political' I mean something in addition to views about specific issues of the day, or party politics.

If the image of the father refers to a person's political capacities, then it is possible to speculate about how 'fatherly' a person is in relation to cultural and political conflicts and issues such as economic inequality or environmental pollution. The term 'father' has to be deliteralized to permit this political reading of personal, clinical material; the patient's general level of humanity or humanitarianism is addressed. Above all, the patient's attitude to power and his or her capacity to use power is highlighted.

Images that we all have of our parents change over time, even when the parents are dead. It is not just because we forgive the parents, or see their better side, or withdraw projections. The parents that the analyst hears about, particularly the father, constitute a message about the ongoing political development of the patient.

The following example shows how a female patient was forced to accept that her apparent concern for her parents and their future masked an appetite for involvement in a more extraverted, social form of caring. The patient talked a lot about her concern for her parents, especially when her father would reach retirement in a few years' time. According to the patient's account, she had herself received inadequate parenting, particularly from her father; in her view, this had led her to become a rather driven career woman. But her parents did not seem to need her input at all, especially her father who was a highly independent person who took little notice of her. It became clear that the key issue here was a conflict between attitudes of extreme dependence and extreme independence. There was little space for interdependence or mutual dependence. The ways in which this overconcerned patient fathered her parents reflected the tension between these idealized and extreme positions of dependence and interdependence. In her fantasy, her parents were going to be economically dependent on her and this would then constellate her own independence. The effect of this was to paralyze her when it came to making plans for her own future on a human as opposed to a career level. You *could* say that she projected her own worries about the future onto the parents. But that would miss something crucial that was lacking in her attitude toward herself, the particular flavor of her blindness about her own future.

The message delivered by the image of her bleakly independent father, who did not need her, was that her style of 'fathering' was deficient. That her parents could cope with the future on their own was the hidden implication of her father's childhood indifference. It was also a hidden political message for her. Now was the time for her to consider her own future and her own values – for instance, the way she equated money and power, and power and caring. Was a change in career indicated, away from commerce and toward some kind of welfare or community work with others? If so, the discoveries made in analysis about how power and caring were linked put her in touch with an important shadow aspect of work in the therapeutic professions.

It would have been easy to restrict analytical exploration to the patient's feelings of having been rejected by her father, or to her problematic identification with him. But, arising from taking the independent image of him that she presented as a message, a different and more politicized interpretive atmosphere arose, permitting her to make changes in her external life, including career changes which themselves took her in a sociopolitical direction. It is interesting that the father image was not a *model* to follow; rather the father of her subjective *past* experience had also formed himself into an emancipatory message that was relevant to her *present* situation, leading to new plans for the *future*. In such a way, the political temperature of the patient was taken and the patient's political development assessed alongside her sexual, aggressive and personality development.

THE POLITICS OF THE PRIMAL SCENE

My *second proposal* about political readings of imagery of the father concerns the primal scene – the image of father and mother together, the image of their intimate relationship, whether in bed or not. (Readers may recall the 'primal scene exercise' from the workshop described in Chapter 3.) I have suggested on several occasions that primal scene imagery functions as a kind of psychic fingerprint or trademark. Now, I want to extend that idea in a political direction, to argue that the kind of image held of the parents' relationship to each other demonstrates, on the intrapsychic level, a person's capacity to sustain conflict constructively in the outer world – a crucial aspect of the person's political capacity. In the image of mother and father in one frame, the scene can be harmonious, disharmonious, one side may dominate the other side, one parent could be damaging the other parent, there will be patterns of exclusion, triumph, defeat, curiosity, or total denial. These great and well-known primal scene themes are markedly political. How they work out in the patient tells us something about that patient's involvement and investment in political culture and his or her capacity to survive therein.

The primal scene is *a self-generated diagnostic monitoring of the person's psychopolitical state at any moment.* The level of political development is encapsulated in the primal scene image. This is why images and assessments of the parental marriage change so much in the course of an analysis. As I said earlier, the parental marriage is not what changes in the majority of instances. Nor is it merely an increase in consciousness on the part of the patient which makes the image change. The image changes because the patient's inner and outer political styles and attitudes are changing. And the specificity of the image communicates what the new styles might be. The parents stand for a *process* as well as for particular attributes and capacities.

The experience of primal scene imagery may be additionally understood as an individual's attempt to function pluralistically, coupling together into a unified whole his or her diverse psychic elements and agencies *without* losing their special tone and functioning. What does the image of the copulating parents represent? The image of the parents in bed is a metaphor for a *coniunctio oppositorum*. This Latin tag can be understood literally as a conjunction of *opposites*. But a more satisfactory reading would refer to a pluralistic engagement with all manner of psychological phenomena and characteristics, many of which appear to us as so unlikely to belong together (to be bedfellows) that they are 'opposites', just as mother and father, female and male, are said to be 'opposites'.

Thus the question of the image of the parents in bed as a coming together of opposites can be worked on in more detail, according to the degree and quality of differentiation a person makes between the images of mother and father. For a *coniunctio oppositorum* only becomes fertile when the elements are distinguishable. In plain language, it's not a *stuck* image of parental togetherness that we see in a fertile primal scene, but something divided and unstuck, hence vital – but also linked, hence imaginable. The psyche is trying to express its multifarious and variegated nature – and also its oneness and integration. Primal scene images can perform this pluralistic job perfectly and the message they carry concerns how well the job is going. Via primal scene imagery, the psyche is expressing the patient's pluralistic capacity to cope with the unity *and* the diversity of the political situation he or she is in.

I do not think that the inevitable reproductive heterosexuality of the primal scene need be taken as excluding people of homosexual sexual orientation. Far from it: I am convinced that the fruitfulness signified in the primal scene, and the problems therein, are completely congruent with homosexual experience. Nevertheless, I do admit that there is a set of cultural and intellectual assumptions that need to be explicated. Why is it that psychological variety and liveliness do not get theorized in homosexual terms? Why is psychological maturity still envisaged in a form of complementary wholeness that requires heterosexual imagery for it to work at all? I can defend my thesis by recourse to metaphor – heterosexuality refers to diversity, otherness, conflict, potential. I could also point out that everyone is the result of a heterosexual union. Nevertheless, there is a question mark in my mind concerning the absence of texts replete with homosexual imagery that would perform the psychological and political functions of primal scene imagery. We might begin a search for the homosexual primal scene.

My overall view is that personal narratives of primal scene imagery, and their working through, demonstrate to a considerable extent a person's capacity to sustain political conflict constructively. (This general point about politics becomes more pertinent when applied to the professional politics of the field of depth psychology. Stuck parental imagery fits the field's symptoms of intolerance, fantasies of superiority, and difficulties with hearing the views of others. If depth psychology's primal scene imagery could be prodded into vigorous motion, perhaps by an active realignment of ideological dialogue, I would feel more optimistic about its future.)

The example I want to give of these ideas concerning political readings of primal scene imagery is the well-known general problem of *not being able to imagine the parents' sexual life at all*, or of having a bland and non-erotic image of it. Clearly, denial and repression play important parts in this, but my argument is that to restrict our understanding to these personal ego-defense mechanisms is to cut ourselves off from the plenitude of collective meanings in primal scene imagery.

Before discussing the non-primal scene, I want to say something about the impact of the primal scene itself upon my speculations about political readings of father imagery. One particular reason for choosing to focus on the primal scene is that we are then invited to address the conventional twinning of man with active and women with passive sexual behavior. This twinning both reflects and, I think, inspires many gender divisions. When individuals access and work on their primal scene imagery, often in fantasy or via the transference in analysis, it is remarkable that the conventional male–active/female–passive divide does *not* invariably appear. Quite the reverse. In fact, it often seems as if the unconscious intention of the sexual imagery associated with the primal scene is to challenge that particular definition of the differences between men and women. Does a challenge to the sexual *status quo* symbolize a kind of challenge to the political *status quo*?

I am also glad that a discussion of the political relevance of a primal scene enables me to reintroduce the mother – but in a transmogrified and politicized form: As an active player in the sexual game, and hence, potentially, as an active player in the political game. Quite literally, she is a *sine qua non*, a without-which-not. Focus on the father is necessary, given the state of developmental psychology, and also of political theorizing. But, eventually, both parents will insist on being in the picture.

Here, I am reminded of the Midrashic story of Lilith. She was, as readers will recall, the first consort of Adam who was created from the earth at the same time as Adam. She was unwilling to give up her equality and argued with Adam over the position in which they should have intercourse – Lilith insisting on being on top. 'Why should I lie beneath you', she argued, 'when I am your equal since both of us were created from dust?' But when Lilith saw that Adam was determined to be on top, she called out the magic name of God, rose into the air, and flew away. Eve was then created. Lilith's later career as an evil she-demon who comes secretly to men in the night (hence being responsible for nocturnal emissions) and as a murderer of newborns culminated, after the destruction of the temple, in a relationship with God as a sort of mistress. Lilith's stories are well documented by scholars of mythology. The importance for us is that the woman who demands equality with the man is forced to leave the Garden and gets stigmatized as the personification of evil.

What of the missing primal scene, the inability to imagine the parents' sexual life that I referred to earlier? I regard this non-primal scene as deriving in the first instance from a colossal fear of the consequences of conflict. (Again, sexual conflict symbolizing political conflict.) For, if the bodies of the parents are not in motion, then psychological and socio-political differences between them, including asymmetries and inequalities, need not enter consciousness. Over time, consciousness of political problematics impacts on the individual's internal processes: His or her capacity to experience different parts of the self in their own particularity and diversity while at the same time sensing that they participate in the whole in a more or less coherent sense of identity. The denied primal scene signifies a loss of faith in the political nature of the whole human organism. Conversely, images of vigorous, mutually satisfying parental intercourse, including perhaps some kind of struggle for power, reveal a private engagement with the conflictual dynamics of the public sphere.

MESSENGERS AS FATHERS

Finally, in these sections on fathers as messengers, the image of 'messenger' itself deserves some attention. We have already encountered the figure of Hermes, messenger of the Gods, elusive harbinger of transformation, guide of souls and tricksterish political theorist. Then there is messenger ribonucleic acid (RNA), whose crucial property of carrying the inherited genetic code is central to biological growth and development. Even in biology and chemistry, and more specifically in the new disciplines of cybernetics and communications theory, the importance of message and messenger cannot be overemphasized. Closer to the field of depth psychology, both structural and systemic family therapy employ variants of communications theory. Given all this, what better way to honor thy father *and* thy mother, than by allowing them to function as messengers?

YOU BE THE DADDY, DADDY

'You be the daddy, Daddy,' said my two-year-old daughter as she plonked two dolls, two rabbits and a mouse on the floor between us. Using a complementary approach of her own, she thereby became the mummy and, as well, Mummy. Later, when I had put the real daughter and our plastic and furry offspring to bed, I fell to musing about 'You be the daddy, Daddy'. Clearly, I am her Daddy and have to be addressed as Daddy. But what differences and similarities are there between 'Daddy' and 'daddy'? It appeared, as the game went on, that other people than Daddies could be daddies for she said at one point, 'I'll be the daddy, Daddy'.

I wondered if this second statement ('I'll be the daddy, Daddy') was an example of someone becoming the father of whatever sex (or age). Even the command 'You be the daddy, Daddy' threw up numerous possible understandings. Perhaps she meant that I should be the father on an impersonal or non-personal level – not the Daddy she knew but the daddy she needed for the game. Not Daddy as daddy but someone whose name just happens to be Daddy playing daddy. A human being drawing on the archetypally sanctioned possibility of being a daddy. Then I thought of psychodynamic explanations: At age two, and recently out of diapers, she was able to project her regressive fantasies into her play children as we cleaned them up, fed them from breast and bottle, and generally babied them. Or, if I'm the daddy, she can be the mummy – and wife. Or she could have been identifying with me, her Daddy, *and* her daddy in the game, as a way of keeping me inside herself during a time of developmental transition. Or she might have been testing that the man she calls Daddy really can be, or really is, a daddy. And what about the pluralistic tensions between two competing statements: 'I'll be the daddy' and 'You be the daddy'?

A posh psychological language in which to express the discoveries that come from playing with (one's own) children does not exist. The discoveries I was making in this game, and in others before and since, overturned the applecart of *social* reality. Though I did not actually think up the idea of the value of confusion in discussions of gender and parenting during this game, it is in the fluid, dramatic, rough-and-tumble of play with daughter and son that the idea has developed and become fleshed out. For these games have a definite social and political impact. It has been a case of Trickster children transforming the political viewpoint of their reactionary father – I do not want to say teaching their father for that sounds too cool and conscious; it all happens at a much less aware level. Nevertheless, what we see in my little tale is the emergence of a female Symbolic, under the aegis of *le nom de la fille*.

The Trickster child is not an Isaac, is not at all trusting of his or her Abraham father. The Trickster child's mission is to change the rules of the game, the power rules, the reality rules, the Symbolic rules. But this revolutionary child cannot remain a revolutionary for ever. Gender certainty arises to challenge gender confusion. Perhaps this is the saddest but greatest trick (or Trick) of all: The child, of whatever sex, becomes a father, of whatever sex. Then the politically grandiose Trickster child, who used to take delight in subversion, changes into the overcautious reactionary father whose pleasure is to be found in saying 'no' to change and whose tragedy is to be found in forgetting that saying 'no' is not the only way to father.

CONCLUDING REFLECTIONS: HEALING THE FATHER

In this chapter and the preceding one, there have been four main variables in motion. These were (1) the father's body, (2) politics, (3) literalism and (4) metaphor. The main persuasive thrust of the chapter was to establish the linkage:

$$\text{father's body} \longleftrightarrow \text{politics}$$

To do this, a linkage in the background argument also had to be made:

$$\text{literalism} \longleftrightarrow \text{metaphor}$$

As we worked through incestuous and aggressive fantasy, we covered the linkage:

$$\text{father's body} \longleftrightarrow \text{literalism}$$

But the socially subversive impact of erotic and aggressive fantasy threw up the linkage:

father's body ⟷ metaphor

Metaphor is an unstoppable force once released from its bottle and politics itself was taken on a metaphorical level, utilizing the symbols and images of intrapsychic and familial process (e.g. the primal scene). The linkage was:

politics ⟷ metaphor

All the time, the unfairness of the material world in which we live, and its limiting effect on human potential, have been in mind. That linkage is simple:

politics ⟷ literalism

These linkages can be put together:

father's body ⟷ politics

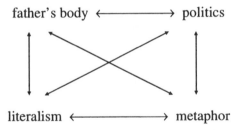

literalism ⟷ metaphor

My intention has been to tone down the level of the material in Part I. From Bezaleel, Machiavelli, the Winnebago Trickster, Hermes, and Adam Smith, we found ourselves in the ordinary world of the family and the father's relations with his partner and their children. We addressed the politics of, in, and springing from the father, and saw him as secretly politically subversive – a subversion we cannot use until we acknowledge its existence. To reach this point, we had to make something constructive out of the confusion that exists in contemporary discussions of gender and parenting. The sex of 'the father' may lead to major differences in emotional process, or it may not; the similarities may come to seem more striking. As our culture has highlighted certain psychosocial themes (father–daughter incest, father–son aggression), these act as filters through which we have to explore incest and aggression between *any* members of the family.

The positive and negative images of the father have a curious connection because they draw on the same pool of imagery. This is markedly physical imagery, and thus the focus comes to be on the father's body. We saw how erotic playback between the father of whatever sex and the daughter of whatever sex inflected political processes and social outcomes, and the same was the case with aggressive playback between the father of whatever sex and the son of whatever sex. I tried to be critical about the exclusive employment of a heterosexist frame of reference.

The idea that, at a metaphorical level, the father functions as a messenger was explored. The concrete presence of an image of the personal father enables us to take a person's political temperature and to assess his or her political development. This notion was illustrated by paternal imagery as it appears in analysis, and also by a political reading of primal scene imagery, especially the missing or non-primal scene, in which one simply cannot imagine one's parents' sexual life.

The mother has not been absent, especially in passages on single-parent families, the primal scene, and concerning her role in the construction of the father relation itself, and the outcome with regard to daughter and son. The challenging effect on maternal psychology of a hopefully temporary but presently necessary preoccupation with paternal psychology was noted. For the most part, though, viewpoints which use a complementary approach to render mother and father into opposites have been eschewed.

At the start of the previous chapter, I stated that my intention was to provide a politically progressive and emancipatory reading of the father – the subversive father. This, I hoped, would lead to a kind of healing of the father by daughter, son and spouse, actively extending to him the benefits (and risks) of erotic and aggressive playback, leading to his discovery of a new primal scene redolent of a plurality of fathers and faith in the possibility of transformation within aggression. What may have been healed is the appalling wound that Robert Bly noted when he pointed out that we lack images of the good father.[14]

It may be that the father can never be healed or altered in the ways that sons, daughters and spouses dream of (and that he may desire for himself). Sometimes, suffering sons and daughters may have to invoke other figures, not necessarily father-figures. Sometimes, as Bly and many others have noted, these will be shamans, mentors, initiate masters. Sometimes these will be male figures, brothers or male comrades in a communal or cooperative project. (We will be looking at men's issues in the next chapter.) Sometimes, I hope, these mentors will be female: Mothers, spouses, daughters, friends. In any case, the potential is in the father to participate in the creation of fresh and different social and political structures. The shift may have to be away from 'change within' to 'change between' and even to 'change out there'. What we call 'deep' psychological change takes place between people and in the external world, as well as in the lonely soul.

Chapter 8

Reflecting on men

Intense interest in the psychology of the father shows that we have reached an extremely interesting point in the evolution of our culture's consciousness concerning *men*. Perhaps for the first time, a category called 'men' can be said to exist, bringing with it a burgeoning 'men's movement'. In the past, it has been men who defined all the other categories that there might be; men themselves were simply part of the intellectual furniture. Now, men are looked at in the ways in which they, historically, have looked at everything else. Men are the object of scrutiny, the object of analysis, the object of dissection on many levels. It is revealing that, hitherto, the only field in which men have been looked at like this has been criminology.

While a monolith called 'men' may not truly exist, there can be little doubt that a crisis exists within masculinity and for men.[1] Differing definitions of masculinity, differing paths to achieve that state, and differing conceptions of what might be done to facilitate the emergence of so-called 'true' masculinity presently coexist in conditions of extreme competitiveness and intense mutual suspicion. Each view of masculinity seeks to knock out the other views and, as a pluralist, I am neither surprised nor dismayed at this state of affairs. However, if, as seems possible, one particular perspective manages to direct people's attention away from the fact that alternative perspectives exist, then that is not a positive thing at all. In this chapter, I try to recover the diversity that resides in 'men', 'masculinity' and the 'men's movement' – without having recourse to the kind of synthesis that would itself constitute a special kind of violent hegemony.

My personal interest in the father needs to be looked at against the particular Western cultural backdrop I have been describing. So, too, does my exploration of male psychology in general, which has led to the setting up of a male psychology workshop under the auspices of the Society of Analytical Psychology in London. This group of around twenty men is composed of analysts and psychotherapists and I have found participation in the group to be emotionally enhancing and intellectually productive. I am in favor of a period in which men work on certain problems in settings restricted to men, though I see this as a temporary phase. There is a parallel to be drawn with the early days of the women's movement in which women-only consciousness-raising groups were a widely accepted vehicle.

However, we should be very careful about drawing parallels between what is happening in the field of the study of men and what has happened and is happening in feminism. On the one hand, there are some striking similarities – and I have mentioned the perceived need for single-sex groups and workshops. Moreover, there are some marked similarities between the social anthropology of the women's movement and what is becoming called the men's movement. For example, there is the intellectual dispute between the essentialists (archetypalists) and those who take a social, constructivist and cultural approach to sexual difference.[2] These disputes lead to patterns of leadership and discipleship – whether sought or unsought – and the resultant schisms are also common to both the women's and men's movements. On the other hand – and this is something that should not be forgotten by men who participate in the men's movement – men and women do *not* start in the same or even similar places. By every political, social and economic indicator most men are in the driver's seat (but not all, if one considers the socioeconomic positions of black men or disabled men or homeless men). Therefore, too much concentration on the vulnerable, sobbing little boy within each powerful man, coupled with too little concentration on the oppressive economic inequality that is bound up with gender division, will lead only to a self-deceiving outcome. (We will return to the connections between men, 'the patriarchy', and capitalism later in the chapter.)

Nowadays men are being seen as 'the problem'.[3] This new stance reverses the trend of centuries in medicine, religion and art in which women – the other sex, the second sex, the dark sex – have been the problem men have set themselves to solve. Men are depicted these days as sexually abusing, domestically violent, planet-despoiling creatures. There is little doubt that the point is a valid one. But, at the same time, a completely different set of images of men has arisen, at least in Western countries. One image of men, called the 'new man', is dramatically different. This is a breed of men who support the rights of women and children and who are ecologically aware and non-violent. From a psychological perspective, we are faced with a split in the cultural image of men. Theory tells us that splits within the unconscious come about when something or someone causes unbearable anxiety. Perhaps our current preoccupation with men is sensed on a collective level as potentially so upsetting to the existing social order that we are afflicted with an anxiety that foments the split between the bad old man and the good new man – between macho-man and the SNAG (the sensitive new age guy). In the previous chapter we saw how a particular version of this split affected discussions of the 'good-enough father' and I argued for an acceptance of a state of affairs in which the stuff of the good father and the stuff of the bad father are taken as the same stuff. Similarly, new men and old men are made out of the same stuff.

The split in the image of men exists not only as a social reality in which there are two or more different kinds of men. The splits also exist within any man living in a culture that seems to support these different kinds of men. The personal and collective dimensions of psychic and social reality are intertwined. Therefore, there are really no averages, which means that the neat divisions we are making into new man and old man do not work. While nearly all attempts to categorize men fail for one reason or another, ironically the impulse to categorize men remains. From a pluralistic point of view, it is important that we do not attempt to mute the competition between the various subdivisions of the category of 'men'. I argue explicitly that it is valuable that there should be a diversity of competing models of masculinity and that men should expose themselves to as many differing models as they can.

In my workshops on fathers and on men, I ask people to do an exercise. I describe a rating scale running from 0 to 10 that represents the continuum from 'old man' to 'new man'. Old man counts as 0 and new man counts as 10. If the participant is a man, he is asked to place himself on this scale. If the participant is a woman (not all workshops are restricted to men), then she is asked to score the most significant man in her life on the scale. Somewhat naively, I thought this would be a straightforward exercise and we would just zip around the room with people saying, 6, 1, 2, 5, 8 and so on. But it did not happen like that.

Many people insisted on giving multiple answers. A man would say that he saw himself as a 2 *and* a 9. Sometimes, this would be expressed more precisely: 'When I'm with a woman, I'm more likely to be a 9, at the new man end, but when I'm with men I find myself a 2 or a 3, right at the old man end.' There was also a good deal of resistance to doing the exercise and there would be queries about whether the father could be counted as a significant man! (Generally, heterosexual women have scored their husbands or partners. Lesbian women have scored their fathers.)

At one particular workshop, the discussion preceding the exercise went on for longer than usual as participants rigorously disputed the paradigm. When it came to one man's turn to score himself he said, 'Look, I'm absolutely fed up with all this farting around. Before we started, I thought I was a 9 but right now I'm a 2!'

One man said, 'I would say I'm a 2. I consider myself traditional but I'm trying to modify myself.' This response is typical; the number of people who mentioned words like 'modify' or 'change' was very high. Some referred to 'improve'. Another man said, 'When I thought about it, I thought 5. I think this isn't out of not wanting to choose, but out of confusion. The struggle, uncertainty and confusion. I don't want to live out a cultural fantasy.' I mused on this reply. Which end of the spectrum contained the cultural fantasy? Or was the spectrum itself a cultural fantasy?

Another man said, 'When you first put the question, I thought 8 or 9. I'm the youngest of three sons and my father was a "disappeared alcoholic". Now I'm in a household where I'm the chief breadwinner, doing all the outside chores. I'm focused on my business. I see myself as slipping back to 6 and falling.' A man said, 'I raised my first son for three months. Now I'm by myself. I was resentful at her breastfeeding. I couldn't wait for it to stop and ease her out. I still have some of that. As a doctor, I work with women, helping with births, etc. I think I'm 2 and 9.'

Many women tended to mock the exercise but – and here the analyst in me speaks – what they actually said is extremely revealing. One woman said, 'I think he's a 2, but *he* thinks he's an 8.' Another said, 'I've been married for thirty-three years. My husband started as a 3 and after bringing up the children, which was terribly important to him, I would think he's a ... 4.' Still another: 'Well, if you push the 1 to 5 to one side and the 5 to 10 to the other side, he's in the abyss.'

I liked the exercise precisely because it is so flawed. It raises the question of whether things have changed in the ways suggested by the images of the new man. Think of the contemporary use in advertisements for baby and child products: Images of a young, attentive, involved father bathing the baby, frolicking on the beach, offering a spoon of food. This handsome, curly-haired male is offered as a new role model. Often, he is naked or stripped to the waist. Then we discover something interesting about his torso – not just that he has no breasts, but that, very often, he has no chest hair either. He is an all-loving, paternal androgyne. Some social scientists would argue that he is a lie as well. From a behavioral standpoint, they say, nothing has changed. Men do not do housework or look after children – and the existence of a few pockets of progressive and well-heeled masculinity should not blind us to that more pervasive reality.

Yet it is clear that *something* is in the process of changing. Without disparaging the view from social science, I think there is a psychological dimension to be considered here that is very difficult to measure which I want to call an 'aspirational atmosphere'. Men may not live up to the rhetoric of their developing ideals, but the tension between the empiricism of the social scientist and the cultural intuition of the depth psychologist needs to be maintained and I want to try to keep both of these competing viewpoints alive.

A social science viewpoint supports the idea that it is very difficult to present a comprehensive and consensual categorization of men. Thinking about maleness and about its cultural extension, masculinity, one has to accept the ineffable plurality of the term 'men'. As I said, there is no monolith that one can address. There is an acute need to achieve a balance between identity and difference as these concepts apply to men.

In some ways and in some respects, there are issues and problems that affect all men alike. So there is an identity here. But in some ways and in some respects there are problems to which men respond quite differently. Difference and identity coexist. The great difficulty, when theorizing about men, is whether to generalize or not. If one issues a general statement, one is firmly in the identity camp. If one issues a statement colored by particularity, one is in the difference camp. I think that this tension, too, has to be lived with. There is an identity of interests, concerns and psychology that affects all men. There is also an immense diversity of interests, concerns and psychologies based, *au fond*, on the plurality of sexuality itself. There is, therefore, an acute need to achieve a balance between identity and difference as these concepts apply to men.[4]

Today, for whatever reason, it seems that nobody talks about masculinity save in relation to notions of change. Even those who seek a timeless definition of the 'archetypal' masculine do so in reaction to the idea that men are changing or have changed and in sorrow that an immutable version of traditional masculinity has been lost. Although I have stated on many occasions that I am utterly in disagreement with the idea that there are archetypal patterns of masculinity and femininity that are potentially available, at differing levels of consciousness, to persons of either sex, I have been interested to note that many accounts of female development include the *changing* nature of her so-called 'masculine' side (animus, in Jungian jargon). The titles of the massive array of books on male psychology and masculinity show this same preoccupation with change, even if the change is said to be of a retrospective kind, meaning cultural change in the direction of what has been the case, as shown, for instance, in Greek myths or Christian symbolism. An example of this is the subtitle to Robert Hopcke's book *Men's Dreams, Men's Healing*. The subtitle says 'A psychotherapist explores a new view of masculinity through Jungian dreamwork'.[5] Books that are most definitely not written from an archetypal perspective show the same tendency. For example, Lynne Segal's authoritative overview has as a subtitle 'Changing masculinities, changing men'.[6] Even a rather conservative psychoanalytic text is entitled *Toward a New Psychology of Men*.[7]

En passant, I want to say something about the explosion of books on men's issues. I have noted nearly one hundred books on men in English since 1985 and no doubt there are many more that I have not seen. Almost every publisher has rushed to get in on this act. Some reviewers have wondered whether it might not be that these books are going to be read primarily by women. Although I understand the point that is being made about male resistance to self-reflection and to change, I would prefer to get a different implication out of this publishing phenomenon. If men are on the move at some level, then, given that they control the sources of economic and political power, including the production of ideology and representations of sexual difference, the factoring in of male political power to the idea of male change could be decisive. In other words, we could be confronted with a social movement as significant as feminism, but with possession of all the resources from which feminism has been excluded.

THE MEN'S MOVEMENT

I want to move on now to discuss the contemporary men's movement and I am going to carry out a dissection of it. I am conscious of the limitations of such an approach because the various subdivisions ultimately overlap. However, unless we try to clarify what is meant by the 'men's movement', it will be difficult to proceed, and we may not realize how multifaceted the men's movement is, or has become. I have been able to identify at least four overlapping aspects of the men's movement. We can call these the *experiential*, the *sociopolitical*, the *mythopoetic*, and the *gay* men's movements. Readers who are familiar with the field are unlikely to find this a particularly radical or disturbing division; I hope such readers will appreciate my intention to begin from diversity rather than from a false and repressive unity.

The *experiential* subdivision of the men's movement operates in an overtly therapeutic mode. Advertisements of groups for men offer the chance to experience feelings and the opportunity for participants to connect up with the small boy-child within themselves. The group offers a chance to cry, a chance to hug, a chance to confess, and so forth. The missing baby boy – big boys don't cry – is often a part of a man's experience of conventional psychotherapy. So, although sometimes the experiential men's movement does not formally operate as therapy, it certainly operates in a therapeutic style. The weakness of the thera-peutically- and experientially-oriented aspect of the men's movement is that it may rest content with superficial persona changes. It is significant that, these days, one encounters mockery about hugging. Hugging not long ago became the symbol of a certain kind of man-to-man relating, and, in its true form, it was once very threatening because it upset our ideas about what heterosexual masculinity is. Nowadays, the practice of indis-criminate hugging has degenerated into a ritual cliché, suggesting that experiential work on male issues can operate only on a behavioral level, so that participants end up merely by producing a different form of socially approved behavior. The remaining virtue of the experiential men's movement has to do with the re-evaluation of relations to women and to the mother and a good deal of work on new and more nurturing models of fathering may also be considered as part of the experiential men's movement.

The second subdivision of the men's movement that I want to discuss, the *sociopolitical* men's movement, is informed by the notion that men are sexist and oppressive. The overt aim of this particular aspect of the men's movement is to make an alliance with feminism. Men can learn from feminism, and should work toward the betterment of social and economic conditions for women, based on an attempt to achieve cooperative and non-hierarchical ways of relating and believing. The sociopolitical men's movement is growing in size in nearly all the Western countries, most dramatically in the United States where there are now over four hundred men's studies courses. But that field is also growing in Europe with extraordinary rapidity. I can illustrate what I have indicated as the main features of the sociopolitical men's movement by quoting extracts from a statement drawn up at the end of a conference organized in 1988 by the British Sociological Association with the title *Men, Masculinities and Social Theory*. This document was a position statement drawn up by the organizers of the conference, which was attended by many of the men who are prominent in the sociopolitical aspect of the men's movement in Britain.[8]

'First, we see it as necessary for men to support the development of feminist scholarship in general, and women's studies in particular. . . . Second, we consider the proper focus for men interested and concerned about gender and gender politics is men, ourselves.' This means that men, save where they have to for academic reasons, should not write about women. Men should write about men, and they should study men. Men have no right to write about women. 'Thirdly, there is no parity between women's studies and the critique of men. While we see women's studies as being by women, of women, and for women, the critique of men is by both women and men.' Women may write about men but men should not write about women. 'Fourthly, men's critique of men, ourselves, needs to be developed in the light of feminism. This critique needs to be anti-sexist, anti-patriarchal, pro-feminist, and gay affirmative. . . . Fifthly, the underlying task of the critique of men is to change men, ourselves, and other men.' Here again we see the preoccupation with change that I mentioned earlier. 'Lastly, we see it as crucial to attend also to the longer-term implications of men studying men.' Among these is the suggestion that if there is research money for studies in gender research, men should refrain from applying for it. This restriction is explicitly stated.

While I have an enormous amount of sympathy with the goals of the sociopolitical men's movement, I do wonder whether this is not a sort of counterphobic or overdetermined kind of response. Each of these propositions basically boils down to a conclusion based upon an awareness of the asymmetry of men/women relations regarding power. Now there certainly is an asymmetry, but whether or not that asymmetry can best be addressed by these kinds of strategies seems to me to be highly problematic. I have to confess I was amazed when I first read this statement, which comes at the end of an excellent book. But the need for action in the face of gendered inequality is surely pressing just now and the sociopolitical men's movement meets the need. For example, men might begin actively to seek out boys and adolescents in need of mentoring and nurturing. They may become active in the pursuit of fathers' rights while, at the same time, working toward the amelioration of the inequalities that afflict women, especially concerning financial support for single-parent families. Behavior connected with the care of children is surely critical here, as I indicated in the preceding chapters. The sociopolitical men's movement can link up with the experiential men's movement to play a part in the redefining of fatherhood that is a necessity for any re-evaluation of masculinity. This might mean deliberate attempts to discredit certain kinds of utterance and act performed by men, leading, for example, to the challenging of the social supremacy of conventional 'male' values.

The material about the sociopolitical subdivision of the men's movement, especially the relation to feminism, makes a very useful link to the third aspect of the men's movement I want to write about – the *mythopoetic* men's movement. Here, I intend to focus on the work of

Robert Bly, the best-known of a number of leaders of the mythopoetic men's movement.

Bly has identified a malaise in young and early middle-aged American men, especially white middle-class men, a kind of shame for their male identity. This shame has been exacerbated by the rise in feminism and the futility of the Vietnam War. As a result, men either turn into wet beansprout-eating wimps, what he calls 'soft males' – or they turn into dry corporate automata. *Iron John* is Bly's book, which has sold over half a million copies in the United States.[9] *Iron John* is based on a Grimm's fairy tale about the discovery of a hairy man at the bottom of a lake in a swampy, chaotic landscape. In the story the hairy man, Iron John, becomes the mentor of the king's son and supports him in a series of adventures in which he undertakes certain tasks, meets psychologically significant people, and gets married.

Bly's concern is that men have lost contact with their primal Dionysian hairy selves. They no longer know how to achieve that ancient Arthurian maleness through which it is possible to be tough, decisive, and at the same time to love poetry, bird-song, and each other without eliciting peer-group sniggers. Our view of what it means to be grown up, Bly argues, has become banal, naive, and corrupted by crass advertising. Bly regrets the disappearance in the West of extrafamilial Iron John instructors, and the loss of initiation rituals which would enhance the mystique of masculinity. Although Bly writes in a passionate and full-blown style, there is a good deal of tough and coherent argument in his book and I do not agree with those who seek to take the entire work as if it were a poem. Even if it were a poem, the assumptions and outcomes of *Iron John* may still be chewed upon.

The fact that I dwell on Bly's position shows how important I think it to be, even if I profoundly disagree with him. At one stage, before Bly visited Britain to promote his book, I had intended to launch a very savage critique of Bly's work. However, I was horrified at the British reviews of the book, most of which simply laughed at it. And I think this really does need to be discussed: Why did so many reviews ridicule the book? The *Guardian* review claimed that he'd unwittingly written a comic masterpiece on the level of *Diary of a Nobody*. He was compared to the Boy Scouts, to the born-again Baptists; his poetry was mocked. One reviewer said 'Bly's toupée is not the cure for men's problems'. It really was amazing to me how much mockery there was. Even on television, the first question Bly was asked concerned how he felt about the ridicule of his work. Faced with this kind of reaction, it was impossible merely to criticize – though I am conscious that, in the United States, Bly has received a fair degree of adulation.

I do agree with Bly that there has been a disastrous demythologization or desacralization of culture. The knock-on effects of the decline of religion have been disastrous for men and their conceptions of masculinity. So I also agree that, for many men on the personal level, there are male wounds to be healed. On the political level, however, I am disgusted (and I think Bly is too) at the oppressive social institutions we see today, and the ways in which all of us are implicated in perverse power relating.

Bly's solutions to these crises are highly problematic. He seems to favor father–son bonding of an old type, male mentoring done by men who are not the father, and much more open relating between men. He seeks to create male initiatory structures leading to contact with the wild man within. Large-scale experimental workshops, involving drumming, chanting, dancing, and nakedness, are the vehicle for this sacred reconnection. It should be noted that Bly has disowned the so-called 'warrior weekends', when men go off into the woods to get in touch with some kind of primal aggression within them.

I have many disagreements with Bly, and not a few worries about his work. But I want to stress that I am not worried by the activities and practices of the men's movement – the weekend workshops, the wilderness retreats, the encounter group techniques, and so on. These encounter group practices seem to me to be completely consistent with the ideas of the men's movement. One reason for my not condemning the practices of the mythopoetic men's movement is that it would surely be a case of beams and motes. As someone whose main activity involves sitting, often in silence, while someone lies on a couch from which they can't see me, doing this three times a week or more, for three years or more, encouraging that person to say whatever comes into his or her head, who am I to call Bly's practices weird? Those who critique the mythopoetic men's movement from the point of view of its practices are barking up the wrong tree. Analysis itself, and psychiatry, which are the most kosher kinds of mental health practices, are often utterly bizarre when viewed without pre-existing assumptions.

I want to divide my critique of the mythopoetic men's movement into five parts. First, I want to address certain delusions of sexual difference. Second, I will discover the relationship of men and politics. Third, I will explore questions of nostalgia, responsibility and initiation. Fourth, I will present some views on idealization and religion. And fifth, legitimizing the problem.

DELUSIONS OF SEXUAL DIFFERENCE

At this stage of the contemporary debate over gender, the focus seems to be on the question of essentialism – whether or not there are innate, universal, unchanging sex-based psychologies. Opposing essentialism is the view that masculinity and femininity are constructed culturally, significantly influenced by socioeconomic pressures, and capable of being understood from a historical perspective as highly mutable. The point here is not which side one takes. The point is that this debate has been fore-closed and prematurely settled within the mythopoetic men's movement, and this is largely due to Bly's writings. I feel it is important to resist any attempt to settle the many questions associated with essentialism.

Bly's ideas about sexual difference need to be questioned. He makes far too sharp a delineation – it's almost a biological difference – between the psychologies and roles of men and women. He underestimates the importance of social and cultural influences, and ignores everything to do with Lacan, feminist theory and social psychology. To justify his argu-ment, Bly depends on what seems to me, as an analytical psychologist, to be a totally out of date, inadequate and reified understanding of the theory of archetypes. In this approach, myths are taken reductively, which limits their usefulness in understanding social and cultural change. For example, Bly does not recognize that if, as he acknowledges, things have changed for men between the 1950s and today, this speaks of something other than archetypes. It speaks of an accelerating cultural process.

Modern archetypal theory is not as archeological or architectural as the version deployed by Bly. There are very real conceptual problems with ideas that depend upon there being a 'bottom' to the psyche – especially when it is a 'male psyche'. Bly writes:

> The upper fifty feet or so of water in the male soul is, as we all know, very roiled and turbid these days. So many roles that men have depended on for hundreds of years have dissolved or vanished. Certain activities, such as hunting and pirating, no one wants him to do any more. The Industrial Revolution has separated man from nature and from his family. The only jobs he can get are liable to harm the earth and the atmosphere; in general he doesn't know whether to be ashamed of being a man or not. And yet the structure at the bottom of the male psyche is still as firm as it was twenty thousand years ago. A contemporary man simply has very little help in getting down to it.[10]

A further delusion of sexual difference has to do with the differing roles that Robert Bly ascribes to mother and father. I am familiar with a vast range of literature on mothering and fathering. But I do not think I have ever met such a sharp distinction as Bly's between what it is that mothers do and what it is that fathers do. Nor do I think I have met an account of mothering and fathering that puts the anatomical sex of the person doing the parenting in such a prominent position. This is extremely problematic. It is also extremely important politically, when one thinks of the theory of the underclass, in which those brought up in single-parent families are given very pessimistic social and psychological prognoses. As I said in Chapters 6 and 7, in my work with single-parent families, I concluded that there are no inevitable psychological problems associated with single parenthood. The main thing single parents and their families suffer from is lack of money.

Bly's personal reasons for writing his book and undertaking his quest are very interesting. I had thought (and had been told) that it was to do with his own father. Indeed, though his avowed interest is in male mentors other than the father, it is notable how frequently his text returns to emotional difficulties connected to the father. Clearly, I share Bly's preoccupation with the father, and I have no problem with the idea that Bly's background, with an overclose relationship with his mother and a cold relationship with an alcoholic father, contributed to his ideas; this kind of connection always exists in psychological theory-making. But then I found material in interviews about his own problems in being a father that I felt I could not ignore. In an interview, Bly said: 'Daughters just seemed to raise themselves. Sons needed a lot of guidance and I had no notion of what to do. I got kind of curious about what a real man is.' On British television Bly said that 'it was sweet and simple to raise daughters'.[11] Now, given what we know about life in the family, I find this an extraordinary basis for Bly's project: That it was sweet and simple to raise daughters. I have a daughter, and I don't think it's sweet and simple . . . .

Re-reading *Iron John*, it is clear that Bly's agenda for the father–daughter relationship is confined to improving her potential to be a partner for a man. There is no awareness of the daughter as a person with a destiny outside the home – in the social, political or economic worlds. When the daughter who stops at home becomes a mother, it is hardly surprising that she becomes a mother from whom a son must escape. As I noted with reference to psychoanalysis in Chapter 7, the idea that a mother might want her son to leave home, in a psychological as well as a behavioral sense, is not entertained.

Thinking about the relations between women and men today, James Hillman, who has associated himself with Robert Bly, said the following:

In America, the rise of women coincided with the murders of Jack Kennedy and Martin Luther King, the disheartenment of the Vietnam war, followed by the Reagan years of greed, pretence, and manipulation, and a profound loss of trust in the institutions to which men devote their working days. . . . The men who had given up their soul to media values, and their spirit to corporate aggression, and their sexual values to jogging and Jaguars, of course they fall prey to strong women.[12]

Of course they fall prey to strong women. Of course! Prey? Strong women? Naughtily, perhaps, I would like to ask who are these men who have sold their soul to media values? Poets and psychologists like power as much as anyone. Hillman's attitude to feminism may be discerned in his prepublication blurb for a book on the goddess as demonstrating a 'feminism that is not ideological'.[13]

Mentioning Hillman leads to a discussion of the ideological role of analytical (i.e. Jungian) psychology in relation to what I have been calling Bly's delusions of sexual difference. I want openly to dissociate myself from seductive and simplistic conceptions of male (or female) development that involve precise numbers of archetypes, usually four, or precise numbers of the stages in growth in the male psyche,[14] or, as I saw in a pamphlet advertising a book, accounts of male development that invite the reader to score himself for mythopoetic heroism! The way in which Jungian psychology has been hijacked by the mythopoetic movement is a disaster that stifles its progressive potentials. Some analysts have not only been hijacked, but are also in the grip of what is called the 'Stockholm Syndrome'. In Stockholm some people were taken hostage in a bank raid and began to identify with the people who had taken them hostage – rather like what may have happened to Patty Hearst in the United States.

Before I first expressed these views in public, I telephoned several analyst colleagues in the United States, male and female, and told them what I was going to do. 'Thank God!' was the usual reply, and 'I'd like to do it myself but I'm too frightened.' The idea that male and female Jungian analysts across the United States are frightened to protest about certain features of the mythopoetic men's movement and the ways in which it has hijacked their discipline is really very worrying indeed.

MEN AND POLITICS

Bly makes interesting use of myth and fairytale. But we need to ask: Who controls these myths politically? Myths are not politically neutral. Who decides which myth is the one to use? My friend and colleague in England, Peter Tatham, has written a quite different kind of book about masculinity.[15] Without succumbing to mythopoetic reductionism, Tatham tells us that his preferred model is Daedalus, the master craftsman and a profoundly anti-heroic figure, able to inspire a plethora of paths to masculinity. Bly's uncritical, mythopoetic use of myth and fairytale fails to disguise a conservative and reactionary element in the mythopoetic men's movement, which has at its heart a backlash against feminism and an uncritical reverence for the nuclear family that harkens back to fundamentalist religions.[16] This acceptance of the benevolence of the nuclear family seems to me to be all the more questionable in view of what we (including Bly) know about men and child sexual (and other) abuse of children of either sex. Bly seems uninterested in discussions of the psychic reality/social reality dynamic as it takes place in the nuclear family. He makes no attempt to remedy the wrongs of the nuclear family; there is no understanding of the nuclear family as a *source* of oppression. The idea seems to be: Get the family working really well, as it used to, with clear-cut divisions between what fathers do and what mothers do, based on clear-cut ('archetypal') divisions between male and female psychology. Then everything will improve. My view is completely different. I believe it is the transgressive styles of family organization – the so-called marginal or deviant lifestyles – that need to be affirmed and put at the center of this debate. What we learn about child–parent relating, for example, by listening to two lesbians bringing up a son together, is far more important than clichés about restoring the father's authority within the family, or achieving the recovery of distinctions between spheres of interest and influence within the family.

There is a further problem about old-style, chauvinistic family men, who are most certainly still the heads of families. As John Rowan, a leading British advocate of the mythopoetic men's movement, but by no means an unquestioning associate of Bly's, has written:

> For [men] who have been down into the pool of femininity, the wild man is valuable as a corrective, or further step. For men who have never done the feminine bit at all, who are unreconstructed male chauvinists, the wild man is simply an invitation to be even more aggressive. This is a real danger.[17]

My last point about men, politics, and the mythopoetic men's movement concerns initiation rites. Male initiation rites do separate the men from the boys. But equally, or even more important, they separate the men from the women. The separation of men from women, the bifurcation around gender, the drawing of a line in the sand, and the compulsory inscription of identity on either side of that line according to anatomy – these actually lie at the heart of oppressive social organization.

NOSTALGIA, RESPONSIBILITY AND INITIATION

Bly bases his argument on an appeal to ancient cultures and traditions, as if these, too, were politically neutral. But, just as myths are not politically neutral, it is not politically neutral to look at ancient cultures, or indeed to fairytales, for solutions to current problems. If we give in to the nostalgic pull for a return to tradition, we end up returning to the very problems that got us to where we are now. *Might it not be better to try to proceed without a cultural model for a while?* Turning to other cultures, turning to other epochs of our own culture, denies present-day men's responsibility for the world as it is. What is more, looking backward severs us from the possibility of there being positive images of men and of fathers in the world in which we live *now*. The unquestioned assumption that life-enhancing fathers can only be found outside our own world and time reinforces the impression that fathers in our culture can only be negative, castrating, inhibited and so forth. I would not suggest that my own project that attempts to explore the vicissitudes of erotic and aggressive playback between parents and children provides a comprehensive answer either, but there is the advantage of retaining a critical and psychological outlook on the political landscape.

The nostalgia that has swept America – half a million books – and Germany – four books on male psychology in the top twenty non-fiction books – is a longing for a past in which men and women each knew their place. The mythopoetic movement gives men latitude to claim that they have nothing to do with the oppressions of the patriarchy. Calling it a 'puerarchy' (as some do) settles absolutely nothing.[18] Nothing to worry about! Real men are not patriarchs, so there's nothing to discuss.

It is disingenuous to divorce 'men' from 'the patriarchy'. Those who attempt to do so argue that the patriarchy is a relatively new form of socioeconomic and political organization. It is claimed that the patriarchy was preceded by a matriarchy, which was often as cruel and controlling as any patriarchy, being not at all soft, sensitive and 'feminine'. The point is, anthropological generalizations like these are wheeled out to serve projects based on either the denigration or idealization of women. Of course men have no monopoly on the ruthless misuse of power! The fact that this is so points up the absurdity of running away from today's world in which men do have power *and* a power complex whereas women have only the complex. Those in the men's movement who look to classical Jungian psychology to provide a theoretical underpinning for what they do and feel will be as disappointed as those in the women's movement were to find that Jungian psychology can often be ahistorical, essentialist, confused between contemporary description and eternal definition, and profoundly conservative. But then again, maybe the present-day North American mythopoetic men's movement wants to be profoundly conservative.

Could we begin to think about the possibility of our existing without a clear-cut model of masculinity, or what it means to be a man? Allowing ourselves to exist in a temporary but creative vacuum might allow a new, antitotalitarian position to emerge. The totalitarian state of mind is one which is orderly, fixed, frightened of subtlety, and unable to tolerate contradiction, complexity, and ambiguity. The nostalgia, the yearning that infuses the mythopoetic men's movement is for this orderly world in which men and women have their place. And this is a totalitarian longing.

Looking for a return to ever-stronger initiatory structures all too often collapses into a search for an eternal culture in which traditions and behaviors are clear-cut and everybody knows their place. Today, maybe for the first time in history, we have the exciting (and risky) possibilities that await us in the absence of initiation structures. Perhaps the manly thing to do nowadays is to try to live without the guidance and structures that defined manliness in the past. My suspicion is that initiation, as defined by Bly, could be yet another goal for a 'Top Dog' or 'Top Gun' to pursue – or purchase. Such men will never (and can never) challenge the system that promoted them to the top of the tree.

Actually, there are probably many more initiation structures in contemporary culture than Bly realizes. What about initiations that go on within the family? What about initiations that go on in sexual behavior and in sexual relationships? What about small-scale, non-decorous initiations? We have lost sight of the fact that what look like pale imitations of 'real' initiations – for instance, officers rising up the hierarchy of an institution, becoming a member of an analytical society, getting married – can, if understood and experienced psychologically, be regarded as perfectly initiatory. Why are these small-scale, everyday, non-decorous, non-eternal initiatory structures not hailed as good? This archetypal reductionism is a problem with what I call 'Zürichocentrism'. Zürichocentrism makes it difficult for people with a Jungian outlook to see that there are non-classical models for growth and development and these do not conform to the lineaments of classical myth or fairytale. They exist in their own, non-decorous right, providing 'mini-rebirths' on an everyday level. Such mini-rebirths involve the inner vision, risk and ordeal that have always characterized initiation.

Haven't there always been complaints about the decline of standards compared to a Golden Age in the past or a Golden Place somewhere else? If we deny other cultures and other epochs anything resembling our own *angst*, then we run the risk of a patronizing racism as we celebrate their so-called 'primitive' virtues. The inherent superiority of the exotic has never been demonstrated and Eurocentric, pseudo-anthropology in Jung's style has surely, by now, been discredited.

To summarize: I am making two frankly contradictory points about men and initiation. First, isn't it exciting that there aren't these structures? And second: There are (if you know how to find them).

In his discussion of initiation, Bly cites the decline of male mentoring. If we take male mentoring absolutely literally, it has to be said that there is a decline; there are, indeed, fewer avenues where older men are sanctioned to help younger men with their development. But do we have to view mentoring so literally? If I look at my own experience, the main mentor I've had has been feminism. I do not only mean females as such. I do not only mean specific theories, books or narratives. The phenomenon of feminism has operated in a mentoring way on me. I am sure I cannot be the only man in that position. I suggest that we need to deliteralize the notion of the mentor.

IDEALIZATION AND RELIGION

I said earlier that the practices of the mythopoetic men's movement can be compared to therapy. But there may be another analogy to draw. At the core of the mythopoetic men's movement I detect a fantasy of forming a new male religion. In *Iron John*, Marie-Louise von Franz is given a very respectful hearing (which is proof of the fact that a deliteralized mentor is a possibility because von Franz seems to be an acceptable mentor, even though she's a woman). It may be that Bly attended von Franz's lectures in Zürich in the late 1950s or early 1960s. This would partly explain the somewhat dated version of archetypal theory and uncritical acceptance of bourgeois values in Bly's work. Be that as it may, at the end of the book von Franz is quoted as saying that the psyche wants a religious figure, a hairy figure, a 'hairy Christ'. Without realizing it, the movement aspires to becoming a kind of religion – a desire that is inflated and dangerous. As with most religions, there are some fantastic idealizations at work here. For example, the notion that 'displaying' a sword can be detached from the social reality of male violence urgently needs to be challenged (I will return to this in the next section). Then there is what seems to be a non-credible idealization of male grief:

> There is a special figure in men that leads them down into one of their great strengths – the power to grieve. There is a grief in men that has no cause. We can feel it in Bach, Rembrandt, Goya, Homer. I don't mean that women do not feel grief, but a man's grief has a separate tone to it.

I fear the consequences if this idealization of masculinity were to be factored into a religious movement. This is where the danger in the mythopoetic men's movement lies – not in the exercises, the chanting and drumming, or the warrior weekends – but in the fantasy of a male religion with a hairy hypermale Christ at its core.

LEGITIMIZING THE PROBLEM

What Robert Bly *advocates* unwittingly forms the best *analysis* of how the patriarchy manages to keep everyone enslaved. Let's take his often-quoted assertion that the Wild Man and male violence are not coterminous. This is the very argument that our culture uses when it tells us that our objections to it are excessively personal, or subjective, or caused by our own psychopathology. The world is not deliberately damaging, we are told. Sure, there is a damaging potential but the violence needs to be read as a 'display' (the showing of the sword, not the use of it).

The same kind of pattern can be noted with regard to what Bly says about the Wild Man's sexuality. We are told in *Iron John* that 'The wild man's legendary sexual prowess, combined with the willing attitude of the maidens, produces an attitude of pure wantonness.' Surely this is not an image of male sexuality that needs awakening from sleep. Bly is prescribing the problematic pattern, not, as he intended, suggesting an antidote. The result is to legitimize what exists already, not to change anything.

Bly's legitimation of what exists can be understood more deeply by introducing an important point made by David Tacey in his review of *Iron John*. Tacey argues the point that Bly's version of masculinity is formed from a 'goddess perspective'. I understand Tacey to mean that Bly has got caught in an unconscious feminine identification (and Tacey has confirmed this).[19] On the cover of the paperbacks of the James Bond books there used to be a blurb quoted from a *Time* magazine review from the 1950s or early 1960s, about James Bond himself: 'What every man would like to be, and every woman would like to have between her sheets.' I think that it may be a case of the Wild Man being not only what every man (including me) might sometimes like to be, but what every man (including me) might sometimes like to have between his sheets. Whether we take a yearning for penetration by the Wild Man on the part of people in the mythopoetic men's movement literally or metaphorically (as symbolizing a form of male initiation), the homosexual cast of the imagery calls into question Bly's unrelenting, revanchist, dogmatic definition of masculinity and the masculine ideal.

CULTURAL FACTORS

Considering the Bly phenomenon and the mythopoetic men's movement in general, I think there are some specifically American cultural factors to consider. Let's reflect on the following statement:

> Megaloid mom worship has got completely out of hand. Our land, subjectively mapped, would have more silver cords and apron strings criss-crossing it than railroads and telephone wires. Mom is everywhere and everything and damned near everybody and from her depends all the rest of the United States. Disguised as good old Mom, dear old Mom, sweet old Mom, your loving Mom, and so on, she is the bride at every funeral and the corpse at every wedding.[20]

It sounds a bit like Hillman or Bly in the 1990s, but this was in fact written by Philip Wylie in 1942 in *Generation of Vipers*, a book which claimed its own inspiration from Jung.

Here is a further quote about Mom:

> From dawn until late at night she finds her happiness in doing for her children. The house belongs to them. It must be 'just so'. The meals on the minute, hot and tempting. . . . Everything is in its proper place. Mom knows where it is. . . . Anything the children need or want, Mom will cheerfully get for them. It is the perfect home. . . . Failing to find a comparable peaceful haven in the outside world it is quite likely that one or more of the brood will remain or return to the happy home, forever enwombed.[21]

This was actually written in 1952, and the writer was the Psychiatric Adviser to the Surgeon General of the Army and Navy of the United States of America. He goes on to say that mothers are guilty of emasculating the nation's soldiers. It is vital to note that the fear of male softness and female domination as undermining cultural health and efficiency is a longstanding trend in the United States. Bly's work must surely be assessed against this background.

THE GAY MEN'S MOVEMENT, HOMOSEXUALITY AND THE FUTURE FOR MEN

My perception of the mythopoetic men's movement is that it displays a longstanding cultural fear of what is felt to be effeminacy. For example, permission for men to cry is sanctioned by the reassurance that these will be 'real men's tears', not the tears of someone 'soppy' (to use an English epithet). But, at the same time, the mythopoetic men's movement expresses the desire of its adherents to be loved by a male figure such as Iron John or the Wild Man or the hairy Christ. We have already discussed the fear of effeminacy within the mythopoetic men's movement in terms of delusions of sexual difference that accentuate separation of function between male and female parents and foster a nostalgic yearning for a much more settled epoch in which men and, especially, women know their places. It is therefore time to discuss male homosexuality, for fear of homosexuality is what drives fear of becoming effeminate.

Homosexuality is in and of itself non-pathological. This is what studies of the evolution of depth psychological theorizing of homosexuality teaches us. Although in the last decade homosexuality has been declared non-pathological, many theories still abound that are little more than dressed-up prejudices, reflecting current preoccupations and underlying attitudes.[22] We also know that the category of 'the homosexual' is a relatively recent one, constructed toward the end of the last century by doctors and also by homosexual emancipators who were keen to demonstrate the existence of 'homosexuals'.[23] We have learned that homosexuality has been the means by which our culture has sought to regulate sexual and other behavior.[24] Specifically, the dominant culture has employed fear and loathing of homosexuality so that men as a group will be tied in to the role of provider in the family. The pay-off for men has been access to social and political power – though groups of working-class men, or black men, or disabled men would certainly dispute that they possess effective political power. We have to take care when generalizing about men. Nevertheless, when considering today's crisis within masculinity, the role of the category of 'homosexual' cannot be underestimated.

A fantasy about homosexuality is still being used to define what is 'really' masculine. In this sense, homosexuality is tagged as effeminate or even as feminine. A homosexual man is therefore a feminine man (maybe even the ultimate 'soft man'). This is a formulation that goes back to Freud and Jung. In Freud's understanding of male homosexuality, a man identifies with his mother and so takes himself, or someone standing for himself, as a sexual object. Homosexuality as a form of narcissistic love. But according to Freud, sometimes the identification with mother is so intense that the boy fantasizes himself to be a woman and seeks someone standing in for the father as a sexual object to be receptively embraced.[25] In Jung's understanding of male homosexuality, similarly, the man identifies with his anima, meaning the internal contrasexual (i.e. feminine) element within himself.[26]

Both Freud and Jung have collapsed sexual object choice into sexual identity. Choosing a man to love does not necessarily mean that a man who does so does it as a sort of woman. The homosexual man is usually sure that he is a man and it does not help to understand him to adduce an interior perspective in which it is claimed, and sometimes 'proved', that he is unconsciously a woman. And, since not only homosexual men can sense themselves unconsciously to be women, this fantasy may be taken as a general feature of the bisexual or bivalent nature of male sexuality, whether it appears in a homosexual or a heterosexual man.[27]

In spite of its strictures against Freud, the mythopoetic men's movement has inherited his conflation of sexual object choice and sexual identity, just as Jung did. 'Feminine' traits are rejected by the movement, not just because they spell mother domination or the triumph of feminism, but because they undermine approved masculine identity (including approved mythopoetic masculine identity) and hence, according to this logic, might lead to the worst thing of all: homosexuality. In sum, the mythopoetic men's movement has become fatally infected with a general version of Freudian speculation and prejudice about homosexuality that is these days being challenged even from within psychoanalysis. It is an example of the way that the work of Bly and his followers has foreclosed on questions of what is meant by masculinity. The enormous diversity within the term 'men', and the enormous diversity within the men's movement itself, are lost when one profile or set of characteristics achieves dominance. Bly's hegemonic sexuality replaces earlier hegemonies of sexuality. Particular aspects of masculinity become subordinate, marginal, deviant, problematic according to whatever hegemony holds sway.

Men certainly need to learn from other men and, in particular, the so-called straight community needs to learn from the gay community. The way in which the gay community has responded to the reality of AIDS, particularly at a time when the illness was thought to be a problem only for homosexuals, offers practical and inspiring models for different variants of masculinity – love between men as a kind of political praxis. Notice the paradox: The group of men regarded by psychoanalysis and Western culture generally as the least 'manly' have become the pioneers, the frontiersmen, the leaders in forging the way through a huge and terrifying territory. In the gay community, one can see novel and original attempts to set up non-hierarchical forms of organization based on love of and between men. There are therefore some links to be made between the gay community and the sociopolitical subdivision of the men's movement. The existence of a thriving gay community undermines a social system that deploys heterosexism to maintain control of women. In family organization and social provision, we see the various connections between heterosexism and male power. Cultural representations of women play a significant role in this. Living a life into which homosexuality has been integrated is in itself a challenge to marriage, the nuclear family and capitalistic social organization. These ideas point up the paucity of any approach to homosexuality that eschews either the psychological or sociopolitical aspects. Indeed, homosexuality is, *par excellence*, the arena in which the personal can be discovered to be political and the political to be personal.

In the previous chapters, I tried to challenge the heterosexist framework within which discussions about family psychology are usually conducted. For instance, I argued that there is no reason to believe lesbians bringing up children will be likely to do a bad job, and that there may be a homosexual primal scene. Indeed, my clinical experience, through a practice in which many patients come from a conventional nuclear family, forbids me even to suggest that the old-style nuclear family ever did a good job. Moreover, it is certainly difficult to theorize around the topic of homosexuality without addressing numerous personal, intellectual and professional issues.

But it does not follow that there is nothing useful depth psychologists can do concerning homosexuality, although I am sure that any search for the precise supposed psychosocial or psychobiological causes of homosexuality is a futile endeavor. It is clear from the immense efforts of the past seventy-five years that a list of etiological factors that would command agreement is a vain hope. Inevitably, the etiological project is utterly implicated in a *psychopathological* project. Neutral exploration of the causes of homosexuality cannot presently take place, at least not within depth psychology. Instead, analysts – gay and straight alike – should try to find out as much as possible about the emotional life and experience of those people whom we should perhaps stop calling 'homosexuals'. On the basis of what is discovered, new theories can be worked out and, in addition, our ideas about heterosexuality will undoubtedly be illuminated and challenged. Nor do I think it is enough to lump homosexuals and heterosexuals together, as Robert Bly does, when he asserts that 'the mythology as I see it does not make a big distinction between homosexual and heterosexual men'.[28] It is another highly revealing example of his sad foreclosing of expressive diversity within masculinity and for men.

MEN, THE MEN'S MOVEMENT, AND WOMEN

Not everything I have written about male homosexuality applies to lesbianism. Lesbians are twice-oppressed – as women, and then as women who have deviated from a norm prescribed for them. As men, male homosexuals seem more able to reap the rewards of participation in capitalistic organization than female homosexuals. More generally, it is by no means clear that the many and varied changes that the men's movement seeks are changes that will have a positive impact on women. In particular, the mythopoetic men's movement, and the model of male development laid out in *Iron John*, do not seem to have much to say about the psychological relations between women and men. We have seen how the mother is stigmatized, and the king's daughter in *Iron John*, whom the protagonist marries, is strictly a cipher. Perhaps the sociopolitical men's movement has gone too far the other way, doing nothing to discourage a taunt (and this is a quote of a criticism of me made at a meeting) that 'they have bowed the knee to the women'. The experiential men's movement seems to be saying that it has nothing at all to do with male violence, sexual abuse, planetary rape and so forth because its members are 'feeling men'. One goal of the men's movement is to try to make men feel 'good' about being men. I must say that I cannot see why one has to feel good about being a man; I feel ambivalent about it.

Concern with sexual harassment has brought the power imbalance between males and females to the fore. So too has the discussion within psychotherapy and other professions about ethical abuses, mostly perpetrated by male professionals against their largely female clientele. It is now clear that it takes acts of consciousness and legislation to try to create a climate in which professional, educational and health matters are not muddled up with sexual and even social contact. A consensus seems to be emerging in which it is agreed that different kinds of relationship often do not belong together. For example, a doctoral student should not be the object of sexual advances by her supervisor because, if a sexual relationship developed, it would lead to the existence in parallel of two incompatible relationships. If the two people truly want to pursue a personal relationship, then steps must be taken by the institution concerned to make it possible for the professional relationship to be taken up by another supervisor without damage to the career of any party. If an analyst and patient find that they do indeed want and seem likely to pursue the kind of relationship that is incompatible with their analytic work and the analyst's professional ethics, the analyst must make it clear that the patient should terminate the analysis and consult another analyst, even to discuss whom to see next. Some would advocate that there should then be a substantial period of time (a 'cooling-off period') in which the two people do not have contact with one another so that the patient can discover whether he or she does in fact want to pursue a personal relationship with his or her analyst. The analyst, too, needs time to explore his or her feelings. A period of one year has been suggested. Others argue that the procedure I have outlined is unsatisfactory; once a professional relationship has been established, then no other kind of relationship, such as a sexual relationship, is *ever* permissible and is always unethical. In either perspective, analytic institutions need to develop procedures to facilitate transfers of patients whose treatments have foundered on this dilemma that can be used in a non-judgmental and therapeutically sound way.

There are some who think that behavioral issues like these, rooted perhaps in the nature of human exchanges, are not important when compared to the major matter of the economic imbalance between men and women. Throughout this book, I have been indicating that I agree that this imbalance is the central background feature to all contemporary discussion of relations between men and women. But I also agree with those who, in a frankly ethical tradition, feel that personal integrity demands that the individual man or woman try to take action in accordance with his or her ideals, even when this feels an almost impossible task. Perhaps the ideal of a partnership between women and men in pursuit of social justice and universal emancipation can never be achieved unless the ethical level is addressed alongside the economic/ political and the individual/psychological levels of injustice and alienation. My own work on the father's body as a potential and actual locus for sociopolitical and ethical transformations, and on the primal scene as representative of political and moral processes within the person, is a step in this direction. Similarly, this chapter on men is intended to address these various levels at once. Let me state in closing, therefore, that the ideal of an ethical partnership between women and men in pursuit of social justice and universal political emancipation is one that I share. Such a partnership cannot be an easy-going one. Women and men are bound to fight and the personal fight cannot be divorced from the continuing political fight. Moreover, men and women share, to varying degrees according to sex, class, race *and* individual circumstances, in a kind of complicity with the grotesque oversimplification and cruelties of patriarchy. But women and men can also share in a rejection of any unified definition of what constitutes 'women' or 'men' and join in a politically significant celebration of the plenitude of meanings inscribed in these words.

Chapter 9

The political person

PERSON-AS-CONTINGENT

In the previous chapters, I think it was confirmed that, in order to make a contribution to political analysis, depth psychology must face the problem that it is not possible to depict a person divorced from his or her cultural, social, gender, ethnic and, above all, economic and ecological contexts. Psychic reality and sociopolitical reality conjoin.

The general point about the *contingency of the person* – that, being embedded in an environment, we are socially constructed beings – has led to the realization that there is very little that is definitely fixed in the human sciences (no single conception of human nature), no fundamental and determining level in the psychological sphere (no agreement on what is given or constitutional in personality), no insulated gender essence (what used to be called masculine or feminine characteristics).[1] Although this perspective, which (following Richard Rorty) we can call in shorthand *person-as-contingent*,[2] is the dominant one in *fin-de-siècle* social science, its counter-intuitive stress on mutability and relativity means that it is still an ideology of and for intellectuals, swimming in a hostile, populist humanistic sea that favors an epistemology of the fixed, the constitutional and the essential. Neither the wider world nor conventional depth psychology, especially psychodynamics, accept that such things as human nature, constitutional personality, and 'true' men or women do not exist. The advantage of contingency theory is that it recognizes that we cannot in principle distinguish between the constructed nature of our intelligible world and the independent structure of the natural world. Person-as-contingent remains a radical perspective which, save for Lacanian psychoanalysis, has seemed inherently hostile to depth psychology. But even Lacanian theorizing is uncomfortable with the full implications of contingency, having translated or, possibly, distorted the notion of contingency into something fixed, constitutional and essential. As Teresa

Brennan points out, the relation of Lacanian contingency to change is 'unpromising'; the Symbolic order is portrayed by Lacan as a 'universal, structural event'.[3]

PERSON-AS-BRIDGE

How, then, is the *person* to be viewed in a way that allows for his or her existence yet acknowledges the crucial significance of the political and cultural dimensions? What is the most appropriate and effective language to use? I do not disagree with those, like Jung or Hillman, who assert that the 'soul has inhuman reaches'.[4] But I wonder if what is meant by 'inhuman' is not sometimes taken in too limited a way: Gods, animals, colors, primary qualities such as beauty. But what if we understand 'the inhuman' as referring to culture, society, the economy, the political system and the environment – and the ways these impact on persons? All of these are inhuman in the sense that they are not purely human productions, and certainly not the personal productions of specific humans. But there is a human aspect to the inhuman. Unfortunately, a tendency has developed in which any exploration of the human person is castigated by Jungians as often as by Lacanians as 'personalistic' or 'egocentric' and as constituting some kind of humanistic/subjectivist takeover of the psyche or unconscious.

Doubtless, there are many nuances here but, as I hope to show, much is lost as far as cultural and political analysis is concerned by an apparently sophisticated refusal to acknowledge fully what is involved in the psychology of the person and of the human subject. We might recall here my remark in Chapter 1 that a culture that is fragmented, fractured and complex is being confronted by a political analysis that is equally fragmented, fractured and complex. Where does that similarly fragmented, fractured and complex entity – the person – fit in?

Perceiving the person as contingent implies a dethroning of the subject, a project carried out in their different ways by Freud, Marx, Jung and Hillman.[5] Lacanian psychoanalysis has also displayed a supposedly new notion of the person as a non-united and 'decentered' human subject. The problem is that the elusive human subject has not gone as far away as is claimed, and, much more important, was never there in the first place – at least not in the way described. Depth psychology in particular and the human sciences in general have to deal with the return of the person, making his or her claim to ontological priority. This is a longstanding and perfectly valid philosophical claim: The person existing prior to body, prior to society, prior to word, prior to image. All of these – body, society, word, image – somehow depend on the notion of the irreducible person.

Clearly, there is more to psychology than the isolated individual human being, or small therapy group, and cultural and political analysis cannot depend solely on findings from clinical work. But the person who is deposed in different ways by the contingency of Lacanian psychoanalysis and the psychologizing of Hillman's archetypal psychology is *not* the only person there is. He or she is instead a distortion of the person as presented in the work of others. If we really were to equate the person with the ego, or with sentimental, humanistic, ahistorical trumpeting of the supremacy of the so-called individual, then hurrah for Lacan and the others for getting rid of a dangerously misleading conception! But this unthinking and reactionary version is not the only possible playing out of the person. The person who needs our attention and therapy has never been like that, never been solely the product of Puritanism, nor snowy white, nor a romantic cliché, nor a humanistic ideal, nor 'the patient', nor the unified being of orthodox psychology, nor Jungian Self, nor Freudian ego. Did those pristine creatures, who certainly deserve a critique, ever exist? Or are they part of a transference onto analysis, onto Freud, Jung and their disciples, that leads to the accusation of intellectual blindness on their part?

The person who stalks contemporary culture, and who is trying to return to its politics, has *always been* a decentered subject, an actor playing many roles in many scripts, characterized by lack, somewhat faded as well as jaded, jerky, marginalized, alienated, split, guilty, empty, Imaginary. The person has *always been* a Trickster in his or her attitude to psychological growth, Machiavellian in his or her understanding of politics. There have always been subpersonalities, though it took psychology to raise them to consciousness. Post-Lacan, we see that *his* Imaginary human subject is the only person there has ever been – Hermetic, anti-heroic, plural. Lacan was describing the case, not discovering its contradiction; he was developing a text, not settling an argument.

In a way, the contemporary critique of the person requires its own psychological critique. Is the specter of naive individualism really so threatening that it calls forth such iron-hard defenses? Why are theorists like Hillman so selective concerning anthropomorphic movements of the psyche itself? I ask, as he has asked: Why does the psyche personify? Why are dreams, fantasies, narratives and memories full of people? It could be said that all these people are metaphors and I certainly would not disagree with that. But, as we saw in the case of 'The father of whatever sex', at the core of the metaphor lies something that has an ongoing life of its own.

When the psyche empowers images of persons, it cannot stop the various qualities of those persons *as persons* from shining through.

I do not think that persons somehow 'create' the social world they inhabit. I am not one of those who turn automatically to the idea of *anima mundi*, soul of or in the world, a fantasy in which the psyche vivifies the material universe – for me, the social world needs no more life than the rich life it already has.[6] Nor do I think the social world is created by projective identification, the colonizing of the world by unconscious phantasy, the modern, infantilized version of *anima mundi* and psychoanalytic heir to the idealist philosophical tradition.[7]

Nevertheless, I think there is something we can do with this de-idealized, putrefied, violent and marvellously rebellious person. The decentered person, understood as a description of what is the case and not as a contradiction of a contrived alternative, is the *means* to fashion a psychological analysis of politics and culture, not an *obstacle* to it. The decentered person is the means by which the world asks for therapy and the means by which depth psychology can provide therapy for the world. For the person makes and is made by the world in a ceaseless generative struggle. Just as the state has not withered away anywhere, the person has not been totally deconstructed. The person is where we find our bridges: Between inner and outer, physical and mental, body and soul, mind and spirit, world and psyche, politics and psychology. And the person, in his or her very existence, deposes the binary base of those oppositions; they are too cut-and-dried. To the fragmentations, fractures and complexities of the culture itself, and to the fragmentations, fractures and complexities of political analysis, we have added those of the person. If we do not allow this person 'in', then the relations between depth psychology and the political world will remain purely formal.

As a pluralist, I accept that the person will have to compete and bargain his or her way back into contemporary discourse. But pluralism is not a dry perspective; passion abides in dialogue and tolerance as much as it does in monologue and fanaticism. Being pluralistic about the presence of the person in contemporary discourse does not mean that people should lose their critical faculties, becoming unable to recognize philosophical differences. But it does mean that we become adept at moving freely through a variety of different discourses (person-as-contingent/person-as-bridge), increasingly reluctant to privilege one mode of expression over another.

Maimonides addressed similar questions to those explored in this chapter.[8] He was puzzled over how to reconcile human creativity, individuality and autonomy with the facts of having been created by God and belonging to the human species. His startling suggestion was that human beings certainly do have autonomous and creative powers but, being created by God, they can only create *in the direction of God*, becoming persons of God. Human creation is a limited kind of creation and headed in a predictable direction. But it is creation nonetheless. To the extent that the person is a player in the political field, we can adapt the structure of Maimonides's argument to suggest that human creation will tend to move *in the direction of social and political activity* because of human immersion in the social and political realms. In other words, we make use of the apparent weakness in the person's case to be heard – that he or she is created by the contingency of the social and political realms. Yes, we are so created. But our powers of creation move, as Maimonides teaches, in the direction of that which has created us.

Part III

The political therapist

In Part III my attention turns to the political role of therapists and analysts. I begin with the results of an international survey by means of a questionnaire on the topic of political material that is brought into the consulting room. Then I explore the strengths and weaknesses of one particular approach to depth psychology – object relations theory – in the formation of a depth psychological approach to politics. I conclude that chapter with a discussion of several different perspectives on group and institutional dynamics. The following two chapters constitute critical reflections on the question of C. G. Jung's alleged anti-semitism and pro-Nazi collaboration. The background to the allegations is the confused and confusing political scene in Europe in the 1930s and so the chapters also stand as a cautionary tale for those depth psychologists interested in the politics of the 1990s. This is not the kind of book that has a tight conclusion, so I have entitled the closing chapter 'Ending and beginning'.

Chapter 10

Political material in the clinical setting
Replies to an international survey

INTRODUCTION

In my analytical practice, I noted that many patients seemed to be introducing political themes more often than they had before. Talking to a few colleagues confirmed that this was also their experience and we tended to put it down to the fact that, since the mid-1980s, the pace of political change in the world appeared to have quickened. But, we also agreed, we were not as sure as we once were how to understand and handle this material. At times, as I noted in Chapter 1, I felt that the usual formulation – that such material needs to be understood symbolically, perhaps as a communication on the transference–countertransference level – was still adequate to guide practice. At other times, it turned out that the patient had a need to talk about some public issue, such as the Gulf War, but had 'learned' that, in analysis, you don't do that. Hence, behind many apparent transference communications there seemed also to be a concern, perhaps still on a psychological level, for the political theme, issue or problem that had been introduced – but in its own right.

I decided that what was needed was a large-scale investigation, by means of a questionnaire, to see if analysts and psychotherapists were experiencing something similar in significant numbers.[1] I therefore obtained the cooperation of fourteen professional organizations in seven countries (the individuals I linked up with are noted in the Acknowledgments). By a variety of means, ranging from direct mailing to piggy-backing on the organization's regular mailing to members, and sometimes making use of pigeon-holes for easy return of the survey form, approximately 2000 questionnaires were sent out. Over 600 forms were returned, making a worldwide return rate of 32 per cent. To be frank, I had not expected anything like this return rate, having been advised that, in the case of a 'cold-call' questionnaire like this one, a return rate of around 10 to 15 per cent would be expected and would be regarded as pretty good.

As Table 10.1 shows, in some cases the return rate was as high as 48 per cent, and even when the recipient had to take specific action to return the questionnaire, such as purchasing an airmail stamp, the return rate was nearly 30 per cent. In fact, in only one instance (the replies from Brazil) was the return rate below 20 per cent. I am not sure how to understand this high return rate, though obviously I am gratified by it. Could it be that the curiosity that motivated me to undertake this project is something that is shared with a great number of colleagues?

Let me move on to say something about the organizations that were included in the survey. Because, as a Jungian analyst, I had the personal contacts to facilitate the practicalities, eight of the fourteen organizations involved are of Jungian analysts. However, three psychoanalytic organizations also took part (two from the United States and one from Britain). Thus comparisons between psychoanalysis and analytical psychology are possible, as well as comparisons between the different Jungian groups and between American and British psychoanalysts. I also included in the survey one of the leading British humanistic psychotherapy organizations and a professional grouping of therapists based in Moscow, which provides further opportunities to explore contrasts according to orientation and location.

Table 10.1 Response rates by organization

	Sent out	Returned	Response rate (%)
British Psychoanalysts	301	129	43
British Jungians	134	59	44
British Psychotherapists	298	100	34
British Humanistics	79	38	48
US Psychoanalysts	491	108	22
US Jungians	166	47	28
Italian Jungians	98	20	20
German Jungians	288	74	26
Israeli Jungians	26	10	38
Brazilian Jungians	54	7	13
Russian Therapists	29	29	100
Worldwide	1,964	621	32

The groups involved were:

1 The *British Psycho-Analytical Society* – the only official psycho-analytic body in Britain and home base of many important thinkers in the field such as Klein, Winnicott, Bion, etc. Hereafter referred to as the *British Psychoanalysts*.

2 The *Society of Analytical Psychology* – the oldest Jungian professional training body in Britain and the largest. The society is characterized in the Jungian world as having the closest links to psychoanalysis of any Jungian group. Hereafter referred to as the *British Jungians*.

3 The *Institute of Psychotherapy and Counselling* – this is the pro-fessional organization of the graduates of the Westminster Pastoral Foundation, which provides professional-level training in psycho-therapy with an eclectic orientation. Hereafter referred to as the *British Psychotherapists*.

4 The *Association of Humanistic Psychology Practitioners* – this is an umbrella body devoted to the maintenance of high standards in humanistic psychotherapy, containing practitioners from a variety of humanistic orientations and training. Hereafter referred to as the *British Humanistics*.

5 The *National Psychological Association for Psychoanalysis* and the *San Francisco Psychoanalytic Institute* were the two American psychoanalytic organizations that I invited to participate in the survey. Although I am aware that, in terms of professional politics, these organizations enjoy very few or indeed no linkages at all, I was advised that it would give a fairer picture of the United States scene in psychoanalysis if two organizations were involved. (In fact, there was no discernible difference between the replies postmarked 'New York' and the replies postmarked 'San Francisco' save for the fact that slightly more New York respondents stated that they were Jewish.) Hereafter referred to as the *US Psychoanalysts*.

6 For similar reasons, I invited three United States professional training organizations in analytical psychology to participate. These were the *Society of Jungian Analysts of Northern California*, the *Society of Jungian Analysts of Southern California*, and the *Chicago Society of Jungian Analysts*. I am satisfied that these three groups provide a representative spread of the trends within analytical psychology in the United States. Hereafter referred to as the *US Jungians*.

7 The *Centro Italiano di Psicologia Analitica* is one of the two Jungian professional training bodies in Italy. There are some ideological differences with the other group but this is not the only reason for the

existence of two organizations. Hereafter referred to as the *Italian Jungians*.

8 The *Deutsche Gesellschaft für Analytische Psychologie* is the German professional training body for analytical psychology. Hereafter referred to as the *German Jungians*.

9 The *Israel Association of Analytical Psychology* is the Jungian professional training body in Israel. Hereafter referred to as the *Israeli Jungians*.

10 The *Sociedade Brasileira de Psicologia Analitica* is the official Jungian professional training body in Brazil. Hereafter referred to as the *Brazilian Jungians*.

11 The *Russian Association of Practical Psychologists* contains a psycho-dynamically oriented professional grouping of therapists based in Moscow. It is not the only such grouping in Russia but it is the one with which I have had contact. Hereafter referred to as the *Russian Therapists*.

Table 10.1 shows the return rates by organization and I would like to comment briefly on these data. I was surprised to get such a high rate of return (43 per cent) from the British Psychoanalysts because – and this is borne out by the results – I imagined that the members of this body would be the most hostile to the survey. Perhaps the high rate of return was helped by the provision of a pre-stamped reply envelope. This was necessary because of the British Psychoanalysts' standing policy of not using their regular mailings to members for non-official purposes. The return rate of 22 per cent from the American Psychoanalysts was achieved in spite of the fact that purchase of an airmail stamp was required. The return rate from Brazil was disappointing because, on a visit there to give lectures, I had gained the impression of the existence of a very high degree of political sensibility. On the other hand, the 100 per cent return rate from Russia speaks for itself. However, I have noticed that the level of work carried out by the Russian Therapists is clearly different from that carried out by members of the other groupings (for obvious reasons – psycho-therapy is only just getting going again in the former Soviet Union). Because of this discrepancy between the Russian Therapists and the rest, and because of the low return from Brazil both in percentage and absolute terms, I have provided two sets of overall figures to facilitate comparison between the data from any one grouping and the data as obtained worldwide. The first overall, global figure is an average of percentages worldwide. The second overall, global figure is an average of percentages worldwide minus Brazil and Russia. Occasionally, it is clear that taking this step was absolutely necessary.

I have listed the participating organizations in a special order so as to facilitate comparison between organizations, groups of organizations, orientations and locations. I keep to this order throughout my account of the replies to the questionnaire.

THE QUESTIONNAIRE

At this point, we should look at the questionnaire and covering letter that were sent out.

Dear Colleague,

QUESTIONNAIRE ON POLITICAL MATERIAL BROUGHT INTO THE CLINICAL SETTING

I am writing to you to ask for your help with a survey I am conducting into the question of political material that is brought into the clinical setting.

I apologise for taking up your time with this but I hope you will feel that this project is worthwhile and timely.

The questionnaire is anonymous but I plan to publish the results in due course.

After giving the matter a good deal of thought, I have decided not to define the term 'politics' in any overall way. Of course, it would be possible to do so and there are many definitions available. It seemed better to let respondents make up their own minds. However, if you feel you would like to discuss what might be meant by 'politics' before answering the questions, do not hesitate to contact me.

The questionnaire is being sent to psychoanalysts, analytical psychologists and psychotherapists in Britain, psychoanalysts and analytical psychologists in the United States, analytical psychologists in Germany, Italy and Brazil, and psychotherapists in Russia. Hopefully a mass of interesting, comparative data will emerge.

I'd like to thank you in anticipation of receiving your completed questionnaire.

Yours sincerely,
Andrew Samuels

Training Analyst, Society of Analytical Psychology, London
Scientific Associate, American Academy of Psychoanalysis
Honorary Research Fellow, Centre for Psychoanalytic Studies, University of Kent

PS: It would be helpful to have your reply within six weeks of receiving the questionnaire. Unfortunately, I do not have the funding to provide a stamped return envelope. I hope you will find the project sufficiently interesting to feel able to airmail me your reply.

1 The questionnaire is anonymous but it would be most helpful if you could give your sex, age, and number of years in analytical/psychotherapeutic practice.

2 If and when your patients/clients introduce political material into their sessions, which themes do they introduce? (please tick)
   International politics
   National politics
   Local (community) politics
   Economic issues (e.g. distribution of wealth, poverty, inflation)
   Third World issues
   Racial or ethnic issues
   Gender issues for women
   Gender issues for men
   Environmental concerns
   Nuclear energy
   Nuclear weapons
   Issues to do with mass media
   Violence in society
   Other issues (please specify)
   (*Note*: It is perfectly OK to tick most or all of these.)

3 Reviewing your practice as a whole, please say which three themes are introduced most frequently (in order of frequency).

4 Does the setting of your work affect the introduction of political material? If you work in private AND institutional settings, what differences have you noticed in this area?

5 Thinking of your patients/clients individually, do you think the themes introduced are connected to the age and sex of the patient?

6 Do you think the themes introduced are connected to the sex and age of the patient relative to your sex and age? (I am interested to see if a correspondence of sex and age between analyst/therapist and patient/client leads to a more frequent introduction of political material.)

7 Generalizing will be difficult, but could you give a list of the possible ways you react to, or handle, or interpret this kind of material?

8 Do you find yourself discussing political issues with your patients/clients?

9 If the answer to question 8 is 'no', why not?

10 If the answer to question 8 is 'yes', which themes mentioned in question 2 have you found yourself discussing with patients/clients in the past 3 years?

11 Has this always been the situation in your practice or have you noticed any changes in the way you work concerning political material?

12 Were matters like those being raised by this questionnaire addressed in your training?

13 If the answer to question 12 is 'yes', was this as part of the formal training (seminars or supervision) or in less formal discussion?

14 Were political issues as such discussed during your training?

15 Were political issues discussed as part of the application process for training?

The following questions are optional but I very much hope you will feel able to answer them.

16 In a few lines, please say something about your own political attitudes. What do you see as having influenced your political attitudes? For example, ethnic/racial background, parental attitudes, socioeconomic background, moral values, religious values, particular event(s), etc. Please specify.

17 Have you ever been politically active (defined in any way you like)?

18 If the answer to question 17 is 'yes', please give brief details.

19 Are you politically active now?

20 If so, in what way?

Thank you for answering these questions. If you would like to comment at any length on the questionnaire and the topics it surveys, please feel free to do so.

SCOPE, HYPOTHESES, VALIDITY

The questionnaire falls into five sections. I will delineate these and say something about the purpose of the questions and my expectations concerning the answers. I will also state briefly what the hypotheses were. In the later parts of the chapter, I will work through the replies question by question.

Questions 1–6 concern overt political material that is brought into the consulting room. This means that the practitioner would have to recognize, by whatever yardsticks, that the material was indeed political. Hence, I provided a list of possible political themes and problems. I was also interested to see if the setting in which the work took place affected the introduction of political material and to explore whether the sex and age of both practitioner and patient made any difference to the prevalence of political material and to its precise nature. My hypothesis was that patients in publicly funded treatment settings would introduce political material more often and that age and sex of either participant would be highly significant.

Questions 7–11 concern the practitioner's understanding and management of such material. My expectation was that for the most part a symbolic, intrapsychic, transferential approach would be taken to political material. However, I expected that there would be important national differences in this and maybe some differences due to orientation. A further hypothesis was that more political themes were being raised at the present time than previously but that the ways in which the practitioners conceptualized and handled such material would *not* have changed very much. I thought that there would be a pattern in which certain specific themes might lead to 'discussion' between practitioner and patient. However, I assumed that only quite small numbers would actually agree or admit to having 'discussed' political issues with their patients and that a picture would emerge of a massive denial of the 'reality' of sociopolitical thematic material that is brought into the clinical situation. In the following pages, we will see how this and other expectations/hypotheses of mine were or were not fulfilled.

Questions 12–15 concern training in analysis, psychotherapy and therapy. I asked (a) whether questions of understanding and managing political material had been covered in training; (b) whether this was done formally or informally or both formally and informally; (c) whether politics as such were discussed during training. As we will see, careless drafting on my part produced some confusion. The hypotheses were that the kinds of issues raised by the questionnaire would most certainly have been raised in training – that is, how to understand and manage overt political material in the treatment situation would have been a topic in training. However, I hypothesized that politics *qua* politics would not have been a part of the training at all.

Questions 16–20 concern the political histories and activities of the respondents. Question 16 invites political credos. Questions 17–20 were intended to ascertain levels of political activity by self-definition. I expected low positive replies to 'Have you ever been politically active?' and 'Are you politically active now?' with a slight, inevitable falling off due to age, increase in responsibilities, etc.

Finally, respondents were invited to comment further on the questionnaire and the topics it surveys. Many did so and their comments fell into two categories: Those which focused on the quality, efficacy and purpose of the questionnaire itself – and those which provided some kind of overall comment that the respondent wished to make on the psychology/politics 'field'. Many respondents took advantage of the invitation to comment freely, often at some length, and I will provide a selection of these comments, as they pertain to psychology and politics, later in the chapter. For the moment, I want to concentrate on the comments that were directly addressed to the questionnaire itself because these are relevant at this point in the chapter, in a section on 'Scope, hypotheses, validity'.

There were quite a number of short comments of a positive or negative kind. For example, a British Psychoanalyst wrote: 'Don't see the point of this', whereas a US Psychoanalyst wrote: 'Great idea – well done'. I do not propose to cite any more of this kind of short condemnations or commendations but to focus on lengthier contributions. However, I must add that a great proportion of the negative comments, and a discernible proportion of the positive comments, came from British Psychoanalysts. That is to say, when invited to comment further on the questionnaire and the topics it surveys, British Psychoanalysts as a group interpreted it as an invitation to judge or assess the survey itself, whereas members of other groups seemed somewhat more inclined to expand on their own thinking on these matters. In general, I must admit that I was simply not prepared for such an active role on the part of the respondents and the whole project has become very much bigger than I anticipated.

Before allowing the respondents to speak for themselves, I will add a note about the conventions I have adopted with regard to quotation from the completed questionnaire. Wherever possible (meaning in virtually every instance) I have quoted the reply in full. After some deliberation, I have decided not to give any demographic information that might identify the respondent to his or her colleagues. I have only indicated to which organization the respondent belongs using the shorthand tags described above. I realize this is a loss but I felt that confidentiality should be preserved. Consequently, details that might identify a respondent have been altered, much as one would disguise the details of a patient about whom one was writing. (The whole matter of confidentiality has thrown up another, surprising problem. Many respondents asked to see an account of my results but did not give their name and address! Others gave name and address without my having asked for this information.) I hope the conventions I have adopted represent a sensible compromise.

Here is a selection of negative comments concerning the questionnaire itself:

> Badly designed questionnaire, waffly, imprecise, questions badly defined, etc. No information about the object of the research. Publish results of what?   *(British Psychoanalyst)*

> None of it is well thought out or well designed or clearly expressed. You don't even define the term 'political'. No reliance could be put on any results.   *(British Psychoanalyst)*

> Hard to understand – don't feel wording well thought out. Feel as though you're trying to prove something you already believe rather than open-mindedly investigate.   *(British Humanistic)*

Here is a selection of positive comments concerning the questionnaire itself:

> I am trained as a social psychologist. Questionnaires have been a part of my professional life for years. About 15 years ago, I became totally disgusted with them. Specifically, I was disgusted with their lack of validity and the way they promote a sort of 'sound bite' mentality. The informality of this one has seduced me into breaking my 15 year avoidance.   *(US Jungian)*

> This is an excellent questionnaire which has made me think about several particular patients and my general approach to my practice in a quite new way. I am grateful for the stimulus to think and, even within the same survey form, to think again. I'd say you've constructively broken a major taboo and I'll be curious to see what follows now. But I predict it could be a far from easy ride!   *(US Psychoanalyst)*

> I like the questionnaire because, among other things, it has caused me to think about items which generally never occupy my attention. I have been involved to some degree in professional politics but I do not personally take to politics and probably have a kind of cynicism that there are very few good leaders whom one can sanguinely endorse.
> *(US Psychoanalyst)*

> Of course it was hard to use a few words only to write about complex issues but it was worth it and I think my work might be influenced by the thoughts this has stimulated – maybe I can bring inner and outer

together a bit more confidently now. Thanks for the unexpected bonus after doing the tedious bit of filling this thing in!

(British Psychotherapist)

This is very interesting and not questions I've been asked prior to this about my practice.   *(US Jungian)*

I'm happy about this questionnaire as it communicates the impression that with other male and female colleagues there are thoughts toward an opening out toward the urgent problems of our time. Motto: 'We're leaving the Ivory Tower'.   *(German Jungian)*

I am afraid that my brief answers do not match the intense way I feel about these issues. A mixture of lack of time and the shape of the questionnaire that is so general. I do think, though, that it is an important theme to be addressed and wish you all the best in your research.   *(British Psychoanalyst)*

Generally speaking, the proportion of positive to negative comments was 70 per cent positive to 30 per cent negative. However, we can safely assume that the negative sentiments were undoubtedly on the minds of many of those who did not reply at all and may also represent the views of some who did complete the questionnaire. We may also assume that those who did not respond contain a relatively high proportion of those who, on reflection, considered the survey pointless, trivial, misguided, etc.

As far as the question of the validity of these findings is concerned, my own view is that, as will become clearer, the results are extremely interesting and destabilize certain assumptions about analytical and therapeutic practice which, I believe, have been widely shared by practitioners and critics alike. I do not for a moment think that the questionnaire replies *prove* anything beyond doubt. But they are, at the very least, extremely interesting and suggestive and, I hope, will not be ignored. I suppose that the challenge I would issue to critics of the whole project of the survey is to ask if it is truly possible *not* to react at all to the findings and to the thoughtful, subtle, complex answers of the respondents that I shall be quoting. It would have been possible to make the questionnaire into a more formal kind of document, using closed category questions, a scoring system, etc. In fact, my Russian colleague, acting on her own initiative, did take the questionnaire and translate it into just such a document. However, the Russian replies were not noticeably easier to 'score' or to assign to categories than the other replies. I suppose I took a calculated gamble in sending out the questionnaire in its present form, realizing, of course, that some of the questions were themselves 'politically' sensitive in professional, psychological (and, especially, psychoanalytic) discourse. That said, the tables that follow do, I think, display a certain reliability of the kind usually associated with statistical reports of replies to question-naires. For those who are put off by tables, I have organized the chapter so that only minimal study of the tables is necessary.

Question 1: Demography

Overall, excluding Brazil and Russia, as Table 10.2 shows, the female–male ratio was 56–44 per cent. Overall, excluding Brazil and Russia, 78 per cent of the respondents were forty-five years old or over. Overall, excluding Brazil and Russia, 72 per cent of respondents had ten or more years of experience. I chose the markers of forty-five years of age and ten years of experience because I had hoped to be able to focus to some extent on what younger and less experienced practitioners were doing and thinking. As it turned out, and no doubt this is due to the fact that analysis/psychotherapy is a career undertaken at a relatively advanced age in many countries, the survey population did not contain as many 'young' practitioners as I had hoped. However, the social circumstances which tend to postpone analytical or psychotherapy training for many individuals cannot explain why it was that so many relatively experienced practitioners chose to answer the survey, and so many relatively inexperienced practitioners did not. Perhaps the data reflect the degree of experience in the various organizations but, by scanning the dates of qualification in the membership rosters of two societies (British Jungians and British Psychotherapists), it is clear that there was more likely a pattern in which the questionnaire itself appealed to more experienced practitioners. Given the recent growth in size of many trainings, particularly in the Jungian world, it is noteworthy that the most youthful cohort do seem to be underrepresented in this survey, except, perhaps, the British Humanistics and the Russian Therapists (see below). The case of the United States Jungians is particularly interesting. While I would have expected that a very high proportion of respondents would be forty-five and over, I would certainly have expected to receive *some* replies from those with less than 10 years' experience. Incidentally, where analyst respondents quoted differing durations of psychotherapeutic or analytic practice, I took account only of their experience as analysts.

(The age spread of the respondents becomes relevant when we reach the replies to questions 5, 6 and, especially, 11. With regard to question 11, which seeks to establish if the situation concerning the practitioner's understanding and handling of political material has changed or remained

Table 10.2 Respondents' sex, age, and years in practice

	M under 45		M 45+		F under 45		F 45+		Total % of replies		Total % of replies		No reply
	<10	10+	<10	10+	<10	10+	<10	10+	M	F	45+	10+	
British Psychoanalysts	5 (4%)	5 (4%)	1 (1%)	44 (34%)	7 (5%)	1 (1%)	10 (8%)	36 (28%)	50%	50%	83%	79%	20 (16%)
British Jungians	3 (5%)	3 (5%)	3 (5%)	9 (15%)	6 (10%)	0 (0%)	4 (7%)	26 (44%)	33%	67%	71%	70%	5 (8%)
British Psychotherapists	4 (4%)	0 (0%)	10 (10%)	8 (8%)	14 (14%)	2 (2%)	44 (44%)	18 (18%)	22%	78%	80%	26%	0 (0%)
British Humanistics	1 (3%)	3 (8%)	3 (8%)	9 (24%)	5 (13%)	4 (11%)	1 (3%)	11 (29%)	43%	59%	65%	73%	1 (3%)
US Psychoanalysts	2 (2%)	4 (4%)	4 (4%)	42 (39%)	4 (4%)	4 (4%)	0 (0%)	40 (37%)	52%	48%	86%	86%	8 (7%)
US Jungians	0 (0%)	0 (0%)	0 (0%)	30 (64%)	0 (0%)	0 (0%)	0 (0%)	17 (36%)	64%	36%	100%	100%	0 (0%)
Italian Jungians	0 (0%)	0 (0%)	0 (0%)	6 (30%)	0 (0%)	6 (30%)	0 (0%)	6 (30%)	33%	67%	67%	67%	2 (10%)
German Jungians	5 (7%)	3 (4%)	3 (4%)	25 (34%)	2 (3%)	3 (4%)	6 (8%)	25 (34%)	50%	50%	76%	78%	2 3%
Israeli Jungians	2 (20%)	0 (0%)	0 (0%)	2 (20%)	0 (0%)	0 (0%)	0 (0%)	4 (40%)	50%	50%	75%	75%	2 20%
Brazilian Jungians	0 (0%)	0 (0%)	0 (0%)	1 (14%)	0 (0%)	3 (43%)	0 (0%)	2 (29%)	17%	83%	43%	50%	1 (14%)
Russian Therapists	6 (21%)	3% (10%)	0% (0%)	0% (0%)	15% (52%)	5% (17%)	0% (0%)	0% (0%)	31%	69%	0%	27%	0 (0%)
Average percentage worldwide	6%	3%	3%	26%	8%	10%	6%	30%	40%	60%	68%	66%	7%
Average percentage worldwide minus Brazil and Russia	5%	3%	4%	30%	4%	6%	8%	33%	44%	56%	78%	72%	7%

the same, there was a divergence of opinion over whether greater experience made one more or less likely to 'discuss' political material or to somehow build an apperception of political 'reality' into clinical work.)

There are a few departures from the 56–44 per cent female–male ratio that are worth discussing. Both groups of psychoanalysts had more males than the average in them. Among the Jungians, the German, Israeli and US Jungians had relatively more males than the other groups. I was not surprised that the British Psychotherapists showed such a preponderance of females as I know that this is a recognized feature of their training intake. Similarly, the fact that the training program of the British Psychotherapists has not been established for as long as the other programs explains the paucity of respondents with ten or more years' experience. Other groups with a significantly high proportion of females over males included the British, Italian and Brazilian Jungians.

The situation of the Russian Therapists is obviously special, demographically speaking, and this is shown by the fact that every respondent was under the age of forty-five.

Questions 2 and 3: Which political themes?

My intention was to get an impression of the whole spread of political themes that are currently being introduced into the clinical situation (question 1). Then I hoped to be able to get some sense of which themes cropped up more often. In the event, as all the themes cropped up to some extent, it was more useful to combine these two inquiries into one, and the result of this is shown in Table 10.3.

Table 10.3 shows how many times each political theme was mentioned in response to question 2 (which asked respondents to say which themes were introduced). In the event, I decided not to use the results from the question about the frequency of specific themes. Rather, I decided to score how often a particular theme was checked on the long list of themes given in question 2. The reasons were that many respondents listed more than three themes in reply to the question concerning frequency or declined to order the themes in any way. Therefore question 3 became redundant and I subsumed it into question 2. The results are much more interesting and comparisons between the organisations are greatly facilitated.

Thus, if we take the British Psychoanalysts as an example, we can see that the theme most often mentioned as occurring was 'gender issues for women' ('women' in Table 10.3). This was followed by 'gender issues for men' ('men'), 'racial or ethnic issues' ('race'). One can chart the issues raised down to 'local (community) politics' ('local pol.') in tenth place.

Table 10.3 Frequency with which specific political themes are introduced

	1	2	3	4	5	6	7	8	9	10	Number of respondents to survey
British Psychoanalysts	women 72	men 43	race 34	violence 31	int. pol. 31	nat. pol. 30	economics 26	environ. 16	nuclear weapons 13	local pol. 12	129
British Jungians	economics 39	women 38	race 24	environ. 22	int. pol. 21	nat. pol. 21	men 21	local pol. 12	violence 10	media 3	59
British Psychotherapists	women 86	economics 54	men 52	nat. pol. 32	race 30	int. pol. 18	environ. 16	local pol. 16	nuclear weapons 10	violence 10	100
British Humanistics	women 33	economics 25	men 24	environ. 15	nat. pol. 10	race 8	media 4	int. pol. 4	local pol. 3	Third World 2	38
US Psychoanalysts	women 70	violence 44	men 44	econ. 42	race 36	nat. pol. 36	environ. 24	int. pol. 18	local pol. 18	media 4	108
US Jungians	women 37	nat. pol. 23	econ. 23	environ. 19	men 18	violence 12	race 6	nuclear energy 2	nuclear weapons 1	Third World 1	47
Italian Jungians	economics 12	violence 12	nat. pol. 9	women 9	men 5	environ. 3	nuclear weapons 3	nuclear energy 2	race 2	int. pol. 2	20
German Jungians	environ. 42	women 31	violence 29	int. pol. 24	men 21	econ. 14	nuclear energy 14	nat. pol. 13	race 8	nuclear weapons 6	74
Israeli Jungians	nat. pol. 10	int. pol. 6	violence 6	race 4	women 4	men 4	economics 2	–	–	–	10
Brazilian Jungians	economics 7	nat. pol. 6	violence 4	women 4	race 2	local pol. 2	Third World 1	–	–	–	7
Russian Therapists	economics 23	violence 18	women 17	men 14	nat. pol. 11	race 3	media 3	local pol. 3	–	–	29

'Gender issues for women' was the most frequently mentioned theme by respondents from five organizations. 'Economic issues' was first in the case of four organizations. The Israeli Jungians most frequently cited 'national politics' and the German Jungians 'environmental concerns'.

A more satisfactory way of organising these findings is to ascertain which specific themes occurred most often in the top three mentioned. If we examine the table we find that 'gender issues for women' is mentioned in the top three 8 times. 'Economics' is mentioned in the top three 7 times. 'Violence in society' is mentioned in the top three 6 times, 'National politics' and 'gender issues for men' are mentioned in the top three 4 times each. 'Racial or ethnic issues' is mentioned in the top three 2 times. 'International politics' is mentioned in the top three 1 time.

This gives a 'league table' as follows:

1 gender issues for women
2 economic issues (e.g. distribution of wealth, poverty, inflation)
3 violence in society
4 national politics
   gender issues for men
5 racial or ethnic issues
6 international politics

It is interesting to note and to reflect on deviations from this order. For example, the British Psychoanalysts placed economic issues in seventh place. It is possible that this reflects something about the socioeconomic status of the patients of British Psychoanalysts because the other three British organizations placed economics either first or second.

The Israeli and Brazilian Jungians placed 'gender issues for women' lower down than other organizations and this may reflect different social situations in these countries. In Israel, it may be that, perhaps due to army service, women have achieved a degree of social equality that they have not in other countries and that gender issues for women are therefore not as pressing. Or, possibly more likely, it may be that so many other issues impinge on the patients of Israeli Jungians that gender issues for women are squeezed out by politics, violence and racial/ethnic issues.

In Brazil, it is possible that concerns over gender issues have simply not reached the pitch or intensity that they have in Europe and North America. Or, as in the case of Israel, there is simply so much else to worry about. The Russian Therapists may, once again, have to be regarded as a special case because, as we will see in a special note written by the coordinator of the survey in Russia, 'gender issues' might well not be regarded as 'political' at all. Nevertheless, in spite of this, the Russian results do not stand out in any way.

From this panorama, I think it is reasonable to argue that national location plays a major part in the political themes that are mentioned in the clinical situation. In which case, the themes that are raised within each patient population may tell us something about the overall state of psychological preoccupation with politics in that population. For example, the regularly high placing of 'economics' at a time of world recession is surely generally significant, as is the high placing of 'violence' in the replies from some groupings.

I had expected 'issues to do with mass media' to figure more prominently and I was struck by the way in which respondents could clearly distinguish between gender issues for women and for men. Of course, the men's movement is still in its infancy, even in the US. The high placing of racial or ethnic issues in the replies from the British Psychoanalysts and British Jungians is also of interest and I had not expected the German Jungians to put environmental concerns first.

To be frank, I think that the best way of getting something out of the replies to questions 2 and 3 is, having understood to what the table refers, to let one's mind float across the results, trying to marry them up with what is known or even believed to be the case in relation to the political scene in the various countries involved in the survey. What I have tried to do in this commentary on Table 10.3 is to indicate the sort of thinking that is possible and to suggest that, to the degree that there is something like a 'national psyche' and to the degree that this will have a political component, the answers to these two questions provide some clues about the state of the national psyches in the countries concerned.

Question 4: Does the setting make a difference?

I was interested to see if the setting – private practice or state/public/institutional/municipal setting – made a difference to the frequency with which political material is introduced. The key columns in Table 10.4 are the fourth and fifth from the left which show the totals for 'yes, there is a difference' and 'no, there is no difference'. Worldwide, 46 per cent said there is a difference and 22 per cent said there is not. However, 32 per cent either did not or could not reply because they worked only in one kind of setting, usually private practice. Worldwide, 21 per cent gave an unspecified 'yes', 13 per cent said there is more political material in institutional settings, and 12 per cent said there is more political material in private practice. It would seem, then, that a majority of respondents

Table 10.4 Does the setting influence the frequency of introduction of political material?

	YES unspecified	More in inst.	More in private	Total Yes difference	Total No difference	No reply
British Psychoanalysts	15 (12%)	16 (12%)	8 (6%)	39 (30%)	54 (42%)	36 (28%)
British Jungians	9 (15%)	12 (20%)	3 (5%)	24 (41%)	0 (0%)	35 (59%)
British Psychotherapists	7 (7%)	32 (32%)	16 (16%)	55 (55%)	14 (14%)	31 (31%)
British Humanistics	7 (19%)	12 (32%)	10 (26%)	29 (76%)	4 (11%)	5 (13%)
US Psychoanalysts	39 (36%)	16 (15%)	6 (6%)	61 (56%)	22 (20%)	25 (23%)
US Jungians	16 (34%)	3 (6%)	0 (0%)	19 (40%)	9 (19%)	19 (40%)
Italian Jungians	6 (30%)	0 (0%)	0 (0%)	6 (30%)	8 (40%)	6 (30%)
German Jungians	3 (4%)	8 (11%)	11 (15%)	22 (30%)	19 (26%)	33 (46%)
Israeli Jungians	0 (0%)	2 (20%)	4 (40%)	6 (60%)	0 (0%)	4 (40%)
Brazilian Jungians	4 (57%)	0 (0%)	1 (14%)	5 (71%)	0 (0%)	2 (29%)
Russian Therapists	6 (21%)	0 (0%)	0 (0%)	6 (21%)	20 (69%)	3 'hard to answer' (10%)
Average of percentages worldwide	21%	13%	12%	46%	22%	32%
Average of percentages worldwide minus Brazil and Russia	17%	16%	13%	46%	19%	34%

who replied to this question noticed a difference but that there is no agreement as to the way in which the difference affects the introduction of political material. The high 'no reply' rate also makes the drawing of any conclusions rather difficult.

In such a situation – where conclusions are difficult to reach – the main points of interest in the results concern discrepancies from the mean. In the following groupings, the proportion of respondents saying 'yes, there is a difference' was high: British Humanistics, US Psychoanalysts, Israeli Jungians and Brazilian Jungians. In order to facilitate speculation as to why this is the case, we have to look at the details of the 'yes' answers. The US Psychoanalysts encountered political material more often in institutional settings, as did the British Humanistics. But the Israeli and Brazilian Jungians encountered political material more often in private practice. I think this last finding reflects certain 'Third World' aspects of life in Brazil, which, in addition to major discrepancies in the distribution of wealth, has a troubled history of abuses of human rights. Maybe it is too risky to speak of politics in a public mental health facility in Brazil. Could the same possibly be true of Israel, and the private setting be a safe place for the expression of sentiments that go against nationalistic fervor? As far as the British Humanistics and US Psychoanalysts are concerned, the high 'yes' answers may reflect the general situation that, in many instances, patients who do not have the resources for private practice are living closer to political realities, especially socioeconomic realities, and hence talk about them more often when they feel free to do so.

However, the same explanation cannot account for the high scores for 'no difference' that were returned by the British Psychoanalysts, the Italian Jungians, and the Russian Therapists. In the case of the British Psychoanalysts, the replies to question 7 showed the existence of a somewhat greater reluctance than average to take the patient's political material as referring to a level of reality must logically lead to downplaying of differences according to setting. I do not understand why the Italian Jungians and the Russian Therapists answered this question in a relatively negative way.

Question 5: Do age and sex make a difference?

I was sure that the majority of respondents would consider that the age and sex of the patient would affect the themes introduced. For example, female patients would focus on 'gender issues for women' and younger patients on 'environmental concerns'. In general, as Table 10.5 shows, this expectation was borne out. Discrepancies from the average are interesting. The British Psychoanalysts returned the highest 'no difference' answer (31 per cent) and once again this reflects the logic of a clinical approach that takes political material on the intrapsychic/symbolic/transference level. However, other groupings, such as the British Jungians and the US Psychoanalysts, returned very high levels of 'yes, there is a difference' answers to this question but *also*, in their replies

Table 10.5 Do the patients' age and sex influence the specific political themes introduced?

	Yes	No	Maybe	No reply
British Psychoanalysts	61 (47%)	40 (31%)	6 (5%)	22 (17%)
British Jungians	39 (66%)	10 (17%)	2 (3%)	8 (14%)
British Psychotherapists	68 (68%)	12 (12%)	14 (14%)	6 (6%)
British Humanistics	34 (89%)	4 (11%)	0 (0%)	0 (0%)
US Psychoanalysts	76 (70%)	22 (20%)	8 (7%)	2 (2%)
US Jungians	33 (70%)	9 (8%)	3 (3%)	2 (2%)
Italian Jungians	15 (75%)	1 (5%)	0 (0%)	4 (20%)
German Jungians	55 (74%)	15 (20%)	0 (0%)	4 (5%)
Israeli Jungians	6 (60%)	2 (20%)	0 (0%)	2 (20%)
Brazilian Jungians	6 (86%)	0 (0%)	1 (14%)	0 (0%)
Russian Therapists	16 (55%)	10 (34%)	3 (10%)	0 (0%)
Average of percentages worldwide	69%	16%	5%	8%
Average of percentages worldwide minus Brazil and Russia	69%	16%	4%	10%

to question 7, had tendencies to note and work with the intrapsychic/ symbolic/transference level. I think that what this points up is the difficulty, and perhaps the importance, of working on more than one level at a time in analysis and therapy. On one level, the sex and age makes a difference because these affect the relationship of the patient to the political world. On another, avowedly internal level, such differences are bound to be regarded as having less significance.

The very high 'yes' return from the British Humanistics is of interest and is what one would expect from an overall orientation to psychology that has distinct 'person-centered' aspects. I do not understand the high 'yes' return from the Brazilian Jungians but, as I have said, the sample was very small.

Many respondents annotated the questionnaire form with the words 'Sex yes, age no' or 'Age yes, sex no' and, on reflection, I wish I had separated the two categories. However, I must record the fact that, of the answers that specifically distinguished between sex and age as factors that affect the introduction of political material, half proposed sex as decisive and half proposed age as decisive.

Question 6: Does sex and age correspondence make a difference?

Question 6 was the third of a series of questions designed to explore the importance of objective factors. Question 4 concerned the setting of work, question 5 the sex and age of the patient. Question 6 introduced the sex and age of the practitioner relative to the sex and age of the patient. On advice, I decided to aim for the modest target of finding out whether respondents thought that their sex and age made a difference at all to the introduction of political material rather than trying to find out in detail what that difference might be. However, as we will see, many respondents clearly thought I should have been more ambitious and gave a variety of opinions on the details of possible correspondences between the sex and age of both participants in therapy and analysis and the introduction of political material.

My expectation was that the combination of sex and age characteristics of practitioner and patient would be acknowledged by the respondents as having an impact. This was strengthened by the results obtained by Question 5 which show that, worldwide, 69 per cent of respondents thought that the sex and age of the patient made a difference. However, as Table 10.6 shows, the replies to this question (question 6) indicate that only 34 per cent worldwide felt that the combination of sex and age of practitioner and patient was significant. In other words, about half of those who felt that the sex and age of the patient were significant in the introduction of political material did not feel that the relationship of their sex and age to those of the patient was significant. I am not sure how justified it would be to interpret this as a reluctance on the part of practitioners to agree that *their own* sex and age make a difference and that they themselves are responsible for the nature and content of the material that they encounter (at least to some extent). Unfortunately, I did not specifically ask 'Do your own sex and age make a difference?' because I thought that question 6 as drawn up carried that burden well enough. On

Table 10.6 Does patient/practitioner sex and age correspondence influence the specific political themes introduced?

	Yes	No	Maybe	No reply
British Psychoanalysts	36 (28%)	61 (47%)	10 (8%)	22 (17%)
British Jungians	21 (36%)	30 (51%)	6 (10%)	2 (3%)
British Psychotherapists	36 (36%)	36 (36%)	26 (26%)	2 (2%)
British Humanistics	17 (45%)	20 (53%)	1 (3%)	0 (0%)
US Psychoanalysts	46 (43%)	50 (46%)	2 (2%)	10 (9%)
US Jungians	12 (26%)	18 (38%)	12 (26%)	5 (11%)
Italian Jungians	9 (45%)	6 (30%)	1 (5%)	4 (20%)
German Jungians	35 (47%)	25 (34%)	8 (11%)	6 (8%)
Israeli Jungians	0 (0%)	8 (80%)	2 (20%)	0 (0%)
Brazilian Jungians	5 (71%)	1 (14%)	1 (14%)	0 (0%)
Russian Therapists	5 (17%)	24 (83%)	0 (0%)	0 (0%)
Average of percentages worldwide	36%	47%	11%	6%
Average of percentages worldwide minus Brazil and Russia	34%	46%	12%	8%

the whole, I think that the answers to the question *do* show a reluctance on the part of a proportion of practitioners to include their own sex and age characteristics in the picture and this is a tendency we will note in the replies to other questions. Many practitioners write with great sensitivity and often with authority about how politics has played a part in shaping their personalities but then are reluctant to take the matter one step further and insert their personalities (politically affected) into their apperception of their work. The image of professional neutrality is clearly still a compelling one.

It is interesting to note that high 'no difference' scores were returned by a whole raft of organizations and it is hard to detect a pattern. The British Humanistics, who had a high 'yes' return when it came to the sex and age of the patient, had a high 'no' return when it came to the combination of sex and age of practitioner and patient. Yet, of all the orientations in the survey, humanistic psychology is surely the least concerned with professional 'neutrality'. The British Jungians returned a slightly higher 'no difference' answer than the British Psychoanalysts and this would imply that the British Jungians, as a group, have a higher commitment to some kind of neutrality which represents a possible departure from Jung's own values.

Moving on to high 'yes there is a difference' returns, I propose to disregard the Brazilian score on the grounds of the small size of the sample.

Although the category of 'maybe' was not offered as an answer on the questionnaire form, it was not hard to see which answers were really 'maybe'. I suspect that if 'maybe' had been an option we would have seen a high number of such answers. I say this because many respondents not only qualified their answers with 'Sex yes, age no' or 'Age yes, sex no', but also made the point that with some patients the combination is tremendously important, with others much less so. A number of respondents thought that a congruence of sex and age made a difference whereas a discrepancy of sex and age did not – without realising that this is, in fact, a 'yes' answer. About the same number thought that discrepancies of sex and age made a difference whereas congruence did not. I think the implication of both sets of opinions – congruence makes a difference, or discrepancy makes a difference – is that the difference is in the direction of *more* political material, more intensely expressed.

Question 7: How do you deal with political material?

This was obviously one of the most important and delicate questions in the questionnaire and, in addition to discussing the statistical presentation of the results, I plan to let the respondents speak for themselves.

As previously indicated, I had expected to find that most respondents would understand and interpret political material on an intrapsychic/ symbolic/transference level. I did not expect that political 'reality' would be validated or gone into very much. As Table 10.7 shows, these expectations were not confirmed.

I found that what I have referred to above as the intrapsychic/ symbolic/transference level was not a sufficiently differentiated category

Table 10.7 Practitioners' responses to political material

	Symbolic/ intrapsychic mentioned	Explore/ meaning mentioned	Symbolic only	Explore only	Total symbolic and explore only	Reality mentioned	Reality only
British Psychoanalysts	84 (65%)	40 (31%)	31 (24%)	30 (23%)	61 (47%)	52 (40%)	4 (3%)
British Jungians	45 (76%)	21 (36%)	2 (3%)	3 (5%)	5 (8%)	51 (86%)	1 (2%)
British Psychotherapists	82 (82%)	32 (32%)	28 (28%)	15 (15%)	41 (41%)	57 (57%)	2 (2%)
British Humanistics	20 (53%)	16 (42%)	2 (5%)	2 (5%)	4 (11%)	33 (87%)	4 (11%)
US Psychoanalysts	68 (63%)	30 (28%)	10 (9%)	2 (2%)	12 (11%)	90 (83%)	10 (9%)
US Jungians	45 (96%)	15 (32%)	9 (19%)	2 (4%)	11 (23%)	35 (74%)	1 (2%)
Italian Jungians	14 (70%)	8 (40%)	3 (15%)	1 (5%)	4 (20%)	15 (75%)	0 (0%)
German Jungians	26 (35%)	32 (43%)	6 (8%)	0 (0%)	6 (8%)	62 (84%)	5 (7%)
Israeli Jungians	10 (100%)	4 (40%)	0 (0%)	0 (0%)	0 (0%)	10 (100%)	0 (0%)
Brazilian Jungians	6 (86%)	2 (29%)	1 (14%)	0 (0%)	1 (14%)	5 (71%)	2 (29%)
Russian Therapists	15 (52%)	6 (21%)	12 (41%)	4 (14%)	16 (55%)	7 (24%)	2 (7%)
Average of percentages worldwide	71%	34%	15%	7%	22%	71%	7%
Average of percentages worldwide minus Brazil and Russia	71%	36%	12%	7%	19%	76%	4%

of response. Scanning the replies, it was possible to note a distinct difference of emphasis between what I have referred to in Table 10.7 as 'symbolic/intrapsychic' understandings, and understandings that refer to an exploration of the political theme mentioned in terms of its *meaning* at whatever level for the patient (in the table, this is referred to as 'explore/meaning').

Let me give a few catchphrases that illustrate the difference of emphasis which I have noted. Later, when I quote the replies verbatim, this difference of emphasis will become even more apparent.

Phrases associated with 'symbolic/intrapsychic' are: Interpret defenses and anxiety; interpret symbolically; take up in terms of transference; relate to inner object relations; understand as projection; internal or unconscious conflict; metaphor or symbol for inner world; ascertain patient's 'use' of material (manipulation); as evidence of psychopathology; inner world material; treat as any other material; neutrality; silence; wait for more.

Phrases associated with 'explore/meaning' are: deepen patient's understanding of issue; explore why patient is interested in *this* issue; why this issue in terms of patient's background; issue as evidence of shared concern affecting patient and analyst.

In addition to the categories of 'symbolic/intrapsychic' and 'explore/meaning', a third category was mentioned in the replies and this is referred to in the table as 'reality'.

Many answers showed an attempt to combine 'symbolic/intrapsychic', 'explore/meaning' and 'reality' approaches.

The table shows the numbers and proportion of respondents that mentioned 'symbolic/intrapsychic', 'explore/meaning' and 'reality'. In addition, the numbers and proportion of respondents who *only* mentioned 'symbolic/intrapsychic', or *only* mentioned 'explore/meaning', or *only* mentioned 'reality' are given.

It is therefore possible to show the numbers and proportion that mention either symbolic/intrapsychic or explore/meaning or both. These are therefore the numbers and proportions of those who do not mention reality at all. Clearly, the numbers and proportions of those who do mention reality include those who *only* mention reality.

A number of comparisons can then be drawn. Most important, perhaps, is the comparison between the proportions of those who do or do not mention reality. A comparison between the proportions who mention 'symbolic/intrapsychic' understandings and those who mention 'explore/ meaning' understandings is also possible. Finally, such comparisons can be made within or between the participating organizations.

It might help if I were to 'talk' the reader through Table 10.7, as it were.

Let us look at the British Jungians. If we go to the fifth column from the left, we will see that 8 per cent of replies mentioned only 'symbolic/intrapsychic' or only 'explore/meaning'. Hence, 8 per cent of replies did not mention the 'reality' of the political theme or issue at all. On the other hand, the sixth column from the left shows that 86 per cent of the replies did mention 'reality' in some way, either in addition to other understandings or alone. It is therefore clear that a large number of respondents from this group have given multiple answers to the question. If we look at the first and second columns from the left we see that 'symbolic/intrapsychic' was mentioned in 76 per cent of replies and 'explore/meaning' in 36 per cent of replies. 'Symbolic/intrapsychic' and 'explore/meaning' were the only replies given in 3 per cent and 5 per cent of answers respectively (third and fourth columns from the left).

We can compare the results from the British Jungians with those of the British Psychoanalysts. If we go to the fifth column from the left, we will see that 47 per cent of replies mentioned only 'symbolic/intrapsychic' or only 'explore/meaning'. Hence, 47 per cent of replies did not mention the 'reality' of the political theme or issue at all. On the other hand, the sixth column from the left shows that 40 per cent of the replies did mention 'reality' in some way, either in addition to other understandings or alone. Once again, large numbers of respondents have given multiple answers. If we look at the first and second columns from the left we see that 'symbolic/intrapsychic' was mentioned in 65 per cent of replies and 'explore/meaning' in 31 per cent of replies. 'Symbolic/intrapsychic' and 'explore/meaning' were the only replies given in 24 per cent and 23 per cent of answers respectively (third and fourth columns from the left).

Making the comparison, the most important difference between these two particular groups is that the British Jungians mention reality over twice as often in percentage terms as the British Psychoanalysts do. The proportion of replies that mention 'symbolic/intrapsychic' and 'explore/meaning' only is six times higher for the British Psychoanalysts. It is therefore possible to claim that a distinct divide in thinking and practice has been revealed. This is further borne out by the percentages of replies citing 'symbolic/intrapsychic' or 'explore/meaning' only: For the British Psychoanalysts these are 24 per cent and 23 per cent respectively; for the British Jungians these are 3 per cent and 5 per cent respectively. Results like these make claims for the similarity of clinical thinking and practice between these two groups difficult to sustain, certainly as far as the handling and interpreting of political material is concerned.

I hope that this somewhat detailed working through of one comparison, which is of interest to me personally, will encourage the reader to undertake his or her own inquiry, depending on his or her own interests, location and orientation. For example, the differences between the British Psychoanalysts and the US Psychoanalysts are as striking as those between the British Psychoanalysts and the British Jungians. US Psychoanalysts mentioned reality in 83 per cent of replies compared to the British Psychoanalysts' 40 per cent. Another example: The British Psychotherapists mentioned 'reality' less often than any group other than the British Psychoanalysts and I must confess that I do not know why.

As I said, it is also possible to explore the situation within a particular group. Let us consider the US Psychoanalysts: 83 per cent mention reality, 63 per cent mention 'symbolic/intrapsychic', 28 per cent mention 'explore/meaning'. We can see that, leaving the almost unanimous mentioning of reality to one side, there is a distinct preference for regarding political material on the level of symbolism, intrapsychic process and transference than in terms of personal relevance or hermeneutical significance for the patient. Both approaches are, of course, utterly psychological but do reflect different emphases and nuances. Going back to comparisons between groups, the German Jungians favor 'explore/meaning' approaches (43 per cent) over 'symbolic/intrapsychic' approaches (35 per cent) when the almost unanimous mentioning of reality is set to one side. (Perhaps I should stress again that the scoring was done in terms of how often any of the three main constructed variables was mentioned in the often very lengthy replies. After that, it was possible to aggregate and see the proportion of 'reality' mentioned to 'reality' not mentioned.)

I was very surprised by how often reality was mentioned as depicting the practitioner's way of understanding and handling political material. I think that the global figure for 'reality' mentioned of 71 per cent is truly amazing and calls into question the notion that analysts and therapists pay no attention to political realities. Similarly, the global figure for approaches that completely eschew the reality factor was 22 per cent and the lowness of this figure bears out my impression that this is a more 'political' profession than had been thought. Even if all the practitioners who did not return the questionnaire form at all are regarded as unlikely to have mentioned reality, that would still leave a total of 22 per cent of the entire mailing of 1,964 as having mentioned reality. All of this adds another, fascinating dimension to the ticklish problem of choosing one's analyst or therapist.

I have organized the presentation of the verbatim responses in a way that reflects the issues that we have been reviewing up to now. First, responses that illustrate the '*symbolic/intrapsychic*' position. Second, responses that illustrate the *'symbolic/intrapsychic' plus 'reality'* position. Third, responses that illustrate the *'explore/meaning'* position. Fourth, responses that illustrate the *'explore/meaning' plus 'reality'* position. Fifth, responses that illustrate the *'reality'* position. I have added a sixth category: Responses that stress the activity or personal involvement of the *practitioner*. Obviously, a number of replies do not completely fit into these categories. But I felt it was better not to split up any of the responses as that would run the risk of distorting meaning even more and also of losing track of the thought processes of the respondent.

'Symbolic/intrapsychic' responses

When someone expresses very strong views I would explore what it is that is being projected out. What this means to the person's psychic functioning – leading up to making some transference or reconstructive interpretation.　　　　　　　　　　　　　　　　　　*(British Jungian)*

I *always* seek the inner overdetermining forces of conflict that the patient is warding off by means of 'political protests' (i.e. rationalizations, etc.).　　　　　　　　　　　　*(US Psychoanalyst)*

I tend to use it more in the context of their internal object relations and their struggle for self-realisation. At other times as direct transference material. I don't seem to have strongly motivated politically clients as yet – perhaps I should think about this!　　*(British Psychotherapist)*

The only way is to understand what it is behind the political presentation and interpret it. Only that.　　　　*(British Psychoanalyst)*

Symbolic – archetypal (e.g. 'Shadow', 'Hermes', 'Ares', 'Wotan'). The political 'reality level' is useless psychologically in therapy and thus a hindrance.　　　　　　　　　　　　　　　*(German Jungian)*

In many cases this is an instance of resistance or of anxiety. I try to analyse it.　　　　　　　　　　　　　　　　　*(Russian Therapist)*

Many times I find patients using some aspect of gender issues, e.g. the biological time-clock, as an external and defensive subject, a way of feeling defeated and limited.　　　　　　　　　*(US Psychoanalyst)*

Although I believe the insights of psychoanalysis are highly relevant to political and social structure and am (broadly speaking) committed to a leftish political set of beliefs, most of the questions you ask seem to me to be based on a very profound misunderstanding of the nature of psychoanalytic treatment in which the analyst's listening to the patient takes place within the framework of the analyst's theory of transference: everything the patient says has meaning in other contexts and much of what he reports and says will be more or less true and relevant in such contexts, *but in the context of the psychoanalytical session the meaning which it is the analyst's job to apprehend is that concerned with what the patient is communicating to the analyst at that moment about the state of his internal (phantasy) relationships and his (phantasy) transference relationship to the analyst.*

Naturally (indeed very often) the patient will turn to political or Political issues from time to time but it is not the analyst's job to take these at face value or to discuss them in the ordinary sense with the patient. While my experience suggests some people (even analysts) can get confused on this point and get caught up in being teachers or counsellors or advisers (or even sympathisers or opponents) in the consulting room I think it is absolutely clear that the principles of psychoanalytic treatment (as they were set out by Freud and subsequently developed by psychoanalysts) do not provide a basis for a psychoanalyst *qua* psychoanalyst to relate to his patient's material except as I set out above.   (*British Psychoanalyst*)

'Symbolic/intrapsychic' plus 'reality' responses

Acknowledge the reality of event and of the reaction to it and also interpret its use – i.e. defensive/distracting or expressive of internal conflict or of a transference communication. Over some universally and immoderately threatening issues such as Chernobyl and the Gulf War (and our Government's attitude to the Gulf War) I would feel that it would be a mark of health if a patient raised it and feel it is worrying if a patient does not do so.   (*British Psychoanalyst*)

To acknowledge patients' view of the reality as they see it and to use it then in a symbolic manner, either transference based, or to illustrate intra-psychic phenomena. I think there has been an increase in this kind of material in the past three years because events have been momentous – e.g. changes in Eastern Europe, the Gulf War, hostage issues, etc. So one's work has had to encompass the patient's and one's own reactions to this 'material'.   (*British Psychoanalyst*)

It depends very much on the patient. With some there can be a discussion based on political realities. With others so many projections are involved that this is impossible and I'd work with the feeling.

(*British Jungian*)

Sometimes, for example if there are piles of uncollected rubbish in the streets, I acknowledge the external reality of the issue. In addition, and sometimes instead, I try to find out what the issue means to the patient. For example, Saddam Hussein was a convenient recipient of projections of the archetypal 'bad father' – someone, it seemed for a time, with considerable power (2 patients). Pollution caused by burning oil wells represented destruction and devastation of earth/mother (1 patient). [British hostage] Terry Waite has been a convenient hero figure (2 patients) – now someone through whom integration of the shadow can take place (1 patient).   (*British Jungian*)

1 interpret as a metaphor for that individual's state
2 discuss it as it is
3 analyse politics psychologically – i.e. is fascism homoerotic?
                                                        (*British Humanistic*)

Some issues (e.g. Terry Waite the British hostage in Beirut) can be treated symbolically, as representing the patient's inner world. Other issues (e.g. cuts in the National Health Service) I treat as part of the environmental reality within which the patient has to live and deal – this does not rule out the symbolic interpretation also.
                                                        (*British Jungian*)

What I try to do is honour the material as a comment on the external world and also to work with it as part of the internal world. Some statement like: 'O.K., so that's what's going on out there. I wonder if it can also tell us something about you?' Also, as a dramatherapist, the work may involve asking the client to take on the role of the politician, endangered species, chauvinist piglet or whatever.
                                                        (*British Humanistic*)

I take them *seriously* as fears and anxieties. I possibly point out opportunities and possibilities for *action* – or I may ask what it means for the patient concerned, how they see the outcome, what their fantasy is of the evolution of the problem, etc.   (*German Jungian*)

Listen and support in some cases. Interpret in others – i.e. 'why are we discussing this issue?'   (*US Jungian*)

I tend to be empathic with the reality of gender prejudice in particular and seek to acknowledge its reality before I interpret the projections into that reality.   (*US Psychoanalyst*)

Interpretation on the subjective level. Only exceptions: during the Gulf

War there were objective elements. But even then there was the subjective interpretation.   (*Italian Jungian*)

'Explore/meaning' responses

According to background of person and inner world.
                                        (*British Psychoanalyst*)

I encourage the patient to explore his views.   (*US Psychoanalyst*)

'I wonder if this is particularly upsetting for you because . . . ' and I link it with the patient's particular situation.   (*British Jungian*)

1 raise consciousness regarding issues,
2 explore meaning from life experience, dream material, etc.,
3 help them to use both in life experience.   (*US Jungian*)

Very interested and attentive and I approach material with loving care. I guide the patient who has a political concern onto the psychic/subjective level which also involves adopting a perspective spanning several generations.   (*German Jungian*)

'Explore/meaning' plus 'reality' responses

I try to validate objective concerns and then try to help individuals understand subjective significance in their own psychology.
                                        (*US Jungian*)

Partly on a realistic level, partly in terms of the patient's background – e.g. war traumas, working through of fears that arise, old defence mechanisms, etc. I also explore what attitude I am fantasized to have (transference).   (*German Jungian*)

I always acknowledge the patient's perceptions and his capacity to have a reasoned, rational political view – and *then* I try to see the opinion in the context of the patient's past and present life.
                                        (*British Psychoanalyst*)

I try (a) to make a link to the life history or the current situation of my patient or (b) to share fears, e.g. about the approaching Gulf War or about an ecological disaster.   (*German Jungian*)

When such material comes to the surface, I try to deal with the client's here and now and his relationship to me and with his responsibilities within the social collective in which he lives.   (*Brazilian Jungian*)

Seeing and understanding it in terms of meaning it carries for the patient but not dismissing political issues as also reality issues (e.g. Gulf War, etc.).   (*British Psychoanalyst*)

I am not afraid of agreeing or disagreeing with my patient, and of recognising the importance of the issues raised both universally and *personally* in the patient. I also look for a 'hidden agenda'. I think I have become more free during the past twenty-odd years to express my own views. I no longer feel that I immediately have to 'interpret' the material in terms of some dogmatic psychological structure.

(*British Psychoanalyst*)

I am more free now to spend some time mentioning politics – but I am always concerned to go on analysing the individual I am with. I might use the political theme as a starting point into unravelling an unconscious process. I think political issues *are* a part of reality and thus ignoring them is ignoring reality, so it is a dynamic issue anyway.

(*British Psychoanalyst*)

Usually in terms of personal meaning for the client and in the transference, but I would acknowledge straightforwardly big issues like hostage release without necessarily interpreting.   (*British Jungian*)

Accept and affirm the reality of politics/sexism/racism but always come back to the relevance of the generalised political issue to *client* and their history, and present situation and so on. How they've been affected and have played a part in being affected by that history/political situation. Sometimes, too, a part of my response may be to accept and stay with the unfairness/awfulness/reality of life.

(*British Psychotherapist*)

I find it very interesting what some people make of external events in terms of their inner world. I also find it remarkable sometimes when earth-shattering events in the outside world do *not* get mentioned in the analysis – and this latter is my preponderant experience.

(*British Jungian*)

I support their perceptions and may link their particular experiences to the general to give a broader perspective *provided* they don't use the general to avoid the particular – e.g. using the word 'racism' to *avoid* looking at their own feelings, behavior, etc.   (*US Psychoanalyst*)

The issue of limits is for me important – i.e. when do you shift to interpreting political beliefs, biases, dreams in terms of developmental history (as opposed to real political conflict)?   (*Israeli Jungian*)

'Reality' responses

I am a woman. Patients of both sexes often bring up issues regarding abortion conflicts, gay bashing and prejudices toward women. At least in New York City, patients and therapists tend to be liberal and belong to the Democratic Party. I tend to listen and agree when patients indicate that Anita Hill seemed to be telling the truth or that gays and women are discriminated against.   (*US Psychoanalyst*)

With patients who go on about some injustice in the community, I might explore what got in the way of taking active measures – e.g. writing to MPs.   (*British Psychoanalyst*)

We live in a special political situation and it influences our state, mood, and actions.   (*Russian Therapist*)

I usually try to welcome the material as their life in the real world, then wonder what it's doing in that session, with me. I have shifted to a more relaxed attitude to reality – but this may reflect a move to [an institutional setting].   (*British Psychoanalyst*)

I feel I've become more forthright and feel it is an important part of life and therefore should enter into what goes on in the analysis also.
                    (*British Psychoanalyst*)

Sometimes suggest attendance at other groups such as consciousness-raising, assertion training, pre-orgasmic groups, etc.
                    (*British Humanistic*)

Unless it has a clear unconscious connection, I deal with it in a real way as a real issue.   (*US Psychoanalyst*)

I most frequently use it to help clients explore their feelings about how they fit into the world today and how this is different from the experience and feelings of other age groups in attitudes to personal and international issues.   (*British Humanistic*)

I do not interpret. I treat it as part of reality and often may share my agreement with patients' values and concerns. In one incident a patient doubted my agreement and would have left if I had not confirmed my agreement.   (*US Psychoanalyst*)

As something natural and inevitable in this mad time.
                    (*Russian Therapist*)

Responses focusing on the practitioner

> I am active in making space for awareness to be kindled about the social and political context of individual concerns – am open if required about my general orientation.   (*British Humanistic*)

> I introduce political material *myself* if it seems to illuminate or extend or integrate more than the inner life. Many of the people I see (I don't call them 'patients' and that is a political decision about equality and avoidance of the medical model of therapy) have become aware of external circumstances which may be a part of their distress. An example: a person feeling that their inner structure was disintegrating. This person having been a long time member of the Campaign for Nuclear Disarmament did not make any connection between this and the disintegration of the USSR, seeming not even to know that the events were happening. A more common example: a man wanting to relate to his feelings but unaware that they had been 'trained out' by the 'big boys don't cry' gender imperative and unaware that he is part of a huge mass of unliberated men.   (*British Humanistic*)

> It's rather me who points to current or historical political links (e.g. environmental problems, the Nazi era).   (*German Jungian*)

> My tactical response is generally to ask them if they've read about the latest depredation in whatever area they select for criticism. My first and best supervisor was Dr N. who entirely understood and wrote a great deal on psychosocial issues.   (*US Psychoanalyst*)

> I react to it with my own opinion and perspective, emphasizing that this is *my* position and perspective.   (*German Jungian*)

> Active listening and on occasions when I feel it appropriate I have mentioned books or articles I have found interesting.
>   (*US Psychoanalyst*)

> Mainly by sharing my own real feelings about similar issues, rarely by interpreting reductively. Sometimes by interpreting archetypally. I seem to have more and longer political discussions each year and I am less defensive about letting it in. It seems now to be a vital place of meeting the patient as fellow citizen trying to construct a reality we both think it important to explore, construe and evaluate.
>   (*US Jungian*)

> I try to re-experience it via empathy. I tentatively give my own assessment of political problems. I very rarely take it as my own

problem though the link to my own psychodynamics that the patient has set up cannot be overlooked.   (*German Jungian*)

I don't exclude political questions from the treatment. I try to clarify how far political attitudes are influenced by neurotically faulty attitudes. After this clarification has been achieved, I encourage my patients to think and act politically.   (*German Jungian*)

Question 8: Do you discuss . . .?

The word 'discuss' prompted some respondents to object that, though they did talk about political issues with their patients, they would not call this 'discussion' because of the implication that this would be the ordinary behavior of friends who 'discuss' politics. I had in mind any relatively prolonged interaction in which overt political content was prominent. I was aware, of course, that such 'discussion' might be a prelude to a move onto a psychological plane in the ways already outlined but I thought it would be interesting to explore the matter in any case, bearing in mind questions 10 and 11 which were intended to see if some particular political themes seemed to lead to more discussion than others, and to ascertain if there was a stable situation regarding practice in this general area.

Table 10.8 contains the data collected from questions 8–11 but I will concentrate on question 8 at this point. Worldwide, excluding Brazil and Russia, 56 per cent of respondents said they did discuss political issues with patients, 44 per cent said they did not. The percentage range of 'yes' answers was from 72 per cent in the case of the US Jungians to 33 per cent in the case of the British Psychoanalysts. Hence, the percentage range of 'no' answers was from 67 per cent in the case of the British Psycho-analysts to 28 per cent in the case of the US (and German) Jungians. I had expected the British Humanistics to return a much higher 'yes' score than they did (55 per cent) and the US Psychoanalysts to return a 'no' score on a par with the British Psychoanalysts (they were ten points less). I had not expected such a high 'yes' response to this question.

Question 9: If not, why not?

The overwhelming reply to this question was that discussing politics was not the job of the psychoanalyst/analyst/psychotherapist/therapist. This view was expressed in varying degrees of intensity and sometimes there was outrage at the question having been asked at all. What is interesting is what those who were outraged would make of the replies of some of their

Table 10.8 Do practitioners discuss political material with patients? Have practitioners changed their practice regarding such discussion?

	Discuss? Yes	Discuss? No	No reply	Same practice	More politics	Less politics	No reply
British Psychoanalysts	43 (33%)	86 (67%)	0 (0%)	85 (66%)	33 (26%)	5 (4%)	6 (5%)
British Jungians	32 (54%)	27 (46%)	0 (0%)	30 (51%)	21 (36%)	8 (14%)	0 (0%)
British Psychotherapists	56 (56%)	44 (44%)	0 (0%)	46 (46%)	42 (42%)	2 (2%)	3 (3%)
British Humanistics	21 (55%)	16 (42%)	1 (3%)	11 (29%)	20 (53%)	3 (8%)	3 (8%)
US Psychoanalysts	46 (43%)	62 (57%)	0 (0%)	58 (54%)	38 (35%)	5 (5%)	7 (6%)
US Jungians	34 (72%)	13 (28%)	0 (0%)	18 (38%)	20 (43%)	9 (19%)	0 (0%)
Italian Jungians	12 (60%)	8 (40%)	0 (0%)	12 (60%)	4 (20%)	4 (20%)	0 (0%)
German Jungians	43 (58%)	21 (28%)	10 (14%)	25 (34%)	36 (47%)	13 (18%)	0 (0%)
Israeli Jungians	6 (60%)	4 (40%)	0 (0%)	8 (80%)	2 (20%)	0 (0%)	0 (0%)
Brazilian Jungians	4 (57%)	3 (43%)	0 (0%)	1 (14%)	4 (57%)	2 (29%)	0 (0%)
Russian Therapists	14 (48%)	14 (48%)	1 (3%)	15 (52%)	9 (31%)	4 (14%)	1 (3%)
Average of percentages worldwide	54%	44%	2%	48%	37%	12%	2%
Average of percentages worldwide minus Brazil and Russia	56%	44%	2%	51%	36%	10%	2%

colleagues because, as noted, the 'yes' replies to the question about discussion were much higher than I expected and, once again, call into question how the profession characterizes itself – not to mention the portrait drawn by its critics.

Question 10: If yes, what themes?

To be frank, this question was a washout because those who answered it wrote 'all of them' so often as to make my project of finding out whether some themes prompted more discussion than others a hopeless task. It seems that if a practitioner does discuss political issues with his or her patients, meaning any relatively prolonged interaction in which overt political content was prominent, then the precise nature of that content is unlikely to have been a reason why the discussion is taking place.

Question 11: Any changes?

The answers to question 11 are contained in Table 10.8. My intent was to see if practitioners were discussing political issues with their patients, for whatever reason, more often than before, or less often than before, or whether the situation has remained stable. From the answers given, it is clear that the question could not be divorced from the one that I had in mind but did not ask in specific terms: 'Are your patients bringing in political material more often than before, less often than before, or has the situation remained stable?' In fact, it is not crucial whether the answers to question 11 are regarded as responding to this unasked, background question or not because one is in any case able to get an impression of how changing or stable the practice situation is regarding the handling of political material from the question that was asked.

Worldwide, excluding Brazil and Russia, the replies showed that 51 per cent felt there had been no changes in their practice or in the way they work. (This is shown in the fourth column from the left in Table 10.8.) Thirty-six per cent felt there had been a change in the direction of 'more politics' in the way they handled political material, whereas 10 per cent felt there had been a change in the opposite direction. Hence, a total of 46 per cent felt there had been a change of one kind or other.

One interesting feature of the replies was that there seems to be a marked divergence of opinion over whether greater experience means that there will typically be 'more politics' in one's practice or whether, typically, greater experience means that there will be 'less politics'. Both claims had their proponents but, as the greater proportion of those who said there had been changes over time said these were in the direction of 'more politics', it would seem that, on a straight majority basis, the consensus might be that more experience means 'more politics'. (I am aware that many non-respondents will want to dispute this formulation.)

The percentage range of 'no change' answers was from 80 per cent in the case of the Israeli Jungians to 29 per cent in the case of the British Humanistics. The percentage range of change to 'more politics' was from 53 per cent in the case of the British Humanistics to 20 per cent in the case of the Italian Jungians. The percentage range of 'less politics' was from 19 per cent in the case of the US Jungians to 0 per cent in the case of the Israeli Jungians and 2 per cent in the case of the British Psychotherapists.

I think it is interesting that 36 per cent of respondents, excluding Brazil and Russia, note that their practices are changing in the direction of 'more politics'.

Questions 12–15: Politics in training

On the basis of what will now have to be regarded as prejudice, I was confident that nothing to do with politics would have been raised in the trainings of the participating organizations. Nevertheless, I thought it would be interesting to test this out. In the questions, I distinguished between the main practice issues covered by the questionnaire (questions 12 and 13) – how to handle political material, do you discuss politics? etc. – and the discussion of politics *per se* in the training (question 14). I was also curious as to whether politics came up during the application process and selection for training (question 15).

At first, I could not understand the discrepancy between the answers tabulated in the first column of Table 10.9 and those tabulated in the fifth column from the left. In the first column we find the results garnered from the question: 'Were matters like these being raised by this questionnaire addressed in your training?' People answered 'yes' and 'no' and I recorded the 'yes' scores because, given my expectation of an almost total absence of concern for politics in the trainings, 'yes' answers were of more interest. But the next question gave a respondent the chance to include any *informal* discussion of the handling and understanding of political material that went on during training. Perhaps this gave participants pause for thought and, as the informal part of the training might not have occurred to them as part of the training, the 'yes' answers to the questions that made space for an informal element were more numerous than those to the previous, more general question.

Table 10.9 Were questionnaire issues discussed in training? Was politics as such discussed in training?

	Yes in training	Yes formal	Yes informal	Yes both	Total yes in training	Politics discussed in training? Yes	Politics discussed on application? Yes
British Psychoanalysts	14 (9%)	10 (8%)	24 (17%)	12 (9%)	46 (36%)	6 (5%)	0 (0%)
British Jungians	15 (25%)	4 (7%)	12 (20%)	4 (7%)	20 (34%)	2 (3%)	0 (0%)
British Psychotherapists	36 (36%)	32 (32%)	14 (14%)	6 (6%)	52 (52%)	34 (34%)	1 (1%)
British Humanistics	18 (47%)	4 (11%)	4 (11%)	16 (42%)	24 (64%)	16 (42%)	8 (22%)
US Psychoanalysts	40 (37%)	14 (13%)	14 (13%)	16 (15%)	44 (41%)	30 (28%)	1 (1%)
US Jungians	18 (38%)	9 (24%)	6 (16%)	3 (8%)	18 (38%)	6 (16%)	1 (3%)
Italian Jungians	1 (5%)	0 (0%)	1 (5%)	1 (5%)	2 (10%)	2 (10%)	0 (0%)
German Jungians	23 (31%)	11 (15%)	13 (18%)	13 (18%)	37 (50%)	29 (39%)	3 (4%)
Israeli Jungians	2 (20%)	0 (0%)	3 (30%)	0 (0%)	3 (30%)	3 (30%)	0 (0%)
Brazilian Jungians	2 (29%)	2 (29%)	0 (0%)	2 (29%)	4 (58%)	4 (58%)	0 (0%)
Russian Therapists	19 (66%)	0 (0%)	0 (0%)	24 (83%)	24 (83%)	24 (83%)	21 (72%)
Average of percentages worldwide	31%	13%	13%	20%	45%	32%	9%
Average of percentages worldwide minus Brazil and Russia	28%	12%	16%	12%	39%	23%	3%

On reflection, I consider that the first column is not a reliable indicator of whether political material and its vicissitudes are addressed in training and I propose to focus on the second, third and fourth columns from the left.

If we look at the fourth column from the left, we see that, including both formal and informal elements, issues like those addressed in the questionnaire were discussed in the trainings attended by 39 per cent of the respondents (worldwide excluding Brazil and Russia). Frankly, I was utterly amazed by this result. However, if we look at the second column from the left, we see that the percentage answer worldwide excluding Brazil and Russia for 'yes' to *formal* coverage of these issues in training was only 12 per cent. Sixteen per cent said that *only* informal coverage took place and 12 per cent specifically answered 'both' – meaning that 28 per cent mentioned informal coverage in some way. So it would seem that a good deal of informal discussion goes on in analytical and psychotherapy trainings over issues concerning how to handle and understand political material brought by patients. There is a discrepancy between the frequency with which this goes on formally and the frequency of informal discussion.

A number of respondents mentioned their personal analysis/psychotherapy as a site of discussion of issues connected with the questionnaire's purview and I regarded this as 'formal' coverage.

The British Humanistics returned the highest 'yes, covered in training' (fifth column from the left) but not the highest 'formal' score which was returned by the British Psychotherapists who, I happen to know, have a seminar on social issues as part of their training program. The various psychoanalytical and Jungian groupings scored around the average with the exception of the Italian Jungians who returned a low 'yes' score (10 per cent).

My personal reaction to these results is that they show, at the very least, that the survey project is timely. The discrepancy between formal and informal coverage is not, of course, a negative phenomenon but it may be interesting to readers to theorize as to why it has arisen.

I will turn now to question 14, which asked if political issues *as such* were discussed in the training programs. Unfortunately, I did not think to repeat the 'formal'/'informal' structure. The replies are presented in Table 10.9, in the sixth column from the left.

The worldwide average, excluding Brazil and Russia, was 23 per cent saying 'yes'. My feeling is that this figure probably includes informal as well as formal elements (though obviously I cannot be sure). I base this on the rather high figure compared to the low 'formal' replies to the earlier questions about the handling of political material and on the possibility that the respondents had been sensitized to informal elements in training by the preceding question that mentioned them.

Some noteworthy high 'yes' answers to the question about political issues being discussed in training: British Humanistics, British Psychotherapists, German Jungians, Israeli Jungians, US Psychoanalysts. Some noteworthy low 'yes' answers: British Jungians, British Psychoanalysts. One would be tempted to put this down to some degree to professional politics and the pecking order. The British Humanistics and British Psychotherapists do not have as high a professional status (broadly understood) as the British Jungians and the British Psychoanalysts. Moreover, the latter two trainings are longer and more expensive. These factors mean that the kind of political intensity associated with being a (professional) have-not might be missing from the British Jungians and British Psychoanalysts. On the other hand, the US Psychoanalysts are not an underprivileged grouping and returned a fairly high 'yes' set of answers (28 per cent). The German Jungians have long been rumored to be the most 'political' Jungian society and this result, together with some other findings of the survey, tends to confirm the rumor.

The Russian answers are fascinating: 83 per cent said the issues addressed in the questionnaire were discussed both formally and informally in training; 83 per cent reported that political issues as such were discussed in training; and, to anticipate the replies to the next question, 72 per cent said that politics came up at their selection interviews. I am sure that readers do not need a commentary from me on these results, but I would say that it is interesting to compare these figures with those garnered by question 8 ('do you discuss?') to which the Russian Therapists returned a less than average 'yes' response. It seems that, as social and political structures change, just about everything connected with the practice of therapy changes. The Russians had a lot of exposure to politics in their training – far more than any other group. But they discuss politics with their patients at a rate below the global average for this tendency.

Moving on to question 15 ('Were political issues discussed as part of the application for training process?'), the worldwide figure, excluding Brazil and Russia, for those saying 'yes' was 3 per cent. The only significant departure from this very low rate was the figure returned by the British Humanistics of 22 per cent.

Question 16: Your political attitudes and influences

Although answering questions 16–20 was optional, 98 per cent of respondents elected to do so. Question 16 was: 'In a few lines, please say something about your own political attitudes. What do you see as having influenced your political attitudes? For example, ethnic/racial background, parental attitudes, socioeconomic background, moral values, religious values, particular event(s), etc. Please specify.'

I will present a selection of the replies to this question by organization rather than attempt any classification in terms of left, right, center, etc. Having read around 600 statements, and having shared some of the material with colleagues, I am sure that this is the best way to cope with the embarrassment of riches.

British Psychoanalysts

Liberal/social democrat background – leads to identification with the oppressed and trodden over victims. Similar to paternal attitudes. Calvinistic/Unitarian/Quaker sympathies. Specific events such as Father's patriotism in Second World War.

Left of centre! The usual . . .

As an analyst and with increasing age, there is a growing concern with political issues; it seems to be concern with the well-being of groups, beyond one's own intimate family and friends, extending to communities, nations and the international community. These groups begin to have more meaning than they did in earlier life when one's concerns were establishing adult identity as a woman, wife, mother and analyst. I am interested in the unexpected capacity to cathect larger groups as one gets older. This is an entirely personal view and may, of course, be atypical.

The questions were searching and quite difficult. I am pleased that you are taking a serious interest in a much neglected area. It is well worth doing.

My parents were both fairly high Tories from an upper middle-class background. My own political views were forged during four years in the army and after the Second World War. I am an agnostic, my parents were devout Church of England. I regard myself as leftish and quite dark green. I am appalled at the way in which the 'civilised' world squanders its resources and pollutes the planet.

I try to be well-informed on political issues, reading political theory and trying to take a psycho-analytic view of history and current events. I find this fascinating, difficult, but seriously worthwhile. I think whatever views I hold are probably influenced by moral values, and ultimately by parental values in the widest sense, although my political views are now different from those my parents held.

I am less a left-wing radical than I was as a young man due I think to my increased wealth and social status but also to the demise of communism. My personal analysis with a Kleinian analyst severely undermined my male chauvinism.

I am more interested in hidden political issues to do with how to think about the privilege of being affluent and western and able to practise and consume psycho-analysis or therapy.

I would say I was 'Socialist/Democrat' – i.e. centre-left. Since my teens – i.e. for 50 years – have moved about this axis, left a bit then right a bit but never far left and certainly never far right. More radical as I get older I think. Influences: socio-economic background, moral values of parents. Events: the depression in the early '20s, the War, decline of the British Empire.

Parental values (former members of the Communist Party) influence me; now liberal-left would be my position – tho' dislike dogma and disappointed that the collapse of the Eastern bloc leaves capitalism appearing so triumphant and unchecked. Imagine I 'should' be more politically active but if I'm honest don't feel inspired, too cynical perhaps to participate more.

Jewish hard-up left-voting family in the '30s. I am atheist but still the child of my parents so far as politics go.

I'm a traditionalist (*tredo, tradere* – to hand over). I see no reason for changing for change's sake. If I'd been brought up as a feminist communist I'd have stayed that way. I am and have been Tory Calvinist!

At present I support the UK Conservative Party. I used to be in government service. I also studied economics. I have not been politically active but I objected to the British Psycho-Analytical Society taking any part, as a Society, in anti-nuclear activity.

I am from [Latin America], Jewish, married with children and grandchildren. With my semi-religious background, growing up in a country with a large black population, I grew up with prejudice and politics inside and outside the home. What with left-wing positions and Zionist ideals, my life and my personality has moulded me into a position of tolerance and awareness of my own stance.

British Jungians

I see myself as rather politically unaware – and feel a bit ashamed of this – no interest at all in party politics. My background is liberal Christian and I have worked in Third World. Although no longer Christian, I would identify with that value system.

Experiencing both privilege and deprivation in Third World countries as a child, having black servants for whom the love clashed with the accepted prejudices. Much of my politics have been about conflict with my father. I have always voted Labour. I feel that my attitudes are changing. There are broadly socialist issues about which I feel strongly. I'm struggling to marry these with self-interest.

Frustrated left-wing. Brought up in [ex-colonial country], identifying with loving servants. Witnessed hypocrisy of family, society. Witnessed immorality in appalling ways. Vaguely religious.

My background was basically Conservative. Voluntary work in S.E. London made me think. I moved left then centre. When Thatcher came to power, I became more politically involved. The Falklands War was important in making me more active.

I used to be more left-wing than I am now. Grew up in [European country] and influenced by 1968, etc. I have been very influenced by recent events in Eastern Europe.

British Psychotherapists

Liberal but also boundaried. Affected by parental attitudes/moral values. I suspect like many of my generation was deeply affected by a post-war National Health Service/Social Services morality based on Judaeo-Christian ethics. Something about outwardly trying to do the best we can for others. I'm not forgetting myself or the shadow. Since often visiting the 'Eastern bloc' I wonder whether a generational morality is affected by more than two generations.

A background in anthropology (and field experience) has greatly influenced my attitude to ethnic, racial, and social diversity issues. Jettisoning my early Church of England background for the Society of Friends/Quakers has given me greater freedom to explore moral/ religious values.

Within months of my birth in 1929, the 'Great Depression' brought about the collapse of my family's independence and confidence in their own resources. As breadwinners, father and grandfather became long-term unemployed. Homes were lost and family roles blocked and confused. No positive socialist ideology or working-class solidarity was available to my family to mediate the meaning of this. Guilt and nihilism developed and swamped what could have been a political sphere. I began consciously to question their social attitudes when I was in my teens and I have been struggling actively ever since.

British Humanistics

If I were a politician I'd be a Green. When I was a schoolboy I almost joined the Young Communist League and copped out when I was told that it would mean that I would not be allowed to visit the USA. I'm white, have domestic servants as parents who have an interesting blend of socialist/working-class and Tory affiliations. I went to a state boarding-school that seemed to pretty much parallel these. I was confirmed into the Church of England when I was still too young to know better and wanted a good daddy. When it comes to religions I still feel close to Marx but I'd like to be a Quaker if I could get by without believing in the Protestant version of god. The 'Cuban Missile Crisis' and my terror at it opened my eyes to global/political issues and the totally inadequate way in which the teachers in charge of me at the time handled these fears left me with a desire to do better and try to help others do so to. Empowerment feels very important to me.

I am very concerned about the environment and the poverty increase in this country. I am from [a European country]. Parents are conservative, upper class. I believe in the good in every person. I am more and more a spiritual rather than a religious person.

US Psychoanalysts

As a Jew I feel I have been more in the liberal tradition. I have identified with the oppressed and was drawn to the study of social psychology as well as clinical psychology. I was impressed by a grandmother who devoted herself to the care and feeding of the poor. The value system of Judaism as represented by the prophets also influenced me greatly.

I have a strong Jewish identity even though I do not have a Jewish name or appearance so it allows patients to be honest about their prejudices which can be difficult for me. I have been asked to speak publicly on female harassment.

All the above helped form my basically liberal (= British Labor) stance, peaking around J. F. Kennedy's election and murder. I saw, at once, that this was the end of liberal politics in the US, indefinitely. Since then I have felt increasingly that politics is a pointless power game which solves no *personal* problems, certainly, and very few others.

1 Being in college in the '60s at Berkeley
2 Being a professor of sociology
3 Being upper-middle class

Background Italian. I personally have struggled for my own personal power. I help my clients to do the same, politically and otherwise.

Left of center. I think the 'apolitical' stance of training in psycho-analysis does a disservice to all, and also produces patients and practitioners with a minimal social conscience, if at all.

Democrat–Liberal. A number of patients were leaders in civil rights and labor activities and therefore these issues were and are often discussed. Events of life have led to inescapable opinions in me.

All of the above have influenced me. I have been a political activist since adolescence – as was my father. Active in certain liberal political issues, civil rights mostly, and more sophisticated/thoughtful anti-nuclear weapons and peace organizations.

Having been born into a large family during our country's Depression, I am most sympathetic to the struggles of the poor, to those oppressed by social and ethnic discrimination, and my political persuasion is Liberal–Democrat. Strong ethical values were important even in the absence of religious dogma.

Liberal–Democrat, pro-environmental concerns, freedom of expression issues, pro-choice (abortion). Pro-Israel but not on West Bank.

I have travelled a great deal and have always been interested in local, national and international politics as well as other issues. My patients, much younger, are more egocentric, less travelled, less aware politically. I think many young Americans (20–35 years of age) are very unaware and very uninformed. Older patients who have more political savvy and who have travelled seem more aware of what is going on around them in the world. I have found most Americans very apathetic to politics. My analyst was very interested and active in all politics. My analytic school did very little. I think that being active in college during the Vietnam War was my first awareness of how we

Americans influenced the world. Being good in history in High School, my father, religious values and my interest in politics influenced me.

My attitudes are colored by being a survivor of World War II and a woman. I have become discouraged in what we can expect from governments but am also reluctant to hand power to private sector without many checks.

The 'Great Depression' occurred during my teens. Also the growth of unionism (CIO) and brutality against strikes in heavy industry during my twenties. At that time I was a writer, so I come by such sensitivity naturally. Hitler also happened!

It is very difficult to discuss my political attitudes and propensities because they are in such flux, and they are not deeply rooted. I would say, roughly speaking, that I was raised as a Jewish liberal and, to a certain extent, am still liberal, but I have been disappointed in liberal leadership in our country and around the world in other democracies. I have many friends who are conservative, and I respect them.

However, one of the big problems is that Americans in general – and I suppose this includes me – have lost their idealization of the capacity of conservatives to make money for any one else but themselves. The American ideal, of course, is a conservative who will trickle down enough money to make the middle class and the poorer classes prosperous. This has been our great disillusionment. I believe that the real problem of the world is not so much political as it is economic – and, alas, nobody seems to understand economics!

Grew up in southern part of United States. Affected very deeply by inequitable distribution of resources between rich and poor. Also taught that this was 'God's will'. Learned early to be suspicious of those in power. My father was in military and I have had an aversion to force.

I am an American liberal Democrat. My parents were humanistic, left-wing, working-class, of Eastern European Jewish origins. I consider my values to have been greatly influenced by them. A combination of history and my new middle-class status makes me more conservative than them, but I hope not less humanistic. I think being poor and Jewish affected my parents and myself in profound ways – I think it enabled them, and now me, to empathize.

I was born into a well-to-do Southern American family in New Orleans *and* I am half Cherokee Indian. Therefore I was always aware of ethnic and racial issues. I was also raised in a strongly religious household with well defined moral values. My first husband was an Anglican clergyman and we were missionaries in the [Caribbean] for four years. All of the above strongly influenced my political attitudes.

US Jungians

As a white male from the South I tended to be oversolicitous toward minorities – especially black. But I also share southern suspiciousness of large government. Have been active in politics in student days and was disillusioned with fanaticism and projection.

I am a far-left liberal and a committed feminist. My family was communist during the '30s and '40s. My parents were both committed to my having full opportunities in the world as a person regardless of my gender.

I am left-leaning, liberal, pro-choice on abortion, pro other women's issues and gay rights. I believe strongly in laws and programs which protect the environment, assure freedom of artistic expression, defend individual freedoms. Am against 'the right to bear arms' and certainly favor gun control. I also believe in global citizenship which includes all forms of ecological-mindedness.

Christian upbringing coupled with poetic sensibility and San Francisco '60s immersion produce pacifistic and liberal position generally.

I consider myself as having been influenced directly by the '30s depression, my Jewish background, being brought up in a liberal activist atmosphere where we felt we, and our efforts, could change the world and the body politic.

Italian Jungians

Left orientation, environmental concerns. My history as an adolescent in 1968, moral values in opposition to the family ones. Specific events: definitely 1968 and the feminist movement.

Liberal (in the English meaning of the word). Naturally, family background, socioeconomic and cultural background influenced me. Then moral and religious values, but then also an irritation with the superficiality and generality of the predominant Catholic and Marxist values that are typically Italian. When I protested against certain Catholic and Marxist values being compulsive, I have also protested against myself.

I am not ruling out getting involved in politics again. But time goes by quickly. In Italy up to about 15 years ago there were very good political/cultural magazines. Now there are only either consumerist magazines or magazines with very limited circulation aimed at very small cultural élites. My dream would be to contribute to the rebirth of a serious political magazine. Ideally the role of the psychologist or analyst could be to draw out individually and deeply rooted needs which are at the same time concrete and common to many. It's a commitment to an educational task. More generally, I think that integration of the traditional analytic attitude – neutrality – with 'taking a stance' is certainly an open issue, at least for me.

German Jungians

Through being a member of the Roman Catholic Church and the processes of change since Vatican II. I was a very early opponent of National Socialism for example. *Religious values.* The experience of the persecution of the Jews, the war, the nuclear threat.

My attitude today: critical rationalism in the sense of K. Popper in reaction to theological indoctrination by the church. Liberal attitude, parental influence. Affected by my later work in the church as a Catholic priest and my later university studies of psychology and sociology. Depth psychology also influenced my political attitudes.

Child and adolescent in the Hitler time and during the war. My parental home was critically distanced (from the Nazis) with a rather cosmopolitan outlook which protected us from total identification. In me, led to pacifist-Christian attitude and an inability to feel 'nationalistic'.

My analysis of Nazis and Jews. Also, fascist tendencies at the analytic institute.

My attitude is left-green oriented. Influenced by the situation in post-fascist Germany, opposition against the many Nazis in high positions, the left-liberal attitudes of my parents that I exceeded when I became more politically left than they.

Students' movement. I was conceived after a rape by a [foreign] soldier and married a [foreigner]. My grandmother was a communist and my mother was very open toward political problems. There was much talk about them in my family. My origins are working-class.

Israeli Jungians

My political attitudes are more democratic-socialist attitudes (left).
Influenced by my parents, my childhood and adolescence (I belonged
to a youth movement that, after the army, joined a kibbutz). I believe
that my political attitudes are *based* on my moral and religious values.

Anti-semitism and the Holocaust influenced my political attitudes with
regard to the possibility of the Jewish people defending themselves
against mass destruction!

Parental attitudes were particularly important – especially father's
liberal, tolerant, socialistic views. Emphasis on humanistic versus
materialistic values. I was also affected by reading certain authors in
early adolescence – Upton Sinclair, etc. Political views have developed
along with personal development – more realistically based – less
theoretical and idealized. As a result in psychiatry I did post-graduate
work and taught in a Dept. of Political Science on personality and
politics and group dynamics in decision making.

Brazilian Jungians

I have always tried to become involved but the government's campaign
against the left prevented me from doing it.

My political attitudes were shaped by my family life. My father was a
member of the Communist Party ('40s and '50s), later becoming a
Socialist. He was a journalist. I was also greatly influenced by my
reading and due to not attending a religious school (which was rare for
a girl of my social class). Politicians came to my house and my father
insisted we had friends from all economic and social and racial classes.

Russian Therapists

I agree with the democratic changes which are going on in the country
but, on the whole, in general, I am very far from 'politics'.

I judge myself to be a liberal democrat. But for me freedom is more
important than social justice. I was active politically during the events
of 19–21 August 1991 [the abortive but crucial coup against
Gorbachev]. Before that I took part in democratic meetings.

I have been involved in attempts to change the place of women in
society. I was involved in the process of getting independence and the
birth of Latvia during January 13–17 1991 in Vilnius. I also joined a

women's organization at university and I am an active member of it. I am in the process of self-actualization as I take part in women's attempts to resolve some of their problems in our society.

I am far from politics (not in principle but in terms of my character), but I am closer to the democrats than to any other group.

In 1970 I participated in reading dissident literature. After 1985 I took part in democratic meetings.

I am not interested in politics but I was in the vicinity of the 'White House' between August 19 and August 21, 1991.

I am somewhat left-wing. I took part in political meetings and put my name to different documents during the period of change in the former Soviet Union.

I used to be active in Komsomol. I was a secretary of an organization of the Communist Party of the Soviet Union.

I am distant from politics but the best, I think, is democratic. I was active during 19–21 August 1991. In the former USSR psycho-analytically oriented work was against official rules so I think that, independent of my personal views, the fact that I did such work could itself be considered as evidence of political activity.

I am mildly liberal but I do not play in political games.

Questions 17–20: Have you ever been/are you politically active?

As one would expect, Table 10.10 shows that there was a falling off in political activity over time. Worldwide, excluding Brazil and Russia, 67 per cent of respondents said they had at some time been politically active. However, political activity now was revealed by 33 per cent – a drop of almost exactly half. Again, as one would expect, there was a move from intense and visible to less intense and visible activity. For example, fund-raising is cited as a 'now' political activity whereas 'Marxism/revolutionary politics, etc.' are cited as 'then' political activities.

But even these bland figures throw up many questions. I think it is significant that nearly a third of the respondents state that they are politically active now. I had expected a much lower figure. The German Jungians are the most presently active (40 per cent), followed by US Jungians (38 per cent). The British Psychoanalysts are slightly more politically active now than the US Psychoanalysts while the British

Table 10.10 Respondents' political activity, past and present

	Yes, have been active	No, never active	Issues mentioned	Yes, active now	No, not active now	Issues mentioned	No reply to any question
British Psychoanalysts	79 (61%)	44 (34%)	Mainstream politics; student politics; pressure groups; nuclear	32 (25%)	91 (71%)	Same as before; financial contributions	6 (5%)
British Jungians	37 (62%)	21 (36%)	Student politics; pressure groups; nuclear; environment	10 (17%)	48 (81%)	Pressure groups; education; environment	1 (2%)
British Psychotherapists	74 (74%)	25 (25%)	Mainstream politics; nuclear; Third World; trade union	26 (26%)	73 (73%)	Social issues; nuclear; environment	1 (1%)
British Humanistics	29 (76%)	9 (24%)	Nuclear; student politics; left-wing politics; gender	10 (26%)	28 (74%)	Environment; peace; mental health; gender	0 (0%)
US Psychoanalysts	70 (65%)	38 (35%)	Civil rights; Vietnam; nuclear; environment	24 (22%)	70 (65%)	Pressure groups; fund raising	14 (13%)
US Jungians	38 (81%)	9 (19%)	Mainstream politics; civil rights; Vietnam; environment	18 (38%)	29 (62%)	Fund raising; pressure groups; peace; environment	0 (0%)
Italian Jungians	16 (80%)	4 (20%)	Student politics; left-wing politics; peace	6 (30%)	14 (70%)	Environment; feminism; political organizing	0 (0%)
German Jungians	50 (68%)	24 (32%)	Peace; mainstream politics; Marxism/revolution; student; women's movement	30 (40%)	42 (57%)	Citizens' pressure groups; anti-racism; professional politics; human rights	2 (3%)
Israeli Jungians	4 (40%)	6 (60%)	Peace; anti-racist/fascist; mainstream politics	3 (30%)	7 (70%)	Peace	0 0%
Brazilian Jungians	Not available	Not available	Not available	4 (57%)	3 (43%)	Multiculturalism; education	0 (0%)
Russian Therapists	6 (21%)	23 (79%)	Communist party; dissident politics	10 (34%)	19 (66%)	Demonstrations; organization; professional politics	0 (0%)
Average of percentages worldwide	63%	36%	–	31%	67%	–	2%
Average of percentages worldwide minus Brazil and Russia	67%	33%	–	28%	69%	–	3%

Jungians are quite a bit less politically active now than either and, indeed, are presently the least politically active organization surveyed. There was a very large falling off between 'then' and 'now' on the part of the British Humanistics and this was also true of the Italian Jungians.

The percentage who said they had been politically active at some time also struck me as quite high (67 per cent worldwide). I wonder if notions that analysis and therapy do not appeal to those with political inclinations are valid.

Any comments?

One hundred and twenty-six respondents (20 per cent) added comments to their completed questionnaire forms. Here is a selection, ordered by the organization to which the respondent belongs.

British Psychoanalysts

> We are political animals, everything we are and do takes place within a political framework. It is impossible to divorce this from the inner world of either our patients or ourselves.

> My firm answer 'no' to Question 9 (Do you find yourself discussing . . .?) makes me wonder whether the questionnaire allows for a clear distinction between political action and political metaphor, also perhaps between being politically active and politically acted upon.

> As a member of the International Physicians Against Nuclear War, I was saying to an Italian psycho-analytic colleague that my patients seldom mentioned 'bombs' – she agreed with me and said nor did hers. But Hannah Segal says that 'nuclear bombs' do come into her material. Why the difference?

British Jungians

> The word 'political' is almost a euphemism. Due to my own politics I think everything is in some sense political and a case of 'some are more equal than others' when it comes to thinking it is possible to speak up on what feels to be a minority issue. It is easier to join a political group and to speak up there than to speak in a work context if one's views do not accord with the assumptive world of the group.

> Interesting and important questions. Made me think again. Clear boundaries, though, I think are necessary between my personal position and my practice of analysis. Under no circumstances would I use the

latter for the expression or exercise of the former, and at times have to use self-analysis to maintain this boundary. There are great dangers in the possibility of the very powerful method and set-up of analysis being an instrument of persuasion instead of being at the service of the patient's individual developmental needs.

British Psychotherapists

I find that as client's therapy progresses, wider issues/concerns feature more often.

I had great resistance to filling this in, but, having done so, I am quite awed by what I discover in myself. Meaning what I said in answer to Question 19 that being a therapist is not just about therapy for me but is a kind of political action and is increasingly becoming more so.

British Humanistics

I think that now you need to approach clients for their views on how their therapists deal with their material in sessions.

I feel this is an important issue. Our culture has tended to dissociate the 'social' from the 'psychological', which I feel is bizarre but has been necessary. Both Marx and Freud developed notions of 'fetishism' – for me this is very significant, and I feel they can be brought together.

US Psychoanalysts

It has interested me and concerned me how much influence – very much like a parent – one has upon patients.

Important issues. In an effort to be non-judgmental, psychoanalysis has developed in recent years with no social conscience or social concerns – this is also inculcated in training.

Psychoanalytic work almost precludes a concern at the moment of the session yet at times I am surprised by the relative absence of relatedness to the world.

US Jungians

I am so glad this is being raised – I feel it (discussing politics) is *the* way to realize the *unus mundus* and to place the discovered self in its true context, as world citizen.

I have been shocked at the a-political bent of our Jungian society from the time I started training. Also at the conservatism. In all other circles of my profession (psychologist) and generally among mental health workers I've found concern about the welfare of the community, society or the world, a humanistic philosophy and concern for humanity. I've sensed that Jungians are very *individual* or archetypal-minded and so introverted as to neglect politics and even disparage those who are concerned. I feel very disappointed about views toward women, therapists abusing patients, etc., which is very slowly changing. Glad to see *your* interest in this topic.

In early days, analysis *was* social critique – far from mainstream or establishment values. If we try to disregard or deny the impact of politics on our clients' lives (and also on our own) by treating all mental experiences as subjective and idiosyncratic, we'll starve our clients.

I'm very glad you are investigating this topic. One of my struggles has been realizing that when I want to use violence to eliminate problems, I've gone over to the enemy, which is no solution. When the U.S. marched into Cambodia, I had to cancel my patients because I was so disturbed. I haven't had to do that recently even though there have been other issues about which I felt deeply. I once had a dream in which Nixon appeared and I woke with a shock in which I asked myself how *I* was violating my office!

When I was practicing in San Francisco, in one week the news of Jim Jones and the mass suicide in Guyana occurred followed by the assassination of Musconi, the mayor, and Harvey Milk. Every one of my patients was deeply disturbed by these events. At the end of the week, I attended a meeting of analysts and candidates in which all of us but one felt we'd been overwhelmed with blood. One analyst was astonished and asked what had happened! I could hardly believe that anyone could live so removed from external events. I wondered what happened with his analysands when they brought up such distressing shadow events. . . .

I've been annoyed by the positions and the assumed omnipotence of opinions from analysts who have never discovered what life is like for 90% of the population. It seems to me that their comprehension comes from being in a superior or advantaged position to 'grant' or give help. An élitist position. They may be politically liberal but not from the experience of having to work for food. I sometimes feel as if they are giving a hungry person a meal of fish, rather than considering how or where this person can learn to fish. This seems to be true for political positions in terms of nations, Third World considerations where the western culture tends to give technology as the fish.

I'll be fascinated when you write about your findings on this research. My hunch is that you are fueling a bonfire.

Italian Jungians

I think my colleague analysts are often rather unconscious of gender and economic issues. Many times I have heard them say 'I am not involved in politics.' I find this an absurd statement.

German Jungians

Since psychoanalytic work absorbs nearly all of my strength, I see my main participation in political work as analytical work. This hopefully has consciousness raising effects, leading to political evolutions, some of which might even be measurable and provable.

I have wondered frequently how apolitical my patients really are. I believe myself to be open to political links and take up political issues, point to questions of political responsibility whenever an opportunity presents itself.

If politics can become 'psychological' then it may be furthered in therapy. But if it remains 'real' (factual, concrete, mundane), then its thematic working through (i.e. discussion) is a professional blunder.

Russian Therapists

I think that for the time being in our country the term 'politics' means something very special and rather narrow. That is why many of my colleagues who were answering the questions were just shocked that 'political' is interpreted as referring to such things as gender issues. For us politics are political struggles which are going on in our country, which are connected with the discussions in the Supreme Soviet, the falling into pieces of the USSR, the problems between former republics of it, the fight against communism. And while many ticked the gender roles or other issues, they were just smiling as this was not politics for them.   (*Written by the coordinator of the survey in Russia*)

CONCLUDING REFLECTIONS

I am aware that, by strictly scientific (or even social scientific) standards, there was a lot wrong with this informal, opinion-seeking questionnaire.

Even so, the results have already prompted thought and discussion and, in a gentle way, I would like to challenge readers to undertake the survey to ascertain its impact themselves. It is clear that, for some respondents, the act of doing the questionnaire was consciousness-raising and even had an effect on their practice.

My overall impression is of a profession in some understandable confusion over politics. We all know that political material can sustain psychological interpretation and we are all, or most of us, trained to take steps to bring such interpretation into being in the analytical/therapeutic relationship. But the situation is by no means so homogeneous and it becomes more and more difficult to generalize about practice, even within a single institution.

I feel reasonably confident in asserting that many practitioners think that the external world does influence what political material is brought and that treating all political material as if it were the same, on the grounds of an internal source, is to take too excessively symbolic an attitude. I think that a high proportion of practitioners recognize this and, as a consequence, engage in 'discussion' (or at least *something*) concerning politics with their patients. The training situation seems to reflect similar anomalies in the way formal and informal elements diverge.

Scanning the statements about political attitudes and influences, one gets a sense that there truly is a 'political history of the person', 'political development' and a 'political here-and-now' of the person. The replies show that politics can be subjected to the same kinds of sensitive, psychological inquiry as any other material and, even more important, that analysts and therapists already know how to do it and are doing it. The levels of past and present political activity were, as noted, higher than what might have been expected.

In sum, it seems to me that there is a marked divide or split in the profession of analysis and psychotherapy. This is not merely a split between those who apprehend the reality of the political and those whose definition of their job concentrates more on what is theorized as part of the inner world. This split certainly exists, and the questionnaire shows it quite clearly. But there is another split, which I see as reflecting something that is simultaneously full of positive potential *and* terribly destructive. This is a split between the *public* apolitical, hyperclinical face of the profession – something that has quite rightly been criticized – and the *private* face of the profession – practitioners all too aware that they have political histories themselves, struggling to find a balance between inner-looking and outer-looking attitudes to what their patients bring to them. The split is between the profession's persona and its own internal reality.

The negative aspect of the split is that whatever insights depth (and other) psychology might have to bring to the political world cannot be taken straightforwardly from the clinical project and hence have to be left to academics and other non-clinicians to provide. It would be better to have *both* clinical and non-clinical contributions. The positive side of the split lies in what could happen were we to recognize its potential existence and bring it (painfully) to full consciousness. Then the engagement of depth psychology and the political world of which I am writing could become a pragmatic possibility and not a pipedream.

I wonder if one of the things that fuels the split, making it impossible for practitioners to go public on the private thoughts and practices that are revealed by this questionnaire, is the existence of psychological theories that themselves incorporate an opposition to the political dimension. That such opposition may well be covert is a factor that adds to the intensity surrounding this taboo on politics. One ideology that could be included in this category is that of object relations and I turn my attention to object relations in the next chapter.

Chapter 11

Object relations, group process and political change

THE OBJECT RELATIONS CONSENSUS

In this book, I have been describing my version of a depth psychological analysis of political and cultural themes, working in terms of the field between psychic reality and sociopolitical reality. This chapter contains a critique in a similar vein of what I hope I can justify calling the 'object relations consensus'. The object relations consensus is proving an active source of attempts to make a psychoanalytic engagement with politics.[1] In this chapter, I want to dialogue energetically with object relations theory, focusing on *the ability of the object relations consensus to function as a base for an analysis of politics or culture*. The claim has been made that, in the object relations consensus, political and social theory has found a brand of psychoanalysis better equipped to engage with political institutions and social relations than classical Freudian theory.[2] It follows – or so the argument runs – that a political analysis that harnesses object relations theory will not suffer from the defects of previous attempts to engage depth psychology with politics.

The chapter is also intended to show some general problems that arise when we employ a psychology derived from clinical work with individuals or small groups to engage on the collective level with social, cultural and political themes. The following two chapters continue to sound a similar cautionary note; they concern the attempts made by C. G. Jung to engage with the politics of the 1930s which went disastrously wrong. For now I will be discussing object relations theory as an example of these problems. Though this movement within psychoanalysis is most strongly represented in Britain, the points I am making are relevant for any other psychology deriving at whatever remove from the psychology of the individual, were it to be employed in political or cultural analysis.[3] (In fact, object relations theory has, by now, spread far beyond Britain.)

First of all, I must explain what I mean by the 'object relations consensus'. I realize that, for some, the portmanteau term will be controversial.

Object relations arose in reaction to what some analysts, mainly in Britain, regarded as an excessive dependence by Freud on quasibiological ways of thinking. In particular, Freud's way of describing instincts seemed to be out-of-date and mechanistic. His model of the mind often used a hydraulic metaphor and this, it was felt, overlooked the emotional quality and feeling tone of internal processes and experiences. In object relations theory, the person is depicted as a creature who seeks relationships (even, synthesizing this view with Freud's, as a creature whose instinct is to relate). The person is a social person. Sometimes, relationships are with whole persons, sometimes with parts of persons; sometimes these 'objects' are external to the self, sometimes they are internal, occupying an internal space or world; sometimes objects which are inside are experienced as if they are outside, via projection, and sometimes, via introjection, the reverse is true. Object relations theory is, therefore, a means of coupling the idea of intrapsychic reality to an interpersonal, relational and social approach to culture: Inner and outer worlds are both given a place.

As object relations theorists continued to depend heavily on Freud's fundamental work, the idea of psychic determinism was by no means jettisoned. This idea holds that later mental events, traits of personality and symptoms are, to a great extent, determined by earlier mental events. In the evolving field of object relations theory, the implication was that the earliest relationships – the earliest object relations – will have a decisive and determining effect upon later relationships. If it is given that relationships (inner and outer) form the mass of human psychological experience, then it would follow that the earliest relationships require the most intense study in recognition of their overwhelmingly important role. And the same would be true if interest was in social relations. Thus, the relationship of the very small baby to his or her mother or breast, both in external reality and in internal reality, had to become the focus of theoretical endeavor, observation and clinical practice. (I would add, in parentheses, that Jung had earlier voiced several of these objections to classical Freudian theory, and developed his own form of object relations theory, subsequently greatly refined by post-Jungian analytical psychologists.[4])

As one would expect, there have been great debates within the object relations consensus that have strained but not broken the general compact. Many of these debates have been between object relations theorists, such as Winnicott and Guntrip, and those psychoanalysts who follow Klein.

The debate has been about diverse matters. One notable argument has been over the question of the importance of the quality of environmental provision (by the real mother). It is claimed (though, in my view, not proved) that Klein did not place enough importance on the real relationships formed in early infancy. The role of the real mother is said to be very sketchily described in her writings. Conversely, Kleinians argue that theorists such as Winnicott have overlooked the vast, innate apparatus that is present in the newborn baby's mind. This colors the infant's experiences of the so-called real mother so that the apparently outer world mother is, in fact (or rather, in 'fact' deriving from fantasy/phantasy) an inner world mother.

Another key dispute is over the status of aggression, and we touched on this in Chapter 7 when discussing the father–son relationship. Klein took up and developed Freud's idea of the death instinct and so, for her, aggression (and destruction) are regarded as primary, innate elements which cannot but affect early and later mental functioning. Winnicott, on the other hand, argued that aggression, while of the greatest importance, is a secondary phenomenon, the result of frustration of the infant by the maternal environment.

It is in full awareness of significant differences like those just mentioned that I propose that a consensus has emerged, taking the form of a synthesis of certain ideas of Winnicott's (and others) and also certain ideas of Klein's (and others). These diverse viewpoints have a great deal in common. What is more, differences of opinion *constitute* and define a field just as they *divide* it. Kleinians and Winnicottians share the same vertices – that is, each knows rather well to what the other side is referring. So argument is possible. If they did not have much in common, argument of the detailed kind that has taken place would not be possible.

I feel confident in asserting that differences of opinion between Kleinians and non-Kleinians define the field of object relations because I have found the same pattern in other fields, notably post-Jungian analytical psychology. My study of the often vicious arguments between the various schools of post-Jungians reinforced the idea that emotional investment in dispute implies an intellectual connection between disputants. In any event, it is worthwhile getting involved in debates within depth psychology because the clash is often as illuminating as or even more illuminating than the contents of one view or other. What often happens in these depth psychological debates is that each side claims that it already owns and uses the best points of the other side. So Winnicottians claim that they have always recognized the significance of innate features in human psychology and Kleinians claim always to have recognized the significance for the infant's emotional life of the quality of the real mothering he or she is receiving. There is a drive toward synthesis based on the grandiosity of each side in the argument.

I have made these opening remarks because I do not want to be thought unaware or disrespectful of the professional and intellectual culture in which I work in Britain and in which Kleinians and non-Kleinian object relations theorists are often at odds. However, several informed and sympathetic observers of the British psychoanalytic scene have also noted the many similarities between the views of the two groups that I have outlined above.[5]

My suggestion is that the object relations consensus, which I have been explaining, has been fashioned out of the very debates within object relations theory that threatened the unity of the theory. Succinctly, the consensus is that there is an interplay between unconscious phantasy and potential on the one hand, and the good-enough personal, facilitating environment on the other. I can see that, for many clinicians and social scientists, the emergence of this consensus was a liberating experience, seeming to resolve, once and for all, not only previous controversial discussions within psychoanalysis, but also the perennial nature versus nurture arguments about human psychology in relation to social process. However, as we saw in Chapter 9, the view that human psychology reflects an interplay between innate and environmental factors, though apparently unobjectionable, denies a great deal. The crucial debate between psyche-as-source and person-as-contingent has been stilled, for the moment, by the object relations consensus in its explicit incorporation, or rather swallowing up, of both perspectives.

OBJECT RELATIONS AND POLITICAL ANALYSIS

I want to be critical and to argue that some of the typical habits of thought of present-day object relations psychoanalysis are not helpful when we come to address political, cultural and social issues. What follows is an unpacking of *certain biases and assumptions* of the object relations consensus, intended to prompt questions about its role in all political and cultural analysis. Inevitably, certain aspects of this critique also open up questions about developmental psychology and clinical analytical technique.

Many applications of object relations theory to social, cultural and political issues require, in the first instance, a problematic dichotomy between what is given (or innate) and what is discovered experientially in the environment. Psychoanalysis is then permitted to resolve this dichotomy into an elegant narrative of marriage – between unconscious phantasy and external object, between preconception and outer reality, between infant and mother, between background and foreground; in post-Jungian theory, between a deintegrate of the primary self and a corresponding external object. It is hard to see how this kind of theorizing helps on the social scale. If we are attempting an analysis of society, then what do we consider *society*'s innate aspects to be? And what constitutes *society*'s environmental factors? The unavoidable way in which innate and environmental realms are first positioned with regard to a single person, so that the object relations consensus can perform its soldering function, makes it difficult to go beyond the individual perspective to a more collective analysis. Psychoanalytic understanding of the ways nature and nurture interact is useful in understanding how people *relate* to the society in which they find themselves (even if this is still a markedly individualistic account). But psychoanalysis, framed in the terms of object relations consensus, is not nearly as useful in an analysis of society *itself*. The assumption that a good-enough environment is all that innate potential of an individual requires to flower, and that this is determined within the nuclear family and in the first months of life, is hopelessly passive in the face of problematic social and political structures. As Martin Stanton pointed out in his review of a book of Kleinian-oriented social theory, wellbeing may not be achievable in a society characterized by alienation. The time-honored values of humanistic ethics are not free of political bias and complicity in the construction of an oppressive and conformist society.[6]

The object relations consensus is biased toward a developmental time-frame. That time-frame is mixed up with a search for whatever seems to be fundamental in the psychology of the individual. This, in turn, leads to a confusion in which the earliest processes, events and relations are regarded as templates for later processes, events and relations. Though no analyst claims that the mother–infant relation is the only important one, there is certainly a hierarchy in existence. Because it seems to come first in time, the mother–infant relation has risen to the top of the hierarchy, leading to the downplaying of other kinds of relations: Father, sibling, spouse, partner, companion, employee, servant, rival, opponent, God. I would go further: Even the search for a psychologically fundamental relation is a flawed project. Does the psyche have to resemble a house, with foundations and upper storeys? Does the psyche have to resemble anything? Or rather, if we want to say that the psyche resembles a house, shouldn't we make room for an acknowledgment that this is one of many possible metaphors? As we saw earlier, *one cannot discount the effect on thought of the raw material of any metaphor employed to facilitate thought.* Houses need foundations and one cannot dispute that. But it is not hard to translate this architectural metaphor into a psychological support for conservative politics. Elsewhere, I proposed a network[7] as an alternative metaphor for the psyche; that, too, would certainly affect political thinking by emphasizing social mutability and the absence of unarguable and unchangeable foundations. There will be innumerable other metaphors, none of them politically neutral.

The idea of development is not to be taken as a 'natural' approach to psychology. 'Development' has its own history and evolution; the idea of personality development is itself subject to contingency. We have to accept that development is an invention and continues to move in the realm of artifice, not to mention fantasy, on the part of developmental theorists. Freud was aware of this. In a remarkable letter to Fliess, written in 1898, he cautions that 'the mirror image of the present is seen in a fantasied past, which then prophetically becomes the present'. Freud admits that the extent of the artifice means that developmental psychology based on psychic determinism can never be wrong – which may explain its persistence even after 'the death of the psychoanalytical past is a *fait accompli*' (in Frank Kermode's words in the 1984 Ernest Jones Lecture). It seems that our infantile world has its roots in adulthood. Yet we need more than one account of 'development' and a plurality of developmental approaches would involve a radical indeterminacy that the object relations consensus eschews.

The object relations consensus is biased toward diachrony: Changes over time are seen as causal, historical, biographical, temporal, chrono-logical, sequential, successive explanations of phenomena in terms of unfolding from specific origins. Now, no contemporary depth psycho-logist can stand outside this tradition; this critique of mine comes from within. But, with cultural and political analysis in mind, I want to question the application of a developmental approach (and its seductive claim for objectivity) to politics. The claim for objectivity may even be intensifying in depth psychology – I am thinking of psychoanalytically influenced experimental work in the laboratory on early mother–infant states, and of the systematic observation of infant–mother interaction at home (which is now a staple in many psychoanalytic trainings). Could psychoanalysis be the heir of Marxism as the wished-for source of a 'scientific' under-standing of social process, and hence subject to all the limitations of such an approach?

The object relations consensus is biased toward causality (again, like Marxism), no matter how subtle this has become. Reference to 'traces' of the real mother, discovered in the clinical setting in the transference experience of the analyst-mother, does not go much beyond a causal explanation nor significantly revise Freud's original insight into transference. Spiral models of development, in which elements of personality commingle in differing ways at different points in life, are caught up in the same developmental imagery as overtly causal models. The spiral is always *going somewhere*, and its development is continuous. Features of modernity – fragmentation, stasis, discontinuity – are overlooked. Diachrony avoids the integrity of the now. No matter how polished the use of object relations becomes, diachronic and causal models of development dominate it. Though I am fed up with the constant New Age idealisation of a less rational and non-human approach to time, the challenge of such ideas to the time-frame of the individual is relevant here. Why should the time-frame of an individual be applicable to whole societies and cultures?

It may be argued that I have missed the point, that infancy itself is only a metaphor, that 'the baby' is just a means of accessing human nature (baby as everyman or everywoman), that the whole range of primitive processes going on in a baby go on in an adult in just the same way (baby as institution, baby as social system). Perhaps that is the *intention* of some theorists, I am not sure, but what has happened is that adults and entire societies are treated (in both senses of the word) as if they were babies; the metaphor is literalized. What is more, the inevitable regressions which take place in analysis, which analysis fosters, are taken concretely as referring to infancy. Taken more symbolically, which they would be if infancy were indeed being understood metaphorically, such regressions would refer to other things, such as regeneration, psychological deepening and additional non-concrete, symbolic aspects of incestuous and aggressive fantasy. Moreover, even if infancy is nothing but a metaphor, we still cannot get out of the past–present linkage because, to repeat the point, the raw material (that is, the imagery) in a metaphor goes on pulsing, suffusing the metaphor on its own raw terms. Claiming that infancy is a metaphor cannot disguise the impact and conditioning effect of the literal infant on every aspect of a psychology that is based on an infancy metaphor. Metaphors stem from the unconscious and, hence, have a powerful life of their own. (In fact, as I have written at length elsewhere, I am very much aware of the utility and benevolence of judiciously deployed reductionism.[8])

The object relations consensus is biased toward complementarity. For example, the image of container/contained has become a key concept, referring to what are claimed to be the characteristics of the mother–infant (or most, or any) relationship. Now, clearly, if two people are in a relationship, one could say that they are contained by the structure of their relationship, or by the typical structure of relationship itself. But that is completely different from seeing it as characteristic of any dyadic relationship that one member should 'contain' the other. Is relationship only about containment? Is that what it is for? What about exchange, bargaining, negotiation, equality – or even torture? Is containment even *the* characteristic of the mother–infant relationship that it is sometimes claimed to be? Does society 'contain' its individual members? Should it? Or is the notion of containment just not adequate to depict the huge range of social relations that exist?

In the rise and general acceptance of containment theory, we can see something numinous and fascinating at work: The *numinosum* is the image of mother and child. As previously mentioned, the *numinosum* is a 'dynamic agency' which 'seizes and controls the human subject, who is always rather its victim than its creator'.[9] A *numinosum* orchestrates the many variables in a particular situation into one overwhelming message, which can be all to the good for, without the presence of the *numinosum* in psychological thinking, there would be no sense of discovery. (I freely admit to having been fascinated by the Trickster.) The *numinosum* certainly fascinates, but it can also tyrannize, and, ironically, it is the numinous image of mother and infant that object relations theory set out to explicate which now tyrannizes it. The professionals have become fascinated, even hypnotized, by the very images that their professional skills uncovered. The numinosity of sex has been replaced by the numinosity of feeding. This leads directly to the tendency, which becomes unavoidable, to treat society and its institutions as if they were babies.

The object relations consensus is biased toward wholeness. I am referring, of course, to the placing of stress on the way in which part-objects do or do not develop into whole objects. Part-objects are undervalued in and for themselves. Experientially, part-objects are often the source of feelings of wholeness, and scanning part-objects for signs of movement toward whole objects suggests that the object relations paradigm is in the grip of a maturation morality and a fantasy of wholeness, and is just as normative as Freud's strictures on love and work or about genitality. The problem is that part-objects are too often regarded as 'things' (ontologically) rather than as processes (epistemologically).

Object relations theory has a particular problem in its refusal to take the emergence of 'persons' in the inner world as other than a kind of part-object madness or, at best, immaturity. (We discussed this in Chapter 7.) Sometimes part-objects *do* develop into subpersonalities and they do perform *as* persons inhabiting the inner world and functioning therein –

for example, as messengers. One can engage in valuable dialogue with those inner persons.[10] What is crucial here is that these Trickster-like states of mind should be valued just as they are, no matter that object constancy is absent.[11] The social and cultural functions of schizoid phenomena – for example, in ritual – deserve recognition. It is not enough to tinker with the order of events in models of development, as some have tried to do, postulating an initial whole object, followed by part objects, followed by whole objects again.[12] The tenor is still unquestionably developmental, moralistic and obsessed by wholeness.

The emphasis laid in the object relations consensus on relationships and their internalization can be seen as apolitical in that the collective level is not mentioned. Even a psychoanalytic narrative of mental health, couched in terms of the structural balance between id, ego and super-ego, displays a greater emphasis on the collective level in that the origins of super-ego are regarded as being, ultimately, collective. My guess is that, in the next few years, we will see an unravelling of the naturalistic fallacy at the heart of the object relations consensus – that is, the way its 'is' has become an 'ought'.

Alongside the normative thrust of the object relations consensus, there is a claim to universal applicability, validity and Truth. But object relations theory cannot be the last word on the human psyche. Object relations arose in particular circumstances and to do a particular job: First, in an England frightened as ever of metapsychology/metaphysics, and, second, to rescue Freud's poetic and humanistic insights from his scientistic aspirations (and those of his translators). The object relations consensus, with its roots in intense ideological conflict within psychoanalysis, has become insulated from those contentious roots and, hence, unable to comprehend that it is still full of its own rhetorical devices and argumentative intents. In the competitive marketplace of psychological thinking, the object relations consensus has one stall among many, and by no means is there a special place reserved for it.

Object relations theories unwittingly perpetuate the political *status quo*. The findings of depth psychologists are, inevitably, embedded in a particular cultural and sociopolitical matrix and hence cannot avoid taking on a prescriptive as well as a descriptive project. Object relations theories focus on intrapsychic and interpersonal explanations for personality development and dysfunction. They tend to rule out sociopolitical or other collective aspects of psychological suffering. The version of personality that object relations theory presents, with its accent on the decisive part played by early experiences, maternal containment, and the move toward the depressive position or stage of concern, is, in many senses, little more than a reproduction of the kind of personality that the culture which surrounds object relations theory already valorizes. If we want to apprehend personality, we have to consider the historical context in which personality exists. For us in the West, this implies that the personality-ideal (to coin a phrase) will reward personality theories that are congruent with our humanistic–romantic–individualistic traditions. Hence, as we will see in this chapter, object relations theory cannot avoid supporting the present-day arrangements over political power and social structures. Moreover, problems in and of the development of personality will be looked at in relation to a normative narrative of development that is not cut off from political pressures. Object relations theories may have attained their popularity, not because they mount a challenge to the existing order, but because of this secret alignment with the existing order. As I say, there is an intense competition over the personality going on.

PROJECTIVE IDENTIFICATION AND THE SOCIAL DIMENSION

I mentioned earlier that there were difficulties with the ways in which object relations psychoanalysis depicts the interaction of individual and culture, and I want to discuss some of them concerning projective identification. The work done on projective identification, whether as early defense, later pathology, or as a means of communication, is something no analyst can ignore. But, as Meltzer noted, there are still questions to be answered about how it 'works', how other people are affected by a person's projections, and how such projections are transmitted.[13] The notion of projective identification is not politically neutral. The Latin verb *proicere* means 'to throw forth', 'to fling forward', 'to throw away', 'to plunge into' and 'to reject, abandon, put off'. The bias is toward throwing and that suggests an empty space between people across which psychic contents are hurled. People are not fundamentally connected in this vision of things; they are momentarily connected when someone plunges something into somebody else. As I said, this ignoring of communality and communion in the name of communication is not politically neutral.

We can challenge this assumption of empty space upon which projective identification depends. We can imagine a kind of social ether in which persons live. If we do this, then the image of the javelin could be replaced by that of the woodworm: Contents from one person burrow through the ether and crawl into the other person.[14] Maybe the image of the ether is itself too ethereal and we need something more earthy. We can get onto a solid plane by re-imagining two (or more) people as two (or more) stalks of a plant feeding off their single rhizome. If we do this, then we have to conclude that *there were never separate people at all*, or at least not to the extent that the idea of projective identification requires. On the contrary, they were always linked. As a phenomenologically oriented psychotherapist put it, 'the fundamental human relation (I–Thou) cannot be reduced to two centers exchanging signals or communications with each other, for there is something "other" than this.'[15]

I do not intend the images of 'ether' or 'rhizome' to become theoretical concepts. The idea was to challenge the primacy of the projection image and, indeed, to point up the fact that theoretical concepts such as projective identification are themselves *images*, and therefore should not be regarded as inherently more sensible, grounded, technical, practical, analytical, etc., than terms that are quite obviously images. (I can see that my providing any image that purports to illuminate unconscious communication is offering a hostage up to fortune.)

Whatever one may think about the psychology of shared states from a theoretical perspective (from an observational standpoint, the question is whether they exist at all), their presence is something that has probably been felt by everyone. Shared states have had a long history in the theories of depth psychology, whether as shared experience or as primary mutuality between people, or even, when viewed as primitive phenomena, as states of undifferentiatedness. Later in this chapter, I will dig out the communal and political referents and implications of those psychological theories, including aspects of object relations theory, that do posit shared states of non-separateness. The concept of projective identification, invaluable though it is in many respects, tends to feed into an approach to politics in which the irreducibly social nature of humanity has less prominence. This is because the concept of projective identification just does not get hold of the collectivity of persons, of where they are already joined together on a psychosocial level, of where things are shared. Hence, projective identification is a relatively weak tool of political analysis.

DISCUSSION

I have been reviewing some problems that I see as hindering the usefulness of the object relations consensus in a psychological analysis of politics. I gave an example of such problems concerning France in 1968 at the start of Chapter 1, and I want now to continue that discussion with further examples. I have avoided giving precise references, though all the material is published, so as to avoid personalizing the debate. Consider the following statements:

[War] allows people and nations to relapse into the very dubious satisfaction of the state of mind Melanie Klein called the paranoid–schizoid position.

In controlling inflation, which it undoubtedly has done, the Thatcher administration can therefore be experienced as one which restored governmental authority over the greedy disorder of the British people.

Our culture suffers from a collective, depressive delusion that is all-bad, all-destructive.

Confronted with the real terror of annihilation, our schizoid defences are increased . . . splitting and projection are increased. There is also a regression to part object relationships, which exclude empathy, compassion and concern.

I want to say right away that, in many respects, I can see the sense in all these statements precisely because I grew up within the traditions of the object relations consensus which underpins them. Nevertheless, even though to say it has meant some self-criticism, these statements reveal the weaknesses of object relations theory in political analysis: The dichotomization of the social into what is innate and what discovered, the assumption of separateness between people as a basic state of affairs leading to dependence on the concept of projective identification, preoccupation with the numinous imagery of the mother–baby relationship, biases toward chronology and the developmental time-frame of an individual, diachrony, causality, complementarity and wholeness, dubious claims for universal validity, and hidden normative and moralistic features.

We see these problems in, for example, the use of words like 'regression' or 'relapse', in the harsh attitude to the paranoid–schizoid position (itself a somewhat paranoid–schizoid attitude?), in the apperception of Mrs Thatcher as a restorative container figure in respect of British (infantile?) greed. Is greed always a disorder? Striking, as well, is the pervasive presence of 'the baby', the one to whom we are supposed to regress and whose very early styles of functioning we are supposed to replicate when we are most threatened. Obviously, the baby cannot be mentioned directly in some of the examples where there is no concrete baby-term that applies to society. So 'society' and 'baby' become almost interchangeable. Equally significant is the moralizing; when the paranoid–schizoid position is offered as an explanation for a particular kind of social or cultural malaise, what is accepted and uncritically assumed to follow is that the depressive position is the only possible basis for a healthier state – and is even the cure. We should be suspicious of ourselves when we find infantile or primitive phenomena in culture, and not get too excited about it. *For were we not looking for infantile or primitive phenomena?* And were these not clearly infecting the eye with which we looked?

I wonder if a society has a psychological age at all. If a society does not have a precise age, then the practice in some psychological analysis of society of taking an early age as the benchmark needs to be questioned. It may be that a society cannot be regarded as adult either – why should these developmental artifices and constructions apply? The emphasis laid on the experiences of babyhood, such as feeding experiences and fantasies, is quite misplaced when it comes to society.

The problem is not only that the world is reduced to 'the baby' or that the fascinating imagery of mother and child has taken over our minds, replacing sex as the dominant strain of imagery therein. The problem has also to do with a certain kind of approach to 'the body'. It is assumed that the baby's earliest experiences are of a bodily kind and that these experiences can, as it were, be retrieved. So, when a society is analyzed as if it were a baby, the literal bodies of mother and baby are maneuvered into place as a metaphoric overlay on social process. The advantage of this is that bodily roots for an individual's social experiences may have been found. The disadvantage is that understandings of social experiences are worked out in a manner limited by already existing understandings of images of the bodies of mother and baby. When Kleinians assert the bodily cast of unconscious imagery and fantasy, they seem to be on safe ground, and it is true that they have fleshed out one segment of an imaginal network. But it is a hugely dogmatic step to claim that all fantasy images merely express bodily experiences, a claim that overlooks the way the unconscious fills with images deriving from *social* relations, institutions and processes – let alone the possibility of the psyche as a source of fantasy images that do not necessarily involve the body at all.

SHARED ELEMENTS IN GROUPS AND INSTITUTIONS

Let us now turn our attention to two themes that have been noted as likely to be important for depth psychological analysis of politics. Both of these arise from object relations theory. The first was mentioned at the end of the section on projective identification: The political and social implications of theories that propose the existence of states of non-separateness between people as non-psychopathological – *the idea of shared experience*. The second theme was introduced at the end of the previous section: The social origins of the fantasy contents of the unconscious – *the idea of shared psychological dynamics*.

After my critical reading of object relations theory, I would like to follow on with an appreciation of those areas of it that have been fashioned into understandings of group dynamics and accounts of institutional process, for example in terms of socially structured defense systems.[16]

Since the end of the Second World War, psychoanalysts and social scientists with a psychoanalytic orientation have studied the group dynamics and social defense systems of groups and institutions such as hospitals or factories. They have done this in a fashion that deliberately attempts to overcome the obvious difficulties encountered in Freud's account of group psychology when it tended to perceive society as a kind of family. The social scientists of the 1940s and 1950s found this naive and too 'psychological'. It is no accident that the criticisms of Freud's theory of group psychology resemble the criticisms of an over-concentration on instinct that led to the emergence of object relations theory – especially the inadequacy of Freud's thinking about the nature of social relating, whether on the personal or group level. It was thought that Freud concentrated too much on movements of libido even if those were understood symbolically.[17]

However, the point that groups, especially very large groups such as societies, cannot be understood by analogous reference to patterns of familial interaction is not really addressed by models of group process based on developmental aspects of object relations. I have been struck by the way the conception of the group takes on varying personifications in object relations theorizing. On the one hand, sometimes the group as a whole is personified as a *parent*, holding and containing its members much as a parent holds and contains an anxious baby. In this personification, the group also persecutes the group members rather like the negative parental objects persecute a baby. The group-as-parent also receives the group members' reparative feelings and gestures.

On the other hand, sometimes the group as a whole is perceived as a *baby*, subject to the internal vicissitudes of persecutory or depressive anxiety. In this personification of the group, the leader may symbolize the parent figure for the group/baby. Or the group/baby might develop parental functions of its own. From the point of view of an understanding of social process, it is not significant whether the group is personified as a parent, or as a baby, or, indeed, as both. The thing I wanted to note was the difficulty in keeping family and individual psychology in a restricted place in narratives of group life.

I return to the themes with which we began and ask how shared experiences in groups come into being and whether there is such a thing as shared psychological dynamics that show up in groups, particularly groups larger and more complex than small therapy groups. I will look at four separate approaches to group process that seem to address these questions and then evaluate them in terms of the possibilities of social and political change. The first two approaches derive from the Kleinian wing of the object relations consensus.

Jaques

Elliot Jaques's work on socially structured defense systems in institutions suggests that individual responses to a shared social situation can mesh together to produce a common psychological response.[18] The meshing of individual responses is carried out by projective and introjective identificatory processes occurring between the members so that, at a certain point, everything relevant has been projected and introjected by the people concerned. Moreover, this common psychological response is not to the institution as it seems to be, but rather to what might be called the unconscious of the institution, meaning the ways its history and the pragmatic restraints on it interact with its conscious goals. As I understand him, Jaques then goes on to make an interesting point. The unconscious of the institution is to be conceived of dynamically. This means that the common psychological response to the institution of the people concerned impacts on the evolving unconscious of that institution. There is therefore a constant movement between shared social experiences of the institution, the meshing of individual responses into a common psychological response, and the dynamic and evolving unconscious of the institution.

If we review this sketch of Jaques's ideas, which I am taking as representative of one kind of object relational work on group and social dynamics, we observe that what Jaques regards as the shared element is *immersion in the same social or institutional situation*. The individuals are not regarded as having been linked already; they are linked by virtue of their *ad hoc* linked social situation. They have to come together into that situation before they can be understood as sharing anything. They come together as individuals and are taken into an institution. Then a hitherto latent capacity to share experience is activated. The pre-existing state of the individuals is separate; sharedness depends on institutions. That is why Jaques needs to hypothesize the importance of projective and introjective identification in the emergence of a common psychological response to a shared social situation.

Bion

Bion's well-known work on basic assumption groups does not underscore the group member's participation in a common social situation in the way that Jaques does.[19] Rather, the three kinds of basic assumption groups (dependency, fight/flight and pairing) are taken as constitutional elements of groups, pre-existing the entry of an individual into a social or institutional setting. Basic assumptions may even be regarded as pre-existing the very formation of groups or institutions. In this sense, the basic assumptions resemble Jung's formulation of the theory of archetypes which, in the classical account, provide a psychological structure for events that have not themselves determined those structures. In Bion's account of group process, the elements that are shared are shared in a Platonic sense, as always existing categories of life itself. As in archetypal theory, if the basic assumptions operate in an unmediated form, the effect is obstructive to psychological balance and to conscious goals (what Bion calls work groups). But, again like archetypes, basic assumptions also have a positive capacity to bring people together in the first place and, hence, they have active and creative roles in the formation of groups and institutions.

Bion's list of the three basic assumptions has always seemed to me to be a preliminary suggestion on his part, and there is no reason why the number of basic assumptions should be limited to three. Conversely, you could say that there is only one basic assumption in group process: Humans enjoy and suffer from groupishness and cannot evade their group fate.

The shared elements in Bion's theory seem to me to be quite different from what is shared according to Jaques. Jaques highlighted the common scene of group process. Bion highlights *the common underlying elements of any group scene*. Nevertheless, both of them are working within the general idea that things can be and are shared. My personal preference is for Bion's version of sharedness because it depends less on projective and introjective identification. In fact, Bion did not develop connections between the basic assumptions and projective identification, an attempt he might have been expected to make. I suppose what is basic to all does not need to be projected from one person and introjected by another. Nor did Bion tie in the basic assumptions with the more developmental perspective characterized as ps $\longleftrightarrow$ d.

Homans

Peter Homans does not write out of an object relations background.[20]

Writing in the United States, his orientation is toward Kohutian self-psychology. But self-psychology shared with object relations theory several of the same objections about Freud's instinct theory and its corollary, ego psychology. Therefore, it is perhaps not surprising to find Homans writing about the relations between the individual and social institutions in terms that are compatible with the object relations consensus. Homans suggests that our culture is a 'culture of fantasy' and that we might try to speak of 'socially shared fantasy'. This is the social context to which the ego relates. But, from his different perspective, Homans has taken the ideas of Jaques and Bion a step further. Jaques identified some psychological consequences of participation in shared social process. Bion identified some of the underlying psychological components in group formation. Homans suggests that the contents of what is shared in social process are socially shared fantasies. What is not clear in Homans's theory – and I think he is trying to keep an open mind about it – is how he would conceive of the coming into being of socially shared fantasies. Are they pre-existent in some way, or primarily social products, or combinations of these, or something else entirely?

Imaginal networks

The fourth example of theorising the shared element in groups and institutions that I want briefly to mention is my own work on the imaginal world and imaginal networks. I think of the imaginal world as the place where the contents of socially shared fantasies are fashioned. I do not think in terms of a complete set of precise, pre-existing images waiting for the right social or institutional context to trigger them off. This is because a crucial characteristic of images is their specificity to certain situations. If images themselves were to be regarded as pre-existing en bloc, then there would have to be so many previously formed images that the idea becomes ridiculous and, anyway, the idea of pre-existing images is philosophically and psychologically dubious. However, I would not see the contents of the imaginal world as *created* by social or institutional contexts; it is a more equal relationship than that. If we were to consider the imaginal world as one pre-existent factor, then we could restrict its relevance to our image-making capacity. It is this *capacity* that pre-exists an entry into the social realm. Hence, imagery that looks like a psychological response to a social situation is also a facet of the construction of that social situation. There cannot be psychological experiences of social reality without images of social reality; social experience is experienced via social imagery. The imaginal world is the place in which shared social fantasy is constantly being freshened, evolving in relation to and as part of the construction of social reality. I would like us to get away from the search for the one thing that is supposed to be fundamental or, pardon the linguistic nonsense, *more* fundamental than other things. Shared social fantasy, a dimension of psychic reality, intermingles with group and institutional dynamics, dimensions of social reality. Social experience is experienced via social imagery.

GROUP PROCESS AND POLITICAL CHANGE

A synthesis of these four viewpoints runs as follows. From Jaques, we learn how a common psychological response develops in individuals to a group, institutional or social situation. From Bion, we learn something of how groupishness is constituted in humans. Homans suggests that there are socially shared fantasies and I elaborate this in terms of an imaginal world whose potential to form images provides us with the contents of socially shared fantasies.

Up to now, I have not attempted to make distinctions between 'group', 'institution', 'social situation' and 'society' – though I have tried to be careful to use the appropriate term with respect to the content and the typical usage of any particular writer. However, when considering the relevance of this body of work on shared elements in group process for an analysis of processes of political change, distinctions between the terms have to be made. To begin with, nearly all the work I have described deals with relatively boundaried situations (and this limitation is also a source of intellectual strength). Even an entire society may be considered a boundaried entity. I think that the limitation needs to be understood in the cultural context of post-1945 Britain when the need to restore and reform social institutions was urgent and at a time when the role of central control, rational planning and social engineering in this task had not yet been discredited. The difficulty is that many social problematics spread across groups, institutions, societies and even cultures.

During the writing of the book, I have been struck by the manner in which the material has organized itself: Not in terms of institutions or situations such as church, army, stock market, class system. Though these kinds of phenomena have by no means been absent from my text, the accent has been much more on social and political *themes and problematics*: Political morality, the market, ecology, poverty. It is very hard to claim such themes and problematics as 'institutions' in the usual sense of the word though, of course, social institutions are implicated in social themes and problems: No poverty without banks. But do the dynamics of a bank as a workplace tell us much about poverty? I am not sure.

A group dynamics specialist or consultant has to work within the confines of the institution as a given. One cannot study the dynamics of a hospital without a hospital to study. But a political approach to social phenomena that accepts the boundaries of such phenomena as givens loses out on what is surely a crucial and valuable aspect of a psychological approach – the manner in which, via association, metaphor and metonymy, boundaries are overridden (in fine Hermetic style). It is the boundary-breaking nature of a psychological analysis that I see as providing the political impetus to accounts of group and institutional process. Of course, I would not go so far as to say that the Tavistock approach as developed by psychoanalysts and social scientists is not psychological. What I am saying is that the parts of psychology that such an approach must eschew – the boundary-breaking parts – are just those parts that make a psychological analysis *political*. The extraordinary body of object relational work on group and social dynamics was created at a certain moment of cultural evolution and social history and therefore chose to engage with institutions-as-found rather than with the problematics and thematics within and through which such institutions functioned.

CAUTIONARY TALES

The use of certain models of the mind derived from object relations theory does not always help attempts to break the psychoanalytical self-proving circle and engage depth psychology with politics. The object relations consensus suffers from a norm-making enmeshment with the numinous images of the bodily relationship of mother and infant, leading to the moralistic advancement of the depressive position as a nostrum for social and cultural ills. However, an extraction from object relations theory of ideas about shared elements in groups and social institutions sharpens up the political utility of object relations theory and, in spite of disagreements, I have tried to link this work with the ground covered by my book.

In the next two chapters, we will continue to observe how hard it is for depth psychology and depth psychologists to make a contribution, particularly in the heat of the moment, to important events in the political arena. For, in these chapters, I will be writing critically about the failure of my own discipline of analytical psychology, demonstrated in Jung's work, to play a constructive and clarifying role in 1930s Europe in the immediate pre-Second World War period. Some of Jung's public behavior and published writings led to accusations of his being an anti-semite and Nazi sympathizer, and I go into these matters. What I want to say here, at the end of a chapter that was critical of object relations theory, is that, though the problems with analytical psychology's engagement with culture are different, they are no less serious. *What I have written concerning the linkage between object relations and political and cultural analysis is relevant for other approaches to the psychology of the political. What I will write about analytical psychology and political and cultural analysis is also relevant for other schools of depth psychology and psychoanalysis. That is why I call this final section 'Cautionary tales'.*

Chapter 12

Jung, anti-semitism and the Nazis

INTRODUCTION

In this chapter and the next one, I try to show that it was Jung's attempt to establish a psychology of nations that brought him into the same frame as Nazi anti-semitic ideology. In addition, Jung was absorbed by the question of leadership. Exploring these ideas as thoroughly as possible leads to a re-evaluation in more positive terms of what Jung was trying to do. Moreover, such an exploration is itself a necessary act of reparation.

In 1988 the London Library, a private institution much favored in intellectual and literary circles, set up an appeal to mark the centenary of the birth of their onetime president, T. S. Eliot. The appeal was to benefit young writers. Instead, a storm of controversy broke out because of the great poet's alleged anti-semitism. Examples were not hard to find. In the poem 'Burbank with a Baedeker: Bleistein with a Cigar' Eliot wrote:

> The rats are underneath the piles.
> The Jew is underneath the lot.
> Money in furs.

In that poem, in thirty-two lines, Eliot compressed a whole range of anti-semitic stereotypes, from the small businessman to the Rothschild-like aristocrat. Or, in the poem 'Gerontion':

> My house is a decayed house
> And the Jew squats on the window
> sill the owner
> Spawned in some estaminet in Antwerp.

The poems were written in the 1920s, but their sting persisted. In 1951, a young Jewish poet, Emanuel Litvinoff, gave a reading, at which Eliot was present, of a poem which included the lines:

> I am not accepted in your parish.
> Bleistein was my relative.

By the time the furore over Eliot had entered the columns of popular newspapers, similar revelations concerning the philosophers Martin Heidegger and Paul de Man were the subject of scrutiny. Questions were also raised, by no means for the first time, about C. G. Jung's alleged anti-semitism and pro-Nazi stance. At least five letters, either attacking or defending Jung, appeared on the correspondence page of the *New York Times* during 1988. A lengthy piece written by a popular American psychiatrist-columnist, critical of Jung, appeared in the *Psychiatric Times* of September 1988. Peter Gay, Freud's most recent biographer, devoted a third of a review published in *The Guardian*, also in 1988, of a recent Jung biography to the subject.

My own experience, as an analytical psychologist interested in relating Jung's work and legacy to that of psychoanalytic thinkers, is that relations between Freudians and Jungians are increasingly hampered by the repeated claims that Jung was a Nazi sympathizer and anti-semite. In 1987, I presented a clinical paper to a study group of the New York Psychoanalytic Institute. The first question concerned Jung's supposed 'admiration of Hitler' (in the questioner's words). I had already noted that the entire audience on that occasion was, or seemed to be, Jewish, a fact which had produced in me a feeling of at-homeness up to the moment of that question.

To accomplish my task, I need to ask the reader to join me in exploring two burning issues that were central to the ideology of fascism in the 1930s. The two themes are (1) the idea of *nation* and (2) the principle of *leadership*.

ON NOT ANALYZING JUNG

Readers of what follows may be disappointed that I scarcely mention Jung's personal psychology or psychopathology – his father-complex, the scars of the break with Freud, his shadow problems, his Swiss bourgeois mentality, and so forth. Nor do I give much space to the abundant personal testimonies that exist, intended to show that Jung cannot be regarded as anti-semitic or to those accounts which prove the contrary, that he had a positive attitude to Jews and helped many Jews to achieve a relationship with their Jewishness for the first time. I must say here that I do not feel any sense of disappointment in Jung, that he has, in some personal way, let me down. Clichés about Jung's shadow problems concerning Jews strike me as rather shallow. I never saw him as 'a perfect leader, a saint, someone who guides us, a guru' so I do not have a reaction when he turns out to be a 'very average collective human being' (to use the dichotomy set out by Adolf Guggenbühl-Craig).[1]

For a while I worried that these omissions added up to a failure of feeling on my part. Obviously, I do not think that we should totally ignore Jung's experiences and experiences of Jung, forgetting the usefulness of a simple answer. Indeed, in the next chapter, I consider Jung the man as an example of a leader or potential leader. But gradually I have come to see that *the true failure of feeling is found when the personal dimension is given too much weight or used to close an awkward issue once and for all.* A similar point was made by the editor of the *Journal of Psychology and Judaism* introducing an issue composed of two major papers on the subject of Jung, anti-semitism and the Nazis.[2] I am sure I am not the only one to have mixed feelings about an analysis-at-a-distance of Jung's internal life (his dreams, for example) that does not observe the rule of 'confidentiality' even to the slightest degree. I simply do not feel that this level of data is the fruitful one. One difficulty with any psychological analysis of Jung the man is that a conclusion that the whole thing is very complicated can almost always be known in advance: Jung, by his own admission (regarding Number One and Number Two personalities), was an extremely complex person who excited equally complex reactions. So, for me, analyzing Jung is not the best way to proceed. Instead, I would like to cast as actors in this drama, not individuals, but *groups*, and suggest that the play is about to-ing and fro-ing between groups: Nazis, Jews, Jungians, Freudians. I was amazed, and sometimes shocked, to discover the extent to which the groups, apparently so different, share a common process.[3]

WAS JUNG ANTI-SEMITIC?

I have chosen to locate my inquiry on an intergroup level, which is where the drama about Jung has been played out, a drama involving Christians as well as Jews, Freudians, Jungians and Nazis. This does not in itself constitute a magic solution to the difficulties inherent in our themes. But it does go some way to rectifying a serious problem with what has been written about Jung to date. We have history.[4] We have attack.[5] We have defense.[6] We have at least half a dozen biographies of Jung. We have the *New York Times* letters. We have pleas for an imaginal approach.[7] But we have virtually no political analysis of this drama. There is very little critical work on the relationship of what is politically dubious in Jung's writings to the general cultural problems of Nazism and anti-semitism.

So, rather than attempt a new analysis of Jung the man (for which, not having met him, I feel I have not the slightest evidential basis), I sought a new use of what I had read. In these chapters, I ask whether there is something in the fundamental structure of Jung's thinking about the Jews, in its heart or essence, that made anti-semitism inevitable. When Jung writes about the Jews and Jewish psychology, is there something in his whole attitude that brings him into the same frame as the Nazis, even if he were shown not to have been an active Nazi collaborator? Is there something to worry about?

My brief answer, in distinction to that of many well-known Jungians, is 'yes' and, as I said, my hope is that by exploring the matter as deeply as I can a kind of reparation will ensue. Then there will be the base from which to explore the full potential of what Jung was trying to do with his psychological thinking about culture in the 1930s.

Many of those who have heard me lecture on this topic have commented that the particular blend of intellect and emotion, logic and image, makes mine a post-modern contribution. Perhaps this is a consequence of exposure to modernism's shadow, the events, language and imagery of the Nazi era. As a Jewish man, I found that writing about Jung and anti-semitism turned into a personal odyssey. Travelling this road has enabled me to stay an analytical psychologist. But I know that, if the source of a thoughtless remark about Jewish people is the *Collected Works* of C. G. Jung, the possible outcome of the idea set loose in the political arena is the concentration camp and the gas chamber. The Jew of whom Jung writes is my relative and sometimes we do not feel accepted in Jung's parish. But this is not a parochial matter, and others than Jews are involved. In 1946 the Foreign Office in London received a document entitled 'The case of Dr Carl G. Jung – pseudo-scientist Nazi auxiliary' suggesting a possible trial as a war criminal. I have seen this document, which did not excite the interest of the civil servants concerned; its significance does not lie in its content, which is familiar, but rather in the degree of political outrage Jung managed to elicit.[8]

Finally, I believe that the manifold strengths and subtleties of analytical psychology are being lost. Such loss results, not only from the alleged Nazi collaboration and anti-semitism (both of which Jung denied), but also from what can sometimes seem like an inability on the part of many Jungians to react to such charges in an intelligent, humane and honest way. Thus, psychoanalysis and other intellectual disciplines are permitted to continue to ignore the pioneering nature of Jung's contributions and, hence, the work of post-Jungian analytical psychologists. As Eli Weisstub puts it:

> There is much to be done in answering some of these criticisms. . . .
> Only in so doing can we (that is, Jungians) get the rest of the world
> analytic community to respect what is valid and valuable and
> significant in Jung's contributions. . . . Trying to preserve a myth about
> 'our leader' will not further this effort.[9]

BACKGROUND INFORMATION

Although what I write is primarily psychological, ideological and critical
– not historical – it may help to provide some background information,
which I will discuss throughout the chapters, for those not familiar with
Jung's activities in the 1930s. I will also try to summarize, but not at this
point critique, some of his ideas about 'Jewish psychology'. These
activities and ideas have been the subject of intense argument from the
1930s to the present day. It has to be said that a definitive factual basis for
clear-cut opinion is extremely difficult, if not impossible to establish.
Nevertheless, when lecturing on the topic of Jung, anti-semitism and the
Nazis, I have found widespread ignorance, even among Jungian analysts,
of what it was that Jung did and said that has caused such a prolonged
outcry. Non-Jungian audiences, on the other hand, have often seemed to
'know' definitely that Jung was 'anti-semitic', a 'supporter of Hitler', and
so on – but not to be aware of the details.

In 1933 Jung took on the presidency of the General Medical Society for
Psychotherapy. This was a professional body with members from several
countries but nevertheless based in Germany and coming under Nazi
control. Jung claimed that he took this post expressly to defend the rights
of Jewish psychotherapists and he altered the constitution of the GSMP so
that it became a fully and formally international (later, 'supranational')
body. The former General Society became the German national member
group. Membership was by means of national societies with a special
category of individual membership (members-at-large). Jews were
already barred from membership of the German national society and so,
under Jung's new provision, were enabled to join the Society via
membership of the individual section. Jung always maintained that his
motives for taking on the presidency were to protect Jewish colleagues in
this way and to keep depth psychology alive in Germany. Freud's books
were burnt and he was 'banned' in 1933.

Jung also became editor of the *Zentralblatt für Psychotherapie*, the
Society's scientific journal. This was one of the leading journals of

psychotherapy in central Europe. Jung said that this was a *pro forma* appointment and he was geographically distant from the editorial offices. He said he did not know that pro-Nazi statements of principles would be inserted for general distribution outside, as opposed to inside, Germany by Professor Göring (a cousin of the Reichsmarschall) who had been made President of the (dominant) German section.

Jung's own editorials and articles in the *Zentralblatt*, extracts of which appear below, have also been a main reason why he has been accused of pro-Nazi sympathies and anti-semitism.

According to Geoffrey Cocks in *Psychotherapy in the Third Reich*, Jung's ideas had 'official approval', he visited Nazi Germany to teach on two occasions, and, as a result, 'German psychotherapists did all they could to link Jung's name with their own activities'.[10] Jung's work was cited by German racial theoreticians and appeared in official Nazi bibliographies. Cocks points out that, following Jung's denunciations in 1938–9 of Hitler and the Nazis, his psychology never became the dominant school under the Nazis.

In an interview on Radio Berlin in 1933, Jung commented:

As Hitler said recently, the leader (*Führer*) must be able to be alone and must have the courage to go his own way. But if he doesn't know himself, how is he to lead others? That is why the true leader is always one who has the courage to be himself, and can look not only others in the eye but above all himself. . . . Every movement culminates organically in a leader, who embodies in his whole being the meaning and purpose of the popular movement.[11]

In his paper 'The state of psychotherapy today', published in the *Zentralblatt* in 1934, Jung wrote:

Freud did not understand the Germanic psyche any more than did his Germanic followers. Has the formidable phenomenon of National Socialism, on which the whole world gazes with astonishment, taught them better? Where was that unparalleled tension and energy while as yet no National Socialism existed? Deep in the Germanic psyche, in a pit that is anything but a garbage-bin of unrealizable infantile wishes and unresolved family resentments.[12]

In the same paragraph, Jung makes the following comments about the Jews: 'The "Aryan" unconscious has a higher potential than the Jewish.' He also states that 'The Jew, who is something of a nomad, has never yet created a cultural form of his own and as far as we can see never will, since all his instincts and talents require a more or less civilised nation to act as host for their development', and that 'the Jews have this peculiarity with women; being physically weaker, they have to aim at the chinks in the armour of their adversary'.

Finally, Jung warns against 'applying Jewish categories indiscriminately to Germanic and Slavic Christendom'. He says much the same in a footnote to the 1935 edition of *Two Essays on Analytical Psychology*: 'It is a quite unpardonable mistake to accept the conclusions of a Jewish psychology as generally valid.'[13] In a separate *Zentralblatt* editorial he had written in 1933 that 'the differences which actually do exist between Germanic and Jewish psychology and which have been long known to every intelligent person are no longer to be glossed over'.[14]

In a letter to his pupil Dr Kranefeldt in 1934, Jung wrote:

As is known, one cannot do anything against stupidity, but in this instance the Aryan people can point out that with Freud and Adler specifically Jewish points of view are publicly preached, and as can be proven likewise, points of view that have an essentially corrosive character. If the proclamation of this Jewish gospel is agreeable to the government, then so be it. Otherwise there is also the possibility that this would not be agreeable to the government.[15]

Jung was not new to speculations about the Jews. In 1918 he had written that the Jew

is badly at a loss for that quality in man which roots him to the earth and draws new strength from below. This chthonic quality is to be found in dangerous concentration in the German peoples. . . . The Jew has too little of this quality – where has he his own earth underfoot?[16]

However, as we will see in a moment, Jung totally rejected the charge of anti-semitism. He said, in a letter to A. Pupato in 1934, that he 'fought Freud's psychology because of its dogmatic claim to sole validity'.[17]

It is interesting to compare these extracts from Jung's writings with the following:
Freud to Abraham in 1908:

Please do not forget that it is easier for you than for Jung to follow my ideas, for in the first place you are completely independent, and then you are closer to my intellectual constitution because of racial kinship . . . I nearly said that it was only by his appearance on the scene that psychoanalysis escaped from the danger of becoming a Jewish national affair.[18]

Freud to Ferenczi in 1913:

> Certainly there are great differences between the Jewish and Aryan
> spirit. We can observe that every day. Hence there would assuredly be
> here and there differences in outlook on life and art. But there should
> not be such a thing as Aryan or Jewish science. Results in science must
> be identical, though the presentation of them may vary.[19]

ATTACKS AND DEFENSES: A DISCUSSION

Having absorbed the contents of the many attacks on Jung, based on the
behavior and writing outlined in the previous section entitled
'Background information', my attention was stirred by the nature of the
equally numerous defenses of Jung that have been put forward. I found
myself reacting to a psychological similarity between the defenses and
attacks. Both defenders and attackers of Jung are sitting in judgment on
him. Both are looking for a 'final solution' to the Jung problem. Between
the cries of 'Let's clear our man once and for all' and 'Let's finish the
bastard off' there is a call for a middle way: Tot up carefully the
competing claims of attackers and defenders so as to reach an apparently
balanced point of view. It is said that the matter can never be settled
decisively. Though it is tempting to join in this Olympian arbitration
between attack and defense, that position can be seen as disengaged,
morally supercilious, politically evasive, pseudo-mature, and, in any case,
as full of a kind of certitude as overt attack or defense! The shadows
surrounding Jung are going to linger, for they want us to pay
psychological attention to them. In the next section, I will let Jung speak
for himself in his own defense.

One particular defense of Jung that is often put forward is that he was
only expressing the attitudes of his time. Many other eminent men and
women were equally guilty of a kind of *trahison des clercs*. Moreover, it
is said that casual, social anti-semitism was apparently so widespread,
normal and acceptable in Jung's culture and time that remarks about the
Jews, even when couched in scientific language, did not seem *outré*.
(Much the same defense has been advanced regarding Eliot, Heidegger
and de Man.) Conversely, Jung has been defended by the argument that he
should *not* be seen as an important man but rather as just a typical,
petit-bourgeois, unthinking, small-minded anti-semitic Swiss burgher.
According to Adolf Guggenbühl-Craig, 'the anti-semitism of Jung was a
sheer banality of the collective he belonged to'.[20]

But these claims, themselves contradictory, actually *stimulate* a search for evidence that would contradict them and, therefore, there is a risk of undermining the intention of defending Jung. For it seems that there could have been other attitudes available to Jung at the time, other choices that he could have made, other viewpoints possible, particularly given that he was not under direct personal threat. Even in Germany, there were the *Judenfreunde*, 'friends of the Jews' – not just the anecdotal good Germans but people actually prosecuted in the courts by the Gestapo for their attitudes and behavior. Then there were the *Rassenschänder*, 'race defilers', who were imprisoned for doing what hundreds and thousands had done quite legally before 1933, as the intermarriage statistics show.[21]

We know from a fascinating letter in the London *Times* on November 13, 1988 – from a typical *Times* correspondent, an Anglican (Episcopalian) clergyman of the old school – that problems faced by Jews were openly and frequently discussed in Germany in the late 1930s.[22] Closer to home, there was the public admonition of Jung by Dr Bally in 1934.[23] In 1935 the Dutch section of the International General Medical Society for Psychotherapy refused to host the annual congress on political grounds. Jung was critical of this decision because, he said, it brought politics into science. In 1936, when Jung was invited to speak at the tercentenary celebrations of Harvard University, and to receive an honorary degree, a public row broke out in the pages of the Harvard *Crimson*, the university newspaper, over the appropriateness of inviting Jung. Gordon Allport felt that Jung's 'scientific integrity' had been 'partially stifled under the Nazi thumb'. Henry Murray defended Jung's independence of thought in very strong terms. The point is that, even at the time, Jung's position was not regarded as unproblematic in intellectual circles.[24] Therefore, Adolf Guggenbühl-Craig's point about Jung being a 'collective intellectual' is a very dubious one. To criticize Jung is not a case of 'present-ism', seeing the past from today's vantage point. He was criticized in similar terms at the time, during the 1930s.

Indeed, the *necessity* of deliberately linking politics with 'science' was on the minds of many intellectuals during this period. It follows that Jung's repeated attempts to divorce the two cannot be regarded as absolutely conditioned by the epistemological climate of the day. For instance, the philosopher and critic Walter Benjamin wrote to Judaic scholar Gershom Scholem in 1937 that he intended to devote a period to an intensive study of Jung's works, not only so as to critique Jung's 'doctrines on archaic images and the collective unconscious', but for openly political reasons. In Benjamin's opinion, Jung had 'leaped to the rescue of the Aryan soul with a therapy reserved for it alone'. This,

Benjamin felt, was an 'auxiliary service to National Socialism [that had] been in the works for some time'. A month later, in the middle of his study period, Benjamin wrote to Scholem that Jung's psychology was 'the devil's work'.[25]

So a result of the claim that the world displayed a universal anti-semitism in the 1920s and 1930s, and that the ideas of Jung and the others were just part of that *Zeitgeist*, has been to constellate a counter-claim, one that is potentially damaging to Jung: Alternative opinions and ways of thinking did exist. Other non-Jewish analysts, who might also have been expected to reflect 'ordinary' anti-semitism, felt the need to get involved in a different way. D. W. Winnicott, for instance, wrote the following letter to Mrs Neville Chamberlain in 1938 urging her to question her husband over his silence on the subject of the Jews and Nazi persecution:

Dear Mrs Chamberlain,

I feel the Prime Minister is too busy to answer questions but I do want to know [something]. Would you try to answer this as many of us are urgently in need of answers that we cannot get . . .

Why does the Prime Minister never mention the Jews. Does he secretly despise them? When in England we say WE, we include Jews who are people like ourselves. I am not asking him to be pro-Jew, but I want to know definitely whether he is or is not secretly anti-Jew . . . at present we seem to be secretly sharing Germany's anti-Jew insanity, and this is not where we want our leaders to lead us.[26]

Many of the articles that appeared in the *Zentralblatt für Psychotherapie* under the banner of Jung's editorship go well beyond 'ordinary', petit-bourgeois anti-semitism. There are repeated attacks on 'Jewish' mental states and a general lauding of 'northern', Aryan psychology. There is a great deal of praise for Hitler and the Nazi party and, in the opinion of some, even coded messages of support for measures such as the extermination of mental patients. In any event, these articles appeared long after the initial confusion over whether a statement of support for the Nazis was to be printed in the *Zentralblatt* proper for 1933 or only in the German national supplement, due in 1934.[27] Jung claimed that it was because of this confusion that his name appeared attached to such a statement. The question is whether Jung knew of the disgusting (and absurd) nature of these further articles published in the years 1933–39. He would have heard some of them at conferences. If he did nothing about it, could it have been because he was completely divorced from the editorial policy and activity of the *Zentralblatt*? But we do know that editorial work *was* carried out in Zürich. C. A. Meier, Jung's associate, wrote to James Kirsch that he personally corrected numerous insulting reviews of 'Jewish books and articles'. Jung, on the other hand, did nothing; according to Meier's account, he left everything to Meier.[28]

Here, Meier's memory is at fault. For, in 1937 Jung wrote to Göring as follows:

> Dr Meier has drawn my attention to your short review of Rosenberg's book. For anyone who knows Jewish history, in particular Hasidism, Rosenberg's assertion that the Jews despise mysticism is a highly regrettable error. I would therefore suggest that we pass over this book in silence. I cannot allow my name to be associated with such lapses.[29]

In the same year of 1937 the *Zentralblatt* published a paper by Victor Frankl, so it seems that Jewish writers could have their work published.

Our sense of relief and desire to applaud the attempts by Jung and Meier to keep the more egregious parcels of anti-semitic thinking out of the columns of the *Zentralblatt* need to be tempered. For the realization that the power to do this was available to the team in Zürich, even after Göring became joint editor in 1936, raises the uncomfortable question of why it was not exercised more often. Are we to assume that, if Jung could keep out anti-semitic ideas that he did not approve of, the anti-semitic ideas of which he did approve are the ones that remain? I do not think that a simple answer exists. I know from experience how complicated the internal politics of a learned journal can be. It has proved very hard to achieve an accurate portrait of how the *Zentralblatt für Psychotherapie* organized itself in these years but, as we will see in a moment, it is vital to establish the degree of involvement Jung had.

Even if Jung played little or no editorial role on the *Zentralblatt*, surely he at least *read* it? He was sole editor from 1933 to 1936 when Göring became joint editor. If he didn't read it at all, did nobody ever tell him what was in it?

In the *Zentralblatt*, there were a number of pieces co-signed by Jung with others. Some of these troubling little pieces are included in the General Bibliography of Jung's writings but are not included in the *Collected Works* (some pieces are not even in the bibliography). The pattern of exclusion of co-signed pieces from the bibliography and/or published works is not consistent and it has been suggested to me that this might reflect doubt in the minds of the editors of the *Collected Works* over whether Jung wrote some of the pieces signed by him with others. In other words, there would be no need to include these pieces in Jung's corpus because it cannot be established that the articles truly expressed Jung's views. However, as far as I can tell, *Jung never disowned any of these pieces, nor protested that his name had been taken in vain.* We should remember that, for much of this time, he was sole editor of the *Zentralblatt* and we have already seen that he could control the content of the journal when he felt strongly about it. My view is that these pieces, co-signed by Jung and apparently not the subject of intra-editorial dissent at the time, may be taken as expressive of his views. (I must add that it is special pleading to argue that, because these pieces are co-signed, they cannot be connected to Jung. Probably the argument is based on the misunderstandings over the statement of pro-Nazi principles that found its way into the *Zentralblatt*, as mentioned earlier. But that piece was neither signed nor co-signed by Jung; it appeared in a journal of which he was the editor.)

I have recently made a study of one of these co-signed pieces which was published in 1934 (following the matter of the pro-Nazi statement that appeared in the *Zentralblatt* in 1933). Maybe Jung was taken by surprise once again and his name used as co-signatory without permission. We simply cannot know for sure but, as stated above, I do not think that such *lèse-majesté* took place for, if it had, Jung or his associates would have done something about it at the time. The contents of this piece make for instructive reading.

The piece is innocuous-looking – a seventieth-birthday greeting to Dr Robert Sommer, one of the co-founders in 1926 of the GMSP, by Matthias Göring and Jung.[30] However, Sommer, according to Geoffrey Cocks, was the 'moving spirit' behind attempts to translate the ideas of 'social and racial hygiene' into the mental health field.[31] Sommer founded an organization in 1923 called *Deutscher Verband für Psychische Hygiene* (German Association for Mental Hygiene). In their birthday tribute, Göring and Jung say of this group that it was a 'comparatively small association before the turning-point, today of extraordinary importance'. The 'turning-point' was, of course, the coming to power of the Nazis.

Göring and Jung go on to praise Sommer's book *Familienforschung, Vererbungs- und Rassenlehre* (which can be effectively translated as Family Studies, Hereditology and Raceology – there are no present-day terms for the last two disciplines). In particular, they praise the new chapter of the book, written in 1927 and added to the existing text of 1907. I wondered why, in 1934, Göring and Jung would go out of their way to praise one particular chapter added in 1927 to a book first published in 1907. Jung certainly knew of Sommer's book, citing it in both the original and the revised versions of a paper on the father (1909 and 1949).[32] But this may have been the first edition. It may not be a *reason*, but we have to recall, as Robert Jay Lifton has pointed out, that from the mid-1930s the

Nazi notion of 'life unworthy of life' became firmly established together with the concept of 'medical killing'.[33] (Eugenics fascinated any thinker concerned with equality and we find proposals for the extermination of 'ethnic trash' in the writings of Bernard Shaw and Friedrich Engels.) In the chapter of Sommer's book specifically referred to by Göring and Jung in the *Zentralblatt* we find many statements along the following lines:

There has been an intrusion of alien blood into the Germanic race.

The morphological differences of human races are in part based on changes in the formation of the skull.

The long-headedness of the so-called Nordic races is of particular importance.

The type of the Nordic race . . . forms a contrast . . . to the backwards sloping forehead of the primitive human races.

Often the formation of the nose is used as a racial criterion in human anthropology. A special emphasis is given to the straight or slightly bow-shaped formation of the nose with regard to . . . . Further, a hook-shaped protuberance is regarded as . . . .

Recently blood research has become of great importance for raceology.

Practical psychiatry is . . . most closely linked with raceology.

The selection of the gifted has to be performed . . . .

There are several possible reasons why – even if he *did* know what was being published in his journal, sometimes over his name – Jung might still have done nothing in contradiction. First, he might have been in full agreement with these views. But, given the Sommer encomium, that would make him an overt Nazi supporter and rabid 'scientific' anti-semite and he denies both of these charges. Second, he might have been playing a long-term political game, continuing his strategy of helping Jewish psychotherapists to go on working. But there is no written or oral evidence that he held back for this reason and, were it the case, I think that there would be some evidence. Third, and I believe this is the answer, Jung's position at the head of the German psychotherapy profession was desirable from the point of view of the development of analytical psychology. The issue here is Jung's leadership. After all, Freud had once written to Jung that psychoanalysis would never find its true status until it had been accepted in Germany. The conquest of Germany was the goal of the psychoanalytic conquistador.[34] History, and Hitler, put that goal within

Jung's grasp, and I shall look at Jung as a conquering leader of the field of psychology in the next chapter.

Whether Jung read the *Zentralblatt* or not, contemporary study of that journal is certainly worthwhile. For example, we find an announcement from Jung's co-editor Matthias Göring that Jung informed the presidents of the national societies of his intention to resign as President of the IGMSP in 'the summer of 1940'.[35] This is at least one year and maybe two years later than many accounts have hitherto suggested and would place the date of the resignation after the start of the war. Similarly, we find that, as late as 1939, Jung is praising the efforts of Matthias Göring to set up institutions 'where the new generation of psychotherapists can be trained in a spirit and atmosphere that offers the best guarantee for the German people (*das Volk*) to be served by these young doctors in the future'.[36]

Another issue of dating on which the *Zentralblatt* sheds light concerns the time at which Jung became involved with the GMSP (as it then was). It appears that Jung became a participant in 1928 and vice-president in 1930. He was not brought in as a distinguished outsider in 1933 but as a distinguished insider.[37]

Similarly, accounts of the proceedings of the congresses of the IGMSP make it clear that Jung was in attendance and, indeed, actually spoke. Therefore he was present to hear Matthias Göring make the following statement at the 1934 congress in Bad Nauheim. Göring began by saying that he expected all members to have studied *Mein Kampf*, going on as follows:

> Today I say that *Mein Kampf* has to be called a scientific book . . . . Whoever reads the book and the speeches of the Führer and studies his way of being will recognize that he has got something that most of us lack: Jung calls it intuition. It is more important than all science. It is because of that that I demand of all of you that until the next congress, which will take place here in Bad Nauheim once again, you study this book and the speeches of Adolf Hitler thoroughly.[38]

Jung's 'not-ordinary' anti-semitism is further demonstrated by his involvement with Jacob Hauer, a professor of Indology and founder in 1933 of the German Faith Movement. Jung co-led seminars with Hauer on Kundalini Yoga in 1932 and was interested in his work. The German Faith Movement was an attempt to construct a religion more in tune with German history and traditions than Christianity, with its Semitic flavor. The new religion would, according to its founder, be different from Christianity on account of the fact that the 'founder of Christianity and its standard documents have reached us from a different racial and cultural area'. Hauer says he could have as easily called his Movement the 'Nordic–Teutonic Faith Movement'. Hauer goes on:

> The German Faith Movement must be understood in close relation with the national movement which led to the formation of the Third Reich. Like the latter, the German Faith Movement is an eruption from the biological and spiritual depths of the German nation. . . .
>
> We want the German people to regard its history and territory with religious devotion. . . . We can see God advancing over German soil. . . . [39]

The translators say, in their introduction to Hauer's book, that one 'odd note' in a typical service of the German Faith Movement would be the expression in a hymn of undying loyalty to Hitler.

It is hard to assess what Jung really thought about the German Faith Movement. In the relevant passage in 'Wotan', published in 1936, he refers to adherents of German Faith Movement as 'decent and well-meaning people' but also analyzes them as 'possessed' by the 'god of the Germans' – Wotan. On the other hand, it is no 'disgrace' to know that the God of the Germans is Wotan 'and not the Christian God'. What is clear is that this is in no way a repudiation or condemnation of Hauer; in fact, the passage could be read as an imprimatur for Hauer's group compared to other new religions.[40]

Another defense of Jung is so interesting that I intend to discuss it in some detail. This defense attempts a divorce of Jung's behavior (including any casually expressed attitudes) from the formal presentation of his ideas in books and articles. These defenders do not excuse Jung's actions but dispute that the true importance of his ideas is affected by them. This defense of Jung can find expression the other way round: though Jung wrote stupid and offensive things about Jews, which he should have corrected, he did not *do* anything that could be regarded as destructive in the real world. The problem with the defense is that, even if one could make such a dissociation between life and work credible in the case of a psychologist, the problem of the influence of the writer's words on the behavior of others still remains an issue. The use of the writer's words by others has to be considered. Obviously the writer cannot prevent exploitation, but he can protest at it. Did Jung?

I disagree with Geoffrey Cocks who, in his pathbreaking history of psychotherapy in Germany during the Nazi era, offers a version of this defense when he writes that 'Jung conceded more to the Nazis by his words than by his actions'.[41] As noted previously, Cocks himself points out that Jung's analytical psychology had official approval and therefore

'German psychotherapists did almost all they could to link Jung's name with their own activities'. From a political, if not a strictly legal standpoint, Jung's professional activities and his psychological theories can be regarded as intertwined. They may not be causally connected in a superficial sense but, if we split them radically, we deny the negative synergy of word and action. If Jung did admit to Rabbi Leo Baeck that he 'slipped up', when they met in Zürich in 1946, then the slip may be understood as referring to this synergy: The influence of thought on action, action on thought. We would not be concerned with Jung's reputation to anything like the same extent if he had merely taken on the presidency of the General Medical Society of Psychotherapy in 1933. Then his efforts to protect the rights of Jewish psychotherapists by altering the constitution of the GMSP (so that it became a fully and formally international body with membership units composed of national societies and a special category of individual membership) would probably seem less controversial. If he had confined himself to the political and institutional arena, then the ingenious way in which his constitutional reforms permitted Jews, barred from the German national society, to practice as individual members would not require justification fifty years later.

But, at exactly the same desperate moment in history, Jung's papers and editorials of the period, dwelling on questions of differing racial and national psychologies and containing disturbing generalizations about Jewish culture and psychology, could easily be misunderstood as supporting Nazi racial ideology. For instance, as we noted earlier, Jews are said 'never to have created a cultural form of their own' but rather to need a 'host nation' for their development. The implication of Jew as 'parasite' (a favorite image of Hitler's) follows on easily (though Jung said he meant something quite specific by the term 'cultural *form*' – see pp. 318–21 below). Similarly, Jews are referred to as 'physically weaker' than others – like women in relation to men. Therefore, like women, they have developed subtle and indirect techniques of attacking and overcoming others. Says Jung, Jews deal with Germans the way women deal with men!

At the very least, the twin presence of action and thought explains why there is such concern today. But I simply cannot persuade myself that the synergy did not exist at the time and is relevant only in terms of our current responses. After all, was not Jung the author of the theory of meaningful coincidences ('synchronicity'), including the idea that the psychic world (his ideas on Jewish psychology, perhaps) and the social world (German politics, perhaps) are acausally intertwined?

Once again, the intended defense is capable of undermining Jung still more.

There are other defenses of Jung which exist and, while I do not want to discuss them in as much detail as the two defenses already mentioned, I will give a brief account.

Many of those who knew Jung recall that he was also generous and, eventually, protective in his personal behavior toward Jews. This seems to be the consensus of most colleagues and personal friends.[42] The snag here is that we are all familiar with the 'some of my best friends are Jews' line; it is quite possible to combine good personal relations with a much deeper prejudice. Further, when Jung writes about the Jews he seems to do it as a member of a dominant and 'positive' race. This can be compared with Freud's position as 'the object of racialist concern who uses and projects this difference onto his perceived enemies and friends'.[43]

Actually, there is in existence a considerable amount of testimony that Jung was not always personally well disposed toward Jews. Michael Fordham, the senior British Jungian analyst, recalls meeting Jung for the first time in 1933 and being treated to a 'harangue' on the Jews and the 'parasitic elements in Jewish psychology'. Jung wondered what the Jews had been feeding on during the forty years in the wilderness. The clear implication was that they were grazing their herds on other people's land. Then Jung said that the Jews were not the same as other races and hence they should wear different clothes so as to emphasize this fact.[44] In similar vein, Jung apparently told an American student of his not to let her daughter marry a Jew as such marriages never worked.[45]

Perhaps the most interesting material that shows Jung as displaying a personal as opposed to an ideological anti-semitism is to be found in a previously unpublished letter from Jung to Mary Mellon written in 1945, a few months after the end of the war in Europe. Mary Mellon was the inspiration and planner behind the Bollingen Foundation which was endowed by her and her husband Paul Mellon. The Bollingen Foundation was undoubtedly the means by which Jung's ideas were disseminated widely in the English-speaking world and the Foundation provided financial support for the publication of Jung's *Collected Works* as well as many other scholarly works in the field of collective and cultural psychology. We may suppose that Jung regarded Mary Mellon, who had been a patient of his before the war, as an important person and patron. In the letter, Jung writes:

you probably have heard the absurd rumor that I am a Nazi. This rumor has been started by Freudian Jews in America. Their hatred of myself went as far as India, where I found falsified photo's [sic] of mine in the Psychological Seminar of Calcutta University. It was a photo retouched in such a way as to make me appear as an ugly Jew with a pince-nez! These photo's came from Vienna! This rumor has been spread over the whole world. Even with us it has been picked up with such alacrity, that I am forced to publish all the things I have written about Germany. It is however difficult to mention the anti-christianism of the Jews after the horrible things that have happened in Germany. But Jews are not so damned innocent after all – the role played by the intellectual Jews in prewar Germany would be an interesting object of investigation.[46]

One thing to note here is Jung's ideational process. It would seem that, in Jung's opinion, the way to ruin a man's reputation is to make him look Jewish and that this tactic was used in an organized way against him by 'Freudian Jews'. It is possible that Jung was temporarily insane or very unbalanced following his heart attack in 1944 but I think we do get an idea of the spleen with which he seems to have regarded Jews.

The second thing to note is the argument in the last two sentences – that it is difficult to discuss the 'anti-christianism' of the Jews and that 'intellectual Jews in prewar Germany' were not innocent. I wonder what Jung saw as the role of intellectual Jews – is he suggesting some kind of responsibility for the 'horrible things' that he knows were done to them? It is difficult to know what to think but the letter is unsettling, to say the least, and needs to be set alongside the idea that Jung was not anti-Jewish in any personal way.

Sometimes, Jung's work is divided up in such a way that the problematic material is quarantined by detaching it from the main body of Jung's writings which are not subject to current critical disapproval. It would help these defenders if the contentious passages and behavior had been the work of extreme youth, say, which they are not. Even so, Jung's work on Judaic themes from, say, 1946 onward is outstanding and can be favorably contrasted with what he had to say on the subject prior to that. But when the problematic material is isolated it is inevitably highlighted. Very little in the way of a defense of Jung is gained by red-lining Jung's work and behavior between 1933 and 1946.

Finally, Jung may be defended by pointing out that it is only human to make mistakes and that his reputation should therefore remain intact. What is more, there are no absolute standards of good and bad behavior, and who are we to judge Jung? One's sympathy for this line of argument should be tempered by the reflection that condemning mistakes in another is not anti-human; it is just as human as making mistakes! If you feel critical of Jung, why not express it? It would be tragic if people were to suppress, or to be prevented from expressing, their real feelings.

One piece of historical information that was recently made widely available has certainly aroused a good deal of anguished feeling in the Jungian community. In 1944, a secret appendix was added to the by-laws of the Analytical Psychology Club of Zürich, limiting the proportion of Jews who could be members at any one time. The quota for full members was 10 per cent and for guest members 25 per cent. The Club was, at that time, the main forum for the discussion of themes of interest to analytical psychology and it was also an important social center for those in Zürich to study or analyze with Jung or one of his collaborators. For whatever reason, this appendix was drawn up and signed by the executive committee and it has become unmistakably clear from massive interview testimony that Jung knew of the quota (though the general membership do not seem to have been told officially). Moreover, the quota for Jews was not removed until 1950. It is not surprising that this information has caused a stir.[47]

JUNG'S SELF-ASSESSMENT

In 1934 the Swiss psychotherapist Gustav Bally published his article critical of Jung's writings and actions in the *Neue Zürcher Zeitung*. Jung published 'A rejoinder to Dr Bally' in the same periodical a few months later. In this piece (and also, in similar vein, in his letters) Jung defended himself as follows:

As to the difference between Jewish and 'Aryan–Germanic– Christian– European' psychology, it can of course hardly be seen in the individual products of science as a whole. But we are not so much concerned with these as with the fundamental fact that in psychology the object of knowledge is at the same time the organ of knowledge, which is true of no other science. It has therefore been doubted in all sincerity whether psychology is possible as a science at all. In keeping with this doubt I suggested years ago that every psychological theory should be criti-cised in the first instance as a subjective confession. For, if the organ of knowledge is its own subject, we have every reason to examine the nature of that organ very closely indeed, since the subjective premise is at once the object of knowledge which is therefore limited from the start. This subjective premise is identical with our psychic idiosyn-crasy. The idiosyncrasy is conditioned (1) by the individual, (2) by the family, (3) by the nation, race, climate, locality, and history. . . .

May it not therefore be said that there is a Jewish psychology . . . which admits the prejudice of its blood and its history? And may it not be asked wherein lie the peculiar differences between an essentially Jewish and an essentially Christian outlook? Can it really be maintained that I alone among psychologists have a special organ of knowledge with a subjective bias, whereas the Jew is apparently insulted to the core if one assumes him to be a Jew? . . . I must confess my total inability to understand why it should be a crime to speak of 'Jewish' psychology. . . .

Are we really to believe that a tribe which has wandered through history for several thousand years as 'God's chosen people' was not put up to such an idea by some quite special psychological peculiarity? If no differences exist, then how do we recognise Jews at all?[48]

In a letter to James Kirsch of 1934, Jung defends himself in a somewhat different manner:

You ought to know me sufficiently well to realize that an unindividual stupidity like anti-semitism cannot be laid at my door. You know well enough how very much I take the human being as a personality and how I continually endeavor to lift him out of his collective condition and make him an individual.[49]

THE QUESTION OF APOLOGY

What did Jung do when he recognized after the war that he might have made a mistake? (Did he recognize it as deeply as all that?, is another question.) Why didn't he listen to Drs Bally and Kirsch? Why didn't he retract? Did he try to make amends?

In 1946 Jung published a slim volume which appeared in English in 1947 as *Essays on Contemporary Events*.[50] In it, Jung republished several of his pre-war papers on Germany and the Nazi phenomenon plus a preface, introduction and epilogue that were specially written for the book. Nowhere in this book does Jung explicitly say that he was caught up in the contemporary atmosphere, that he became a devotee of Wotan, that he became so excited by the potential of the Aryan unconscious that he developed a corresponding 'problem' about Jews. He does not retract anything, nor apologize for anything. But, in the preface to the book, he does refer to the 'violence of the impact of world events on the individual analyst'.[51] In the introduction Jung writes of the need to know that 'your worst enemy is right there in your own heart'.[52] Elsewhere, Jung was writing, also in 1946, of the shadow as 'the thing a person has no wish to be' and yet, somehow, *is*.[53] One could go on to say, as Jung did, that for anything or anyone to have substance and worth, he, she or it would have to possess a shadow.

It is my belief that *Essays on Contemporary Events* represents some sort of attempt on Jung's part to rehabilitate himself. However, I know from talking with many Jungian analysts that the question of an explicit expression of regret by Jung, in a clear, substantial and published form, is a very painful issue.

There is little doubt that Jung minded very much that his reputation and standing had been undermined by what he said and did in the 1930s. Recently available correspondence between Jung and his American supporters between 1947 and 1950 show Jung more-or-less orchestrating a concerted campaign to clear his name. Not for the first time, any notion that Jung could rise 'above' such things as personal reputation has to be dispelled.[54]

Once again, I must part company with Adolf Guggenbühl-Craig. His idealization of Jung is revealed when he asserts that Jung, as a 'genius', '*let* himself be drawn into the collective madness' (emphasis added).[55] I think he was *drawn in*, he did not decide to do it, any more than analysts *decide* to let their patients affect them. Then he failed to comprehend his 'countertransference'.

Certain of Jung's ideas can themselves be explained and clarified and hence made less objectionable. For instance, when he writes that the Jews have no cultural forms of their own, he obviously cannot mean that they have no culture at all. The remark about the Aryan unconscious having a higher potential than the Jewish unconscious can be taken in two ways. The alarming way is to hear Jung as saying that Aryans can go higher and further than Jews. The more reassuring way is to hear Jung as saying that Aryans have a long, long way to go before they reach the level that Jews have reached. But, as Jewish civilization is so much older, Jews may have already fulfilled much of their cultural potential. Is Jung suggesting that we should not expect all that much more from them? Reassurance tips back into alarm.

Finally, there is the question of forgiveness. In 1946, Jung managed to convince Leo Baeck of his bona fides. Baeck, in turn, convinced Gershom Scholem to attend the Eranos conference in 1947 and accept a collegial relation to Jung; the conference was on Jewish mysticism.

JUNG AND THE PSYCHOLOGY OF THE NATION

I will argue that the main difficulty with Jung's work in the general area of national psychology is an unwarranted expansion of his psychology, and hence his authority as a leading psychologist, into complicated fields

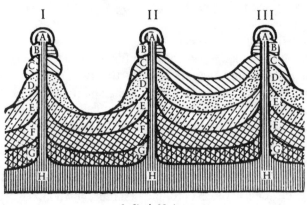

I. Single Nations
II and III. Groups of Nations (e.g., Europe)

A. Individual   E. Groups of People
B. Family   F. Primitive Human Ancestors
C. Tribe   G. Animal Ancestors
D. Nation   H. Central Force

Figure 12.1 Jacobi's 'psychic genealogical tree'

Source: Diagram from Jolande Jacobi, *The Psychology of C. G. Jung* (New Haven: Yale University Press, 1973), diagram XI, p. 34. Copyright © 1973 by Yale University Press. Reprinted by permission of Yale University Press.

where psychology on its own is an inadequate explanatory tool, especially concepts like the 'collective unconscious'.

To handle the obvious fact of cultural differences in the forms the archetypes of the collective unconscious assume, Jung asserted that there is a 'collective psyche limited to race, tribe, and family over and above the "universal" collective psyche'.[56] This concept of a restrictedly collective level of psyche is depicted in Jolande Jacobi's book *The Psychology of C. G. Jung*, published in 1942 with Jung's express approval, by a 'psychic genealogical tree' (Figure 12.1). She describes the diagram as follows:

> At the very bottom lies the unfathomable, the central force out of which at one time the individual psyche has been differentiated. This central force goes through all further differentiations and isolations, lives in them all, cuts through them to the individual psyche.

Resting upon this 'unfathomable ground', Jacobi arranges different strata; there are eight in all, arranged like the layers of a cake: The central force, animal ancestors, primitive human ancestors, groups of people, nation, tribe, family, individual. Though Jacobi does not use the word 'race', it is clear from the text as well as from Jung's remarks quoted above that this is what is meant by 'groups of people' (also referred to in the English translation as 'human groups' and in a later, post-war edition as 'ethnic groups' – in the German original, it is *Volksgruppe*).[57]

The hypothesis of a racial layer in Jung's model of the collective psyche has caused as great a furore as his alleged anti-semitism. As a result, a serious charge of racism has been levelled against him and against his psychology. According to most modern definitions, racism involves dividing humankind into distinct and hierarchically gradeable groups on the basis of biological or quasibiological characteristics. A racist is therefore someone who believes that people of a particular race, color or origin are inherently inferior, so that their identity, culture, self-esteem, views and feelings are of less value and may be treated as less important than those of the groups believed to be superior.[58]

We have to ask: Does Jung's idea of a racial layer of the psyche conform to this definition?

In a paper entitled 'Jung: a racist', Farhad Dalal thoroughly surveyed Jung's writings, especially on Africa and Africans.[59] He concluded that Jung was indeed a racist in that he thought that blacks were inferior and not just different. Dalal understood Jung to be saying that Africans lack a complete layer of consciousness altogether, that whites are inherently less 'primitive' and that therefore individuation is reserved for them alone, and that it is methodologically correct to use modern Africans to exemplify the psychologist's assertions about the prehistoric human.

Reviewing now the whole question of Jung's racism, I am conscious of an opportunity lost, not only by me in my reply to Dalal,[60] but by Jung himself. As so often with Jung, it is the intuitive cast of his thought which causes the difficulty. Jung's psychological intuitions about the malaise in Western culture were important, but his thinking was handicapped by the means he had available for the communication of his intuitive insights. I certainly do not mean to join in knee-jerk defenses of Jung here, but we should recognize that, alongside the unfortunate excursions into racial typology, we can also discern the seeds of a surprisingly modern and constructive attitude to race and ethnicity. For example, in 1935 Jung argued against the imposition of 'the spirit' of one race upon another, referring to a Eurocentric, judgmental approach to other cultures.[61] Here and elsewhere in Jung's writings, there is also a respect for and interest in the evolution of different cultures.

But it is clear that something goes very wrong with Jung's thought when he goes beyond the boundaries of psychology into what has been termed *racial typology*. When Jung's African stays an imaginal African, the African of dreams, or when Jung studies African myth, he makes a creative though politically limited contribution to social thought. But when Jung generalizes about African *character*, and does so from a solely psychological point of view, ignoring economic, social, political and historical factors, then he spoils his own work, inviting the severe criticism he has received. This literalism also plagues his comments about Jews in the 1930s, when the political reality of Jung's own position broke down any possibility of his 'Jews' being safely metaphorical.

What was it that led Jung to spoil his own work, leaving him open to the charge that his theories resemble Nazi ideology? When Jung ceases to serve the psyche and finds a new lodestar in the politics of psychotherapy in Germany, he can scarcely avoid being linked to the Nazis and castigated as an anti-semite. We have to look beyond the general danger of a racial psychology to find an explanation of Jung's behavior and attitudes in the 1930s. *It is far too vague and facile a conclusion to advance Jung's own racism as the linkage between analytical psychology and Nazi ideology.* There is more in Hitler's theorizing that resembles Jung's than its undeniably racist element. There is also a comprehensive political and historical theory that is hard to disentangle from the racial ideas. The political dogma also uses a *nationalistic* vocabulary and focuses on the idea of the nation.

The key questions that require answers are these: Why did Jung get involved with German political affairs *in the way he did*? Why did he feel *obliged* to publish his thoughts on 'Jewish psychology' at such a sensitive moment? Was there anything in the *structure* of his work that made his active involvement an inevitability? Simply to dismiss Jung as a racist does not help us to address these issues. If we want to know more about Jung, the Nazis, and anti-semitism, then, without in any way minimizing the question of Jung's racism, we have to explore the idea of the nation as it appeared, not only in National Socialism, but also in analytical psychology.

Look again at the layers in Jacobi's diagram. Notice that at layer D, 'nation', a quality change has come into the diagram. The introduction of the idea of the nation leads inevitably to the introduction of economic, social, political and historic factors. For the 'national level' of the psyche, unlike levels such as those of the 'animal ancestors', involves an economic, social, political and historical construct of relatively modern origin: the nation. I hope it becomes clearer why I stress that 'race' is too general a theme to serve as an overarching backdrop to the drama which has engulfed Jung. When we look a little more closely at Jung's not-absolutely-collective layer of the collective unconscious, we find that it is not 'race', not 'tribe', and not 'family' that engage Jung, but *nation*. Jung makes numerous references to the 'psychology of the nation' and to the influence of a person's national background, saying that the 'soil of every country holds [a] mystery . . . there is a relationship of body to earth'.[62]

When Jung wrote about America and the Americans in 1918, he introduced the idea that the land in or on which an individual lived influenced the psyche and the psychological development of that individual. 'The mystery of the American earth' was so powerful that, according to him, it had even changed the physiognomy of the citizens. The skull and pelvis measurements of second-generation Americans were becoming 'indianized'.[63] Consideration of this absurd idea shows that Jung is not thinking solely along racial lines, for the immigrants from Europe and the indigenous Indians come from *different* races. No – living in America, living on American soil, *being part of the American nation* all exert profound psychological and, according to Jung, physiological effects. Though the effects may be described along roughly racial lines, they have not been caused by race; it is 'the foreign land' that has 'assimilated the conqueror'.[64] Mary Loomis, a contemporary American Jungian analyst, has written in similar terms about 'the phenomenon of the Native American influence on the psyche' of Americans of European (and presumably African) descent.[65]

There is an important case that Jung wrote about in 1937, a significant date considering the topic of this chapter. A young woman from Europe had been born in Java. As an infant she had a local woman as an *ayah* (which Jung takes to mean a wet-nurse, though the term often describes a nanny). The patient returned to Europe to go to school and quite forgot her childhood, including her one-time fluency in Malay. During the analysis, the patient's dreams included imagery of a marked Indonesian kind. Jung claimed that 'tantric philosophy' (which he read while writing the case up) was most helpful in understanding his patient's dynamics. At one point in the case history, Jung comments that the patient had 'sucked in the local demonology with the *ayah*'s milk'.[66] Here again, the argument is not based on race but on the idea that 'earth and native culture constitute the matrix from which we evolve', to use Loomis's words. For Jung, earth plus culture equals nation.

In my view, Jung's account of the relations between a nation and the individuals who are part of it is simplistic. For example, he frequently asserts that 'nations are made up of individuals'[67] or that 'the psychology of the individual is reflected in the psychology of the nation'.[68] Statements like these form the basis for Jung's argument that there is a 'psychology of the nation'.

However, as early as 1921, the writer and critic Robert Musil had pointed out that the idea that 'the will of the nation does not represent the sum of its individuals is nothing new . . . it has been an often-discussed and carefully investigated subject'.[69] In the same paper, entitled '"Nation" as ideal and as reality', Musil makes the observation that what happens is that a style of thinking suitable for addressing an invariant category (such as race) is employed in an unsuitable context of speculation about a highly variable social construct (such as nation).[70] Though 'race' is itself also a culturally constructed category, it is clear what Musil is getting at, and we can see the relevance of his point for Jung's thought about national psychology. To the extent that race implies, or has come to mean, something biologically determined, it must be distinguished from concepts such as 'nation'. For, on the level of nation, there are no equivalents to the existence of genetically determined features of race (for example, color of the skin). Once again, reviewing Musil's ideas, we can see that Jung was not merely 'a man of his time' whom it is silly to contradict with the benefit of hindsight; other thinkers held other views at the time.

Furthermore, nationalism has as its social and political functions the *overriding* of individual distinctions, often including the overriding of so-called racial differences within a single state. Far from being a phenomenon that is somehow secondary to the individual, the nation sets its stamp on her or him through its ideology and power structures – a closely textured web of assumptions about society and the individual's place in it, about morality (what Durkheim called 'collective conscience'), about the rules and concepts of behavior, about politics, about life itself. Although nationalism requires the equation of state and people, the one is not 'made up' of the other and to say that they are is to fall victim to false consciousness. Of course, we should not forget that defining the differences between 'nation', 'state', and 'people' is still a thorny problem. Germany's divided condition used to be referred to as 'two states, one nation'.

The modern version of 'nation' stems from the late eighteenth and early nineteenth centuries. The idea gradually arose that nationality was a natural possession of everyone and that a person could only participate in civic and political life as part of a nation. It has been argued that it was only when large-scale colonization produced encounters on a mass level with other cultures and colors that the idea of nation came into being, the 'Other' defined the 'Self' as a nation.[71] Just as political allegiance had hitherto not been determined by nationality, so civilisation had not been regarded as nationally defined. During the Middle Ages, civilization defined itself religiously and, in the Renaissance and Enlightenment periods, the classical cultures of Greece and Rome became the yardsticks. When civilisation started to be defined on the basis of nationality, it was felt for the first time that people should be educated in their own mother tongue, not in the language of other civilisations. Poets and scholars began to emphasize cultural nationalism. They reformed the national language, elevated it to literary status, and celebrated the traditional past of their native culture for nationalist ends.

The German nation, as a cultural and political phenomenon, did not exist in these terms before the rise of Prussia at the end of the eighteenth century. German cultural nationalism has been portrayed as stressing instinct over reason, the power of historical tradition over modernization and democracy, the historical differences between nations over their common aspirations.[72] If we analyze typical nationalist ideology (Germany being only one example), we find that much more is involved than emphasis on the geographical unit. We also find an emphasis on some kind of ethical principle, or at least ethical expression, and this is usually couched in comparative (and self-congratulatory) terms: Our soldiers are the bravest, the quality of our family life is the finest, we have the best constitution or royal family, we have a special relationship to higher forces, our articles of manufacture are of the highest quality, our upper lips the stiffest. In other words, *nationalism always involves a form of psychological expression and self-characterization. It follows, therefore, that nationalism elicits the services of psychologists*, who can readily succumb to the notion that this particular cultural project needs their help.

It is my contention that, in C. G. Jung, nationalism found its psychologist and that, in spite of his theoretical concern with the racial unconscious, it is as a psychologist of nationhood that we should also understand Jung's statements about political problems. He was a psychologist who lent his authority to nationalism, thereby legitimizing ideas of innate, psychological differences between nations. Jung's admittedly problematic pan-psychism,[73] the tendency to see all outer events in terms of inner, usually archetypal dynamics, the neglect in his writing of economic, social, political and historical factors, finds its most extreme reductive expression in the phrase 'the psychology of the nation'. Unfortunately, even among contemporary Jungian analysts, one finds direct echoes of Jung's contempt for everything that is not psychology: 'Nations constitute a powerful phenomenon and, like all important psychological phenomena, they cannot be explained; they can only be approached by mythological images', according to Adolf Guggenbühl-Craig writing in 1991.[74] He goes on to make the following claim, which I see as typical of the arrogant psychological reductionism that ruined

Jung's attempts to bring depth psychology to bear on the events of his day: 'All the other explanations, based on economics and sociology, look impoverished compared with the tremendous mythological images by which Jung approached National Socialism.'[75] I regret such statements for they make the much-needed interdisciplinary work on culture, society and politics harder to organize.

With these insights in mind, Jung's offensive generalizations about Jews can be understood more profoundly. There are hardly any references to 'Aryans' in Jung's *Collected Works*. But there are numerous references to Germany and, indeed, to most of the countries of the world. There are also frequent uses of the term 'Germanic', and at first glance it might seem that Jung has made the important distinction between Germany the nation state and Germanic culture, an identifiable, communal and ethnic tradition established over a very long time, to which Jung was committed because it was his chief cultural source. Had Jung consistently made this distinction, we would be able to distinguish clearly the racial from the nationalistic trends in his thought.

Unhappily, the situation is extremely confused, and this confusion cannot all be laid at the door of Jung's English translator. In the index to Volume 10 of the *Gesammelte Werke*, under '*Germanisch*' we find '*s. auch Deutschland*'. In 'Wotan', which is the piece of Jung's where the distinction is probably most needed, we find a sentence which has been correctly translated in the following manner: 'Wotan is a *Germanic* datum of first importance, the truest expression and unsurpassed personification of a fundamental quality that is particularly characteristic of the *Germans*.'[76] Later in the same text we find a reference to 'the Germans who were adults in 1914', so it does seem that Jung had a specific historical and geographical entity in mind when he writes of Germans and Germany. At one point, Jung even refers to himself as a 'Germanic', if we attend to the German language original![77] But, after the war (and even before it), Jung often recalled that he was Swiss, in contradistinction to being German. It follows that modern nations were very much in his mind, as well as large-scale supranational cultural groupings.

Sensing and recasting Jung as the psychologist of nations does not do away with the problem of his racism. But I suggest that his nationalism is the more important factor in understanding the theoretical overlap which occurs, often at a feeling as much as at a thinking level, between Jung and those Nazis whom he so often asserted did not have his political support and whom, in common with other citizens of Western democracies, he came to fear and hate without reservation.

Jung got into trouble less because of Nazi politics than because of his attempt to write a psychology of nations. We have already seen how complex are the historical, economic, political and cultural forces which go into the development of a nation and its nationalism. Jung's mistake was to expand his role as a psychologist to the point where he could seem to regard the nation as an exclusively psychological fact to be observed solely from a psychological point of view. Jung's uncritical psychologizing is illustrated in his favorable response to Count Hermann Keyserling's somewhat eccentric books, two of which he reviewed in the 1920s and 1930s. In these popular works, Keyserling opined that each nation has a definite psychological character and that each contributes one feature to a sort of world personality. In one of these reviews Jung writes that 'the "nation" (like the "state") is a personified concept that corresponds in reality only to a specific nuance of the individual psyche ... [The nation] is nothing but an inborn character.'[78]

Jung was influenced by C. G. Carus, the German Romantic philosopher of the early nineteenth century, who thought that the relation of the passage of the sun to any given area influenced the character of those living there. According to Carus, one of the first formulators of the idea of the unconscious, new inhabitants of a geographical area acquire the characteristics of its previous, unrelated inhabitants. By this hypothesis, possession of land, central to nationhood, is elevated to a mystical level. Here I would say that Jung followed Carus rather closely, as in his remarks about the 'mystery' to be found in a country's soil. The Germans, according to Carus, acquire and recapitulate the development and achievements of the Caucasians, Persians, Armenians, Semites (sic), Pelasgians, Etruscans, Thracians, Illyrians, Iberians, Romans, and Celts. Carus is not advancing a racial theory, for literal biology plays little part in his formulations. For Carus, even though he was a philosopher, and for his follower Jung, the concern is with psychology, not biology.

But Jung went so far in this direction that his ideas about national psychology degenerate into nothing more than a glib typology. His method is to assemble lists of complementary characteristics to serve as stepping stones toward a definition, whether of German or of Jew – exactly the same method that he used to define the psychological attributes of the two sexes.[79] The emphasis is on what a Jew *is*, rather than on what being a Jew is like. Jung's focus is on the predefining of difference via a classification by characteristics. He does not say much about the experience or living out of difference. Just as with the sexes, we find Jung promoting the ethos of complementarity so that any two opposite lists can be combined to produce an absolutely wonderful sounding 'wholeness'. Jew and German seem to constitute two halves of a whole: Rational, sophisticated, erudite city-dweller complementing irrational, energetic, earthy peasant-warrior. This fantasy of 'opposites' is presented as something factual, as if revealed by an empirical, psychological method. At no point does Jung admit to being part of a myth-making process, nor does he claim a metaphorical intent, though it is convenient nowadays to claim that Jung's writings on nations were just 'fantasy' and hence only part of his stock-in-trade as a psychologist.

But is what Jung writes really psychology, or is it the use of psychological terminology and Jung's authority as a leading psychologist to convert anecdote, prejudice and desire into definitory, typological statements? I shall return to that question at the end of the next chapter but for now I'd like to ask my readers to hold the idea of Jung as a psychologist of nations in their minds for a while so that I can turn my attention to certain relevant aspects of the political theories of Adolf Hitler. Remember, up to now we have been discussing the hypertrophy of psychology, *its* expansionism, *its* search for *Lebensraum*, 'living space'.

Chapter 13

Nations, leaders and a psychology of difference

JUNG, HITLER AND THE PSYCHOLOGY OF THE NATION

It is interesting to note that Hitler did not regard Germany as being composed purely of 'Aryans'. Rather, he hoped to increase the Aryan proportion of the population through genetic selection, deportation and extermination. As I mentioned earlier, throughout Hitler's writings it is clear that there is a pronounced nationalistic as well as a racial component in his thinking. (This is also true of nineteenth- and twentieth-century anti-semitism in general, as the Dreyfus affair showed.[1])

Re-reading Hitler confronts us with a coldly paranoid logic. Hitler regarded all history as consisting of struggles between competing nations for living space and, ultimately, for world domination. The Jews, according to Hitler (who got it from Lueger), are a nation and participate in these struggles with the principal goal of world domination. Hitler thought that this was because the Jews did not possess living space, an identifiable, geographical locality. Therefore, it is the world or nothing for them. In fact, for Hitler, the nationalism of the Jews is 'denationalization, the inter-bastardization of other nations'.[2] The Jewish nation achieves its goal of world domination by denationalizing existing states from within and imposing a homogeneous 'Jewish' character on them – for instance, by its *international* capitalism and by its equally *international* communism. So, in Hitler's thinking, there is a tussle between wholesome nationhood and its corrupting enemy, the Jews. (The question of the nationhood of the Jews is still a pressing problem, especially in the context of Middle Eastern politics, as my Israeli colleague Gustav Dreifuss has reminded me.)[3]

Thus, a crucial aspect of *Hitler's* thinking is that the Jews represent a threat to the inevitable and healthy struggle of different nations for world domination. There is an uncomfortable echo to Hitler in *Jung's* view that each nation has a different and identifiable national psychology of its own that is, in some mysterious manner, an innate factor. Merely to juxtapose these two points of view would be distasteful and it is certainly not my intention to make a straightforward comparison of Hitler and Jung, nor to suggest that Hitler influenced Jung. But if we go on to explore *the place of the Jews in Jung's mental ecology*, to try to find out where they are situated in his perspective on the world, then we have to ask whether there is a similarity in the underlying structure of the assumptions about nations, history and culture in these two views. Readers will recall that my intention has been to see whether there is anything in Jung's thinking about the Jews that must lead him to anti-semitism, perhaps forcing honest women and men to give up their interest in analytical psychology.

My perception is that the ideas of nation and of national difference form an interface between the Hitlerian phenomenon and Jung's psychological approach to culture. For, as the psychologist of nations, Jung's theorizing was threatened by the existence of the Jews, this strange nation without land and, hence, in Jung's words of 1918, lacking a chthonic quality, a good relation to the earth.[4] Jung's whole approach to the psychology of the nation was threatened by this nation without cultural forms – that is, without *national* cultural forms – of its own, and hence, in Jung's words of 1933, requiring a 'host nation'.[5]

What threatens Jung in particular can be discovered by inquiring closely into what he means when he describes, as he often does, 'Jewish psychology'. His use of the term is dramatically inconsistent.

First, there is Jewish psychology defined as the typical psychological characteristics to be found in a typical Jewish person, and not found in a typical member of another ethnic or racial group. Jung argues that everyone is affected by his or her background, and this leads to all kinds of prejudices and assumptions: 'Every child knows that differences exist.'[6] One can disagree or agree with Jung's views on what the psychology of Jews is like; I have already said that I do not consider such views to be psychological in a professional sense. The observation that there are differences in cultural tradition is not the same as the assertion that there are differences in the actual process of psychological functioning and I do not think Jung manages to validate the latter assertion.

Jung's second use of this term 'Jewish psychology' has a different and even more provocative implication. Here he is referring to systems of psychology developed by Jews like Freud and Adler, systems that claim universal applicability and truth. Such a psychology is a 'levelling psychology' in that it undermines the idea of national differences.[7] Such a psychology has erred in applying 'Jewish categories . . . indiscriminately to German and Slavic Christendom'. We are tempted to make the 'unpardonable mistake [of] accepting the conclusions of a Jewish psychology as generally valid'.[8] It is not Freud's psychoanalysis that is the problem here but *Jewish* psychoanalysis – rather a different thing.

At this point, we have to bring in the fourth group in the drama that has surrounded Jung – Freudians – to add to the Nazis, the Jews, and the Jungians. Is Jung saying that the theories of psychoanalysis reflect Jewish psychology, meaning typical Jewish character traits, as exemplified in Freud himself? If so, he surely goes far beyond his habitual position that all psychological theorizing is a 'subjective confession'. Even the prejudice-ridden personal friction between Jung and Freud, which undeniably existed, would not explain why, for Jung, this became his reading of the whole of psychoanalysis. It seems that, for Jung, with his current interest in national psychology, there is an extra ingredient: The Jews as a group, typified by Freudian psychoanalysis, represent a strain of *psychological* denationalization, levelling out all national psychological differences. Psychoanalysis therefore occupies a place in Jung's mind *analogous* to the place occupied in Hitler's mind by capitalism and communism. The great fears are, respectively, of 'levelling' and of 'denationalization'. Jung and Hitler react to the Jews in differing ways of course, but the levelling aim of Jewish psychology and the denationalizing aim of Jewish political and economic activity represent a similar threat to each of them. So each develops a similar theme.

For Hitler, it takes the form of an obsession with a Jewish 'spirit', functioning as a pestilential bacillus, undermining the very idea of nation. For Jung, it takes the form of a depiction of a Jewish psychology, capable of being imposed on all other ethnic groupings and, above all, on all other national psychologies. Jung was afraid that the Jews – Freud (and Adler) and their followers – would take over psychology, disregarding its rightful soil in German Romantic philosophy. This would be the inevitable cultural carpetbagging of a people without a national land or nationhood of their own.

Jung's ideas that psychoanalysis imposed itself on psychological differences and that this was a specifically Jewish psychological trait appear to have persisted to the end of his life. In 1955, he wrote to Dr Hans Illing that Freud was

> profoundly Jewish to the extent that he never submitted to a personal analysis, which does not prevent him from claiming that his psychoanalytical judgments are valid for every one else. This corresponds exactly to the Jewish idea of God. . . .

Jung's explanation is that there is a 'chosen people complex'.[9]

Jung's psychological expansionism can be seen as counterpointing Hitler's geopolitical expansionism. The former results from Jung's claim that psychology needed rescuing from the danger posed by 'Jewish psychology'. The latter results from Hitler's claim that Europe needed rescuing from the danger posed by Jewish communism or Jewish capitalism.

At one point Jung seems to have had a direct connection in mind between psychoanalysis (his worry) and communism (Hitler's worry). In 1919, in a letter to Sabina Spielrein not yet published in English but available in German, Jung castigates Freud and Lenin in the same sentence as 'disseminators of the rationalistic darkness which might yet extinguish the small lamps of reason'. Jung cannot understand why Spielrein is so upset at the death of Karl Liebknecht, the leader of the communist Spartakusbund in Germany who, together with Rosa Luxemburg, was murdered in January 1919. Concerning the 'lamps of reason', Jung goes on to say that 'whoever betrays this light to power or cleverness will become a parasite (Schädling)'. We might want to ask what Jung has in mind when he writes of the Schädling in 1919.[10]

It is in this general area that we may understand the response of those who have picked up on the uncomfortable resonances in Jung's writings to something they have already learned to hate in Hitler. Only when we have understood the basis in the collective mind for the association of Hitler's thinking with Jung's can we begin to explicate the enormous divergences between them. Then we can restore the humanity to Jung's quite dissimilar cultural project.

Regarding the question of the possession of national land, I mentioned earlier that Jung's use of the phrase 'cultural forms' rather than 'culture' is significant. It can be seen that, for Jung, the missing elements in Jewish history and experience that would have made the emergence of Jewish cultural forms possible are those of nation and land. In a letter to C. E. Benda of 1934 he writes

Between culture and cultural form there is, as we know, an essential difference. The Swiss, for instance, as you rightly remark, are a people with a culture but no cultural form of their own. For this, you rightly remark, certain conditions are needed, such as the size of a people and its ties to the soil, etc. . . . A people with no ties to the soil, having neither land nor homeland is commonly called nomadic.[11]

Writing to James Kirsch in the same year, Jung once again emphasized the importance of land and nationhood to the creation of cultural forms by pointing out that Jewish cultural forms might come into being in Palestine.

Jung makes the interesting point in this letter that the Jews often become the carriers or even promoters of the culture in which they live, something that was certainly true of pre-war Germany.[12] However, I think many, including Jaffé who has otherwise defended Jung, would agree that at this time he did not know enough about Jewish culture to make some of these assertions. Be that as it may, the issue here has been to clarify the nature of the threat the Jews present to Jung's conception of national psychological difference.

It is fascinating to report that Jung's and Hitler's differing but similar fears have, quite recently, entered the academic mainstream. In his book *Black Athena*, Martin Bernal argues that, contrary to conventional wisdom, classical Greek civilization has its deepest roots in Afroasiatic and Semitic cultures.[13] But these influences are usually ignored – according to Bernal – for racist reasons. What is more, Bernal undermines the claim that the Classical Greeks were originally 'Aryans' who moved down from the north. The Greeks, beloved of Freud, Jung, Neumann, Hillman *et al.*, were, putting it crudely, African, Egyptian, Phoenician and Semitic.

From the other end of the intellectual spectrum, genetic researchers have managed to link everyone alive today to a fully human common ancestor – 'a woman who lived in Africa 100,000 to 300,000 years ago'. The theory is known as the 'Noah's Ark' theory. The report I have of this research concludes: 'Whether or not everyone descends from a recent African Eve . . . , [the] Noah's Ark theory suggests that all of today's races are closely related – so closely related that there can only be one "superior" race: the human one.'[14]

JUNG AND LEADERSHIP

I have criticized Jung for using his leadership and authority as a psychologist for non-psychological purposes. I used the words 'Jung's leadership' deliberately to raise the question of where Jung stood as a leader and in relation to the theory and practice of leadership. The whole subject of leadership, as already stated, forms the second overarching backdrop to my material.

That Jung had a desire for leadership and behaved like the leader of a movement is still a contentious claim to make within analytical psychology. Many Jungian analysts, recognizing Jung's exceptional gifts, try to put him beyond a power drive, and, therefore, beyond the opportunism to which he is often accused of succumbing in his dealings with the Nazi establishment regulating psychotherapy in Germany in the

1930s. Yet if we look at Jung's earlier career, the part played by Jung's own desire for power in bringing about the break with Freud is often underestimated (and here I *am* engaging psychologically with Jung the man). Jung himself was emphatic that, unlike Freud, he had no ambitions to be a leader and was not interested in forming a school of psychology, in actively spreading his ideas, or taking part in the training of analysts. In *Jung and the Post-Jungians*, I sought to show that Jung displayed many of the features of a typical leader: sometimes maintaining his rule by dividing his followers, selecting individuals for particular support (often by writing forewords for their books), and eventually laying down rather tough academic criteria for the professional training of analysts.[15] In 1935, Jung explicitly claimed Drs Kranefeldt, Heyer and Adler as 'members of my school'.[16] How can we reconcile this skillful dissemination of influence with Jung's claim to be a solitary thinker and his corollary exclamation 'Thank God I'm Jung and not a Jungian'? Jung's denial that he participated in the making of Jungians is often repeated by those most closely associated with him. I think that Jung's technique was to flatter his followers by maintaining that he did not want disciples; therefore those involved with Jung could never have been mere disciples.

It can be argued that Jung succeeded in relegating his leadership ambitions to his shadow. If so, then we see a projection of something personal in Jung's interest in the *Führer*. But I want to contribute something more profound than the 'wild' assertion or psychological cheap-shot that Hitler was Jung's shadow. After all, in what has been described as the 'decade of the dictators', it is certainly not simply a personal issue for Jung. The image of the dictator could fascinate him without its being a projection of unmet needs for recognition and dominance in depth psychology.

In the late 1930s Jung was a prime mover in efforts to unite the psychotherapies behind a common program and he drew up a list of propositions concerning the theory and practice of psychotherapy.[17] These 'Fourteen Points', also known as 'Views Held in Common', were Jung's attempt to bring unity to depth psychology. We can see now that the seemingly inherent tendency of depth psychology to fragment into warring groups made this a forlorn hope, practically speaking. But we may well wonder at the idealistic and even arrogant aspects of the use of the political catchphrase dating from the time of the formation of the League of Nations to characterize this effort. Was this an attempt to make Jungian analysis the generic psychotherapy? We know that Jung wanted to be the dominant psychological theorist of the day. He regarded his approach to analysis as *subsuming* those of Adler and Freud (for instance, in his paper 'Problems of modern psychotherapy').[18] Any Jungian analysis would include the relevant features of an analysis of each of the other schools, although the vital final stage of analysis known as 'transformation' was said to be possible only in Jung's approach. Had the Fourteen Points caught on, Jung would have become the leading theorist of all psychotherapy.

Bearing these reflections in mind, we can turn our attention to Jung's comments about *political* leadership, for example in the famous interview by Dr Weizsacker on Radio Berlin in 1933. Jung told his listeners, using the key word *Führer*, that 'every great movement culminates in a leader'.[19] Even more interesting is Jung's opinion that the prerequisite for successful leadership is self-knowledge: 'If [the leader] doesn't know himself, how is he to lead others? That is why the true leader is always one who has the courage to be himself.'[20]

Matthias von der Tann has made a careful linguistic analysis of Jung's remarks in this interview.[21] It was only in 1987 that the full German text of the interview once again became available in the public domain, and an important result of von der Tann's research is to highlight how the English translation consistently mutes Jung's imagery, making his remarks altogether more statesmanlike and less inflammatory than they really were.[22] Von der Tann demonstrates that on many occasions Jung uses words and phrases that would have had a particular connotation for German listeners. These words and phrases echo Nazi ideology and propaganda and can be said to constitute a message: Jung is in agreement with what our present leaders are trying to bring about. (Incidentally, the official translation of the English *Collected Works of C. G. Jung* contains several similar examples of sanitization.)

Strangely, we find Jung speaking of Hitler as if Hitler could become a leader conscious of his position, as if Hitler could become an analyzed leader. Where does this idea originate? Jungian analysts-in-training are often reminded that it was Jung who was the first to insist, in 1913, that a prospective analyst be analyzed.[23] Among the many reasons for this requirement is the observation that the patient can go only so far as the analyst has gone, psychologically speaking. So the analyst's neurosis is the brake on the patient's growth – or, as Jung said of the leader, transposing the analytical dictum to the political arena, 'if he doesn't know himself, how is he to lead others?'. In the interview, we can hear how Jung reconciles his seeming acceptance of the *Führerprinzip* (the principle of unquestioned leadership) with his lifelong advocacy of Swiss-style democracy. For I really cannot think of a better short definition of individuation than 'having the courage to be oneself'.[24] There seems to be some kind of connection in Jung's mind between the analyst and the political leader. Jung has transposed psychology to the top table, to the world stage.

By 1939 Jung had changed some of his views about leadership. In a letter to an American youth, which came to light via a train of extraordinary coincidences in 1991, Jung responds to the question: 'Can anything good come from a dictatorship?' with the unequivocal statement that 'there is no such thing as a liberal dictatorship'. In this letter, Jung seems rather fatalistic about the political process itself: 'We all ought to be happy if we just happen to have no revolution, no war and no epidemics.' (I do not know how to assess Jung's opinion in this letter that 'if conditions become better, the people become worse'. He might have been thinking of the dangers of mindless affluence – or there might be shards of an anti-democratic tendency in such a view.[25])

With the politics of intellectual endeavor in mind, I would ask if there is anything wrong with a great thinker trying to influence other people, promote his work, and be a leader. Why do Jungians continue to deny that Jung was actively involved in the ideological marketplace – for instance, in 1930s Germany where the banning of Freud left a vacuum in depth psychology? There is obviously some strange investment in sticking to Jung's public version of himself: An unworldly, even other-worldly, poetic genius, naively indifferent to the institutional dynamics of his profession, as well as to politics in general, a man who had almost to be forced to become President of the IGMSP. One has only to read the Freud–Jung letters, in which Jung reveals himself as an enthusiastic psychoanalytic politician to understand where the naïveté really lies. After all, Jung did not display much hesitation when asked by Freud to become President of the International Psychoanalytical Association.

Jung was certainly not completely dominated by his desire for leadership. He did seem able to value other people's points of view and he had a great capacity to tolerate uncertainty and not knowing. He is believable when he says that 'agreement would only spell one-sidedness and desiccation' and that we need many theories before we get 'even a rough picture of the psyche's complexity'.[26] But Jung's élitism is always just below the surface – nature is, after all, 'aristocratic'.[27] The idea of leadership (like that of the nation) forms part of a psychological backdrop to the interplay of Nazis, Jews, Jungians and Freudians that we have been examining. Indeed, in some form this theme pervades *all* these groups. Nazi claims to leadership result in the installation of the Führer with the final solution; there are time-honored Jewish claims to moral primacy as the chosen people; the Freudian Committee, set up in part to ensure that defectors were not taken seriously, illustrates Freudian desires for hegemony; and Jung tried to organize world psychotherapy under his 'neutral' leadership.

ANALYTICAL PSYCHOLOGY AND RENEWAL

At this point, I would like to restate what, for me, is the key question to ask when considering Jung, anti-semitism and the Nazis. Is there anything in Jung's habitual way of thinking that leads to anti-semitism? I think there is – and it is found in the way Jung employs his ideas of the nation and about leadership. These ideas are ideograms with damaging potential and I have tried to show that Jung deployed them in an insufficiently critical manner.

But what about the future of analytical psychology? Specifically, what about the future of analytical psychology – and depth psychology generally – as a means of developing an analysis or critique of political processes?

Reviewing the troubled and tragic history of psychoanalysis in Germany, Robert Wallerstein, then President of the International Psycho-analytical Association, used these words: 'We need to underline the implicit invitation (nay, demand) that all of us in psychoanalysis reflect together on what this means for our common humanity and where our psychoanalytic identities can fit meaningfully into it.'[28] Similarly, can analytical psychologists employ psychological and critical reflections on Jung, anti-semitism and the Nazis in such a way that some kind of renewal can result? Could this then lead to a more productive engagement of depth psychology with the public sphere?

Since Jung's death in 1961, analytical psychology *has* sought to renew itself from without – through contact with psychoanalysis, religion, classical mythology, even theoretical physics. But what about attending to renewal from within, through seeking those discoveries that come from a self-directed, psychological and critical attitude toward the events and ideas of the past? Can analytical psychology learn from its founder's experiences? I suggest that renewal will not occur until Jungians resolve their work of mourning for Jung. This will lead, eventually, to our giving him up. Jungians are not alone in having problems in disidentifying from the great man who still dominates their discipline. As Wallerstein said, in a presidential address to the Freudian group: 'For so many of us, Sigmund Freud remains our lost object, our unreachable genius, whose passing we have perhaps never properly mourned, at least not in [an] emotional fullness.'[29]

Only when Jung the man, the flawed (and hence overanalyzed) leader, has been mourned can anything be learned from 'Jung' the social and cultural phenomenon. If this could be done, and if we were then to attempt to sketch out a program of renewal for analytical psychology, what would that program look like?

DEPTH PSYCHOLOGY, DIFFERENCE, AND NATIONALISM

To begin with, I think it would help if analysts and therapists (of all persuasions) were to cease expanding the national boundaries of the psychological kingdom and try to work cooperatively with their colleagues in the social sciences. This would mean stopping the abuse of our authority when we advance definitions of the typical psychology of this or that group – whether Jews, Germans, African Americans, homosexuals, women, or men. Whether we like it or not, as Jung's experience in the 1930s demonstrates, depth psychology and politics are connected. As a signal of our stopping this abuse, we should consider expressly allying ourselves to so-called marginal and minority groups, for that is the category where we ourselves belong. Such groups are often demoralized and disorganized; sometimes they suffer from a kind of social invisibility (mentally handicapped people, for instance). We could contribute our limited but profound expertise to the achievement of their goals. Jung aligned himself with and sought power; we should align ourselves with the powerless. We would do this by using our therapeutic capacity to work with the inexpressible in a clarification of the psychological experience of being Jew, German, African American, homosexual, woman, man. We would assist such groups in getting behind the defensive stereotypes imposed by a threatened dominant culture as we explore the nature of difference itself. Analysts and therapists may even find unnamed cultural groupings, somehow overlooked by social theory.

Some general issues arise from a depth psychological exploration of the psychology of cultural difference. Sometimes, and for some individuals, membership of a minority or marginal group will be of supreme importance, psychologically speaking. At other times, and for other people, it may turn out that the issue is one of sharing in the psychological assumptions and cultural traditions of the majority. It may well be that, on occasions, both of these positions will hold true. Then a pluralistic analysis would suggest that there is a competitive tension between being *alike* (sharing in *one* set of psychological assumptions and cultural traditions) and being unalike (invested in a particular set out of *many* sets of psychological assumptions and cultural traditions).

Refining this point about the competitive tension between identity and difference, as I hinted in Chapter 1, it is by no means certain that all the members of a particular group will share in the same psychological experiences. Group homogeneity cannot be assumed. For example, if a psychocultural group is identified by means of a religious background (it could be the Jews), we should not forget the differences introduced into the picture by differences in age, class, sex, geographical origin and so forth. Trying to express this pluralistically brings in that most psychologically pregnant word 'some'. Some Jewish experiences are experienced by all Jews, some are specific to specific kinds of Jews. Moreover, in any one Jew, is there not an inevitable tension between what he or she has in common with other Jews and, still within the experiential area of Jewishness, what he or she does not have in common with other Jews?

Even this point about the 'someness' of cultural experience requires fine tuning. For the groups that I have been discussing have a fragile existence. They are themselves culturally and politically constructed; they are historically contingent entities while, at the same time, having social ontology and psychological reality. (This conundrum for groups is analogous to that faced by the individual, discussed in Chapter 9. There, I expressed it in terms of a competitive tension between psyche-as-source and person-as-contingent.) The psychological life of a cultural group is, in many respects, strengthened and fostered by the worry that the group itself is evanescent, having no 'real' existence.

The creation of a psychology of difference does not only apply to the social situation of minority or marginal groups; it may also help us to understand the workings of groups that have ample access to the corridors of power and hence can grab a disproportionate share of the cake.

It is subversive work, breaking the contemporary taboo on the discussion of difference (racial, national, ethnic, gender, class). But it has to be done. After all, many of the most convincing objections to Freudian theory rest on a rejection of its supposedly universal generalizations which are in fact suffused by the specific ambience of *fin de siècle* Vienna. Analytical psychology has to free itself from similar cultural blunders rooted in Germanic ideas of Nation and Leadership that obscure other things that we know about nations and leaders. In fact, the entire Eurocentric cast of depth psychology, its own historical and cultural location, will have to be examined. In Chapter 5, I discussed psychological aspects of economic development in the so-called Third World countries and the relevance of depth psychology to non-European political and cultural processes was explored. I agree with those who dispute the universality of the findings of psychoanalysis (for example, the Oedipus complex).

I have not been arguing that there are *no* differences between nations (or between races, or between sexes, or between classes). I am insisting, rather, that it is crucial that these differences not be defined or predefined. It is impossible to classify such differences; they are an unknown. The analyst is not an authority or teacher who has *a priori* knowledge of the psychological implications of the patient's ethnic and cultural background. Rather he or she is a mediator who enables the patient to experience and express his or her *own* difference.[30] When it comes to cultural difference, analysts should privilege individual experience over universal and abstract formulations. As I said earlier, analysts are good at getting people to talk about what they implicitly know but have not yet consciously expressed. Joseph Henderson's refinement of Jung's layers of the collective unconscious, leading to the hypothesis of a 'cultural unconscious', will be helpful here.[31]

However, we still lack an adequate account of the role of collective psychology in a complicated, multifactorial situation. What is more, the cultural unconscious, as an idea, needs further thought. For example, is the cultural unconscious a kind of repository of cultural experience – a storehouse of difference? Or is it the means, already existing as a potential, by which the human psyche gives birth to cultural difference? Or both?

I think that Jung himself was trying, with an inadequate methodology and hence with very mixed results, to do a kind of analysis of cultural difference. In 1934 he wrote to A. Pupato:

> The question that I broached regarding the peculiarities of Jewish psychology does not presuppose any intention on my part to depreciate Jews, but is merely an attempt to single out and formulate the mental idiosyncrasies that distinguish Jews from other people. No sensible person will deny that such differences exist, any more than he will deny that there are essential differences in the mental attitude of Germans and Frenchmen . . . . Again, nobody with any experience of the world would deny that the psychology of an American differs in a characteristic and unmistakable way from that of an Englishman.[32]

Jung's focus on the idiosyncrasies that constitute difference led him to speculate on the origins of difference. His most evolved view is that difference stems from: (1) the individual, (2) the family, (3) the nation, race, climate, locality and history. Psychology is one factor among many and hence *the germ of a multidisciplinary approach is here.*

Moving out of the consulting room, depth psychologists could initiate a psychological exploration of a world in which racial strife is as destructive as national strife. Such a world urgently needs a psychological model for practice in which difference is truly valued, in which diversity need not become the reason for schism, and in which competition and bargaining – between race, class, sex, nation – are given a new valency: As normative and as mutually enriching. Moreover, there may even be a distinctly political value in trying to understand difference more profoundly. In the same letter of 1934, Jung wrote to Pupato that

> I would consider it most fortunate if, for example, Germany and France took the trouble to understand each other's characteristic values. But the way things are, each explains the other in terms of the assumptions of its own psychology, as you can convince yourself daily by reading the French and German newspapers. That people are also all alike is by this time a familiar fact, but it leads to no end of misunderstandings. These come from the differences, which should therefore be a worthy subject of investigation.[33]

Here we can make *creative* use of that rejection by Jung of the imposition of the psychology of one group upon another.[34]

Alongside the many problems with Jung's ideas about nation and race that we have been tracking, there are also the seeds of a productive and useful approach to difference. Even if Jung's list-making method and his ideology of complementarity are suspect, his intuitions of the importance of exploring differences, preserving them, even celebrating them, remain intact. When I write of the renewal of analytical psychology, I mean just that: Reconnecting to Jung's intuition about the importance of difference, but being firm about staying unhindered by excessive dependence on complementarity, on the dogma of 'the opposites', on oppositional thinking and, above all, on essentialism – the argument that things are as they are because it is only natural for them to be that way. It is not enough simply to accept or reject 'the opposites'. We have now to try to make a psychological theory *about* them so as to explain their immense psychopolitical power. We have to explain how oppositions such as Jew/German, homosexual/heterosexual, black/white, female/male, thinking/feeling actually work on the cultural level. What kind of profound split in humanity and human ideation is being carried by these opposites? What can we learn from fantasies of bringing them together in some kind of conjunction? What political negotiations are possible between the members of the pairs – and then between the pairs themselves, when they are not seen as functioning in isolation? If we make a psychological theory that explains some of these political issues, then we might be better placed to examine, and dispute, what is really meant by 'marginal'. In Chapter 6, I suggested that single parents are performing a kind of cultural laboratory work for everyone in the field of family organization, and in Chapter 5 I proposed that Third World industrial strategies have a psychological resonance for cultural processes in the developed world. In Chapter 8 I argued that the gay men's movement has generated forms of social organization and thinking that constitute a critique of existing forms. Becoming less dependent on 'the opposites' enables us to relocate the marginal to the center of imaginative and progressive political activity. A depth psychological analysis may foster a redrawing of the map of social structure, leading, on the political level, to an urgently needed reallocation of economic resources. For what distinguishes marginality is, in many cases, the absence of economic clout.

As far as differences in national psychology are concerned, we must resist the temptation to indulge in national typology and offer to a multi-disciplinary endeavor *only* what we have learned as depth psychologists. If we do this, then another role for depth psychology emerges. Generalizations about national character and psychology, from all manner of sources, can be interpreted as a form of myth-making crucial to a sense of *Gemeinschaft* (community). National characteristics, or rather what are claimed as national characteristics, are revealed as metaphors and as part of the contemporary quest for *Gemeinschaft*. There is, these days, a yearning for a pre-industrial time, when societal relations seemed to be governed by tradition and agriculture rather than by politics and commerce. The question of the psychological influence of the earth can be tackled psychologically and understood as a group's attempt to express its uniqueness, its own national difference. Even Jung's stress on 'earth' rather than race contains an exceedingly powerful anti-racist potential, making a pluralistic vision of society psychologically viable. For the earth sustains people of different backgrounds, permitting us to realize that the differences that we inherit, culturally and biologically, are of value. Do not modern desires for national identity reflect just that?

It is a matter of the very shape and texture of the countryside: 'the old track fading on the hillside, the tumbled stone of a Saxon steading, winter sunlight on new ploughland, the strip of dark beneath the trees, the names repeating in a country churchyard'.[35] That's one person's vision of England. Or, from a letter written by a Japanese scholar to his Prime Minister: 'The Japanese spirit is to be found in sacred old rocks and pine trees ... only the Japanese know instinctively how to live in harmony with nature.'[36] The Romantic nature of such nationalistic expressions should not obscure their potentially revolutionary nature or their feel for history. Though clearly in reaction to the evolution of modern societies, there is an aura of renewal and group regeneration that has a political significance; it need not lead inevitably toward fascism.

However, we should recall that there is no such thing as a single, immutable 'pure' national character; a belief in national purity can have only one disastrous outcome. The problem is exemplified in the word 'blood'. When Jung writes that there is a Jewish psychology based on 'blood and history',[37] we need to see through 'blood' to understand it as referring also to the shared history of a connected group of people. But sometimes blood is meant literally, and then the image of purity is bound to arise.

When the idea of national purity is abroad, then we are bound to forget the mutability of nationhood, the ways in which, over time, nations define and redefine themselves. If humanity did begin in one part of Africa, then it is clear that the world as we find it is one station on an unknowably long journey. In Europe, the rise and decline of city-states, empires and supranational federations is well documented but, as this mutability is anxiety-provoking, it can easily be set aside. In India and in Africa, patterns of tribal organization and separation often turn out to be of surprisingly recent origin. Nations are ideas; Charles de Gaulle spoke of 'une certaine idée de la France'. The mutability of nationhood is another reason why the presence of depth psychologists is required: Nation is a coruscating fantasy. But Jung's conception of the role of the psychologist was insufficiently questioning of the apparent fixity of contemporary national arrangements.

I wrote much of this chapter prior to 1989, before the massive political changes in Europe had taken place and before the Baltic and Russian moves to secede from the Soviet Union had got under way. I could not have known then the extent to which discussion of nationalism and issues of national psychology would be in the foreground. For example, the question of German reunification positively reeked of an immense anxiety about the true nature of German national psychology (something that was more-or-less assumed to exist). Though unease about German national psychology is usually admitted to be subjective, difficult to catch in the nets of rationality, it is obviously an exceedingly potent factor in the debate.

Close on the heels of the upsurge of nationalism in Europe comes that classic, perennial parasite on nationalism – anti-semitism. Whether in the rise of Pamyat in the Soviet Union, or the character defamation of the

Hungarian Free Democrats as a Jewish party (heavily defeated in the first free elections), or the demonstrations in Poland in 1990 for a Europe 'free of Jews', or the post-revolutionary murmurings in Rumania of getting rid of the Magyars and Jews, or the desecration in 1990 of Bertolt Brecht's tombstone in East Berlin (it was daubed with the words 'Jewish pig' though he was not Jewish) – and not forgetting the wave of anti-semitism in France at the same time or the scarcely disguised blaming of Jews in America for the materialistic excesses of the Reagan era – it is clear that whatever threatens and upsets people about the Jews has upped its work-rate once again. There has even been a resurgence of openly expressed anti-semitism in Germany in 1992. I feel that the content of these two chapters, ostensibly about Jung, the Nazis and anti-semitism in the 1930s, takes on a new, wider and more pressing political significance. Could it be that images of the Jews that were active in the 1930s are also the problem today: The nomads with no cultural forms of their own; the Wandering Jews; world citizens; international communists (now, incredibly, reviled for their Marxism in the former Soviet Union and Eastern Europe); wily international capitalists; scholars with a poor relation to the earth but nevertheless protected by their internationally recognized PhDs? Could it be these images of the Jews, the same ones that threatened both Jung and Hitler, these images of the enemies of national differences, that are the problem for today's nationalists?

Whatever the problem really is, there is no use in merely speaking out against nationalism because that would be a simplistic and unrealistic response to such a complicated matter. Rather, we need to make a psychological distinction between different aspects of nationalism, or, putting it another way, between different nationalisms. On the one hand, we have nationalism serving a positive collective psychological function, socially progressive, historically liberalizing and democratizing, reconnecting people to their roots and traditions, celebrating differences in a cornucopia of languages. Nationalism is preferable to world empire or the played-out game of geopolitics dominated by the superpowers. But, on the other hand, we have what could be called 'spiritualized nationalism', the creed of the *Kulturnation*, with the emphasis on kinship, blood, people (*Volk*), earth – the whole mysterious, mystifying Romantic lexicon. Spiritualized nationalism obliterates the social contract, constitutional rights, the political dimensions of life itself. What is collective and held in common is decreed by birth and not by consent. As Saint-Just said, before his execution during the French Revolution, 'There is something terrible about the holy love of one's nation, for it is so excessive that it sacrifices everything to the public interest, without mercy, without fear, without humanity.' We must be careful lest those who possess what is claimed to be a common tongue allow that claim to take precedence over civil rights and constitutional government. This is particularly pressing in the context of the break-up of the Soviet Union. In addition, world economic developments are promoting migration and population movements on such a massive scale that reliable ethnolinguistic homogeneity is ceasing to exist in many areas. Hence, pluralism of language and multi-ethnicity must be accommodated within a nationalistic framework. This requires an agnostic nationalism.

As far as Germany in the 1930s was concerned, nationalism was anything but agnostic. We can see that, without enemies, the *Volk* could not exist. Perhaps this dependence on the Other for national definition was particularly marked in German nationalism dating from the end of the eighteenth century and due to specific features of German political evolution. From a psychological perspective, the creation of an entity other to the nation facilitates the expression of national aggression because the national Other then serves as the object of aggression (what philosophers call an 'intentional object'). The role of plain projection is also important; the *Volk*-identified nation evacuates what is sensed unconsciously to be its undesirable features into designated enemies (without and, as in the case of Germany and the German Jews, within). Complementarity plays its usual suspect role so that German virtues are complemented by Jewish vices. Though the *Volk* may sometimes seem all-powerful, it can be, and maybe usually is, manipulated by a leader or leadership class.

The Germany of the 1930s performed a collective psychological function for the rest of the developed world which, in some respects, the Holocaust continues to perform in our time. The great economic depressions of the 1920s and 1930s brought suffering in all the industrialized societies to ruling class and proletariat alike. The kind of national organization Hitler was evolving salved desires for retaliation and rage against the invisible Fates of economic forces on the part of both rulers and ruled. Those classes with aspirations for economic and political leadership saw these brought into concrete form by the alliance of the *Führerprinzip* with German industrial power. Classes with little or no economic power could identify with the world historical role assigned by Hitler to members of his *Volk*. Even the final solution met both these sets of needs.

As Germany was not the only country to suffer economic depression, this argument might also explain the ambivalence of the world community toward Hitler's expansionism; an ambivalence that continues to provoke guilt – a guilt that contributes to a preoccupation with the Holocaust. For the Holocaust was not only the supreme crisis of nationalism, anti-semitism and racism, it was also a crisis for industrialism and for modernity itself.

I can see no alternative to saying that, at the present time, we do not have a satisfyingly full answer to questions of the influence of national (or ethnic, or racial, or class) background upon individual psychology, or the part played by what we call 'psychology' in the formation of what we call 'nation'. Depth psychologists can join with scientists, social scientists and environmentalists in a study of these matters. If they do join up in this way then I think Jung's contribution will prove seminal and valuable: 'Nationalism – disagreeable as it is – is a *sine qua non*, but the individual must not remain stuck in it. On the other hand, in so far as he is a particle in the mass he must not raise himself above it either' (Jung in a letter to James Kirsch written in 1934).[38]

We have to use our judgment and make a distinction. The idea of nationalism, like the idea of race, can lead to paranoia and chauvinism – but it also leads to the undoubtedly healthy and positive desire not to be dominated by something or someone felt as foreign: A foreign suffocating mother, a foreign castrating father, a foreign, disciplinarian super-ego, a foreign, uncomprehending psychological theory. We cannot eliminate competition and division between nations. But why should we? A pluralistic political psychology can demonstrate that competition and division, mediated by bargaining, are productive paths to follow. It may even be that the nation is rather a good milieu for the development of psychological pluralism on the social scale. On one level, the nation contains the various competing interest groups. On another level, the nation itself has to compete politically with all the interest groups that are associated with it. In the spirit of pluralism, the nation has to compete for its special privileges. The nation has a kind of oneness to it – and the nation itself is also part of a kind of manyness.

If certain features of nationalism can be raised to consciousness and identified, leading to a deliberate attempt to counteract them, and if this is done with the knowledge that a degree of failure is inevitable and not totally damning, then we could go beyond the conventional condemnation of nationalism and, by implication, of the idea of the nation. For it would be pointless simply to replace the idealistic approach to nationalism of the 1930s with an overly-pessimistic judgment.

If a nation is to function as a locus and as a midwife of psychological pluralism, it has to try to avoid developing a fixed list or classification of what are its psychological characteristics. Or, given that such lists often exist, let us say that they exist as reference points, part of myth-making, things to be seen through. We should certainly see through ideas like Jung's that nations consist of the sum of individuals. Then we become more conscious of the relative autonomy and psychological impact of the form of national organization itself. It follows that psychologists should study constitutions and voice their reactions to them. But psychologists should also take care not to muddle genetic invariants like race with changing social constructs like nations. Frankly, I am not sure that there is anything at all, in either a psychological or a social analysis, that depends on race alone. Therefore, as I hinted earlier, 'race' is itself also a construct. Nevertheless, the temptation that Musil noted in the 1920s, to muddle race and nation, is still with us.

Similarly, we need to be careful not to construct national ideals (for instance, ideals of where the nation is headed) out of what is perceived as the past history of the nation. If we are going to be idealistic, then let us be idealistic in a true sense and not manufacture ideals out of yesterday's arrangements and events. This is not to ignore history, but rather to assign to history a more fruitful role than as the manufactory of ideals that are then converted into spuriously 'eternal' structures (Platonic, archetypal) that are claimed to govern political developments in the future.

CONCLUDING REFLECTIONS

My hope is that finding echoes of Jung in Hitler and Hitler in Jung, emotionally wearing though it is, will lead to a decision to try to make a contribution to a contemporary political celebration of difference.

Then depth psychology can joyfully renounce the top table, the level of nation states – for we have seen what a terrible mess it makes when it tries to sit there. But depth psychologists do not need to retreat behind the barricade of 'the clinical'. Depth psychologists can simultaneously go on with an analysis of politics. To do it, I think they need to stand up with the materially disadvantaged and the socially frightened, as well as sit down with educated analysands. They should be engaged when a Law of Return is passed and small ethnic groups gain or regain their lands; hence, they should be engaged when an *intifada* erupts. They *should* be concerned with promised lands, as well as with sovereign nation states; with the people as well as with their leaders.

Clinicians may have to question the milieux in which many of them work, for private practice with a privileged clientele is not politically neutral. This mode of working has affected depth psychological thinking. Clinicians may have to question their automatic preference for the inner world, and this tendency to make 'inner' and 'outer' or 'private' and 'public' into polar opposites, rejecting multidisciplinary work as 'un-analytical'. As we saw, all images can be read politically.

Before the war, Hitler proclaimed all German modern art to be 'decadent'. Officially approved realistic art was sponsored. Two exhibitions were organized – one of the degenerate and one of the official art. The degenerate exhibition was viewed by two million people, still the world record for any single art exhibition, whereas less than four hundred thousand attended the official exhibition.[39]

In these last two chapters, I have exhibited the decadent and degenerate side of analytical psychology. This has been a cautionary tale for depth psychologists who seek to analyze politics and culture. I tried to show that it was Jung's attempt to establish a culturally sensitive psychology of nations that brought him into the same frame as Nazi anti-semitic ideology. In addition, Jung was absorbed by the question of leadership. Exploring these ideas as thoroughly as possible leads to a kind of reparation, for I think that post-Jungians do have reparation to make. Then it is possible to revalue in more positive terms Jung's overall project. We must couple a less simplistic methodology and a more sensitive set of political values to Jung's intuitions about the centrality of a psychology of cultural difference. If we do so, then analytical psychology has something to offer a depth psychology that is concerned with processes of political and cultural transformation.

Chapter 14

Ending and beginning

Gradually, I have become aware that it is not enough merely to describe the political as a psychoid phenomenon, meaning that it is constituted out of intersections of psychic reality and social reality. Politics is also a transpersonal activity and, like most transpersonal activities, politics points in what can only be described as a spiritual direction.[1] Depth psychology is not a religion, though it may be the heir to some aspects of conventional religion. The project of factoring the psychological into the political seems to want to be done in quasi-religious language. Perhaps this is because depth psychology, politics and religion all share, at some level, in what I referred to in Chapter 2 as the fantasy of providing therapy for the world. The very word 'fantasy' must, I am sure, have made problems for some readers. It certainly is a struggle to work the perception that fantasy is not pathological into an understanding of the necessarily utopic role of fantasy in political discourse.

Sometimes, I see depth psychology as a new monasticism, meaning that, just as the monks and nuns kept culture in Europe alive during the so-called 'dark ages', so, too, in their often rigorous way, the depth psychologists are keeping something alive in our own age. However, as we found on numerous occasions in this book, the values that depth psychology keeps alive are difficult to classify. They do not always have the ring of absolute Truth (though such a possibility is not ruled out); nor are they based on a fixed account of human nature (though that is what is invariably being attempted, time and again). In its discovery of values and value in that which other disciplines might reject, depth psychology helps to keep something alive in the face of threats ranging from state hegemony to vicious market forces to nostalgic longings to return to a past in which it is assumed that the old certitudes of nation, gender and race would still hold.

We sometimes hear calls for a global ethic or a global sense of responsibility to be placed at the heart of political theory and the political process. My question is: How can this be done without some kind of psychological sensitivity and awareness? Such sensitivity and awareness may not be easily measurable by the sturdy tools of empiricism but reveal themselves in dream, in parental and primal scene imagery, in an understanding of a person's own political history and development. Hence, clinical work on oneself is permitted an interplay with political work in one's society.

My working out of a 'clinical' model with which to engage political problematics is intended to make every citizen into a potential therapist of the world. An active role for the citizen-cum-therapist is highlighted and nowhere will this be more apparent than in relation to experts (myself included). The active, generative, inventive, compassionate potential of the more marginalized groups of the world population is not being tapped and, as I see it, in order to tap into that kind of energy we need a discourse of politics that can accommodate the unpredictability of subjectivity.

What I am after is indeed a 'poor' politics, a politics of subjectivity that does not eschew alterity, a politics that would privilege contributions made by women, children, the economically disadvantaged, gays and lesbians, members of ethnic minorities, people living in unconventional families – and just people.

The cultural diversity of 'people' is not a disaster; it is a challenge and an opportunity. 'People' are all actors in a kind of identity game but this does not mean that values and a sense of meaning or purpose are banned from the game. In this book, I have tried to keep the game as open as possible, but also as humane as possible. Whether in connection with the market, the environment, an expanded conception of politics – or in connection with the father, male psychology and the political development of the person – openness and hybridity are themselves values. We saw the importance of openness in relation to Jung's intuitively accurate but conceptually disastrous essays into the area of nationalisms. Today, the nation is stressed in two opposite directions: In the direction of all manner of global, transnational influences – and by a multiplicity of competing internal diasporas composed of ever more assertive minorities.

But up to now, as Paul Roazen has noted, 'theoretical inquiry in the field of contemporary political psychology has been relatively neglected'.[2] Perhaps one reason for this is the fear of the collapse of a more-or-less reputable field into a more-or-less disreputable one. For, sad to say, depth psychology has not caught on in political science as it might have done. There comes a point when it is not enough to state reassuringly that depth psychology is in any case a constant background presence in contemporary culture, or to espouse the fancy that depth psychology generated the intellectual happenings of the twentieth century. There is a desire on the part of depth psychologists for a more affectionate response to depth psychology by the wider community, not to mention the academy. Depth psychology wants there to be a therapy for the world. The world is dubious. So depth psychology softens its 'message' and its style in a vain attempt to gain acceptance, to become reputable. What I mean to point up is the way in which the role of the irrational in political discourse has been minimized and denied by the kind of psychology whose hallmark it is. Depth psychology surely has to get back to the excitement of its avowedly risky project and make its contribution on the basis of that, rather than on the basis of a prettified and secretly normative and moralistic distortion of itself. After that, exegetical sobriety may be able to carve out its own place.

I have tried not to collapse one discourse into another. I have acknowledged the discovery of a two-way process between depth psychology and politics as the original intent to illumine the political turned into a searching exploration of the clinical. Though the relationship between psychic reality and sociopolitical reality exists, movements within each realm take place in different ways and at different rates of change. Hence, my book has had to negotiate a tension between respect for historical specificity and context on the one hand and the limitless, playful vitality of imagination and fantasy on the other. I believe that this tension, far from being a coherence-wrecking problem, is itself of axial cultural and political significance, indicating the tensions that lie within the political psyche itself.

Notes

1 The mirror and the hammer: The politics of resacralization

1 Sigmund Freud, 'Post-scriptum to a discussion on lay analysis'. *SE* 27: 235. *SE* refers to The Standard Edition of the *Complete Psychological Works of Sigmund Freud*, 24 vols, ed. and trans. James Strachey *et al.* (London: Hogarth Press and The Institute of Psycho-Analysis, 1953–73). References are given by volume and page numbers.

2 The term 'human sciences' derives from Wilhelm Dilthey's distinction between *Naturwissenschaften* and *Geisteswissenschaften*. Dilthey placed psychology among the human sciences. See Michael Ermarth, *Wilhelm Dilthey: The Critique of Historical Reason* (Chicago: Chicago University Press, 1978).

3 Sigmund Freud, 'The claims of psycho-analysis to scientific interest'. *SE* 13: 185–6.

4 C. G. Jung, Preface to *Essays on Contemporary Events*. *CW* 10: p. 11. *CW* refers to the *Collected Works* of C. G. Jung, ed. Herbert Read, Michael Fordham and Gerhard Adler. Trans. R. F. C. Hull (London: Routledge and Kegan Paul; Princeton, NJ: Princeton University Press, 1953–77). References, save where indicated (as in this note), are by volume and paragraph number.

5 Jane Temperley, 'Psychoanalysis and the threat of nuclear war'. In *Crises of the Self: Further Essays on Psychoanalysis and Politics*, ed. Barry Richards (London: Free Association Books, 1989), p. 259.

6 This attitude was exemplified in some of the (often rather abusive) responses I received to the questionnaire on political material brought into the consulting room (see Chapter 10 for a report on this international survey).

7 See Jeffrey Masson, *Against Therapy* (London: Collins, 1989) and James Hillman, 'The yellowing of the work'. In *Personal and Archetypal Dynamics in the Analytical Relationship* (Proceedings of the Eleventh International Congress for Analytical Psychology), ed. Mary Ann Mattoon (Einsiedeln, Switzerland: Daimon Verlag, 1991). Hillman has also expressed his views in numerous newspaper interviews and in James Hillman and Michael Ventura, *We've had a Hundred Years of Psychotherapy and the World's Getting Worse* (San Francisco: Harper, 1992).

8 I am thinking of embarrassing 'psychoanalytic' books like Leo Abse,

Margaret, Daughter of Beatrice (London: Cape, 1989). In this work, the author, a Labour Member of Parliament, 'analyzes' Mrs Thatcher. From more professional sources, I am thinking of remarks made during the Gulf War about the phallic symbolism of cruise missiles, etc.

9 Anthony Giddens, *Modernity and Self-Identity: Self and Society in the Late Modern Age* (Cambridge, Cambs.: Polity Press, 1991).

10 Ibid., pp. 181–5.

11 For accounts of the difficulty in translating *Nachträglichkeit* into English and other languages see the whole issue of the *International Review of Psycho-Analysis* 18: 3 (1991).

12 This was at the 1990 conference of the International Association for the History of Psychoanalysis in London.

13 Freud's phrase was contained in a letter to Wilhelm Fleiss. See *The Complete Letters of Sigmund Freud to Wilhelm Fleiss 1887–1904*, ed. Jeffrey Masson (Cambridge, Mass. and London: Harvard University Press, 1985), p. 320.

14 Exodus 37, 1–5.

15 Thomas Mann, *Confessions of Felix Krull, Confidence Man*. Trans. Denver Lindley (Harmondsworth: Penguin, 1958).

16 See Andrew Samuels, *The Plural Psyche: Personality, Morality and the Father* (London and New York: Routledge, 1989), pp. 194–215. In that chapter, entitled 'Original morality in a depressed culture', I make connections between depression and unimaginative approaches to political problems.

17 *The Times*, November 22, 1990.

18 Kevin Phillips, *The Politics of Rich and Poor: Wealth and the American Electorate in the Reagan Aftermath* (New York: Random House, 1990), p. xvii.

19 For a statement of the main details of the 'underclass' theory see Charles Murray, 'Underclass' in *Family Portraits*, ed. Digby Anderson and Graham Dawson (London: Social Affairs Unit, 1990). For a critique of the theory see Sue Monk, *Escaping the Underclass* (London: National Council for One Parent Families, 1990). The debate has been extensively reported, see Anna Coote, 'Mother and father of a battle' (*The Guardian*, September 26, 1990) and Sarah Boseley, 'Trauma that can last a lifetime' (*The Guardian*, January 31, 1990). It seems clear that the debate has been raging in Britain and the United States. My position is that the 'underclass' theory is fuelled as much by moral panic engendered by a threat posed to 'normality' by single-parent families as by anything else.

20 *The Times*, November 15, 1991.

21 The problem was addressed in dramatic form in Tariq Ali and Howard Brenton, *Moscow Gold* (London: Nick Hern Books, 1990).

22 *The Times*, November 15, 1991.

23 C. G. Jung, *Psychology and Religion. CW* 11: 6.

24 Rudolf Otto, *The Idea of the Holy*. Trans. James Harvey (Oxford and London: Oxford University Press, 1923), p. 58.

25 See also Andrew Samuels, *Plural Psyche*, Chapters 4–6, especially Chapter 6, 'Beyond the feminine principle', in which I discuss problems with equating anatomy and psychology and critique essentialisms purporting to be based on archetypal theory.

26 Donald Williams, Review of David Barash, *The Hare and the Tortoise: Culture, Biology and Human Nature. San Francisco Jung Institute Library Journal* 8: 1 (1988), p. 27.
27 Ian Craib, *Psychoanalysis and Social Theory: The Limits of Sociology* (London and New York: Harvester Wheatsheaf, 1989), pp. 7–11.
28 Ibid., pp. 2–3.

2 Subjectivity and political discourse: The contribution of the clinic

1 See Eric Rayner, *The Independent Mind in British Psychoanalysis* (London: Free Association Books, 1991), Michael Gorkin, *The Uses of Countertransference* (Northdale, NJ: Jason Aronson, 1987), Edmund Slakter (ed.), *Countertransference: A Comprehensive View of Those Reactions of the Therapist to the Patient that may Help or Hinder the Treatment* (Northdale, NJ: Jason Aronson, 1987), Patrick Casement, *On Learning from the Patient* (London: Tavistock, 1985). In 1991 a new journal was started called *Psychoanalytical Dialogues: A Journal of Relational Perspectives* which is intended to focus on transference–countertransference interaction.
2 For a fuller account of the research project see Andrew Samuels, *The Plural Psyche: Personality, Morality and the Father* (London and New York: Routledge, 1989), pp. 143–74.
3 For a discussion of this by an analytical psychologist, see Renos Papadopoulos, 'Jung and the concept of the other'. In Renos Papadopoulos and Graham Saayman (eds), *Jung in Modern Perspective: The Master and His Legacy* (Bridport, Dorset: Prism, 1991).
4 Christopher Bollas, *The Shadow of the Object: Psychoanalysis of the Unthought Known* (London: Free Association Books, 1987), pp. 201–3.
5 C. G. Jung, 'Problems of modern psychotherapy'. *CW* 16: 163. This paper was written as early as 1929.
6 Paula Heimann, 'On counter-transference', *International Journal of Psycho-Analysis* 31, 1950.
7 Sigmund Freud, 'The unconscious'. *SE* 14: 194.
8 Robert Langs, *The Listening Process* (New York: Jason Aronson, 1978).
9 Heinrich Racker, *Transference and Countertransference* (London: Hogarth, 1968).
10 Michael Gorkin, *Countertransference*, pp. 81–104 on 'disclosure'.
11 Jacques Lacan, *The Seminar. Book 1. Freud's Papers on Technique. 1953–1954*. Ed. and trans. John Forrester (Cambridge, Cambs.: Cambridge University Press, 1988), pp. 30–3.
12 Christopher Bollas, *Shadow of the Object*, p. 205.
13 Judith Hubback, 'Uses and abuses of analogy'. In Judith Hubback, *People Who Do Things To Each Other: Essays in Analytical Psychology* (Wilmette, Ill.: Chiron Publications, 1988). Paper first published in 1973.
14 Martin Stanton, *Sandor Ferenczi: Reconsidering Active Imagination* (London: Free Association Books, 1991), p. 64.
15 Robert Musil, 'Helpless Europe'. In Burton Pike and David Luft (eds and trans) *Precision and Soul: Essays and Addresses* (Chicago: Chicago University Press, 1990). Paper first published in 1922.

16 See Richard Kuhns, *Psychoanalytic Theory of Art* (New York: Columbia University Press, 1983), Ellen Spitz, *Art and Psyche* (New Haven, Yale University Press, 1985).

17 See Karl Figlio, 'Oral History and the unconscious', *History Workshop* 26 (1988).

18 John Forrester, *The Seductions of Psychoanalysis: Freud, Lacan and Derrida* (Cambridge, Cambs.: Cambridge University Press, 1990), p. 240.

19 Friedrich Nietzsche, *The Anti-Christ*. Trans. Frederick Hollingdale (Harmondsworth: Penguin, 1972), p. 123.

20 See Joan Chodorow, *Dance Therapy and Depth Psychology: The Moving Imagination* (London and New York: Routledge, 1991); Kristina Stanton, 'Dance movement therapy: an introduction', *British Journal of Occupational Therapy* 54: 3 (1991); Wendy Wyman, 'The body as a manifestation of unconscious experience', unpublished (1991); and especially Ilene Serlin, 'Kinaesthetic imagining: A phenomenological study', unpublished (1989).

21 Juliet Mitchell, *Women: The Longest Revolution* (London: Virago, 1984), p. 117.

22 Alan Sheridan, 'The death of the author'. In *Ideas from France: The Legacy of French Theory* (London: Free Association Books, 1989), p. 42.

23 See Judith Butler, *Gender Trouble: Feminism and the Subversion of Identity* (London and New York: Routledge, 1990); Richard Feldstein and Judith Roof (eds), *Feminism and Psychoanalysis* (Ithaca, NY: Cornell University Press, 1989); Hugh Silverman (ed.), *Philosophy and Non-Philosophy since Merleau-Ponty* (London and New York: Routledge, 1988); Robin Cooper *et al.* (eds), *Thresholds Between Philosophy and Psychoanalysis: Papers from the Philadelphia Association* (London: Free Association Books, 1989); Jane Flax, *Thinking Fragments: Psychoanalysis, Feminism, and Postmodernism in the Contemporary West* (Berkeley and Los Angeles: University of California Press, 1990); Margaret Whitford, *Luce Irigaray: Philosophy in the Feminine* (London and New York: Routledge, 1991); David Macey, *Lacan in Contexts* (London: Verso, 1988); Linda Nicholson (ed.), *Feminism/Postmodernism* (London and New York: Routledge, 1990). For two further perspectives, different from each other and from the above, see Cornelius Castoriadis, *The Imaginary Institution of Society* (Cambridge, Cambs.: Polity Press, 1987) and George Atwood and Robert Stolorow, *Structures of Subjectivity: Explorations in Psychoanalytic Phenomenology* (Hillsdale, NJ: Analytic Press, 1984).

24 Ann Scott.

25 Beatrix Campbell, *Wigan Pier Revisited: Poverty and Politics in the '80s* (London: Virago, 1984).

26 Heinrich Racker, *Transference*; George Atwood and Robert Stolorow, *Subjectivity*; Samuels, *Plural Psyche*; Michael Fordham, *New Developments in Analytical Psychology* (London: Routledge and Kegan Paul, 1957); Margaret Little, '"R" – the analyst's total response to his patient's needs', *International Journal of Psycho-Analysis* 38, 1957; D. W. Winnicott, 'Metaphysical and clinical aspects of regression within the psycho-analytical set-up'. In D. W. Winnicott, *Through Paediatrics to Psycho-Analysis* (London: Hogarth, 1975), paper first published in 1955.

27 Patrick Casement, *Learning*.
28 Russell Jacoby, *The Repression of Psychoanalysis: Otto Fenichel and the Political Freudians* (New York: Basic Books, 1983), p. 103.
29 Ludmilla Jordanova, 'Fantasy and history in the study of childhood', *Free Associations* 2, 1985.
30 Russell Jacoby, *Repression*, p. 32.
31 See also Andrew Samuels, *Plural Psyche*, Chapters 1 and 12 and Andrew Samuels, 'Pluralism and training', *Journal of the British Association of Psychotherapists* 22 (1991).
32 Robert Stolorow and George Atwood, Review of *The Plural Psyche: Personality, Morality and the Father* by Andrew Samuels, *International Review of Psycho-Analysis* 18: 1 (1991), pp. 99–100.
33 See Andrew Samuels, *Plural Psyche*, pp. 143-93 for a fuller account.
34 See Andrew Samuels, 'What is a good training?', *British Journal of Psychotherapy* 9: 3 (1993). In this paper, I suggested that we could assess a 'good' training in terms of authenticity, openness, and pluralism. By authenticity, I meant the extent to which the training has got a workable balance between employing 'experts' from outside to do the teaching and supervision and making use of its own graduates to do the work. By openness, I meant the removal of all impediments to entry to training based on ethnic background, sex, sexual orientation, and socioeconomic factors. I also suggested that this was not only a matter for entry to the training but that these themes should be borne in mind throughout the training itself. By pluralism, I meant to indicate the desirability of factoring teaching based on existing disputes in the field into the program.

I made the following practical suggestions (with the proviso that these ideas were to be taken as 80 per cent literal/pragmatic and 20 per cent imaginative/ stimulating): (1) not organising the training in a linear, historically sound way but in terms of disputes; (2) using dispute as a teaching tool by hiring teachers on the basis of their proven *inability* to get along; (3) focusing on polemical books and texts; (4) employing a proportion of inexperienced teachers; (5) distinguishing between the social and ideological functions of leadership (to the degree that this is possible) so that powerful figures in the training organization do not have too much power to say which views are 'right' or 'wrong'.

I also suggested that we start to think in terms of 'plural interpretation' of clinical work, taking up the theory first mooted in Andrew Samuels, 'Parents as messengers', *British Journal of Psychotherapy* 7: 4 (1991).

3 Depth psychology and politics

1 Andrew Samuels, *The Plural Psyche: Personality, Morality and the Father* (London and New York: Routledge, 1989).
2 Howard Levine *et al.* (eds), *Psychoanalysis and the Nuclear Threat: Clinical and Theoretical Studies* (Hillsdale, NJ: Analytic Press, 1988).
3 Review of above (note 2) by Alexander Gralnick, *International Journal of Mental Health* 20: 1 (1990).
4 I have not been able to find a precise reference for this statement. I would be most grateful if any reader who can supply the reference would do so.

5 See Michel Foucault, *The Archeology of Knowledge*. Trans. by Alan Sheridan (London: Tavistock, 1972). Tony O'Connor summarizes Foucault's main positions as follows: 'There is no timeless or universal view of philosophy. . . . Any particular criterion of truth can function as part of a certain episteme, which means it will always involve a political or ideological position . . . if situations are to be changed in a controlled way, whether this involves the development of some branch of knowledge, or some aspect of society, or both, this will be best achieved by means of a grasp of the situation and a mastery of the means available for changing it. Lest it be considered that this overly neutralizes Foucault's position, let me stress that in practice the situation of change will be rather turbulent. Conflicts and tensions will tend to be features of change, as the new theories and practices work to establish their own spaces and institutions. Those who hold power will tend not to be anxious to relinquish it. . . . ' In Hugh Silverman (ed.), *Philosophy and Non-Philosophy since Merleau-Ponty* (London and New York: Routledge, 1988), pp. 150–1.

6 For example, C. G. Jung, *The Undiscovered Self. CW* 10: 536. Also Melanie Klein, 'On mental health', *British Journal of Medical Psychology* 33 (1960).

7 See Robert Hinde, *Animal Behavior: A Synthesis of Ethology and Comparative Psychology* (Oxford: Oxford University Press, 1970).

8 C. G. Jung, 'On psychic energy' (1987). *CW* 8: 100–13.

9 Alexandra Kollontai, *Love of Worker Bees*. Trans. by Cathy Porter (London: Virago, 1977).

10 See Lawrence Kohlberg, 'Moral development'. In *International Encyclopedia of Social Science* (New York: Macmillan Free Press, 1968); James Fowler, *Stages of Faith* (San Francisco: Harper and Row, 1981); Richard Keegan, *The Evolving Self* (Cambridge, Mass.: Harvard University Press, 1982).

11 See Andrew Samuels, *Plural Psyche*, Chapter 2.

12 Chris Oakley, 'Introducing an incomplete project'. In Robin Cooper *et al.* (eds), *Thresholds between Philosophy and Psychoanalysis: Papers from the Philadelphia Association* (London: Free Association Books, 1989), p. 4.

13 C. G. Jung, 'The transcendent function'. *CW* 8. For a definition of 'compensation' see Andrew Samuels *et al.*, *A Critical Dictionary of Jungian Analysis* (London and New York: Routledge, 1986).

14 As in the case of James Hillman.

15 Tom Steele, personal communication, 1991.

16 Sigmund Freud, *Introductory Lectures on Psycho-Analysis. SE* 16: 446. 'We have abandoned hypnosis only to rediscover suggestion in the shape of transference.'

17 E. H. Carr, *What is History?* (Harmondsworth: Penguin, 1964), pp. 107–8.

18 See Rozsika Parker and Griselda Pollock, *Framing Feminism: Art and the Women's Movement 1970-1985* (London and New York: Pandora, 1987).

19 Quoted in Rozsika Parker and Griselda Pollock, *Framing Feminism*, p. 46.

20 See my Introduction to Andrew Samuels (ed.), *Psychopathology: Contemporary Jungian Perspectives* (London: Karnac Books, 1989; New York: Guilford, 1991).

21 Roger Scruton, *A Short History of Modern Philosophy from Descartes to Wittgenstein* (London: Routledge and Kegan Paul, 1984), pp. 281–84.

22 For example Luigi Zoja, *Drugs, Addiction and Initiation: The Modern Search for Ritual* (Boston: Sigo Press, 1989).
23 David Miller, *The New Polytheism* (Dallas: Spring Publications, 1981), pp. 83–5.
24 For example Anthony Stevens, *Archetype: A Natural History of the Self* (London: Routledge and Kegan Paul, 1982).
25 See 'psychoid' in Andrew Samuels *et al.*, *Critical Dictionary*.
26 C. G. Jung, *The Psychology of the Transference*. *CW* 16: 373. See 'teleology' in Samuels *et al.*, *Critical Dictionary*.
27 Sigmund Freud, *The Future of an Illusion*. *SE* 21: 51.

4 The lion and the fox: Morality, Trickster and political transformation

1 I have used the George Bull translation of *The Prince* (Harmondsworth, Penguin, 1961).
2 See 'shadow' in Andrew Samuels *et al.*, *A Critical Dictionary of Jungian Analysis* (London and New York: Routledge, 1986): '"The thing a person has no wish to be" (Jung, *CW* 16: 470). . . . Over and over again Jung emphasizes that we all have a shadow, that everything substantial casts a shadow, that ego stands to shadow as light to shade, that it is the shadow that makes us human. . . . Jung professed to deal with the shadow in a way different from the Freudian approach which he said he found limited. Recognising that the shadow is a living part of the personality and that it "wants to live with it" in some form, . . . involves coming to terms with the instincts and how their expression has been subject to control by the collective. . . . In other words, it is impossible to eradicate shadow; hence the term most frequently employed by analytical psychologists for the process of shadow confrontation in analysis is "coming to terms with the shadow".'
3 Problems met when writing about the Trickster are described by John Beebe, 'The Trickster in the arts', *San Francisco Jung Institute Library Journal* 2: 2 (1981).
4 See John Beebe, 'Trickster' and William Willeford, *The Fool and His Sceptre* (Evanston, Ill.: Northwestern University Press, 1969).
5 Paul Radin, *The Trickster: A Study in North American Mythology* (New York: Schocken, 1972). First published in 1956.
6 C. G. Jung, 'On the psychology of the Trickster figure'. *CW* 9: 477.
7 Heinz Kohut, *The Analysis of the Self* and *The Restoration of the Self* (New York: International Universities Press, 1971 and 1977).
8 See *'puer aeternus'* and *'senex'* in Andrew Samuels *et al.*, *Critical Dictionary*. These are not developmental terms – you can have babies with senex-type qualities of wisdom, moderation, etc., and we all know older people who are *puers* or *puellas*.
9 John Beebe, 'Trickster', p. 39: 'The Trickster manipulates the other men to the point that even their lack of confidence in him is betrayed.'
10 Thomas Cleary (ed. and trans.), *The Tao of Politics: Lessons of the Masters of Huainan* (Boston: Shambhala, 1990). For a fuller version of my account of

moral process see Andrew Samuels, *The Plural Psyche: Personality, Morality and the Father* (London and New York: Routledge), Chapter 11.

11 *The Times*, January 25, 1991 headline: 'Saddam's box of tricks a match for Powell's hi-tech tools'. The Iraqis were making use of subterfuge and camouflage.

12 According to the British *Social Trends 1991*, half the money earned in Britain goes to the richest fifth of all households. The poorest fifth get 2 per cent of the nation's wealth. The gap between rich and poor has widened since 1977: The poorest fifth have had their proportion of the total income halved, while the richest fifth have seen theirs increase by 16 per cent. Allowing for taxes and benefits, the richest fifth get 44 per cent of the total national income, up from 37 per cent in 1977. In 1989, the richest 1 per cent of the population owned 18 per cent of the wealth, up from 17 per cent the year before. The richest half of the population owns 94 per cent of the wealth.

The children of unskilled workers in Britain are twice as likely to die in their first year as those of professional parents. Unskilled manual workers are twice as likely as professionals to suffer from long-term heart disease, digestive problems and nervous complaints.

Similar figures for the United States may be found in Kevin Phillips, *The Politics of Rich and Poor: Wealth and the American Electorate in the Reagan Aftermath* (New York: Random House, 1990).

13 Personal communication, November 1986.

14 Ludmilla Jordanova, *Sexual Visions: Images of Gender in Science and Medicine between the Eighteenth and Twentieth Centuries* (London and New York: Harvester Wheatsheaf, 1989), p. 9.

15 G. S. Kirk, *The Nature of Greek Myths* (Harmondsworth: Penguin, 1974). Quoted in Ludmilla Jordanova, op. cit., p. 182. Hans Blumenburg writes that myths are characterized by a combination of a 'high degree of constancy' and a 'pronounced capacity for marginal variation'. So 'myths are not like "holy texts", which cannot be altered by one iota' (quoted in Drucilla Cornell, 'The doubly prized world: Myth, allegory and the feminine', *Cornell Law Review* 75: 3 (1990).

16 All quotations are taken from the translation by Charles Boer, *The Homeric Hymns* (Dallas: Spring Publications, 1979).

17 Thomas Cleary, *The Tao of Politics*.

18 Mircea Eliade, *The Quest: History and Meaning in Religion* (Chicago: Chicago University Press, 1969), p. 157.

19 Jean Bethke Elshtain, 'The passion of the "Mothers of the Disappeared" in Argentina', *New Oxford Review*, January–February 1992.

20 Rozsika Parker, *The Subversive Stitch: Embroidery and the Making of the Feminine* (London: Women's Press, 1984; New York: Routledge, 1990).

21 Jean Bethke Elshtain, 'The passion of the "Mothers"', p. 10.

22 See *New Left Review* 185 (1991).

23 Quoted in Robin Blackburn, 'Socialism after the crash', *New Left Review* 185 (1991).

24 R. W. Johnson, Review of C. Lemke and G. Marks (eds), *The Crisis of Socialism in Europe* (Durham, N. Carolina: Duke University Press, 1991). In *London Review of Books*, March 12, 1992.

25 Quoted in Steven Lukes, Review of Robin Blackburn (ed.), *After the Fall: The Failure of Communism and the Future of Socialism* (London: Verso, 1992). In *New Statesman and Society*, March 6, 1992.
26 *The Guardian*, July 2, 1991.
27 Ibid.
28 Charles Louis de Secondat Montesquieu, *The Spirit of Laws* (London: Fontana, 1973).
29 Source: Report of the United Nations Development Program (UNDP) 1992. The report states that the gap between rich and poor countries has doubled in the last thirty years and the richest fifth receive 150 times the annual income of the poorest fifth. The report concludes that this is a recipe for global social unrest.
30 Richard Wilkinson, 'Inequality is bad for your health'. Summary of research, *The Guardian*, June 12, 1991.
31 Ibid.
32 Frans de Waal, *Peacemaking Among Primates* (Cambridge, Mass.: Harvard University Press, 1989).

5 Against nature

1 See *The Times*, May 6, 1992.
2 Margaret Atwood, *Surfacing* (London: Virago, 1972).
3 J.-K. Huysmans, *Against Nature*. Trans. Robert Baldick (Harmondsworth: Penguin, 1959. Originally *A Rebours*, 1884).
4 See note 12 to Chapter 4 for statistics.
5 See note 29 to Chapter 4 for statistics.
6 Margaret Atwood, *Survival: A Thematic Guide to Canadian Literature* (Toronto: Anansi Press, 1972).
7 A *nekyia* is a form of temporary regression in which a person makes contact with his or her internal world at the expense of a loss of contact with external reality. In myth and legend, this is represented by a journey downward or into darkness – the 'night sea journey'. According to Jung, 'regression is not necessarily a retrograde step in the sense of a backwards development, but rather represents a necessary phase of development. The individual is, however, not consciously aware that he is developing; he feels himself to be in a compulsive situation that resembles an early infantile state or even an embryonic condition within the womb. It is only if he remains stuck in this condition that we can speak of involution or degeneration.' In 'On psychic energy'. *CW* 8: 67–78.
8 For an account of the woman equals nature theme see Ludmilla Jordanova, *Sexual Visions: Images of Gender in Science and Medicine between the Eighteenth and Twentieth Centuries* (London and New York: Harvester Wheatsheaf, 1989).
9 See Anne Baring and Jules Cashford, *The Myth of the Goddess: Evolution of an Image* (London: Viking, 1991).
10 See Andrew Dobson, *Green Political Thought* (London: Harper Collins, 1990), pp. 201–2.
11 Francine du Plessix Gray, Introduction to Margaret Atwood, *Surfacing*, p. 6.

12 For example George Woodcock, *Surfacing, A Reader's Guide* (Toronto: General Paperbacks, 1991).

13 Margaret Atwood, *Survival*, pp. 202–4.

14 Keith Thomas, *Man and the Natural World: Changing Attitudes in England 1500-1800* (London: Allen Lane, 1983).

15 Ibid., p. 301.

16 See James Lovelock, *Gaia: A New Look at Life on Earth* (Oxford: Oxford University Press, 1982).

17 Cabiri were dwarf-like, phallic creatures who served the Great Mother goddess, especially in her guise as the Terrible Mother. They could be dangerous to her opponents.

18 Raphael Kaplinsky, *The Economies of Small* (London: Intermediate Technology Press, 1990).

19 Kurt Hoffman and Raphael Kaplinsky, *Driving Force: The Global Restructuring of Technology, Labor, and Investment in the Automobile and Components Industries* (Boulder, Colorado: Westview Press, 1988), pp. 36-40.

20 Ibid. (1978), pp. 64–9.

21 See Gertrude Goldberg and Eleanor Kren (eds), *The Feminization of Poverty: Only in America?* (Westport, Ct.: Greenwood Press, 1991). Amartya Sen argues that we are dealing with a case of millions of 'missing women'. Given equivalent health care, nutrition, etc., women will live longer than men. The fact that, in the Third World, they do not live longer than men shows that they are not getting equivalent levels of health care, nutrition, etc. Hence, on an institutional level, the feminization of poverty in the Third World, and maybe in the industrially advanced nations as well, is a kind of murder. See Amartya Sen, 'Women's survival as a development problem', *Bulletin of the American Academy of Arts and Sciences* XLIII: 2 (1989).

22 Oscar Wilde, 'The soul of man under socialism'. In *Complete Works of Oscar Wilde* (London: Book Club Associates, 1978), p. 1010.

23 See W. G. Hoskins, *English Landscapes: How to Read the Man-made Scenery of England* (London: British Broadcasting Corporation, 1973) and John Barrell, *The Dark Side of the Landscape: The Rural Poor in English Painting 1730–1840* (Cambridge, Cambs.: Cambridge University Press, 1980).

24 I have in mind that an 'environmental actor' would move to central stage, ceasing to be part of what Bataille calls 'the heterogeneous'. See Georges Bataille, *Visions of Excess: Selected Writings 1927–1939* (Minneapolis: University of Minnesota Press, 1985).

6 Fathers

1 John Beebe, 'The father's anima'. In Andrew Samuels (ed.), *The Father: Contemporary Jungian Perspectives* (London: Free Association Books, 1985; New York: New York University Press, 1986), pp. 101–5.

2 D. W. Winnicott, 'Hate in the countertransference'. In *Through Paediatrics to Psycho-Analysis* (London: Hogarth Press, 1975). Paper first published in 1949.

3 Quoted in Douglas Cooper and Gary Tinterow, *The Essential Cubism: Braque, Picasso and their Friends* (London: Tate Gallery, 1983), p. 266.

4 Andrew Samuels, 'The psychology of the single parent'. Unpublished research carried out for the Family Welfare Association, London, 1975–77.

5 See H.M. Stationery Office, *General Household Survey 1989*; National Council for One Parent Families, *Tomorrow's Parents, Yesterday's Values* (London: National Council for One Parent Families, 1987); Frances Logan, *Homelessness and Relationship Breakdown: How the Law and Housing Policy Affects Women* (London: National Council for One Parent Families, 1986).

6 David Smith (ed.), *Understanding the Underclass* (London: Policy Studies Institute, 1992).

7 See Margaret Mahler, 'A study of the separation-individuation process', *Psychoanalytic Study of the Child*, 1971.

8 Juliet Hopkins, 'The observed infant of attachment theory', *British Journal of Psychotherapy* 6: 4 (1990), p. 465.

9 D. W. Winnicott, 'The effect of psychotic parents on the emotional development of the child'. In D. W. Winnicott, *The Family and Individual Development* (London: Tavistock, 1968), p. 73.

10 D. W. Winnicott, 'What about father?'. In D. W. Winnicott, *Getting to Know Your Baby* (London: Heinemann, 1944), p. 32.

11 John Forrester, *The Seductions of Psychoanalysis: Freud, Lacan and Derrida* (Cambridge, Cambs.: Cambridge University Press, 1990), p. 110.

12 Ibid., pp. 110–11.

13 See Daniel Stern, *The Interpersonal World of the Infant: A View from Psychoanalysis and Developmental Psychology* (New York: Basic Books, 1985).

14 Page du Bois, *Sowing the Body: Psychoanalysis and Ancient Representations of Women* (Chicago: University of Chicago Press, 1988), p. 188.

15 See Andrew Samuels, *The Plural Psyche: Personality, Morality and the Father* (London and New York, 1989). Chapter 6, 'Beyond the feminine principle', contains a much expanded account of my views of gender and depth psychology.

16 Teresa Brennan, Introduction to Teresa Brennan (ed.), *Between Psychoanalysis and Feminism* (London and New York: Routledge, 1989), p. 3.

17 Donald Meltzer, *The Apprehension of Beauty: The Role of Aesthetic Conflict in Development, Art and Violence* (Strath Tay, Perthshire: Clunie Press, 1988), p. 65.

18 Quoted in Margaret Whitford, 'Rereading Irigaray'. In Teresa Brennan (ed.), *Between Psychoanalysis and Feminism* (London and New York: Routledge, 1989), p. 109.

19 Ibid., p. 109.

7 Political readings of paternal imagery

1 See C. G. Jung, *Symbols of Transformation. CW* 5.

2 See Andrew Samuels, *The Plural Psyche: Personality, Morality and the Father* (London and New York, 1989), p. 188: 'Freud's conception of eros underwent numerous modifications. Laplanche and Pontalis point out that the

place of sexuality in Freud's thinking changed radically. First, it was seen as a problematic and subversive force. Then, when Freud developed his idea of the life and death instincts, it was the death instinct that was "the problem" and, strangely, sexuality that which helped to overcome it. In fact, Freud did not always equate sexuality and genital activity; he wrote of his concept of libido as identical to "the Eros of the poets and philosophers which holds all living things together" (in 1920). Eros is also referred to in terms of a "more and more far-reaching combination of the particles into which living substance is dispersed" (in 1923). This suggests that Freud's evolving concept of eros, even prior to the dual instinct theory, was rather broad. In 1910 he stated that "libido not only refers to genital sexual drives but also to everything covered by *lieben* (to love)".'

3 See Andrew Samuels, *Plural Psyche*, pp. 188–9: 'Jung, too, used "eros" in a number of different ways. Sometimes he equates eros with sexuality or eroticism (as late as 1943). More often, he writes of eros as an archetypal principle of psychological functioning – connectedness, relatedness, harmony, and named for Eros the lover of Psyche and son of Aphrodite. Sometimes the principle eros is referred to as a "feminine" principle. This implies a complementary relationship with a "masculine" principle (*logos*, "the word", rationality, logic, intellect, achievement.'

4 See Andrew Samuels, *Plural Psyche*, pp. 188–9: 'We can identify five aspects of eros. First there is eroticism as an adjunct to reproduction. Then there is the possibility of lust. Thirdly, the partners perceive each other as individuals; hence, caring, romantic, and esthetic factors come into play. This occurs alongside projective and introjective process. Next we can speak of a spiritual dimension and each partner is deeply enhanced by the presence and impact of the other. Finally, an awareness dawns of a relationship quality that is very hard to define. Jung's word for this was *sapientia* or wisdom.'

5 Women's magazines focus on the difficulty and necessity of combining different roles into a satisfying whole. For example, promotional material produced in 1992 for *She* magazine states that '*She* is a woman, *She* is a lover, *She* is a worker, *She* is a mother – *She* is for the women who juggle their lives.' Sometimes, the whole issue is boiled down into the horrible over-simplification of 'Superwoman' or 'Supermom'. Nevertheless, the balancing act required of modern women (and also of modern men) is perhaps the hottest issue in daily life.

6 More material from Beatrice's analysis can be found in Andrew Samuels, *Plural Psyche*, pp. 87–9.

7 Gerda Siann, *Accounting for Aggression: Perspectives on Aggression and Violence* (London and Boston: Allen and Unwin, 1985).

8 More material from this analysis can be found in Andrew Samuels, *Plural Psyche*, pp. 87–9.

9 Ernest Jones, 'Early development of female sexuality'. In *Papers on Psychoanalysis* (London: Baillière, Tindall and Cox, 1950). Paper first published in 1927.

10 *The Guardian*, February 9, 1991.

11 Personal communication, 1991.

12 Ibid.

13 See C. G. Jung, *Memories, Dreams, Reflections* (London: Collins and Routledge and Kegan Paul, 1963), pp. 207, 211.
14 Robert Bly, *Iron John: A Book about Men* (Reading, Mass.: Addison-Wesley, 1990), p. 107.

8 Reflecting on men

1 An excellent overview with an accent on diversity is Lynne Segal, *Slow Motion: Changing Masculinities, Changing Men* (London: Virago, 1990).
2 For an account of 'essentialism versus constructivism' see Rosemarie Tong, *Feminist Thought: A Comprehensive Introduction* (London: Unwin Hyman, 1989).
3 For instance Heather Formaini, *Men: The Darker Continent* (London: Mandarin, 1991). The title of the book suggests that men are even worse than Africans, denizens of the 'dark continent'! Racism is thereby deployed to serve the author's thesis that 'men are fearful of intimacy and commitment'. Klaus Theweleit, *Male Fantasies* (Cambridge, Cambs.: Polity Press, 1987) claims to access the intrapsychic processes of men by an exploration of the life of the *Freikorps* – private armies that roamed Germany and served the cause of domestic repression in the aftermath of the First World War – a direct precursor of the Nazis. Once again, the verdict is damning and makes use of guilt by association.
4 For an account of the identity/difference theme in terms of political philosophy see William Connolly, *Identity/Difference: Democratic Negotiations of Political Paradox* (Ithaca, NY: Cornell University Press, 1991).
5 Robert Hopcke, *Men's Dreams, Men's Healing: A Psychotherapist Explores a New View of Masculinity through Jungian Dreamwork* (Boston: Shambhala, 1990).
6 Lynne Segal, *Slow Motion*.
7 Robert Friedman and Leila Lerner (eds), *Toward a New Psychology of Men: Psychoanalytic and Social Perspectives* (New York: Guilford, 1986).
8 Jeff Hearns and David Morgan (eds), *Men, Masculinities and Social Theory* (London: Unwin Hyman, 1990), pp. 203–5.
9 Robert Bly, *Iron John: A Book about Men* (Reading, Mass.: Addison-Wesley, 1990).
10 Robert Bly, *Iron John*, pp. 229–30.
11 Interview with *Harpers and Queen*, March 1990. Interview on BBCtv, September 18, 1991.
12 Interview with *Harpers and Queen*, March 1990.
13 Jacket copy of Anne Baring and Jules Cashford, *The Myth of the Goddess: Evolution of an Image* (London: Viking, 1991).
14 For example, Robert Moore and Douglas Gillette, *King, Warrior, Magician, Lover: Rediscovering the Archetypes of the Mature Masculine* (San Francisco: Harper, 1990).
15 Peter Tatham, *The Makings of Maleness: Men, Women, and the Flight of Daedalus* (London: Karnac; New York: New York University Press, 1992).
16 The term 'backlash' is taken from the title of Susan Faludi, *Backlash: The Undeclared War Against Women* (New York: Crown, 1991; Chatto and

Windus, 1992). I think Faludi is right to cite the mythopoetic men's movement and Bly's work as part of an undermining of the (really rather limited) gains made by women in the period 1960–90 (pp. 339–45).

17 John Rowan, *The Horned God: Feminism and Men as Wounding and Healing* (London and New York: Routledge, 1987), p. 111.

18 Robert Moore and Douglas Gillette, *King, Warrior, Magician, Lover.*

19 David Tacey, 'Attacking patriarchy, redeeming masculinity', *San Francisco Jung Institute Library Journal* 10: 1 (1991).

20 Quoted in Barbara Ehrenreich and Deirdre English, *For Her Own Good: 150 Years of the Experts' Advice to Women* (London: Pluto Press, 1979), p. 213.

21 Quoted in Barbara Ehrenreich and Deirdre English, *For Her Own Good*, p. 210.

22 Kenneth Lewes, *The Psychoanalytic Theory of Male Homosexuality* (New York: Meridian, 1988).

23 Jeffrey Weeks, *Sexuality and its Discontents* (London and New York: Routledge, 1985).

24 Michel Foucault, *The History of Sexuality* (London: Allen Lane, 1979–88).

25 Sigmund Freud, *Three Essays on the Theory of Sexuality. SE* 7: 125–245; *The Ego and the Id. SE* 19: 1–66.

26 C. G. Jung, 'Definitions' in *Psychological Types. CW* 6: 809–11.

27 Andrew Samuels *et al.*, *A Critical Dictionary of Jungian Analysis* (London and New York: Routledge, 1986).

28 Robert Bly, *Iron John*, p. x.

9 The political person

1 See note 23 to Chapter 2 for titles that cover this field.

2 See Richard Rorty, *Contingency, Irony and Solidarity* (Cambridge, Cambs.: Cambridge University Press, 1989), p. 3: 'About two hundred years ago, the idea that truth was made rather than found began to take hold of the imagination of Europe. The French Revolution had shown that the whole vocabulary of social relations, and the whole spectrum of social institutions, could be replaced almost overnight. This precedent made utopian politics the rule rather than the exception among intellectuals. Utopian politics sets aside questions about both the will of God and the nature of man and dreams of creating a hitherto unknown form of society.'

3 Teresa Brennan, Introduction to Teresa Brennan (ed.), *Between Psychoanalysis and Feminism* (London and New York: Routledge, 1989), pp. 2–14.

4 James Hillman, *Re-Visioning Psychology*, p. 173.

5 For example, James Hillman, *Re-Visioning Psychology* (New York: Harper and Row, 1975). Hillman follows Jung here. Richard Rorty, *Contingency*, p. 3, comments (in a continuation of the quote in note 2): 'At about the same time, the Romantic poets were showing what happens when art is thought of no longer as imitation but, rather, as the artist's self-creation.' Most of Jung's work is in this tradition.

6 See James Hillman, 'Anima Mundi: the return of soul to the world', *Spring* 1982.

7 For example, several of the chapters in Barry Richards (ed.), *Crises of the Self: Further Essays on Psychoanalysis and Politics* (London: Free Association Books, 1989).
8 See Moses Maimonides, *Guide of the Perplexed* (Philadelphia: Jewish Publication Society of America, 1938).

10 Political material in the clinical setting: Replies to an international survey

1 Some previous questionnaires that I know of: Fred Plaut, 'Analytical psychologists and psychological types: Comment on replies to a survey'. *Journal of Analytical Psychology* 17: 2 (1972); Judith Hubback, 'The assassination of Robert Kennedy'. In Judith Hubback, *People Who Do Things to Each Other: Essays in Analytical Psychology* (Wilmette, Ill.: Chiron Publications, 1988) (first published in 1970); Andrew Samuels, *The Plural Psyche: Personality, Morality and the Father* (London and New York: Routledge, 1989), Chapter 9 'Countertransference and the *mundus imaginalis*'. Plaut was investigating analysts' use of typology, Hubback the reactions of patients and analysts to the assassination of Robert Kennedy, Samuels the type and frequency of countertransference reactions.

11 Object relations, group process and political change

1 See Barry Richards (ed.), *Capitalism and Infancy: Essays on Psychoanalysis and Politics* (London: Free Association Books, 1984); Barry Richards (ed.), *Crises of the Self: Further Essays on Psychoanalysis and Politics* (London: Free Association Books, 1989); Paul Hoggett, *Partisans in an Uncertain World: The Psychoanalysis of Engagement* (London: Free Association Books, 1992); C. Fred Alford, *Melanie Klein and Critical Social Theory* (New Haven, Ct.: Yale University Press, 1989); Michael Rustin, *The Good Society and the Inner World: Psychoanalysis, Politics and Culture* (London: Verso, 1991).
2 See Ian Craib, *Psychoanalysis and Social Theory: The Limits of Sociology* (London and New York: Harvester Wheatsheaf, 1989).
3 For example, see a piece that critiques the developmental research of Daniel Stern in terms that resemble my critique of object relations: Philip Cushman, 'Ideology obscured: Political uses of the self in Daniel Stern's infant', *American Psychologist*, March 1991.
4 See Andrew Samuels, *Jung and the Post-Jungians* (London and Boston: Routledge and Kegan Paul, 1985), pp. 148–54.
5 For example, Jay Greenberg and Stephen Mitchell, *Object Relations in Psychoanalytic Theory* (Cambridge, Mass.: Harvard University Press, 1983); James Grotstein, 'An American view of the British psychoanalytic experience: psychoanalysis in counterpoint', *Melanie Klein and Object Relations* 9: 2 (1991).
6 Martin Stanton, review of C. Fred Alford, *Melanie Klein and Critical Social Theory. Times Higher Education Supplement*, April 27, 1990.

7 See Andrew Samuels, *The Plural Psyche: Personality, Morality and the Father* (London and New York: Routledge, 1989), pp. 39–47.

8 See Andrew Samuels, *Plural Psyche*, pp. 15–39.

9 C. G. Jung, *Psychology and Religion. CW* 11: 6.

10 See John Rowan, *Subpersonalities: The People Inside Us* (London and New York, Routledge, 1990).

11 See Fred Plaut, 'Object constancy or constant object?'. In Andrew Samuels (ed.), *Psychopathology: Contemporary Jungian Perspectives* (London: Karnac Books, 1989; New York: Guilford Publications, 1991). Also in Fred Plaut, *Analysis Analysed* (London and New York: Routledge, 1993). Paper first published in 1975.

12 See James Astor, 'The breast as part of the whole: theoretical considerations concerning whole and part-objects', *Journal of Analytical Psychology* 34: 2 (1989).

13 Donald Meltzer, *The Clinical Significance of the Work of Bion* (Strath Tay, Perthshire: Clunie Press, 1978), p. 23.

14 The view of most modern physicists that the universe consists to a great extent of 'cold, dark matter' that is difficult or even impossible to observe directly strikes me as an intellectual descendant of the idea of the 'ether'. Moreover, the view seems to be that there is no 'empty space' in the universe. If so, then those who postulate empty space between people should be regarded as on the defensive and we are entitled to ask for proof that such a depiction is indeed the case.

15 Chris Oakley, 'Introducing an incomplete project'. In Robin Cooper *et al.* (eds), *Thresholds Between Philosophy and Psychoanalysis: Papers from the Philadelphia Association* (London: Free Association Books, 1989), p. 4.

16 Elliot Jaques, 'On the dynamics of social structure: a contribution to the psychoanalytical study of social phenomena deriving from the views of Melanie Klein'. In Eric Trist and Hugh Murray (eds), *The Social Engagement of Social Science: Volume 1: The Socio-Psychological Perspective* (London: Free Association Books, 1990). Paper first published in 1953.

17 See the relevant entries in R. D. Hinshelwood, *A Dictionary of Kleinian Thought* (London: Free Association Books, 1989).

18 Elliot Jaques, 'On the dynamics of social structure'.

19 Wilfred Bion, *Experiences in Groups* (New York: Basic Books, 1961).

20 Peter Homans, *The Ability to Mourn: Disillusionment and the Social Origins of Psychoanalysis* (Chicago: Chicago University Press, 1989).

12 Jung, anti-semitism and the Nazis

1 Adolf Guggenbühl-Craig, 'Jung and anti-semitism'. In Mary Ann Mattoon (ed.), *Personal and Archetypal Dynamics in the Analytical Relationship* (Einsiedeln, Switzerland: Daimon, 1991), p. 495. As the chapter progresses, the reader will become aware of the differences of opinion between myself and Adolf Guggenbühl-Craig.

2 See Reuven Bulka, Editorial, *Journal of Psychology and Judaism* 6: 2 (1982).

3 See Christopher Hampton, *George Steiner's The Portage to San Cristobal of*

A.H. (London: Faber, 1983), pp. 67–84 for a disgustingly inventive depiction of the common processes of Jews and Nazis.

4 For example Aniela Jaffé, 'C. G. Jung and National Socialism'. In Aniela Jaffé, *Jung's Last Years* (Dallas: Spring Publications, 1971); Geoffrey Cocks, *Psychotherapy in the Third Reich: The Göring Institute* (London and New York: Oxford University Press, 1985).

5 For example Robert Haymond, 'On Carl Gustav Jung: psycho-social basis of morality during the Nazi era', *Journal of Psychology and Judaism* 6: 2 (1982); Paul Stern, *C. G. Jung: The Haunted Prophet* (New York: Braziller, 1976).

6 For example Ernest Harms, 'Carl Gustav Jung – defender of Freud and the Jews: a chapter of European psychiatric history under the Nazi yoke', *Psychiatric Quarterly*, April 1946; James Kirsch, 'Carl Gustav Jung and the Jews', *Journal of Psychology and Judaism* 6: 2 (1982).

7 Wolfgang Giegerich, 'Postscript to Cocks', *Spring* 1979.

8 I would like to thank Ann Casement for her help in obtaining this material.

9 Eli Weisstub, personal communication, 1990.

10 Geoffrey Cocks, *Psychotherapy in the Third Reich*, p. 129.

11 C. G. Jung, *C. G. Jung Speaking*. Ed. William McGuire (London: Thames and Hudson, 1978), pp. 773–9.

12 C. G. Jung, 'The state of psychotherapy today'. *CW* 10: 354.

13 C. G. Jung, *Two Essays on Analytical Psychology*. *CW* 7: 240n.

14 See *CW* 10: 1014.

15 Published in *International Review of Psycho-Analysis* 4: 3 (1977).

16 C. G. Jung, 'The role of the unconscious'. *CW* 10: 18.

17 C. G. Jung, *Letters*. Ed. Gerhard Adler (London, Routledge and Kegan Paul, 1973–4).

18 Sigmund Freud and Karl Abraham, *A Psycho-Analytic Dialogue: The Letters of Sigmund Freud and Karl Abraham 1907–1926* (New York: Basic Books, 1965).

19 Quoted in Ernest Jones, *The Life and Work of Sigmund Freud* (New York, Basic Books, 1955), vol. 2, p. 149.

20 Adolf Guggenbühl-Craig, 'Jung and anti-semitism', p. 495.

21 See Sarah Gordon, *Hitler, Germans and the 'Jewish Question'* (Princeton, NJ: Princeton University Press, 1984).

22 *The Times*, November 13, 1988.

23 See Gustav Bally, 'Deutschstämmige Psychotherapie?', *Neue Zürcher Zeitung* 343 (1934).

24 I am grateful to Sonu Shamdasani for showing me the relevant *Harvard Crimson*.

25 Gershom Scholem (ed.), *The Correspondence of Walter Benjamin and Gershom Scholem 1932–1940* (New York: Schocken, 1989), pp. 197, 203.

26 See *D. W. Winnicott, The Spontaneous Gesture: Selected Letters*, Ed. F. Robert Rodman (Cambridge, Mass.: Harvard University Press, 1987), p. 4.

27 The story is told most memorably in Aniela Jaffé, 'C. G. Jung and National Socialism'.

28 Quoted in James Kirsch, 'Jung and the Jews', p. 117.

29 C. G. Jung, *Letters*, vol. 1, p. 238. I am indebted to John Beebe for pointing out this letter and for the information about Victor Frankl.

30 *Zentralblatt für Psychotherapie* 7: 3 (1934). The GMSP was not formally incorporated until 1928.
31 Geoffrey Cocks, *Psychotherapy in the Third Reich*, p. 46.
32 C. G. Jung, 'The significance of the father in the destiny of the individual'. *CW* 4.; Robert Sommer, *Familienforschung, Vererbungs- und Rassenlehre*, 3rd edition ('Dritte durch Rassen- und Stammeslehre vermehrte Ausgabe') (Leipzig: Barth, 1927). The new chapter was entitled 'Raceology and racial history' (pp. 344–499).
33 See Robert Jay Lifton, *The Nazi Doctors: Medical Killing and the Psychology of Genocide* (New York: Basic Books, 1986). I am deeply indebted to Gottfried Heuer for following up the matter of Sommer, deciding to obtain the second edition of his book, and making the translations that follow. Matthias von der Tann also provided background information for which I am thankful.
34 See C. G. Jung, *Letters*, p. 156; William McGuire (ed.), *The Freud/Jung Letters* (London: Hogarth and Routledge and Kegan Paul, 1974), pp. 13, 38, 126, 166.
35 *Zentralblatt für Psychotherapie* 12: 3 (1940).
36 *Zentralblatt für Psychotherapie* 11: 3 (1939). I am grateful to Matthias von der Tann for alerting me to the existence of this piece.
37 See Geoffrey Cocks, *Psychotherapy in the Third Reich*, pp. 46–7. In his book, Cocks paints a picture of the GMSP as being concerned from its beginnings with the 'spiritual' dimension, anti-Freudian, and part of a particular kind of German Protestant movement within the professions. This is important because it contradicts the idea that the GMSP was some kind of consensual, umbrella body. In the debates which always characterize the field of psychotherapy, the GMSP was most certainly *parti pris* (see Cocks, pp. 47–9).
38 In Karen Brecht *et al.* (eds), *Hier geht das Leben auf eine sehr merkwürdige Weise weiter . . . : Zur Geschichte der Psychoanalyse in Deutschland* (Hamburg: Kellner, 1985). Published on the occasion of the 34th Congress of the International Psychoanalytic Association held in Hamburg in 1985. This was the first Congress held in Germany since the Holocaust. Gottfried Heuer translates the title as 'Here life continues in a rather strange way'. My thanks to him for providing and translating this material. Jung was definitely present at the meeting in Bad Nauheim in 1934 because his Presidential Address is summarized in the *Zentralblatt für Psychotherapie* 7: 3 (1934). The Editors of the *Collected Works* believe Jung's address to have been republished as a paper entitled 'Contribution to a discussion on psychotherapy' (in *CW* 10: 1060ff.).
39 Jacob Hauer *et al.*, *Germany's New Religion: The German Faith Movement*. Trans. Scott-Craig and Davies (London: Allen and Unwin, 1937), pp. 18–19, 28–9, 55. I am grateful to Sonu Shamdasani for providing this material.
40 The passage I mention may be found in *CW* 10: 397–8. See William McGuire, *Bollingen: An Adventure in Collecting the Past* (Princeton, NJ: Princeton University Press, 2nd edition, 1989), pp. 26, 39, 46. I think McGuire is wrong to summarize (on p. 26) that 'Jung criticized Hauer in his essay "Wotan"'.
41 Geoffrey Cocks, *Psychotherapy in the Third Reich*, p. 134.
42 Gerhard Adler, Gustav Dreifuss, James Kirsch, personal communications 1977–91.

43 Sandor Gilman, personal communication, 1992.

44 Michael Fordham, unpublished autobiography.

45 Jung was supposed to have said this to Mary Foote who repeated it to others and put it in her diary. This is the only time in these chapters on Jung and anti-semitism where I adduce unsubstantiated anecdote. Every other reference is fully sourced or was a direct personal communication.

46 I am grateful to the Jung Estate for permission to publish extracts from this letter and to William McGuire for providing me with a copy of it.

47 See Aryeh Maidenbaum, 'Report from New York'. In Mary Ann Mattoon (ed.), *Personal and Archetypal Dynamics*, pp. 468–70.

48 C. G. Jung, 'A rejoinder to Dr Bally'. *CW* 10: 1025–8.

49 C. G. Jung, *Letters*, p. 161.

50 Under my editorship, *Essays on Contemporary Events* was reassembled and republished in the *Collected Works* translation of the various constituent pieces (London: Routledge; Princeton, NJ: Princeton University Press, 1988).

51 C. G. Jung, *Essays*, p. xv.

52 C. G. Jung, *Essays*, p. 8.

53 *CW* 16: 470.

54 Sonu Shamdasani has provided me with copies of numerous letters between Jung and his supporters, and between various supporters, as they put together a public relations campaign to protect his name in the United States. I am grateful to Sonu Shamdasani for sight of this archival material.

55 Adolf Guggenbühl-Craig, 'Jung and anti-semitism', p. 497.

56 C. G. Jung, *The Relations between the Ego and the Unconscious. CW* 7: 235.

57 Jolande Jacobi, *The Psychology of C. G. Jung* (London: Kegan Paul, Trench, Trubner, 1942), p. 33.

58 For example, Ellis Cashmore, *A Dictionary of Race and Ethnic Relations* (London: Routledge, 1984). Also British Government reports such as the Swann Report and the Rampton Report.

59 Farhad Dalal, 'Jung: a racist', *British Journal of Psychotherapy* 4: 3, 1988.

60 Andrew Samuels, Reply to Farhad Dalal, 'Jung, a racist'.

61 C. G. Jung, *CW* 7: 240n.

62 C. G. Jung, 'The role of the unconscious'. *CW* 10: 19.

63 Ibid., para. 18.

64 C. G. Jung, 'Mind and earth'. *CW* 10: 103. Written in 1927.

65 Mary Loomis, 'Balancing the shields: native American teaching and the individuation process', *Quadrant* 21: 2 (1988).

66 C. G. Jung, 'The realities of practical psychotherapy'. *CW* 16: 557ff.

67 *CW* 10: 45.

68 *CW* 7, p. 4.

69 Robert Musil, '"Nation" as ideal and as reality'. In Burton Pike and David Luft (eds), *Precision and Soul: Essays and Addresses by Robert Musil* (Chicago: Chicago University Press, 1990), p. 105.

70 Ibid., p. 106.

71 Martin Banton, *The Idea of Race* (London: Tavistock, 1977), p. 13.

72 Henry Kohn, *The Idea of Nationalism* (Oxford: Oxford University Press, 1967).

73 *CW* 8: 29.

74 Adolf Guggenbühl-Craig, 'Jung and anti-semitism', p. 496.
75 Ibid., p. 497.
76 *CW* 10: 389, emphasis added.
77 Matthias von der Tann, personal communication, 1989.
78 *CW* 10: 921.
79 See Andrew Samuels, *The Plural Psyche: Personality, Morality and the Father* (London and New York: Routledge, 1989), pp. 107–22.

13 Nations, leaders and a psychology of difference

1 Marcus Marrus, 'Popular anti-semitism'. Catalogue of *The Dreyfus Affair: Art, Truth and Justice*. Exhibition, Jewish Museum, New York (Berkeley: University of California Press, 1987).
2 Sarah Gordon, *Hitler, Germans, and the 'Jewish' Question* (Princeton, NJ: Princeton University Press, 1984), p. 94.
3 Personal communication, 1990.
4 *CW* 10: 18.
5 *CW* 10: 353.
6 *CW* 10: 1029.
7 *CW* 10: 1029.
8 *CW* 7: 240n.
9 C. G. Jung, *Letters*. Ed. Gerhard Adler (London, Routledge and Kegan Paul, 1973–4), Vol. 2, p. 48.
10 Aldo Carotenuto, *Sabina Spielrein: Tagebuch einer heimlichen Symmetrie* (Freiburg: Kore, 1986), pp. 222–3. I am grateful to Gottfried Heuer for drawing my attention to the German edition of Carotenuto's book and for making the translation.
11 C. G. Jung, *Letters*.
12 C. G. Jung, *Letters*.
13 Martin Bernal, *Black Athena: The Afroasiatic Roots of Classical Civilisation* (London: Free Association Books, 1987).
14 *The Economist*, August 13, 1988.
15 Andrew Samuels, *Jung and the Post-Jungians* (London and Boston: Routledge and Kegan Paul, 1985), pp. 1–22.
16 *CW* 10: 1060.
17 *CW* 10: 1072.
18 *CW* 16.
19 *C. G. Jung Speaking*, ed. William McGuire (London: Thames and Hudson, 1978), pp. 73–9.
20 Ibid., p. 77.
21 Matthias von der Tann, 'A Jungian perspective on the Berlin Institute for Psychotherapy: A basis for mourning', *San Francisco Jung Institute Library Journal* 8: 4 (1989).
22 *C. G. Jung Speaking*, pp. 73–9.
23 *CW* 4: 586–7.
24 See Andrew Samuels *et al.*, *A Critical Dictionary of Jungian Analysis* (London and New York: Routledge and Kegan Paul, 1986). Entry on 'individuation'.

25 I was visiting Vancouver and staying with Jungian analyst John Allan who told me the following story: 'For several years in the early 1980s, I used to co-lead a group for the University of California at Santa Cruz to the C. G. Jung Institute at Kuznacht. As part of this program, participants would write a brief outline of their objectives and in some cases we would call them to seek clarification at various points.

'In one such case I called a young man and was informed that he would be unable to come. As we talked he asked me if I would like a copy of an old letter of Jung's. He related how he had been hitch-hiking through Kansas and dropped into a bar for a beer. He struck up a conversation with an older man in his late fifties and soon they were chatting about Jung. As it turns out, the older man had written Jung a letter in late 1938 saying that he was an American youth who thought that one answer to the world's problems was for countries to be run by "liberal dictators". What did he (Jung) think? A few months later Jung wrote back. The man in the bar still had a copy of the letter which he gave to the "hitch-hiker" who in turn sent me a copy.'

I suggested to John Allan that the letter be published and we are grateful to the Jung Estate for permission to quote extracts from the letter. (First published in *Journal of Analytical Psychology* 37: 2 (1992).)

26 *CW* 15: 198.

27 *CW* 7: 198, 235. *CW* 17: 343, 345.

28 Robert Wallerstein, 'Psychoanalysis in Nazi Germany: historical and psychological lessons', *Psychoanalysis and Contemporary Thought* 11: 2 (1987), pp. 360–1.

29 Robert Wallerstein, 'One psychoanalysis or many?', *International Journal of Psycho-Analysis* 69: 1 (1988), p. 9.

30 Stan Perelman, personal communication, 1989.

31 Joseph Henderson, *Cultural Attitudes in Psychological Perspective* (Toronto: Inner City, 1985).

32 C. G. Jung, *Letters*.

33 Ibid.

34 *CW* 7: 240n.

35 Quoted in Ian Buruma, 'England, whose England?', *The Spectator*, September 9, 1989.

36 Ibid.

37 *CW* 10: 10.

38 C. G. Jung, *Letters*.

39 From the catalogue of the exhibition *Stationen der Moderne* (Berlin, 1988).

14 Ending and beginning

1 See John Rowan, *The Transpersonal: In Psychotherapy and Counselling* (London and New York: Routledge, 1992).

2 Paul Roazen, 'Nietzsche and Freud: two voices from the underground', *The Psychohistory Review*, Spring 1991, p. 333.

Bibliography

Abse, Leo, *Margaret, Daughter of Beatrice*. London: Cape, 1989.

Adler, Gerhard (ed.), *C. G. Jung: Letters*. London: Routledge and Kegan Paul, 1973-4.

Alford, C. Fred, *Melanie Klein and Critical Social Theory*. New Haven, Ct: Yale University Press, 1989.

Ali, Tariq and Brenton, Howard, *Moscow Gold*, London: Nick Hern Books, 1990.

Astor, James, 'The breast as part of the whole: theoretical considerations concerning whole and part-objects', *Journal of Analytical Psychology* 34: 2, 1989.

Atwood, George and Stolorow, Robert, *Structures of Subjectivity: Explorations in Psychoanalytic Phenomenology*. Hillsdale, NJ: Analytic Press, 1984.

Atwood, Margaret, *Survival: A Thematic Guide to Canadian Literature*. Toronto: Anansi Press, 1972.

Atwood, Margaret, *Surfacing*. London: Virago, 1972.

Bally, Gustav, 'Deutschstämmige Psychotherapie?', *Neue Zürcher Zeitung*, 343, 1934.

Banton, Martin, *The Idea of Race*. London: Tavistock, 1977.

Baring, Anne and Cashford, Jules, *The Myth of the Goddess: Evolution of an Image*. London: Viking, 1991.

Barrell, John, *The Dark Side of the Landscape: The Rural Poor in English Painting 1730–1840*. Cambridge, Cambs.: Cambridge University Press, 1980.

Bataille, Georges, *Visions of Excess: Selected Writings 1927–1939*. Minneapolis: University of Minnesota Press, 1985.

Beebe, John, 'The Trickster in the arts', *San Francisco Jung Institute Library Journal* 2: 2, 1981.

Beebe, John, 'The father's anima'. In Samuels, Andrew (ed.), *The Father: Contemporary Jungian Perspectives*. London: Free Association Books, 1985; New York: New York University Press, 1986.

Bernal, Martin, *Black Athena: The Afroasiatic Roots of Classical Civilization*. London: Free Association Books, 1987.

Bion, Wilfred, *Experiences in Groups*. New York: Basic Books, 1961.

Blackburn, Robin, 'Socialism after the crash', *New Left Review* 185, 1991.

Bly, Robert, *Iron John: A Book About Men*. Reading, Mass.: Addison-Wesley, 1990.

Boer, Charles (trans.), *The Homeric Hymns*. Dallas: Spring Publications, 1979.

Bollas, Christopher, *The Shadow of the Object: Psychoanalysis of the Unthought Known*. London: Free Association Books, 1987.

Boseley, Sarah, 'Trauma that can last a lifetime', *The Guardian*, January 31, 1990.

Brecht, Karen *et al.* (eds), *Hier geht das Leben auf eine sehr merkwürdige Weise weiter . . . : Zur Geschichte der Psychoanalyse in Deutschland*. Hamburg: Kellner, 1985.

Brennan, Teresa (ed.), *Between Psychoanalysis and Feminism*. London and New York: Routledge, 1989.

Bulka, Reuven, Editorial, *Journal of Psychology and Judaism* 6: 2, 1982.

Buruma, Ian, 'England, whose England?'. *The Spectator*, September 9, 1989.

Butler, Judith, *Gender Trouble: Feminism and the Subversion of Identity*. London and New York: Routledge, 1990.

Campbell, Beatrix, *Wigan Pier Revisited: Poverty and Politics in the '80s*. London: Virago, 1984.

Carotenuto, Aldo, *Sabina Spielrein: Tagebuch einer heimlichen Symmetrie*. Freiburg: Kore, 1986.

Carr, E. H., *What is History?* Harmondsworth: Penguin, 1964.

Casement, Patrick, *On Learning from the Patient*. London: Tavistock, 1985.

Cashmore, Ellis, *A Dictionary of Race and Ethnic Relations*. London: Routledge, 1984.

Castoriadis, Cornelius, *The Imaginary Institution of Society*. Cambridge, Cambs.: Cambridge University Press, 1987.

Chodorow, Joan, *Dance Therapy and Depth Psychology: The Moving Imagination*. London and New York: Routledge, 1991.

Cleary, Thomas (ed. and trans.), *The Tao of Politics: Lessons of the Masters of Huainan*. Boston: Shambhala, 1990.

Cocks, Geoffrey, *Psychotherapy in the Third Reich: The Göring Institute*. London and New York: Oxford University Press, 1985.

Connolly, William, *Identity/Difference: Democratic Negotiations of Political Paradox*. Ithaca, NY: Cornell University Press, 1991.

Cooper, Douglas and Tinterow, Gary, *The Essential Cubism: Braque, Picasso and their Friends*. London: Tate Gallery, 1983.

Cooper, Robin *et al.* (eds), *Thresholds between Philosophy and Psychoanalysis: Papers from the Philadelphia Association*. London: Free Association Books, 1989.

Coote, Anna, 'Mother and father of a battle', *The Guardian*, September 26, 1990.

Cornell, Drucilla, 'The doubly prized world: Myth, allegory and the feminine', *Cornell Law Review* 75: 3, 1990.

Craib, Ian, *Psychoanalysis and Social Theory: The Limits of Sociology*. London and New York: Harvester Wheatsheaf, 1989.

Cushman, Philip, 'Ideology obscured: Political uses of the self in Daniel Stern's infant', *American Psychologist*, March 1991.

Dalal, Farhad, 'Jung: a racist', *Brititish Journal of Psychotherapy* 4: 3, 1988.

de Waal, Frans, *Peacemaking Among Primates*. Cambridge, Mass.: Harvard University Press, 1989.

Dobson, Andrew, *Green Political Thought*. London: Harper Collins, 1990.

du Bois, Page, *Sowing the Body: Psychoanalysis and Ancient Representations of Women*. Chicago: University of Chicago Press, 1988.

Ehrenreich, Barbara and English, Deirdre, *For Her Own Good: 150 Years of the Experts' Advice to Women*. London: Pluto Press, 1979.

Eliade, Mircea, *The Quest: History and Meaning in Religion*. Chicago: University of Chicago Press, 1969.

Elshtain, Jean Bethke, 'The passion of the "Mothers of the Disappeared" in Argentina', *New Oxford Review*, January–February 1992.

Ermath, Michael, *Wilhelm Dilthey: The Critique of Historical Reason*. Chicago: University of Chicago Press, 1978.

Faludi, Susan, *Backlash: The Undeclared War Against Women*. New York: Crown, 1991; London: Chatto and Windus, 1992.

Feldstein, Richard and Roof, Judith (eds), *Feminism and Psychoanalysis*. Ithaca, NY: Cornell University Press, 1989.

Figlio, Karl, 'Oral History and the unconscious', *History Workshop* 26, 1988.

Flax, Jane, *Thinking Fragments: Psychoanalysis, Feminism, and Postmodernism in the Contemporary West*. Berkeley and Los Angeles: University of California Press, 1990.

Fordham, Michael, *New Developments in Analytical Psychology*, London: Routledge and Kegan Paul, 1957.

Formaini, Heather, *Men: The Darker Continent*. London: Mandarin, 1991.

Forrester, John, *The Seductions of Psychoanalysis: Freud, Lacan and Derrida*. Cambridge, Cambs.: Cambridge University Press, 1990.

Foucault, Michel, *The Archeology of Knowledge* (trans. Alan Sheridan). London: Tavistock, 1972.

Foucault, Michel, *The History of Sexuality*. London: Allen Lane, 1979–88.

Fowler, James, *Stages of Faith*. San Francisco: Harper and Row, 1981.

Freud, Sigmund. References are to The Standard Edition of the *Complete Psychological Works* of Sigmund Freud, 24 vols (ed. and trans. James Strachey *et al.* London: Hogarth Press and the Institute of Psycho-Analysis, 1953–73.

Freud, Sigmund and Abraham, Karl, *A Psycho-Analytic Dialogue: The Letters of Sigmund Freud and Karl Abraham 1907–1926*. New York: Basic Books, 1965.

Friedman, Robert and Lerner, Leila (eds), *Toward a New Psychology of Men: Psychoanalytic and Social Perspectives*. New York: Guilford, 1986.

Giddens, Anthony, *Modernity and Self-Identity: Self and Society in the Late Modern Age*. Cambridge, Cambs.: Polity Press, 1991.

Giegerich, Wolfgang, 'Postscript to Cocks', *Spring* 1979.

Goldberg, Gertrude and Kremen, Eleanor (eds), *The Feminization of Poverty: Only in America?*. Westport, Ct: Greenwood Press, 1991.

Gordon, Sarah, *Hitler, Germans and the 'Jewish Question'*. Princeton, NJ: Princeton University Press, 1984.

Gorkin, Michael, *The Uses of Countertransference*. Northdale, NJ: Jason Aronson, 1987.

Gralnick, Alexander, Review of Levine, Howard *et al.* (eds), *Psychoanalysis and the Nuclear Threat: Clinical and Theoretical Studies*. In *International Journal of Mental Health* 20: 1, 1990.

Gray, Francine du Plessix, Introduction to Atwood, Margaret, *Surfacing*. London: Virago, 1972.

Greenberg, Jay and Mitchell, Stephen, *Object Relations in Psychoanalytic Theory*. Cambridge, Mass.: Harvard University Press, 1983.

Grotstein, James, 'An American view of the British psychoanalytic experience: psychoanalysis in counterpoint', *Melanie Klein and Object Relations* 9: 2, 1991.

Guggenbühl-Craig, Adolf, 'Jung and anti-semitism'. In Mattoon, Mary Ann (ed.), *Personal and Archetypal Dynamics in the Analytical Relationship*. Einsiedeln, Switzerland: Daimon, 1991.

Hampton, Christopher, *George Steiner's The Portage to San Cristobal of A.H.* London: Faber, 1983.

Harms, Ernest, 'Carl Gustav Jung – defender of Freud and the Jews: a chapter of European psychiatric history under the Nazi yoke', *Psychiatric Quarterly* April 1946.

Hauer, Jacob *et al.*, *Germany's New Religion: The German Faith Movement* (trans. Scott-Craig and Davies). London: Allen and Unwin, 1937.

Haymond, Robert, 'On Carl Gustav Jung: psycho-social basis of morality during the Nazi era', *Journal of Psychology and Judaism* 6: 2, 1982.

Hearns, Jeff and Morgan, David (eds), *Men, Masculinities and Social Theory*. London: Unwin Hyman, 1990.

Heimann, Paula, 'On counter-transference', *International Journal of Psycho-Analysis* 31, 1950.

Henderson, Joseph, *Cultural Attitudes in Psychological Perspective*. Toronto: Inner City, 1985.

Hillman, James, *Re-Visioning Psychology*. New York: Harper and Row, 1975.

Hillman, James, 'Anima Mundi: the return of soul to the world', *Spring* 1982.

Hillman, James, 'The yellowing of the work'. In Mattoon, Mary Ann (ed.), *Personal and*

Archetypal Dynamics in the Analytical Relationship (Proceedings of the Eleventh International Congress for Analytical Psychology). Einsiedeln, Switzerland: Daimon, 1991.

Hillman, James and Ventura, Michael, *We've had a Hundred Years of Psychotherapy and the World's Getting Worse*. San Francisco: Harper, 1992.

Hinde, Robert, *Animal Behavior: A Synthesis of Ethology and Comparative Psychology*. Oxford: Oxford University Press, 1970.

Hinshelwood, R. D., *A Dictionary of Kleinian Thought*. London: Free Association Books, 1989.

Hoggett, Paul, *Partisans in an Uncertain World: The Psychoanalysis of Engagement*. London: Free Association Books, 1992.

Hoffman, Kurt and Kaplinsky, Raphael, *Driving Force: The Global Restructuring of Technology, Labor, and Investment in the Automobile and Components Industries*. Boulder, Colorado: Westview Press, 1988.

Homans, Peter, *The Ability to Mourn: Disillusionment and the Social Origins of Psychoanalysis*. Chicago: University of Chicago Press, 1989.

Hopcke, Robert, *Men's Dreams, Men's Healing: A Psychotherapist Explores a New View of Masculinity through Jungian Dreamwork*. Boston: Shambhala, 1990.

Hopkins, Juliet, 'The observed infant of attachment theory', *British Journal of Psychotherapy* 6: 4, 1990.

Hoskins, W. G., *English Landscapes: How to Read the Man-made Scenery of England*. London: British Broadcasting Corporation, 1972.

Hubback, Judith, *People Who Do Things To Each Other: Essays in Analytical Psychology*. Wilmette, Ill.: Chiron Publications, 1988.

Hubback, Judith, 'The assassination of Robert Kennedy'. In Hubback, Judith, *People Who Do Things To Each Other: Essays in Analytical Psychology*. Wilmette, Ill.: Chiron Publications, 1988.

Hubback, Judith, 'Uses and abuses of analogy'. In Hubback, Judith, *People Who Do Things To Each Other: Essays in Analytical Psychology*. Wilmette, Ill.: Chiron Publications, 1988.

Huysmans, J.-K., *Against Nature* (trans. Robert Baldick). Harmondsworth: Penguin, 1959. Originally *A Rebours*, 1884.

Jacobi, Jolande, *The Psychology of C. G. Jung*. London: Kegan Paul, Trench, Trubner, 1942.

Jacoby, Russell, *The Repression of Psychoanalysis: Otto Fenichel and the Political Freudians*. New York: Basic Books, 1983.

Jaffé, Aniela, 'C. G. Jung and National Socialism'. In Jaffé, Aniela, *Jung's Last Years*. Dallas: Spring Publications, 1971.

Jaques, Elliot, 'On the dynamics of social structure: a contribution to the psychoanalytical study of social phenomena deriving from the views of Melanie Klein'. In Trist, Eric and Murray, Hugh (eds), *The Social Engagement of Social Science: Volume 1: The Socio-Psychological Perspective*. London: Free Association Books, 1990.

Johnson, R. W., Review of Lemke, C. and Marks, G. (eds), *The Crisis of Socialism in Europe*. Durham, N. Carolina: Duke University Press, 1991. In *London Review of Books*, March 12, 1992.

Jones, Ernest, 'Early development of female sexuality'. In *Papers on Psychoanalysis*. London: Baillière, Tindall and Cox, 1950.

Jones, Ernest, *The Life and Work of Sigmund Freud*. New York: Basic Books, 1955.

Jordanova, Ludmilla, *Sexual Visions: Images of Gender in Science and Medicine between the Eighteenth and Twentieth Centuries*. London and New York: Harvester Wheatsheaf, 1989.

Jordanova, Ludmilla, 'Fantasy and history in the study of childhood', *Free Associations* 2, 1985.

Jung, C. G., Except where indicated, references are by volume and paragraph number to the *Collected Works* of C. G. Jung, 20 vols (ed. Herbert Read, Michael Fordham and Gerhard Adler; trans. R. F. C. Hull). London: Routledge and Kegan Paul; Princeton, NJ: Princeton University Press, 1953–77.

Jung, C. G., *Memories, Dreams, Reflections*. London: Collins and Routledge and Kegan Paul, 1963.

Jung, C. G., *Letters* (ed. Gerhard Adler). London: Routledge and Kegan Paul, 1973–4.

Jung, C. G., *C. G. Jung Speaking* (ed. William McGuire). London: Thames and Hudson, 1978.

Kaplinsky, Raphael, *The Economies of Small*. London: Intermediate Technology Press, 1990.

Keegan, Richard, *The Evolving Self*. Cambridge, Mass.: Harvard University Press, 1982.

Kirk, G. S., *The Nature of Greek Myths*. Harmondsworth: Penguin, 1974.

Kirsch, James, 'Carl Gustav Jung and the Jews', *Journal of Psychology and Judaism* 6: 2, 1982.

Klein, Melanie, 'On mental health', *British Journal of Medical Psychology* 33, 1960.

Kohlberg, Lawrence, 'Moral development'. In *International Encyclopedia of Social Science*. New York: Macmillan Free Press, 1968.

Kohn, Henry, *The Idea of Nationalism*. Oxford: Oxford University Press, 1967.

Kohut, Heinz, *The Analysis of the Self* and *The Restoration of the Self*. New York: International University Press, 1971 and 1977.

Kollontai, Alexandra, *Love of Worker Bees* (trans. Cathy Porter). London: Virago, 1977.

Kuhns, Richard, *Psychoanalytic Theory of Art*. New York: Columbia University Press, 1983.

Lacan, Jacques. In Forrester, John (ed. and trans.), *The Seminar. Book 1. Freud's Papers on Technique. 1953–1954*. Cambridge, Cambs.: Cambridge University Press, 1988.

Langs, Robert, *The Listening Process*. New York: Jason Aronson, 1978.

Levine, Howard *et al.* (eds), *Psychoanalysis and the Nuclear Threat: Clinical and Theoretical Studies*, Hillsdale, NJ: Analytic Press, 1988.

Lewes, Kenneth, *The Psychoanalytic Theory of Male Homosexuality*. New York: Meridian, 1988.

Lifton, Robert Jay, *The Nazi Doctors: Medical Killing and the Psychology of Genocide*. New York: Basic Books, 1986.

Little, Margaret, '"R" – the analyst's total response to his patient's needs', *International Journal of Psycho-Analysis* 38, 1957.

Logan, Frances, *Homelessness and Relationship Breakdown: How the Law and Housing Policy Affects Women*. London: National Council for One Parent Families, 1986.

Loomis, Mary, 'Balancing the shields: native American teaching and the individuation process', *Quadrant* 21: 2, 1988.

Lovelock, James, *Gaia: A New Look at Life on Earth*. Oxford: Oxford University Press, 1982.

Lukes, Steven, Review of Blackburn, Robin (ed.), *After the Fall: The Failure of Communism and the Future of Socialism*. London: Verso, 1992. In *New Statesman and Society*, March 6, 1992.

McGuire, William (ed.), *The Freud/Jung Letters*. London: Hogarth and Routledge and Kegan Paul, 1974.

McGuire, William (ed.), *C. G. Jung Speaking*. London: Thames and Hudson, 1978.

McGuire, William, *Bollingen: An Adventure in Collecting the Past*. Princeton, NJ: Princeton University Press, 2nd edition, 1989.

Macey, David, *Lacan in Contexts*. London: Verso, 1988.

Machiavelli, Niccolò, *The Prince* (trans. George Bull). Harmondsworth: Penguin, 1961.

Mahler, Margaret, 'A study of the separation-individuation process', *Psychoanalytic Study of the Child*, 1971.

Maidenbaum, Aryeh, 'Report from New York'. In Mattoon, Mary Ann (ed.), *Personal and Archetypal Dynamics in the Analytical Relationship*. Einsiedeln, Switzerland: Daimon, 1991.

Maimonides, Moses, *Guide of the Perplexed*. Philadelphia: Jewish Publication Society of America, 1938.

Mann, Thomas, *Confessions of Felix Krull, Confidence Man* (trans. Denver Lindley). Harmondsworth: Penguin, 1958.

Marrus, Marcus, 'Popular anti-semitism'. Catalogue of *The Dreyfuss Affair: Art, Truth and Justice*. Exhibition, Jewish Museum, New York. Berkeley: University of California Press, 1987.

Masson, Jeffrey (ed.), *The Complete Letters of Sigmund Freud to Wilhelm Fliess 1887–1904*. Cambridge, Mass. and London: Harvard University Press, 1985.

Masson, Jeffrey, *Against Therapy*. London: Collins, 1989.

Mattoon, Mary Ann (ed.), *Personal and Archetypal Dynamics in the Analytical Relationship*. Einsiedeln, Switzerland: Daimon, 1991.

Meltzer, Donald, *The Clinical Significance of the Work of Bion*. Strath Tay, Perthshire: Clunie Press, 1978.

Meltzer, Donald, *The Apprehension of Beauty: The Role of Aesthetic Conflict in Development, Art and Violence*. Strath Tay, Perthshire: Clunie Press, 1988.

Miller, David, *The New Polytheism*. Dallas: Spring Publications, 1981.

Mitchell, Juliet, *Women: The Longest Revolution*. London: Virago, 1984.

Monk, Sue, *Escaping the Underclass*. London: National Council for One Parent Families, 1990.

Montesquieu, Charles Louis de Secondat, *The Spirit of Laws*. London: Fontana, 1973.

Moore, Robert and Gillette, Douglas, *King, Warrior, Magician, Lover: Rediscovering the Archetypes of thee Mature Masculine*. San Francisco, Harper, 1990.

Murray, Charles, 'Underclass'. In Anderson, Digby and Dawson, Graham (eds), *Family Portraits*, London: Social Affairs Unit, 1990.

Musil, Robert, 'Helpless Europe'. In Pike, Burton and Lufts, David (eds and trans), *Precision and Soul: Essays and Addresses*. Chicago: University of Chicago Press, 1990.

Musil, Robert, '"Nation" as ideal and reality'. In Pike, Burton and Lufts, David (eds and trans), *Precision and Soul: Essays and Addresses*. Chicago: University of Chicago Press, 1990.

National Council for One Parent Families, *Tomorrow's Parents, Yesterday's Values*. London: National Council for One Parent Families, 1987.

Nicholson, Linda (ed.), *Feminism/Postmodernism*. London and New York: Routledge, 1990.

Nietzsche, Friedrich, *The Anti-Christ* (trans. Frederick Hollingdale). Harmondsworth: Penguin, 1972.

Oakley, Chris, 'Introducing an incomplete project'. In Cooper, Robin *et al.* (eds), *Thresholds Between Philosophy and Psychoanalysis: Papers from the Philadelphia Association*. London: Free Association Books, 1989.

O'Connor, Tony, 'Foucault and the transgression of limits'. In Silverman, Hugh (ed.), *Philosophy and Non-Philosophy since Merleau-Ponty*. London and New York: Routledge, 1988.

Otto, Rudolf, *The Idea of the Holy* (trans. James Harvey). Oxford and London: Oxford University Press, 1923.

Papadopoulos, Renos, 'Jung and the concept of the other'. In Papadopoulos, Renos and Saayman, Graham (eds), *Jung in Modern Perspective: The Master and His Legacy*. Bridport, Dorset: Prism, 1991.

Parker, Rozsika and Pollock, Griselda, *Framing Feminism: Art and the Women's Movement 1970–1985*. London and New York: Pandora, 1987.

Parker, Rozsika, *The Subversive Stitch: Embroidery and the Making of the Feminine*. London: Women's Press, 1984; New York: Routledge, 1990.

Phillips, Kevin, *The Politics of Rich and Poor: Wealth and the American Electorate in the Reagan Aftermath*. New York: Random House, 1990.

Plaut, Fred, 'Analytical psychologists and psychological types: Comment on replies to a survey', *Journal of Analytical Psychology* 17: 2, 1972.

Plaut, Fred, 'Object constancy or constant object?'. In Samuels, Andrew (ed.), *Psychopathology: Contemporary Jungian Perspectives*. London: Karnac Books, 1989; New York: Guilford, 1991.

Plaut, Fred, *Analysis Analysed*. London and New York: Routledge, 1993. Paper first published in 1975.

Racker, Heinrich, *Transference and Countertransference*. London: Hogarth, 1968.

Radin, Paul, *The Trickster: A Study in North American Mythology*. New York: Schocken, 1972.

Rayner, Eric, *The Independent Mind in British Psychoanalysis*. London: Free Association Books, 1991.

Richards, Barry (ed.), *Capitalism and Infancy: Essays on Psychoanalysis and Politics*. London: Free Association Books, 1984.

Richards, Barry (ed.), *Crises of the Self: Further Essays on Psychoanalysis and Politics*. London: Free Association Books, 1989.

Roazen, Paul, 'Nietzsche and Freud: two voices from the underground', *The Psycho-history Review*, Spring 1991.

Rodman, F. Robert (ed.), *D. W. Winnicott, The Spontaneous Gesture: Selected Letters*. Cambridge, Mass.: Harvard University Press, 1987.

Rorty, Richard, *Contingency, Irony and Solidarity*. Cambridge, Cambs.: Cambridge University Press, 1989.

Rowan, John, *The Horned God: Feminism and Men as Wounding and Healing*. London and New York: Routledge, 1987.

Rowan, John, *Subpersonalities: The People Inside Us*. London and New York: Routledge, 1990.

Rowan, John, *The Transpersonal: In Psychotherapy and Counselling*. London and New York: Routledge, 1992.

Rustin, Michael, *The Good Society and the Inner World: Psychoanalysis, Politics and Culture*. London: Verso, 1991.

Samuels, Andrew, *Jung and the Post-Jungians*. London and Boston: Routledge and Kegan Paul, 1985.

Samuels, Andrew (ed.), *The Father: Contemporary Jungian Perspectives*. London: Free Association Books, 1985; New York: New York University Press, 1986.

Samuels, Andrew *et al.*, *A Critical Dictionary of Jungian Analysis*. London and New York: Routledge, 1986.

Samuels, Andrew (ed.), Jung, C. G., *Essays on Contemporary Events*. London: Routledge; Princeton, NJ: Princeton University Press, 1988.

Samuels, Andrew, *The Plural Psyche: Personality, Morality and the Father*. London and New York: Routledge, 1989.

Samuels, Andrew (ed.), *Psychopathology: Contemporary Jungian Perspectives*. London: Karnac Books, 1989; New York: Guilford, 1991.

Samuels, Andrew, 'The psychology of the single parent'. Unpublished research carried out for the Family Welfare Association, London, 1975–77.

Samuels, Andrew, Reply to Dalal, Farhad, 'Jung, a racist', *British Journal of Psychotherapy* 4: 3, 1988.

Samuels, Andrew, 'Pluralism and training', *Journal of the British Association of Psychotherapists* 22, 1991.

Samuels, Andrew, 'Parents as messengers', *British Journal of Psychotherapy* 7: 4, 1991.

Samuels, Andrew, 'What is a good training?', *British Journal of Psychotherapy* 9: 3, 1993.

Scholen, Gershom (ed.), *The Correspondence of Walter Benjamin and Gershom Scholem 1932–1940*. New York: Schocken, 1989.

Scruton, Roger, *A Short History of Modern Philosophy from Descartes to Wittgenstein*. London: Routledge and Kegan Paul, 1984.

Segal, Lynne, *Slow Motion: Changing Masculinities, Changing Men*. London: Virago, 1990.

Sen, Amartya, 'Women's survival as a development problem', *Bulletin of the American Academy of Arts and Sciences* XLIII: 2.

Serlin, Ilene, 'Kinaesthetic imagining: A phenomenological study'. Unpublished, 1989.

Sheridan, Alan, 'The death of the author'. In *Ideas from France: The Legacy of French Theory*. London: Free Association Books, 1989.

Siann, Gerda, *Accounting for Aggression: Perspectives on Aggression and Violence*. London and Boston: Allen and Unwin, 1985.

Silverman, Hugh (ed.), *Philosophy and Non-Philosophy since Merleau-Ponty*. London and New York: Routledge, 1988.

Slakter, Edmund (ed.), *Countertransference: A Comprehensive View of those Reactions of the Therapist to the Patient that may Help or Hinder the Treatment*. Northdale, NJ: Jason Aronson, 1987.

Smith, David (ed.), *Understanding the Underclass*. London: Policy Studies Institute, 1992.

Sommer, Robert, *Familienforschung, Vererbungs- und Rassenlehre*. 3rd edition, Leipzig: Barth, 1927.

Spitz, Ellen, *Art and Psyche*. New Haven: Yale University Press, 1985.

Stanton, Kristina, 'Dance movement therapy: an introduction', *British Journal of Occupational Therapy* 54: 3, 1991.

Stanton, Martin, Review of C. Fred Alford, *Melanie Klein and Critical Social Theory*. *Times Higher Education Supplement*, April 27, 1990.

Stanton, Martin, *Sandor Ferenczi: Reconsidering Active Imagination*. London: Free Association Books, 1991.

Stationen der Moderne, exhibition catalogue. Berlin, 1988.

Stern, Daniel, *The Interpersonal World of the Infant: A View from Psychoanalysis and Developmental Psychology*. New York: Basic Books, 1985.

Stern, Paul, *C. G. Jung: The Haunted Prophet*. New York: Braziller, 1976.

Stevens, Anthony, *Archetype: A Natural History of the Self*. London: Routledge and Kegan Paul, 1982.

Stolorow, Robert and Atwood, George, Review of Samuels, Andrew, *The Plural Psyche: Personality, Morality and the Father*, *International Review of Psycho-Analysis* 18: 1, 1991.

Tacey, David, 'Attacking patriarchy, redeeming masculinity', *San Francisco Jung Institute Library Journal* 10: 1, 1991.

Tatham, Peter, *The Makings of Maleness: Men, Women, and the Flight of Daedalus*. London: Karnac; New York: New York University Press, 1992.

Temperley, Jane, 'Psychoanalysis and the threat of nuclear war'. In *Crises of the Self: Further Essays on Psychoanalysis and Politics* (ed. Barry Richards). London: Free Association Books, 1989.

Theweleit, Klaus, *Male Fantasies*. Cambridge, Cambs.: Polity Press, 1987.

Thomas, Keith, *Man and the Natural World: Changing Attitudes in England 1500–1800*. London: Allen Lane, 1983.

Tong, Rosemarie, *Feminist Thought: A Comprehensive Introduction*. London: Unwin Hyman, 1989.

Trist, Eric and Murray, Hugh (eds), *The Social Engagement of Social Science: Volume 1:*

The Socio-Psychological Perspective. London: Free Association Books, 1990.

Von der Tann, Matthias, 'A Jungian perspective on the Berlin Institute for Psychotherapy: a basis for mourning', *San Francisco Jung Institute Library Journal* 8: 4, 1989.

Wallerstein, Robert, 'Psychoanalysis in Nazi Germany: Historical and psychological lessons', *Psychoanalysis and Contemporary Thought* 11: 2, 1987.

Wallerstein, Robert, 'One psychoanalysis or many?', *International Journal of Psycho-Analysis* 69: 1, 1988.

Weeks, Jeffrey, *Sexuality and its Discontents*. London and New York: Routledge, 1985.

Whitford, Margaret, 'Rereading Irigaray'. In Brennan, Teresa (ed.), *Between Psychoanalysis and Feminism*. London and New York: Routledge, 1989.

Whitford, Margaret, *Luce Irigaray: Philosophy in the Feminine*. London and New York: Routledge, 1991.

Wilde, Oscar, 'The soul of man under socialism'. In *Complete Works of Oscar Wilde*. London: Book Club Associates.

Willeford, William, *The Fool and His Sceptre*. Evanston, Ill.: Northwestern University Press, 1969.

Williams, Donald, Review of Barash, David, *The Hare and the Tortoise: Culture, Biology and Human Nature*, *San Francisco Jung Institute Library Journal* 8: 1, 1988.

Winnicott, D. W., 'What about father?'. In *Getting to Know Your Baby*. London: Heinemann, 1944.

Winnicott, D. W., *The Family and Individual Development*. London: Tavistock, 1968.

Winnicott, D. W. 'The effect of psychotic parents on the emotional development of the child'. In *The Family and Individual Development*. London: Tavistock, 1968.

Winnicott, D. W., 'Metaphysical and clinical aspects of regression within the psycho-analytical set-up'. In *Through Paediatrics to Psycho-Analysis*. London: Hogarth, 1975.

Winnicott, D. W., 'Hate in the countertransference'. In Winnicott, D. W., *Through Paediatrics to Psycho-Analysis*. London: Hogarth, 1975.

Woodcock, George, *Surfacing, A Reader's Guide*. Toronto: General Paperbacks, 1991.

Wyman, Wendy, 'The body as a manifestation of unconscious experience'. Unpublished, 1991.

Zoja, Luigi, *Drugs, Addiction and Initiation: The Modern Search for Ritual*. Boston: Sigo Press, 1989.

Name index
Compiled by Richard House

Subject index
Compiled by Richard House